the Cooking Light® way to LOSE WEIGHT

Compiled and edited by
Anne C. Cain, M.P.H., M.S., R.D.

Oxmoor
House®

Library of Congress Catalog Number:
 2003103413
ISBN: 0-8487-2807-6
Printed in the United States of America
First printing 2003

Oxmoor House, Inc.
Editor-in-Chief: Nancy Fitzpatrick Wyatt
Executive Editor: Katherine M. Eakin
Art Director: Cynthia R. Cooper
Copy Chief: Catherine Ritter Scholl

The *Cooking Light* Way to Lose Weight

Results in weight loss may vary. Check with
your physician about weight-loss goals and
before making any changes in your diet.

Editor: Anne C. Cain, M.P.H., M.S., R.D.
Editorial Assistant: Dawn Russell
Senior Designer: Emily A. Parrish
Publishing Systems Administrator:
 Rick Tucker
Director, Production and Distribution:
 Phillip Lee
Books Production Manager: Leslie Johnson
Production Assistant: Faye Porter Bonner
Contributors:
Cooking Light Projects Editor: Mary Simpson
 Creel, M.S., R.D.
Cooking Light Production Editor: Hazel R.
 Eddins
Copy Editor: Dolores Hydock
Illustrator: Melanie Magee
Indexer: Mary Ann Laurens
Intern: Sarah Miller
Photographers: Colleen Duffley,
 Susan Salinger, Walt Seng

To order additional publications, call
1-800-765-6400 or visit **oxmoorhouse.com**

Cooking Light®
Vice President, Editor: Mary Kay Culpepper
Executive Editor: Billy R. Sims
Managing Editor: Hillari Dowdle
Senior Food Editor: Jill G. Melton, M.S., R.D.
Senior Editor: Alison Mann Ashton
Senior Writer: Robin Mather Jenkins
Projects Editor: Mary Simpson Creel, M.S., R.D.
Editorial Coordinator: Carol C. Noe
Associate Editor: Phillip Rhodes
Associate Food Editor: Krista Ackerbloom
 Montgomery, M.S., R.D.
Assistant Food Editors: Julie Grimes, Ann
 Taylor Pittman
Assistant Editor: Rachel Seligman
Contributing Beauty Editor: Lauren McCann
Senior Editor/Food Development Director:
 Ellen Templeton Carroll, M.S., R.D.
Art Director: Susan Waldrip Dendy
Assistant Art Director: Maya Metz Logue
Designers: Fernande Bondarenko, J. Shay
 McNamee
Assistant Designer: Brigette Mayer
Senior Photographer: Becky Luigart-Stayner
Photographer: Randy Mayor
Senior Photo Stylist: Lydia DeGaris-Pursell
Photo Stylists: Melanie J. Clarke, Jan Gautro
Photography Assistant: Karry Hosford
Studio Assistant: Kiersten Atkinson
Test Kitchens Director: Vanessa Taylor Johnson
Food Stylist: Kellie Gerber Kelley
Assistant Food Stylist: M. Kathleen Kanen
Test Kitchens Staff: Sam Brannock, Kathryn
 Conrad, John Kirkpatrick, Tiffany Vickers,
 Mike Wilson
Copy Chief: Maria Parker Hopkins
Copy Editors: Jennifer Southall, Tara Trenary
Production Manager: Liz Rhoades
Production Editor: Hazel R. Eddins
Production Assistant: Joanne McCrary
Research Assistant: Dani Leigh Clemmons
Office Manager: Rita K. Jackson
Editorial Assistants: Cindy Hatcher,
 Heather W. Johnson
Correspondence Editor: Michelle Gibson
 Daniels
CookingLight.com
Editor: Maelynn Cheung
Managing Editor: Jason Burnett
Assistant Editor: Jennifer Middleton

TABLE OF CONTENTS

Part 4: Get Started on Your Weight-Loss Lifestyle   103

Part 5: Supermarket Savvy and Secrets from the Test Kitchens   125

Foreword

By definition, a tool is something that helps you complete a job. And this book, *The Cooking Light Way to Lose Weight*, is a very real and effective tool to help you realize the goals you set for yourself. Full of stories, tips, and recipes from America's top magazine for great food and healthy living, this book—and your own motivation—can aid you in changing your life.

Like so many things in life, losing weight is at the same time both simple and difficult. The formula is certainly uncomplicated: Consume fewer calories each day than you expend. Simply put, to be successful, you need to eat less and exercise more. However, fitting that "simple" equation into daily life is a challenge for many of us.

The reasons why it's difficult to eat less are usually personal: You have a hungry family to feed that doesn't like "diet" food, your days are too hectic, you have obligations with family and friends that revolve around food, or you need soothing on a nerve-jangling day.

As editor of *Cooking Light*, I know the magazine's philosophy has always been that deliciously healthful food can fit into the fast-paced lives (and suit the demanding tastes) of today's families. Our Superfast recipes, quick menus, and recipes for on-the-go meals make it simple to decide on a dinner tonight that will make everybody happy. And our lightened offerings for special occasions such as birthdays, parties, and holidays taste fresher and brighter than the fat-and-calorie-laden originals. After all, the magazine professes that an intelligent indulgence—say, a sensibly-sized slice of cake or a cup of lightened chocolate mousse—is not a luxury, it's a necessity.

Indeed, the magazine's position on exercise is that it's a necessity, too. Bodies were made for movement. When you incorporate exercise into your day, the benefits of burning more calories have a ripple effect: You become more confident, you acquire new strength, and you're revived with increased energy. What's more, the exercise needn't be strenuous to be effective. Setting off on a walk around the block can literally be the first step in the right direction.

Of course, the next step involves taking charge. On the cover of every issue of *Cooking Light* are the words, "Eat Smart, Be Fit, Live Well." They're three sides of a healthy-living triangle, really. Each is dependent on the other two. When you eat smart and aim for fitness, living well comes easily. Identifying your goals—not just for weight loss, but for the whole of your life—is key to success on every level.

That said, this book represents something of a change in direction for *Cooking Light*. Weight loss per se has never been the magazine's reason for being. But our readers who do lose weight consistently tell us that *Cooking Light* helps them in their efforts. People who seek a fresh start—and the encouragement to keep going—rely on the magazine's exercise routines, menus, and recipes. Along the way, they realize that they've embarked not on a diet but on a whole new way of living, a way that naturally incorporates vibrant fitness, deliciously healthful eating, and the many pleasures they bring.

And that is what *Cooking Light* magazine and this book are all about.

Mary Kay Culpepper
Vice President, Editor
Cooking Light magazine

About Our Recipes

Glance at the end of any *Cooking Light* recipe, and you'll see how committed we are to helping you make the best of today's light cooking. With six chefs, four registered dietitians, three home economists, and a computer system that analyzes every ingredient we use, *Cooking Light* gives you authoritative dietary detail. We go to such lengths so you can see how our recipes fit into your healthful eating plan. When you're trying to lose weight, the calorie and fat figures may help most. But if you're keeping a close eye on the carbohydrate, sodium, cholesterol, and saturated fat in your diet, we provide those numbers, too. And because many women don't get enough iron or calcium, we can help there, as well. There's also a fiber analysis, since fiber plays a role in weight loss as well as disease prevention.

Here's a helpful guide to put our nutrition analysis numbers into perspective. Remember, one size doesn't fit all, so take your lifestyle, age, and circumstances into consideration when determining your nutrition needs. For example, pregnant or breast-feeding women need extra protein, calories, and calcium. And men over 50 need 1,200mg of calcium daily, 200mg more than the amount recommended for younger men.

In our nutritional analysis, we use these abbreviations:

sat	for saturated fat	**CHOL**	for cholesterol
mono	for monounsaturated fat	**CALC**	for calcium
poly	for polyunsaturated fat	**g**	for gram
CARB	for carbohydrates	**mg**	for milligram

Your Daily Nutrition Guide

	women ages 25 to 50	women over 50	men over 24
Calories	2,000	2,000 or less	2,700
Protein	50g	50g or less	63g
Fat	65g or less	65g or less	88g or less
Saturated Fat	20g or less	20g or less	27g or less
Carbohydrates	304g	304g	410g
Fiber	25g to 35g	25g to 35g	25g to 35g
Cholesterol	300mg or less	300mg or less	300mg or less
Iron	18mg	8mg	8mg
Sodium	2,400mg or less	2,400mg or less	2,400mg or less
Calcium	1,000mg	1,200mg	1,000mg

The nutritional values used in our calculations either come from The Food Processor, Version 7.5 (ESHA Research), or are provided by food manufacturers.

Part
1

No-Diet, No-Denial Weight Loss

Learn why indulgence may be the best way to lose
weight permanently and never feel denied.

Chapter 1

Eating Satisfaction Guaranteed

Discover how eating well really is the secret
to permanent weight loss.

Imagine a food guru, wise in the ways of weight loss. You've climbed a mountain to meet the wise one—or at least it feels like you have, since your search for slimness has probably taken you through the peaks and valleys of dieting, the "highs" of losing weight, and the seemingly inevitable "lows" of regaining it.

You want to lose weight—and keep it off. You want to discover the secrets of weight loss—what really works. You ask him to advise you. And since he knows his stuff, these are the pearls of wisdom he utters.

- There are no bad foods. None. You never need to feel guilty about eating a food you like.
- Eating enjoyment is the key to weight loss. Pleasure and satisfaction are natural. Denial is unnatural—and it is the road to binging.
- You can cut fat without cutting taste.
- Think positively—weight loss and better health are easy to achieve with enjoyable food choices and regular exercise. You can lose weight. You will lose weight.
- And then he would leave you with this last piece of sage advice: Read *The Cooking Light Way to Lose Weight*. Everything you need—surprising secrets of successful weight loss, slimming and delicious recipes—is between the covers of that book.

WHY THE NO-DIET, NO-DENIAL APPROACH WORKS

We did talk to food gurus. Dozens of them—professors of nutrition at colleges and universities, leading dietitians, food scientists, health-savvy chefs, and doctors who treat their patients with healing foods. Those "pearls of wisdom" you just read are the distillation of what they told us and the essence of what you'll find in this book—a unique and effective philosophy of weight loss that is best summed up in the phrase "Positive Eating." And positive eating is definitely not about dieting and denial.

"You don't need to learn how to diet," says Joan Salge Blake, M.S., R.D., L.D.N., a nutrition professor at Boston University's Sargent College of Health and Rehabilitation Sciences. "You need to learn how to eat."

"Often, a person thinks she needs to eat special foods or undertake a special regimen to lose weight," says Salge Blake. "But nobody can maintain such a 'special' approach to everyday eating. After you lose your weight, you'll return to the eating pattern that got you into your predicament in the first place—which is why 95 percent of dieters regain the pounds they shed. What you need is a new eating pattern that you can live with, a lifelong eating pattern that is healthful and enjoyable."

And Salge Blake says the only thing you should deny yourself while eating healthfully is denial itself. "You should never make any food forbidden," she says. "A 'forbidden' food is put on a pedestal and given more power than it deserves. Go ahead and have a small amount of a rich food you love, like chocolate, or a modified, low-fat, low-calorie version of a 'fattening' food. But if you feel you can't have it, you'll think about the food all the time, and eventually you will eat it—and may eat more than is healthful or waist-friendly."

There are no bad foods. None. You never need to feel guilty about eating a food you like.

In fact, you should emphasize the foods you like, says William Hart, Ph.D., R.D., assistant professor of nutrition and dietetics at Saint Louis University. "Any time you try to restrict the foods you're used to, you're less likely to stick with any healthy changes you're trying to make." Instead, says Dr. Hart, use recipes that give you slightly modified, low-fat, and very tasty versions of your favorite foods—the type of recipes found in the pages of *The Cooking Light Way to Lose Weight*. (Both Salge Blake and Hart are big fans of *Cooking Light*, by the way.) "This is the ideal way to lose weight and keep it off," he says.

Regular physical activity is another important component of successful weight loss, says Lawrence Cheskin, M.D., Director of the Weight Management Center at Johns Hopkins University in Baltimore, Maryland. "But that doesn't mean running marathons or becoming a star athlete," he says. "It means consciously increasing physical activity during the day, such as parking your car a little further from your destination, or using the stairs instead of the elevator." And walking—at whatever speed you feel comfortable—is the best daily exercise for burning calories, he says. Well, those are exactly the type of exercise recommendations you'll find in this book.

In fact, let's take a moment and talk about what you can look forward to in these pages.

- The Power of Positive Eating. You'll discover that healthful and enjoyable food choices—filling fruits and vegetables, beans and whole grains, healthy fats, low-fat dairy foods, the right amount of protein, and good-for-you sweets—are the way to lose weight.
- The Happy Days of No-Diet Weight Loss. Surprise—it's easy to make the daily choices that trim the pounds and re-energize your life.
- Helping Your Family Be Healthy. Many of today's kids are dangerously over-weight. We tell you how to make weight loss a family affair.
- Jump (or Walk, or Swim) for Joy. If exercise isn't enjoyable, you're not going to stick with it. Here are fun ways to burn extra calories, along with a 12-week fitness plan.
- The Top 10 Weight-Loss Challenges. Everybody faces them. We tell you how to beat them.
- Recipes, Recipes, Recipes! They're quick and easy to make. They're delicious. They're low in fat. And there are hundreds of them, for every meal and occasion. (Plus, menu plans that make them simple to include in your everyday schedule.)

We know you're ready to use this book—and start losing weight! But before you begin, here's a final, inspiring thought from Dr. Hart.

"Everyone who wants to lose weight should have hope. You can control your food intake and enjoy what you're eating. You don't have to deprive yourself—just modify recipes for the foods you love, while keeping them delicious. Add a little exercise, and you'll be healthier, happier—and really achieve your weight-loss goals."

In other words—on the road to lasting weight loss, your eating satisfaction is guaranteed!

—Bill Gottlieb

Chapter 2

Diets Don't Work

Ditch the diet and discover the real secret to weight loss.

Diet is one of those four-letter words most people want banned from their vocabulary. Yet, according to The American Dietetic Association (ADA), Americans spend billions of dollars each year on weight-loss products and services. "People are looking for miracles," says Kathleen Zelman, R.D., a spokesperson for the ADA. "And there are all kinds of schemes that promise results."

THE DIET DU JOUR

It seems like every week there's a new weight-loss product or program on the market. You see the commercials with scores of "before" and "after" pictures and happy, thin spokespeople running around the screen touting the virtues of the most recent diet plan. Or you spy a new weight-loss book on the best-seller list, and you think, if millions of people have tried it, could it be that bad? Before you're tempted to spend a lot of money on the latest weight-loss fad, review the checklist on page 17 and you'll probably find it's not worth the investment.

> The best way to shed pounds is this simple advice: Eat a varied, balanced diet and exercise regularly.

If you're wondering whom to trust, or where to go to find credible information, look no further. The editors of *Cooking Light* are committed to bringing you reliable weight-loss information that is based on sound science. Not only is *Cooking Light* America's leading food magazine, the staff includes four registered dietitians and an editorial advisory board made up of physicians and certified fitness specialists. These experts make sure that the information you get is current, accurate, and realistic. For more information, go to CookingLight.com; AOL Keyword: Cooking Light.

FAD DIET FOLLIES

Patty, 48, a reformed dieter, knows the pitfalls of fad dieting all too well. "I've tried all kinds of diets," she says. "The problem was as soon as I stopped the diet, I gained all my weight back and then some." Between diets, Patty would binge on candy, keeping bags of sweets stashed away in her desk drawers at work. "I would buy 10 to 15 bags of candy during a holiday and just keep eating from those bags until the next holiday. Then I'd buy 15 more bags of candy and do the same thing." Patty fell victim to one of the biggest problems with diets—they offer so many restrictions people often binge on "bad" foods. This puts the pounds back on, prompting another diet, and continuing an unhealthy loss and gain cycle.

After going on and off diets most of her life, Patty decided to change the way she ate. Patty enrolled in a program that taught her how to make healthy changes she could maintain for a lifetime. "I realized that it wasn't what I ate, it was how much I ate," Patty says. "I learned I can eat anything I want, as long as I eat it in moderation. I learned to make changes in my eating habits that I could live with." Patty's changes are not only helping her lose weight, they are helping her achieve a healthier life for her and her husband. Patty knows that she can stay healthy for a lifetime with the skills she's learned, and she's celebrating her victory of keeping off thirty pounds for more than a year. Patty's success is due to the fact that she learned how to make permanent lifestyle changes rather than relying on a "quick-fix" diet. Research shows that people who choose fad diets with no weight-maintenance component tend to gain back all the weight they lost as soon as they go off the diet.

"The real secret to losing weight and keeping it off comes down to a mathematical equation," Zelman says. "Calories in minus calories out equals calories gained or lost. That translates to pounds gained or lost. If you eat more calories than you use, you'll gain weight." So the best way to shed pounds is this simple advice: Eat a varied, balanced diet and exercise regularly. Let *Cooking Light* show you how to do just that, without giving up the foods you love. The only things you'll be saying "no" to are dieting and denial.

—*Michele Mann*

Fad Diet Checklist

❑ Does it rely too heavily on a particular food or nutrient? If so, it's not a good idea. Eating a variety of foods is essential in adequately getting all the nutrients your body needs.

❑ Who's writing it? Just because it's on the radio or television, or even on the best-seller list, doesn't mean the diet is sound. Many times you'll find an entrepreneur or celebrity who's looking to cash in on the lucrative weight-loss market. Or health professionals may be endorsing the diet, but their backgrounds aren't in nutrition. Be sure to investigate the "expert" behind the product.

❑ Does it include exercise? Any weight-loss program that does not emphasize physical activity as essential to weight loss is not worth a second glance.

❑ Does it sound too good to be true? If a weight-loss product or book promises a significant weight loss in a short amount of time, or makes any other outlandish claims, avoid it.

The Secret to Long-Term Weight Loss

High-protein, low-carbohydrate diets are all the rage. In fact, so many people have gone on them that researchers took note. Are these diets merely quick fixes, or can they keep weight off over time?

"We studied more than 2,000 people who had maintained a weight loss of 30 pounds or more for at least a year, and we found that less than 1 percent were following a low-carbohydrate diet," says Holly Wyatt, M.D., assistant professor of medicine at the University of Colorado-Denver.

Another related study found that even those who do lose weight—over the short term—on a high-protein, low-carbohydrate diet eat 1,000 fewer calories a day than they did before dieting. "In the end, losing weight is about monitoring total calories," Wyatt says. "But you can eat a larger volume of food on a high-carb, low-fat diet, and that may explain why so many more people use those guidelines for a lifetime."

The bottom line: Don't believe the high-protein hype. Most people maintain long-term weight loss by eating a high-carbohydrate, low-fat diet—and watching the number of calories they consume.

Chapter 3

What You Gain
When You Lose

Losing weight is not just about fitting
into a smaller pair of jeans—it's
about being on the road to better health.

When 58-year-old Jeanne Price decided it was time to lose weight, she knew it wasn't going to be easy. "I've dealt with a weight problem all my life," she says. "I had come to terms with that and become content with who I was—extra pounds and all." But all that began to change when she had a mild stroke a week after her 31st wedding anniversary. Not long after the high blood pressure that signaled the stroke was diagnosed, Jeanne was also diagnosed with type 2 diabetes. "It was definitely a wake-up call," she says. "I knew that being overweight was beginning to affect my health, but I was still in denial. I wasn't ready to make a change." It wasn't until she became a grandmother that reality set in. "I want to be around for graduations and weddings, and, more importantly, I want to enjoy my grandchildren right now." So with the support of family and coworkers, Jeanne joined a group that is teaching her to make smarter food choices, and she is starting to walk at a local park a few times a week. "I feel better," she says. "But the best part is my blood pressure is down and so are my blood sugar levels." Jeanne admits her doctors are thrilled, and so is she. "I have more energy and I'm accomplishing my goals. That makes me feel wonderful."

If you are overweight, you already know that your weight can affect both your physical and emotional health. The bright side is that losing even a few pounds can lower your overall health risks and leave you feeling better—body and soul.

LOSING TO WIN

Losing weight doesn't guarantee you a clean bill of health, but shedding the pounds will start you off in a healthier direction. And the best news is that you don't have to lose as much as you might think to get some major health benefits. Losing as little as 10 percent of your weight can lower your risk for developing heart disease, high blood pressure, diabetes, and cancer.

There are also some studies that show that being obese increases the risk of certain cancers. While it's not clear whether weight loss alone can reduce that risk, it does appear that increased physical activity and a healthy diet are likely to reduce the cancer risk.

Though health professionals aren't certain how far-reaching the benefits of losing weight are on your health, there is certainly no drawback to adopting a healthier lifestyle. "The jury may be out on clinical evidence of all the health benefits of losing weight," says Colleen Doyle, M.S., R.D., director of nutrition and physical activity for the American Cancer Society. "But there's no downside to being physically active and achieving a healthy weight."

When Women Gain Weight

It's no news that many women spend much of their adult lives waging war against unwanted pounds. It might surprise you to learn, though, that research from various universities presented at the North American Association for the Study of Obesity has pinpointed three key times when a woman may be most vulnerable to unwanted weight gain:

(1) the onset of her first menstrual period,
(2) after pregnancy, and
(3) when she is approaching or after menopause.

While the initial menstrual-cycle gain is courtesy of Mother Nature and puberty, the pounds that creep on after giving birth and undergoing menopause are linked to food and exercise—specifically, too much of the former and too little of the latter. And as a postmenopausal woman ages, her metabolism begins to slow down, meaning she needs more physical activity than before to burn the same number of calories. But it's important to remember that the need for fewer calories does not mean the need for fewer nutrients.

So take heart in the fact that you are not alone if you have experienced weight gain during any of these three important times in your life. Some of this weight gain is normal (and maybe even healthy), but don't let it get out of control. These are the times of your life when you need to pay special attention to eating healthy foods and making sure that you are physically active.

GAINING SELF-ESTEEM

One of The American Dietetic Association's primary strategies in weight management is encouraging people to eschew appearance or a number on a chart as their main motivation for losing weight, and focus on becoming healthier. And a recent study that tracked the reasons why women lose weight and keep it off showed that women who kept the weight off for the long haul recognized that gaining weight was directly related to how they felt about themselves. So once they accepted themselves as they were, they were more realistic about their weight-loss goals and their motivations for losing.

Taking an honest look at your life may be the push you need to start setting weight-loss goals. That often is the beginning of a new outlook and a new look. "People have different weight-loss needs," says Sheah Rarback, M.S., R.D., a spokesperson for The American Dietetic Association. "But setting weight-loss goals and achieving them is a boost in self-esteem for anyone. Anytime you accomplish a goal you've set for yourself, you should feel good about who you are."

8 REASONS TO BE A LOSER

When you lose as little as 10 percent of your weight, you can improve your health in the following ways.

1. Lower your cholesterol levels
2. Lower your risk for developing diabetes
3. Lower your risk for developing cancer
4. Lower your blood pressure
5. Lower your risk for developing heart disease
6. Lower your risk for having a stroke
7. Have more energy
8. Have a greater chance of living a long, healthy life

Chapter 4

What Is Your Healthy Weight?

Believe it or not, there's no
such thing as an "ideal weight."

H ow much do you weigh? It's a question that triggers all kinds of negative emotions, especially in women—guilt, shame, frustration, resignation. According to a recent survey, 67 percent of women over 30 want to lose weight. While it is true that the incidence of obesity is increasing in the United States for both men and women, some of this desire for weight loss is due to unrealistic expectations about weight. Do you have a number fixed in your head that is your "perfect weight?" If that number is what you weighed when you graduated from high school, this weight might not be realistic. But just because you can't get back into the jeans you wore in high school, there's no reason to think that you can't achieve a healthy weight.

A healthy weight is about more than just appearance—it's about feeling good and avoiding health problems. A healthy weight is not simply the numbers on the scale— it's about how much of your weight is fat and where that fat is located. It's also about body shape and heredity. A healthy weight is a weight that is right for you.

FINDING YOUR BEST WEIGHT

Despite what we see on television, in magazines, and in movies, there is no such thing as a "perfect body" or ideal weight. Rejoice in your uniqueness and the shape that is you, and work at making the most of what you have.

When you are setting your weight-loss goals, it's important to be mindful of your body shape. Most people fall into one of three categories: (1) ectomorph (thin and willowy), (2) endomorph (round and curvy), or (3) mesomorph (muscular and athletic). For the most part, your body shape is determined by genetics, and one shape is not any healthier than another.

21

Even though a healthy weight depends on much more than just numbers on a scale, those numbers are a place to start. One tool to help you determine if your weight is in the healthy range is the Body Mass Index, or BMI. The BMI correlates closely to body fat percentage, so it's a better way to determine healthy weight than the older "ideal weight" charts. Instead of suggesting an ideal weight, this index can help you see if your weight is in a healthy range. Use the chart on page 23 to determine your BMI. It's important to remember that body weight and body fat are not the same thing. A person can be in the healthy weight range but still have a high percentage of body fat. Or an athlete with a lot of muscle mass and very little fat might have a weight that is above the normal range.

To Determine Your BMI:

1. Find your height in inches on the left side of the table on page 23.

2. On the row corresponding to your height, find your current weight.

3. Look at the numbers at the very top of the column to find your BMI.

4. Use the BMI and Health Risk section at the bottom of page 23 to determine your health risk. If your result is above the healthy limit, you can determine your target weight by finding a healthy BMI for your height and running the numbers in reverse on the chart.

Size Up Your Shape

Along with weight, where you carry fat is an indicator of health risk. People who tend to store fat around the waist (apple-shaped) are at higher risk for heart disease than people who tend to store fat on the hips (pear-shaped). To figure out if you are an "apple" or a "pear," calculate your waist-to-hip ratio.

Waist-to-Hip Ratio

1. Using a tape measure, measure your waist at its smallest point.

2. Measure your hips at the widest point of your buttocks and hips.

3. Divide the waist number by the hip number.

Waist-to-Hip Ratio and Health Risk

1.0 or more = apple shape = greater risk of heart disease

Less than 1.0 = pear shape = lower risk of heart disease

Less than 0.8 = normal for women

Less than .95 = normal for men

Body Mass Index (BMI)

BMI	19	21	23	25	27	30	32	34	36	38
Height				Weight (pounds)						
58"	91	100	110	119	129	143	152	162	172	181
59"	94	104	114	124	134	149	159	169	179	188
60"	97	107	117	127	138	153	163	173	183	194
61"	101	111	122	132	143	159	169	180	191	201
62"	103	114	125	136	147	163	174	185	196	206
63"	107	119	130	141	152	169	181	192	203	214
64"	111	123	135	146	158	176	187	199	211	223
65"	114	126	138	150	162	180	192	204	216	228
66"	118	131	143	156	168	187	199	212	224	236
67"	121	134	147	159	172	191	204	217	229	242
68"	125	139	152	165	178	198	211	224	238	251
69"	128	142	155	169	182	203	216	230	243	257
70"	133	147	161	175	189	210	224	237	251	265
71"	136	150	164	179	193	214	229	243	257	271
72"	140	155	170	185	199	221	236	251	266	281
73"	143	158	174	189	204	226	241	257	272	287
74"	148	164	179	195	210	234	249	265	281	296

BMI and Health Risk

Below 18.5 = Underweight

18.5 to 24.9 = Healthy Weight

25.0 to 29.9 = Overweight

30+ = Obesity

For example, if you are 5 feet 7 inches tall (67") and weigh 147 pounds, your BMI is 23. This means that you are in the healthy weight range and have a reduced risk of developing a weight-related disease, such as heart disease or Type 2 diabetes. If you are in the overweight weight range, you are at moderate risk, and if you are in the obese range, you are at high risk.

GET REAL

Although your weight is only one measure of your health and fitness status, the numbers on the scale are an indication about what is going on with your body. If you are gaining weight, is it because you've added more muscle? (It's true—muscle does weigh more than fat.) Or are you gaining because you stopped exercising and started eating more potato chips?

It's important to gain a good perspective about your weight. You don't need to have unrealistic expectations about losing down to a weight that is not achievable based on your body size and shape. But neither do you want to ignore the fact that you might be heading for a unhealthy weight.

READY, SET, GOAL

If you want to lose weight, here are some tips for setting realistic goals.

- Set action goals rather than result-oriented goals. For example, set a goal of walking three to four times each week rather than a goal of losing 5 pounds each week. When you focus on the behavior change, the results will follow.
- Be specific. Instead of making your goal "to walk more," make your goal to walk for 30 minutes, three times a week.
- Set small, short-term goals. If you want to have a goal of pounds lost, make your goal a manageable one, such as "lose 1 to 2 pounds a week" rather than "lose 50 pounds." A reasonable and safe rate of weight loss is 1 to 2 pounds per week.
- Judge your progress by changes in your body shape, not numbers on the scale. Who cares how much you weigh when you've gone down two skirt or pants sizes?
- Let health be your goal instead of just weight loss. A weight loss of just 10 percent is enough to lower high blood pressure, cholesterol, and triglycerides. Weight loss and exercise can also help lower blood sugar.
- Be realistic. If you are a large-boned, muscular person, it's not practical to try to look like a willowy super-model.

Chapter 5

Beyond the Scales

How much you weigh isn't as important as how much body fat you have. There are a number of simple ways to determine your percentage of body fat, but here's one man's account of having his body fat measured the most accurate way.

"OK, time for a dunking," Zeb Kendrick announces. In my skimpy Speedo bathing suit, I step into what looks like a summer-camp kiddie pool in a basement room on the Temple University campus in Philadelphia, where Kendrick conducts body composition research. At his direction, I rub my body down to get rid of air bubbles, then position myself, the water line chin-high, on a submerged scale not unlike the ones butchers use to weigh a side of beef. Kendrick instructs me to lean forward, put my face in the water, and exhale as fast and hard as I can to expel the air from my lungs. I repeat this procedure several times. "Blow out the candles," hollers Kendrick, like a coach rallying an athlete.

It isn't easy. I hold each exhale for five or six seconds, but it seems to be much longer than that. From swimming, I'm comfortable in the water, but with all the gadgetry and people poking their noses in the room, I feel like some specimen being sacrificed for the greater good.

More like my own good, actually. Fifty-two years old and in decent shape—or so I think—I'm here at Temple's Biokinetics Research Laboratory to undergo what's considered to be one of the true tests of good health: **hydrostatic weighing**, the most accurate means of measuring a person's body fat. "The gold standard," Kendrick, former director of the lab, calls it. Essentially, my weight in air will be subtracted from my weight in water using a formula devised at the University of Minnesota after World War II—which explains all the dunking, rubbing, and blowing I'm submitting myself to.

Study after study has linked excess body fat with a variety of diseases and conditions, including diabetes, heart disease, hypertension, gallbladder problems, and arthritis. Keeping fat off only gets harder as you get older. On average, people lose 3 to 5 percent of muscle mass every decade after age 25; after 50, muscle can really take a dive. Less muscle can mean more fat: For every pound of muscle we lose, we burn 50 fewer calories per day. No wonder the jelly roll around my waist is expanding.

THE NUMBERS TO BEAT

An accurate body-fat reading is much better than total weight as an indicator of physical health because it allows you to figure out how much of your heft is desirable muscle and bone, and how much is flab. For instance, according to a bathroom scale, someone with a broad frame might be considered overweight but have a desirable fat level. Or the scale could say pretty much the same thing it's said for 20 years, but physical evidence—a tight waistband, as in my case—signals that something may be amiss.

At Temple, some of the people tested regularly by Kendrick include military personnel and local professional athletes, members of the Philadelphia 76ers and Eagles among them. Thankfully, though, you don't have to be as lean as a drill sergeant or power forward to be considered healthy. The target body-fat levels determined by the American College of Sports Medicine are surprisingly realistic. (See the chart on page 28.) For men, anything between 11 percent and 17 percent is considered optimum; 25 percent and higher may be cause for concern. Because women naturally have higher fat-to-muscle ratios than men do, target body-fat levels for women tend to be higher as well: 19 to 22 percent is considered optimum; 30 percent and higher indicates a potential health threat. Those figures are actually estimates; science being what it is, the true standards are more complicated, broken down not just by gender but also by age in order to account for declining metabolisms such as mine. For instance, 21.3 percent body fat is considered good for my peers, men ages 50 to 59; guys in their 40s, however, must answer to a higher standard. For them, 19.6 percent is good (your doctor should have access to the more detailed standards).

> For every pound of muscle we lose, we burn 50 fewer calories per day.

As precise as this all sounds, though, all types of body-fat testing—even hydrostatic weighing—are subject to error. In addition, the 25 percent and 30 percent cutoffs for health risk are based on epidemiological studies, which don't clearly establish cause and effect, says Gary Hunter, Ph.D., an expert on body composition at the University of Alabama at Birmingham. But he emphasizes that a man or woman at the upper end of the acceptable category may want to take measures to reduce his or her body fat. For example, those folks who fare poorly during Kendrick's testing are generally asked to reduce calories by 10 to 15 percent and to walk, bicycle, or perform some other type of moderate aerobic exercise four to five times a

Weight training helps build muscle and bone, and it increases your body's metabolism.

week. The goal, Kendrick says, is a weight loss of 2 to 3 pounds per week for the first two weeks, and 1 pound a week after that. Weight training, or strength training, two or three times a week may also be recommended; it helps build muscle and bone, and it increases your body's metabolism.

Finally, I climb out of the tank, dry off, and wait for Kendrick to complete his computation. At last, Kendrick returns to the room, clipboard in hand, with the result for which I'd consented to expose my body to this room full of scientists. He gives it to me straight: 12.8%. Not exactly pro-basketball-worthy, but nonetheless it's a figure that puts me in the "superior" category for people my age. This is a score that validates my good health and, most importantly, my low-intensity exercise program.

—*Marc Bloom*

FIND OUT WHAT YOU'RE MADE OF

Here are several ways to get your body fat measured, in order from most to least reliable.

- **Hydrostatic weighing,** an extremely accurate way to measure fat. You're placed in a specially designed pool, and your weight in air is subtracted from your weight in water. It's available only at a few college laboratories and other sports-medicine complexes nationwide. The cost varies; Temple University charges $50, for example.

- **Air displacement,** a possible heir apparent to hydrostatic weighing because of its accuracy and ease of use. As you sit comfortably in a cocoonlike contraption called a Bod Pod, computerized pressure sensors determine the amount of air displaced by your body. The five-minute test typically costs between $25 and $50; it's available at more than 60 health clubs, universities, weight-control clinics, and sports-medicine complexes.

- **Skin-fold analysis,** in which calipers are used to "pinch" three body parts where fat accumulates: chest, abdomen, and thigh for men; triceps, thigh, and hip for women. For accuracy, the calipers should be spring-loaded to squeeze at a constant pressure. You can get the test done at many health clubs and fitness centers.

- **Bioelectrical impedance,** similar in cost and accuracy to skin-fold analysis. A weak electrical current passes through electrodes placed on your ankles and wrists. An instrument measures resistance to the current and produces a figure for fat-free mass. It's offered at some health clubs.

- **Infrared interactance,** where infrared radiation passes through a fiber-optic probe at your biceps. Reflected energy produces the body-fat measurement. Because only one part of the body is used, it's not as reliable as other methods. It's also hard to find; it may be available through some colleges or personal trainers.

- **"Fat-o-meters," "body-fat analyzers," or "body-fat scales,"** devices usually found in drugstores and health-product catalogs, generally deliver only ballpark figures. The margin of error is high because they have not been tested with large populations.

Recommended Body-Fat Levels

	Women	Men
Low/Acceptable	14 to 18%	6 to 10%
Optimum	19 to 22%	11 to 17%
Acceptable	23 to 30%	18 to 25%
Too High	More than 30%	More than 25%

Chapter 6

A Pound
of Prevention

Middle-age spread is alive and well, and actually not
all that bad for your health—if you keep a handle on it.

O h, there were signs. The day you cursed the dryer for suddenly shrinking your
favorite pair of jeans. The switch from sleekly tailored suits to sweaters tied
around the hips, untucked shirts, and elastic-waisted, wide-legged pants. At first, you
chalked it up to your evolving fashion sense. After all, you couldn't be gaining
weight; you were so faithful to your morning-walk workouts. Your eating habits
hadn't really changed throughout your 30s, either; the master of moderation, you
managed to enjoy yourself without overindulging. So you were understandably
shocked and disheartened to discover that, as your
40th birthday approached, you'd kicked up a few
notches on the bathroom scale.

**A modest weight gain
is inevitable—at least
for women—and can
actually be beneficial.**

You're not alone: Chances are, your friends in
their late 30s and early 40s have put on an extra
couple of pounds themselves. Blame it on Father
Time, not a lack of willpower. Age-related physi-
cal changes beginning in the middle 30s cause both men and women to grow heavier.
And while there are ways to keep your weight under control as you hit midlife, some
researchers say a modest weight gain is inevitable—at least for women—and can
actually be beneficial.

MUSCLE MATTERS

The formula for weight gain is really simple: Eat too much, move too little. That
holds true in midlife, too, but your aging body makes it easier to do both, says
Miriam Nelson, Ph.D., director for the Center for Physical Fitness at the

Friedman School of Nutrition Science and Policy at Tufts University. "Beginning in the mid-30s, you lose ⅓- to ½-pound of muscle each year," she says. "Muscle drives your metabolism. So if you're losing muscle each year, your metabolism goes down." That means the 2,200 calories per day you easily burned when you were 25 are too much at 35—and the excess gets stored as fat. On the exercise front, it's as if you're trying to run up a down escalator: You have to work harder for your gains because your body is losing muscle while you're trying to build it.

GOOD GAIN

Both men and women have to contend with age-related muscle loss and fat gain. But women lose twice as much muscle as men and gain twice as much fat per year after age 35—about 1½ pounds annually. In addition, some research suggests that hormonal differences make midlife weight gain more of a factor for women. Studies as far back as 1975 have shown that as women's bodies produce less estrogen with aging, their fat cells take up some of the slack, actually producing the hormone themselves. This causes the cells to grow larger starting in the mid- to late-30s as a woman approaches menopause. Even women who are physically active see these changes.

A modest midlife weight gain may help a woman's body stay healthy through menopause. There is evidence from the National Institute on Aging that women who are heavier at midlife have stronger bones and fewer hip fractures. Other studies suggest that women who are heavier at midlife sleep better, experience fewer hot flashes, and have smoother skin. So you might be healthier in the long run if you accept some weight gain.

You don't have to resign yourself to carrying an extra 15 to 25 pounds, though—as little as 2 to 5 pounds can be enough to protect you. But know this: Your body will probably want to gain more than that. Left to its own devices, the average woman's body will have lost 2½ pounds of muscle, gained 7½ pounds of fat, and need 200 fewer calories per day by her 40th birthday. That's not to mention lifestyle changes that might also affect your weight: Demanding careers, increasing family responsibilities, and other stressors can encourage you to eat more and exercise less.

THE STRESS FACTOR

Chronic stress, such as that resulting from a divorce, caring for an aging parent, or dealing with a difficult teenager, may lead to a more troubling type of weight gain. Dr. Pamela Peeke, assistant clinical professor of medicine at the University of Maryland School of Medicine, suggests that what she calls "toxic" stress not only provokes your appetite for high-fat, high-carbohydrate foods, but also that the accumulated fat collects deep in the abdomen rather than on the surface. Peeke says this type of fat is different from the superficial fat gained naturally as women approach menopause. Both men and women are susceptible to this deep-abdominal fat, which increases risks for heart disease, stroke, diabetes, and some types of cancer.

Peeke's suggestion that chronic stress contributes to deep-abdominal fat is still under much debate. But regardless of how it plays out in future research, taking steps to keep midlife weight gain under control can only benefit your health—as long as you approach it the right way. That means adjusting your exercise program, stress-handling strategies, and eating habits to go along with the changes in your body. Here are a few techniques for keeping midlife weight gain to a minimum.

Walk a different way. If you've been faithful to your walking routine for years, your muscles adapted to the activity long ago. Surprise your body with something different: cycling, swimming, cardio-kickboxing, inline skating. If you just can't give up walking, find a hilly route, try walking up stairs, or mix in some jogging—anything to make it more interesting for your muscles and therefore increase your metabolism.

Go for an hour, four days a week. Aerobic-exercise sessions need to last an hour to get maximum fat-burning effectiveness. Work up to this gradually to protect yourself from injury. If you're unaccustomed to exercise, fitness experts recommend starting with 20 minutes a week and increasing by no more than 10 percent each subsequent week. This strategy also helps prevent the novice exerciser's main enemy: burnout. If you're switching to a new activity, sustain it for 30 minutes; increase by 10 percent weekly.

Eat smaller, more frequent meals. Smaller meals and snacks can help stabilize blood sugar, keep energy high, and prevent overeating. Some dietitians recommend eating at least five times a day. Keep in mind, though, that you probably need 200 to 400 fewer calories overall per day than you did when you were younger. Use snacks to help work in healthful foods you may run low on in the course of the day: fruits, vegetables, and foods rich in calcium and fiber.

Make smart choices. The best way to keep your weight under control at any age is to eat sensibly—just like your mother told you. You don't have to be a scientist to know how to eat right. Go back to basics. Eat vegetables, fruits, and whole grains. That's what works.

Eat when you're hungry. And don't eat when you're not. That may seem self-evident, but staying connected to your body's food needs can help you keep a handle on your appetite. When you sit down to a meal, eat a quarter of your portion, pause, and check in with your body: Are you satisfied? If not, eat another quarter, and ask that question again.

Make muscle. The best way to combat age-related muscle loss—and therefore rev up your metabolism—is strength training. Research has shown that women who begin strength training in their 70s can build their muscles back to what they would have been if they were 40 years younger—and that works for men as well. Two days of strength training a week was all it took.

Don't diet. Engaging in regular physical activity is more important than dieting for keeping your weight under control in midlife. This advice particularly applies to women because dieting threatens female fat cells' ability to produce estrogen. It may be that undernourished fat cells actually grow larger in defiance.

—Lisa Delaney

Part
2

Healthy Weight-Loss Success

from the readers of
Cooking Light

"Our success, to be real, must contribute to the
success of others."—*Eleanor Roosevelt*

Chapter 7

Weight-Loss Inspirations

These *Cooking Light* readers have experienced real and significant weight loss, the *Cooking Light* way. Listen as they share their stories, advice, and insights so that you, too, can successfully lose the weight you want to lose.

The Best Time of My Life

JeAnne Swinley · **Age** 30 · **Height** 5'5" · **Before** 338 pounds
After 195 pounds (and still losing) · **Time It Took** 2 years

Words of Wisdom "Everyone has their own recipe for success. The one consistent thread is that you must take the time to find out what works for you. Find your path, that is, what you feel you can work with long-term, not just what will work long enough for you to squeeze into that party dress."

Sometimes it's best to get out of the way of a good story and let a person speak for him or herself. Such is the case with JeAnne Swinley's tale. JeAnne regularly shares her insight on CookingLight.com's "Healthy Living" bulletin board, where she leads a lively discussion on weight-loss support. Read on for the account of her struggle, in her own words.

"On September 13, 2000, I began a journey that would alter the course of my life. I have always joked that dieting attempts were the best time markers of my life. When things were going well, there was always a new diet to try. I would eagerly buy into the new plan, do a month's worth of healthy food shopping and spend Sunday chopping carrot sticks and celery, preparing a week's worth of chicken breasts and tuna.

"When life stopped being perfect (somewhere between day 2 and day 10 of a new diet), I would toss the broiled chicken and grapefruit aside as I reached for the pint of ice cream, swearing off deprivation forever and insisting I had everything I wanted.

"Still, despite people telling me I would never get the terrific job, the great husband, or achieve any of my other dreams as long as I was fat, I spent 20-plus years proving them wrong. I gained and lost the same 50 pounds, and each time I put on a little more. Nonetheless, I landed a wonderful job in an investment bank, I pursued writing and music interests. And I also fell in love and married the most incredible man, who from day one has been my number one fan.

"After being married a few months, I finally got tired of being sick and tired. I was kidding myself that at 338 pounds I had the same energy as my 160-pound husband. I thought about our future together and how I wanted our lives to be filled not only with love, but also with adventure and just plain fun. I didn't want to be held back by a cumbersome body.

"I knew inside me there was a free spirit, a risk taker who wanted to live for a long time, enjoying all of what life had to offer with the person she loved. But this time had to be different: I had to accept that I was a foodie with food issues. I was going to have to resolve my issues while still enjoying food in all its variety and glory.

"I started a weight-loss program and a few months later discovered *Cooking Light*, both the magazine and the Web site. *Cooking Light* introduced me to new flavors and foods, accurate portions, and exercise ideas. All these things had a domino effect on my weight loss and still contribute to my success.

"I have lost 195 pounds and still have more to lose—but the rest is just icing on the cake. Don't get me wrong, it is incredibly hard work to change habits that took years to create. But I have successfully changed my relationship with food without killing my love of it."

"This is the single most important thing that I could have done for me and me only. It has been life-changing."

MORE WORDS OF WISDOM

JeAnne has plenty of solid insights and strategies that inspire no matter how much weight you aim to lose. Here are a few pearls.

Support Systems: Choose people to be in your life whom you can count on to anchor you through difficult times. Leave the naysayers alone and ask for encouragement and support only from those who can give it.

Journal: Writing down what you eat is one of the most helpful ways to be accountable.

Rewards: I celebrate at 10- and 25-pound increments. I give myself training sessions, jewelry, CDs, manicures, etc.

Scales: Scales are deceiving. Instead, measure your body regularly to mark progress in inches lost and pay attention to how clothes feel.

Deprivation: Don't do it. It's about portion control and finding a balance with food and exercise.

On perfection: Life is stressful and strange things happen. Being successful at weight loss long-term means accepting that you are not perfect and that you can choose to eat or not to eat. Once you've made that choice, be at peace and move on.

On setbacks: There are always little setbacks; life is just like that. To overcome them, don't rely solely on motivation, which is fleeting. Perseverance and patience are what pays off in the long run. Don't wait three days or three months to get back in the swing of things—do it immediately.

On living life lighter: I had never thought of myself as a wallflower, but there are some things that I can do now that I definitely couldn't do as a 338-pound woman. To feel liberated from that weight physically is indescribable. I feel strong as an Amazon and invincible!

A Strong Skinny

Casey Blumenthal · **Age** 49 · **Height** 5'4½"
Before 132 pounds · **After** 107 pounds · **Time It Took** Half her life

Words of Wisdom "There is no secret and no easy way to success. It's simple: Calories in must be less than calories out to lose weight. Use aerobic exercise and weight resistance to increase your caloric consumption and burn fat, and balance your diet with a lot of fresh fruits, vegetables, whole grains, moderate protein, and lower fats. This is the only recipe for long-term success and true physiological wellness."

So many of us struggle with the butterfly syndrome: We know that our true selves are trapped within an ill-fitting casing and crave the day when we can break out. Dropping excess weight is one of the most powerful ways to shed that shell and the resulting joy can be life-altering. That's how it was for Casey Blumenthal.

Though Casey's weight-loss saga was just that—an ongoing battle waged most of her life—when she struck the right healthy lifestyle formula, she was finally able to wear the body she always knew she had inside. Being comfortable in your own skin took on a whole new meaning for this fit forty-something. Take a listen:

"I was a chubby child in a family of thin people," says Casey, "and the subject of enough jokes that I wanted a different body. I started taking ballet as a 5-year-old and was always in the back row but I wanted to be up front.

"When I was 12 years old, my mother and I were shopping for a bathing suit,"

"When I finally could see muscles emerging from all my weight training and aerobic work, there was the person I knew I was meant to be at last!"

Casey continues. "And after a day of staring in dressing room mirrors, I was near tears. My mother told me she would help me lose weight if I did what she told me."

Casey's mom, a well-meaning woman disciplined enough to cut her own chocolate candies in half, ran a "from scratch" family kitchen and began serving her daughter smaller portions. She also limited the child's desserts and snacks. Casey would ask her mother before eating anything and within two months, the little girl had lost 15 pounds. Though she maintained her moderate weight through high school, Casey never truly accepted her new shape—maybe because she wasn't exactly in the driver's seat, maybe because a poor body image had been implanted so early.

Regardless of the reason, Casey yo-yoed for years, picking up the freshman 15 in college, adding another five pounds here and there, then losing extra weight from illnesses contracted while traveling in Mexico and Asia. While she'd never recommend such unlucky souvenirs as the ideal way to jumpstart a healthy lifestyle, the last bout did just that for her.

"As the pounds disappeared," says Casey of her go-round with malaria, "I moved into a long-term lifestyle that took off the rest of my extra weight,

and I stayed there. What I found most interesting during that time," says Casey, who reached her 30s at the height of the aerobics craze, "was that I discovered a reservoir of self-discipline. I never knew that I had such stick-to-it-iveness, but it emerged in full force—especially when I started working out in the weight room. I loved the feeling of control and strength it gave me and I reveled in how my body felt as I pushed it to its limits."

A fitness buff was born. Casey, who is married to a former professional skier, works full-time and credits her success to consistent "hearty weight training" and aerobic activity—she's either skiing, spinning, hiking, mountain biking, ice dancing, or taking a variety of fitness classes at least four to five times a week. That, plus a healthy, low-fat diet gleaned from 13 years as a *Cooking Light* subscriber, helped the pounds "melt away."

As for that body image, check out this turnaround: Remember the 5-year-old Casey on the back row in ballet? She's a 49-year-old on the front row of the dance classes she now takes. "I feel like I'm my true self," she says, smiling. "Yeah, I'm kinda skinny, but I am a strong skinny."

Sister Act

Deena and Meredith Beard · **Ages** 29; 31
Height 5'10"; 5'6" · **Before** 182; 178 pounds · **After** 159; 144 pounds
Time It Took About a year; 8 months

Words of Wisdom "I maintained at one weight for eight months before moving into the final stretch. That was OK, though, because this is a life change and I don't need to rush." (Deena)

"Losing weight did take over my life for a while, but when you're making a positive change, that isn't such a bad thing." (Meredith)

Deena

Not enough can be said for the good that a pal can do a person. And when it comes to tackling a challenge like reshaping your lifestyle, your eating habits, and overhauling your self image with weight loss—well, let's just say doing it with a friend is twice as nice.

That's just what Deena Beard and her sister-in-law Meredith discovered a few summers ago. Deena, two inches shy of six feet, had recently seen a picture of herself and was shocked. "I knew my clothes were tight," Deena says of her size

"After a week of eating light meals that didn't skimp on taste, I was good to go."

then, "but I was telling myself that I hid it well because I was tall. Not true."

Fast forward to a family beach trip soon after and Deena was in for shock number two: Her sister-in-law Meredith had lost nearly 20 pounds since the last time they had seen one another. And being the team player that she is, Meredith had brought along her copies of *Cooking Light* and other weight-loss materials to share with anyone who was interested. After a week of eating light meals that didn't skimp on taste, Deena was good to go.

"I made tofu chocolate mousse," says Deena, "and after that I was inspired." For help in getting on the right path, she followed her sister-in-law's example, incorporating exercise, low-fat recipes, and portion control into her daily routine. Plus, she set small, incremental weight-loss goals so as not to overwhelm herself by losing the weight all at once. The two women, separated by a few state lines, reinforced the other's commitment—and motivation—via e-mail.

"Meredith was an incredible inspiration," says Deena. "She started a few months before me and was so good at staying focused! She exercises all the time and has lots of great tips and recipe ideas. I knew that if she could do it, I had no excuse not to try as well."

Though she may have been a rock for Deena, Meredith had her own struggles to contend with. Initially, she entered into

Meredith

"My family and friends were the most important factors in my success."

her plan with four other friends who lived nearby, all of whom made getting fit and healthy a major life priority. "They were an amazing support group," says Meredith. "Once Deena started as well," continues Meredith, "family support became more important, since she knew what I was going through. She celebrated when I was doing well and encouraged me to keep going when I was discouraged. It made me feel good about what I had accomplished when I was able to share advice and encouragement with Deena."

In the end, Meredith lost nearly 35 pounds. And Deena, after losing 10 pounds and holding there for nearly eight months before she felt confident enough to keep on, is just shy of her 27-pounds-lighter goal.

What advice do they have to share? Because they both still have cravings, and neither of them cares for artificially low-fat, low-calorie, or fat-free foods, they both use lighter, natural ingredients in flavorful recipes. "I try to make healthier versions of my comfort foods so that I know I can still have them," says Deena.

"And I spent a lot of time figuring out what I could eat to satisfy my cravings (mostly for chocolate) without going overboard," says Meredith, who admits that having reached her goal brings its own challenges. "Although I have changed my attitude about food," she says, "it's still tempting to say 'I'm done losing weight,' and celebrate by eating everything I want."

But she's not slipping back into old habits just yet. Maybe it's because of the self-esteem she's built through this whole process; maybe she doesn't want to let herself or her family and cohorts down. Or maybe it's because she incorporated one of the best fail-safes in any lifestyle overhaul—a support network that buoys her through thick and thin.

Dressed for Success

Sandra Lira · Age 57
Height 5'5" · **Before** 165 pounds · **After** 135 pounds
Time It Took 6 months

Words of Wisdom "Plan out a week's worth of meals in advance. I found that sitting down on a Sunday and making a list of recipes and groceries for each day (even lunches) made it easier to stay focused. I also kept a calendar in full view where I logged in any exercise that I did—even a little 10-minute walk."

Forget the scale. If you want to know how you're faring in the battle of the bulge, head to the closet. There it comes down to the ultimate truth: Is it a skinny or fat jeans day? Whichever pair wins out can determine your mood for the day, a scenario Sandra Lira knows all too well.

"I could be the poster person for yo-yo dieting," says Sandra, who calls Alberta, Canada, home. "I not only own a skinny and fat wardrobe, I also have clothes for the in-between stage."

It was her so-called fat wardrobe that put her over the edge one day. "I had managed to get myself to the point where dressing to go out was literally painful," says Sandra. "When even the fat side of my wardrobe didn't fit, when my energy level and self-esteem were at an all-time low, that's when I decided to lose weight.

"I had been ignoring what was happening to my body," says Sandra, who had previously tried all sorts of diets, from eating only cabbage to downing nothing but fat-free soup. She even went so far as to invest $400 on weight-loss pills. "I think I must have been getting pretty desperate," she admits. "But finally my emotional side decided to take a stand. And stand I did, in front of the mirror, which I had avoided for a full year."

That quality time in front of the looking glass sealed the deal. "It was as if a light bulb went off in my head," says Sandra. "I knew what I had to do, but I wasn't totally sure what avenue to follow." What diet? What exercise plan? I was certainly not prepared to go back to a gym atmosphere in my overweight, out-of-shape condition."

So Sandra took matters into her own hands, getting back to the basics she, a one-time aerobics instructor, knew to be true: A healthy lifestyle begets a healthy weight. "I started on a low-fat meal plan and scheduled two 20-minute walks per day," she says. "In less than two months, I had lost 20 pounds."

"What worked for me in the end," she explains, "was to realize that I had to look at my eating as a lifetime lifestyle change, rather than the old 'Well, I'll diet for a month or two and then.' I guess this is why *Cooking Light*'s low-fat, low-calorie recipes really appealed to me. I didn't feel as though I was denying myself anything. The taste is still there, just without the fat and the calories.

"The nicest thing is that I have managed to keep the extra pounds off," says Sandra. "I recently quit smoking and was very concerned about possible weight gain. Not happening! I have increased my exercise regimen to include aerobics and weight training. I feel younger now than I did when I was 30!"

> "We have to realize that it is energy in, energy out. So an hour-long aerobics class doesn't justify that order of French fries. Well, that is unless they are the low-fat fries that I eat now!"

Sensible Indulgences

Heidi Myers · **Age** 31 · **Height** 5'2"
Before 144 pounds · **After** 111 pounds
Time It Took 4 to 5 months

Words of Wisdom "There is no immediate gratification with weight loss—it's truly a lesson in patience and in planning."

It's no secret that one of the most daunting, depressing words to surround weight loss is "diet." Those four little letters conjure up a prison of deprivation filled with bland, fist-sized portions of not a whole lot. What's a food lover to do?

"Don't deprive your-self," says Heidi Myers, a self-proclaimed foodie who had been over-weight her entire life and wanted a turnaround as she stood on the thresh-old of her 30s. "I L-O-V-E food. All kinds of food," she says emphatically. So imagine her relief when her first *Cooking Light* cookbook arrived, the very day she joined a weight-loss program. "Not only did the cookbook make it easy to follow my plan, but the recipes are also wonderful. I didn't feel like I was giving up a thing."

In part to save her hus-band from boring "diet" food, and in part to satiate her own adventurous palette, Heidi turned to the wild stuff. "I realized that ethnic and exotic cui-sine was the best way for me to lose weight," she says. "Using spices and fresh ingredients lends a lot of flavor but not calories."

So Heidi began trying out new recipes three, then four, then five nights a week and

"The healthier your menu is, the more fresh and flavorful it is. Try new spices. Be adventurous. You never know what you might discover."

pretty soon she had a new lifestyle, not to mention a new cooking repertoire. "I began using ingredients that I never even knew about before," she says, "like different peppers and other produce, whole grain couscous, all sorts of condiments."

And there were some surprises with the old standards as well: "I never knew how much I enjoyed grilled or steamed fish," Heidi says. "I always thought I hated fish! I just didn't know how to prepare it to enhance the flavors."

Heidi was amazed with how quickly healthy eating became a way of life. "I now crave veggies and fruit instead of chips and candy," she says. "And I truly don't feel like I am giving up anything when I eat well. Rather, I much more enjoy whole grains, fresh produce, and lower-fat meats. It's a rare day that I crave something fried or fat-laden. And when I do give in, I'm reminded of how heavy and sluggish those meals make me feel, which cures me from craving them for quite a while."

Just as important as staying on track is how you treat yourself when you make the occasional "bad" choice. "Know that you never 'fail' or 'fall off the wagon'," says Heidi, who once backtracked a little herself, putting on a few pounds near her 30th birthday. "It happens, but just don't allow one bad choice to become an excuse to stop caring."

To stave off unhealthy urges in the first place, Heidi—who lost that reclaimed weight—follows a few strategic rules. She plans out her menu weekly, and in the beginning, wrote down every piece of food that went into her mouth, which allowed her to differentiate between empty calories and healthy choices. On the flip side, she always makes room for dessert a few nights a week, indulging sensibly with low-fat alternatives. And she has one indulgent meal a week. "You'll soon find out that even though what you are choosing that night is more decadent than what you had the rest of the week," Heidi says, "you no longer consider the unhealthy choices regularly."

The end result of all her efforts is manyfold. "I am stunned at how creative and adventurous I am with my cooking," says Heidi. "And I knew from the beginning I was doing this for me—to be happy and healthy. I'm still amazed with myself."

Mother Knows Best

MaryKay Lawrence · **Age** 37
Height 5' 5½" · **Before** 185 pounds · **After** 149 pounds
Time It Took 8 months

Words of Wisdom "My approach was not to 'diet and lose weight.' I tried an overall lifestyle change instead. The nicest part was that I was enjoying good food and nice walks and the change happened without me even realizing it. All of a sudden I was back in my size 10 jeans and I felt great!"

Mothers-to-be, who are generally advised to gain between 25 and 35 pounds to help ensure their baby's health, often find themselves in a sticky situation: They must eat enough for two, but not so much that they jeopardize their own health and happiness. When you're battling hormones and cravings, not to mention the hassles of daily life, this can be a daunting balancing act—just ask MaryKay Lawrence.

For four-and-a-half years, MaryKay ran an espresso café and art gallery in Roseville, Minnesota. When her routine of long hours, little exercise, and catch-as-catch-can eating paired up with her first pregnancy, it was a combo that took her from her normal size 10 to a size 16. About four months after her son Jake was born, MaryKay (who had stopped working) took the added pounds to task.

"After months of living in the whirlwind of new motherhood, I was ready to find my old body and a bit of my old mental self," says MaryKay. "Plus," she adds, "I wanted back

"It was the happiest day when I pulled on my pre-pregnancy jeans! I called everyone!"

in my old wardrobe."

She began studying her pile of *Cooking Light* magazines, which had been neglected throughout her pregnancy. "I cut out recipes, logged onto the Web site and stocked my quite-empty kitchen with many of the *Cooking Light* basics. I was surprised how easy it was to make unique, tasty, and healthy meals."

That MaryKay is naturally blessed with motivation and an optimistic attitude helped immensely. Witness these two scenarios: When she noticed using fresh vegetables—as opposed to those that are canned or dried—really did make a difference in a dish's taste, she planted her first gardens, one for vegetables and one for herbs. And because her family now relies on husband Dale's income alone, each week she bakes muffins and breads and cooks homemade soup for him to take into the office. The payoff in both cases? Healthy living and money saved.

If MaryKay doesn't sound like the average exhausted and overwhelmed new mom, take heart; even the mighty have tough times. "My initial setback was the inability to consistently exercise," says MaryKay, who believes in the water, sleep, exercise, healthy eating, and vitamins approach to weight loss and maintenance. "Taking care of a newborn does not allow for trips to the gym." So the Lawrences bought at-home equipment and now MaryKay works out as Jake naps in the morning. "It was the best decision we could have made," she says.

Roadblock number two came in the form of discipline. When MaryKay left any one strategy out of the equation—exercising regularly but not sleeping well, for instance—the weight came off slowly or not at all. "Once I incorporated them all into my life as habit," she says, "it worked and I didn't even realize I had made a life change."

Now MaryKay's so productive about the home her family and friends call her Martha—as in Martha Stewart. One of her favorite stories is how her mother remarked after hearing of yet another great meal: "You must be gaining more weight with all of that cooking." "Not at all," MaryKay was able to say. "In fact, we're losing weight!"

So how does MaryKay plan to stick with her new lifestyle? The recipe seems to be equal parts diligence and perspective. "Little setbacks, such as Jake's colds and sleepless nights can cause me to miss one or more of my new daily habits," admits MaryKay. Without skipping a beat she adds, "The key is to do what you can and start each day anew."

Sounds just like the sort of advice great moms are known for.

—*Melissa Bigner*

How to Be a Weight-Loss Success Story

Want to know what it takes to be a success story? Here's the advice that a *Cooking Light* reader sent.

- Educate yourself. Learn about both diet and exercise. You can do one without the other but it's much harder and the results won't come as quickly.
- Plan your meals ahead. That goes especially for lunches and includes snacks.
- Keep a food journal. Be brutally honest.
- Don't starve yourself. Your body needs food, and not eating will make you sick.
- Talk to your doctor or nutritionist. Ask about taking multi-vitamins and/or calcium.
- Look into weight training. Muscles burn calories just being there, and healthy bones are extremely important.
- Find a workout buddy. Don't go at it all alone.
- Try a personal trainer. Go to one long enough to get you headed in the right direction.
- Forget the scale. Stop thinking in terms of a magic number and instead, focus on eating right, exercising, and keeping your heart healthy.
- Find your motivation. This varies from person to person.
- Don't expect instant results. You didn't put the weight on overnight, and you won't lose it overnight either.

Chapter 8

Jump-Start
Healthy Habits

See how this active woman sets a healthy
example for her family with exercise and her passion
for balanced and sensible eating.

You wouldn't know it to look at her now, but nine years ago, Sheila Agnew Burke made a life-changing decision. "The business was piling up," she recalls of that time. "I was working long hours and just eating any kind of way." She was still Sheila Agnew then, just-turned-40, divorced, and the single mother

Sheila walks three miles a
day with her neighbor
friend.

of a college-age daughter. She was juggling two businesses on Chicago's South Side—a party-supply store and the event-planning business that would grow into Innovative Custom Event Designs, the company she runs today.

Though she had been physically active throughout her 20s and 30s, the stress from her work load caused her to take on some bad habits—poor eating and little exercise. She put on 25 pounds. It didn't help that she was also too busy to continue what once had been regular just-for-fun bicycle rides to and along Lake Michigan.

She resolved to change her ways. "I had a choice: I could either stay that way, or I could get back to wearing the clothes that I had before," says Sheila, who's always considered herself fashionable. "I decided to get back into shape."

She began walking three miles a day with a neighbor friend, mostly on the track at nearby Chicago State University. She continued to eat the same foods because her diet had always been fairly healthful, but scaled back on what had become supersize portions. Within months, Sheila was back to her old "perfect size 10" self, and felt perfect, too. Just as importantly, fitness walking and sensible eating had evolved from obligations to lifetime habits, easy to keep up even after relocating to Ohio almost five years ago with her daughter Ilika; granddaughter Tyler; and new husband Rodney Burke.

Three to five times every week now, Sheila makes the drive to Blacklick Woods Metro Park, three miles from her home in suburban Columbus, and briskly race-walks a four-mile trail. In bad weather, she works out at home, exercising along with ESPN2's Crunch Fitness and BodyShaping programs or, more recently, practicing videotaped Tae-Bo routines. On Saturdays, she and a small group of women do circuit weight training. Walking remains Sheila's favorite exercise activity, though, and nothing beckons more than the gravel-and-blacktop loop that meanders through an oasis of beeches, maples, sycamores, and buckeyes on the east border of the state's capital city.

You won't see her zoned out listening to a CD or cassette, either. "I like hearing nature," Sheila says. "I like hearing the birds chirp." She also likes the time to think. "Work, life—you can pretty much meditate on anything"—including what her long-held commitment has done for her and the people around her.

ALL IN THE FAMILY

Most nights, those closest to Sheila gather around the dinner table, where she shares the other healthful passion in her life—balanced and sensible eating. Her family, which now includes another granddaughter, Makhia, is completely happy with meals based on fruit, vegetables, fish, chicken, and turkey. Sheila downplays her skills in the kitchen, but her talents, especially stir-frying, have proven sufficient to keep her crew happy. And they don't miss conventional, red-meat-heavy meals—not even husband Rodney, who, in his bachelor days, used to routinely polish off a 24-ounce steak just before going to bed.

For someone who "never ate turkey bacon in my life prior to meeting Sheila," Rodney admits it tastes pretty good; ditto ground turkey as a substitute for ground beef in pasta dishes. Such flavorful alternatives and the deft application of spices have made cutting back on his former red meat habit surprisingly painless. "Now I eat red meat twice a week, if that," he says. "And it's kind of controlling my weight."

ROLE MODEL FOR FITNESS

Those 25 extra pounds Sheila walked away from in Chicago have never returned. "I feel great physically. I feel great about my appearance. I enjoy the compliments I get from both men and women, and, most of all, I like to help motivate others," she says. In fact, she's become, literally, a model of the healthy life. Revlon has used her at style shows to demonstrate a product that highlights gray hair. And women of various ages marvel at her fitness. "I just had a young girl ask me last week what I do to stay in shape," Sheila says.

She inspires the home team, too. Rodney gets his walks on the golf course, and Ilika occasionally joins her mother on a morning jaunt. Sheila recently helped teach 7-year-old Tyler to ride a bike, running up and down the street beside her. Nine years ago, at 40, that might not have been possible. Today, almost anything is.

—Bill Beuttler

5 WAYS TO STAY MOTIVATED TO WALK

1. **Write it down.** Keeping track of your walking program with an exercise diary helps keep you focused on your goals.
2. **Entertain yourself.** Listen to music, walk with a friend, take a stroll with your dog—do whatever it takes to make walking interesting.
3. **Have a destination.** Using your walk as a commute to work or as a way to run errands makes the exercise seem useful as well as healthful. If you feel that you're doing something useful, you'll have a much greater tendency to do it.
4. **Walk in a nice place.** Plan your route through a park, past historic landmarks, or to other interesting sites.
5. **Reward yourself.** Give yourself a pat on the back for a job well done, but don't do it with food or anything else that may be counter-productive to reaching your goals. New walking shoes and a trip to the movies are positive reinforcements, and fun.

Chapter 9

Cook Together, Lose Weight Together

Cooking together, even with a little creative separation,
is a great way to enjoy the art of healthy living.

I t is a typical Saturday night at Mark and Annette Shideler's secluded home in
Mount Sinai, Long Island, New York. Old friends will arrive for dinner in an
hour. In the meantime, the flurry of chopping, mixing, seasoning, and measuring is

Mark likes to read a
recipe once, then do his
own version.

so intense (although paced to Al Jarreau's casual
jazz on the stereo) you'd think somebody had
brought in an extra kitchen.

And you would be right. Mark and Annette
love to cook so much—both for health and pleasure—that while renovating their 100-year-old
Adirondack-style home, they customized the
kitchen with his-and-hers work stations. Time to
call a marriage counselor? Hardly. In a world of
separate checking accounts, vacations, bathrooms,
and e-mail accounts, a kitchen counter of one's own
can definitely be a sign of togetherness.

GETTING IT TOGETHER

Working together at the art of healthy living has come naturally to Mark, marketing
director for a St. Louis-based bison ranch, and Annette, technology coordinator for
a local school district. Even their approach to fitness is relaxed and well-integrated
into their everyday routine. Separately, Mark walks their Yorkshire terrier, Baggins,
twice a day ("he comes and gets me when it's time for us to walk," Mark says) while
Annette power-walks through the neighborhood three times a week. Together, the

Annette cooks strictly "by-the-book" when she's in the kitchen.

couple does a mix of sit-ups, body bends, and other calisthenics each morning. "Because my job is fairly stressful and extremely fast-paced, it's important to rev up my metabolism in the morning to prepare for work," Annette says.

Well matched as they are now, it's still a wonder the couple ever got together. "I like to joke that ours is a mixed marriage," Mark says. "Our backgrounds are as different as can be." He was reared in Kansas City "in the house of Ozzie and Harriet" on meat and potatoes; first-generation Italian-American Annette grew up on Long Island, imbued with a cuisine famous for its passions and flavors. It took a blind date 10 years ago to bring their separate ways together.

LET'S DO IT MY WAY

When it gets down to the countertop (or tops), it's easy to see the true synergy this pair has developed. They agree on the importance of eating healthfully, of cooking with less fat and salt, and on using the best and freshest ingredients they can find. But they also have their idiosyncrasies: Mark is an improviser and a big fan of The Galloping Gourmet—he'll hear or read a recipe once and then do his own riff—while Annette is strictly by-the-book. So there's often her way and his.

As joint ventures go, this is precisely the point. You don't have to agree all the time; you can make your case, maintain respect, go on about your business, and have a lot of fun along the way.

IT'S ALL IN THE KITCHEN

From virtually the instant the Shidelers moved into their house 10 years ago, they knew one key to happiness lay in the design of their kitchen. A long, dark, and windowless throwback to the 1950s, the space accommodated the usual one cook, not two who see cooking as a fun, essential component of healthy living. Looking at the low ceiling, faded ruby-red linoleum, paneled cabinets, laminate countertops, and the single sink, they knew there was just one solution: Gut it.

They sketched out something more compatible with their lifestyles: dual work stations, plenty of countertops, and a big bay window. To overcome the cramped feeling, they raised the ceiling a foot and leveled the hardwood floors. Granite countertops and backsplashes strike a balance between form and function. And for the kitchen's work engines, they chose a combination gas cooktop and electric oven large enough to manage several courses at once.

WHAT TWO CAN DO

"Dinner's served!" Annette announces. The guests—friends they've known for more than 25 years—make their way from the fireside living room into the dining room. Annette makes a quick kitchen detour to help Mark put the final touches on the first course. He fills each bowl with soup; she adds the garnish, a sprinkling of chives, and serves. Now what has come together is about to be torn asunder, dish by dish, and happily so.

—Kim Goad

TWO COOKS, ONE KITCHEN

If you'd like to try a two-cook kitchen in your home, Lee Woodall, an Atlanta-based certified kitchen designer, offers this advice.

Consider your needs. "You'll have to think about how you prepare food and how you use the appliances and countertops in your kitchen," she says. "Are you cooking for convenience? For pleasure and hobby? The answers will dictate the best way to make your kitchen more user-friendly."

Let it flow. Understanding the flow of traffic through your kitchen can help you plan an efficient layout that'll keep you happily cooking side-by-side. "If you're bumping into each other or find the things you need are often out of reach, focus on creating a layout that eliminates those problems."

Dollars and sense. Customizing for two cooks can cost anywhere from hundreds of dollars for simple fixes to thousands for dual stoves. "The most common problems are lack of counter space or the need for another sink, and those are relatively inexpensive," Woodall says.

Chapter 10

Spread the Word: Healthy Is Happy

From the vast Texas Panhandle, Becky McKinley spreads her inspiration about healthy living and low-fat cooking as a caterer, columnist, and mother.

W e've all heard about community involvement, but what if your community is the Texas Panhandle? Then you might want to follow the example of Becky McKinley, a mother of three who has made it her business and her mission to tell everyone in the vast region who can read, watch TV, attend a cooking class, or

come to a party that a healthy lifestyle is just too easy, happy, and energizing to pass up. Today, in her spacious Amarillo home, she's teaching one of her low-fat cooking classes to 20 members of the Texas Cattlefeeders' Association Board Wives.

As the wives settle into her dining room, Becky tucks a mixing bowl under one arm, stirs the several pots on her stovetop, and makes a last-minute check that all the ingredients are in place. First she'll demonstrate, then they'll eat. And Becky knows that no matter how well she makes the case that low-fat cooking is as friendly to beef as it is to chicken, fish, veg-

Becky shows her friends that healthy food can taste good.

gies, or desserts, the true test will be in the taste. When lunch is served—beef tenderloin, balsamic-glazed onion sandwiches, cream-of-leek soup in puff pastry, and chocolate angel food cake topped with cream-cheese ice cream—some of the women are openly skeptical. "It looks good," they murmur, "but will we like it?" The verdict comes with the first mouthful. "This is low-fat?" one of the women wonders aloud.

Becky smiles. Happens every time.

MAKING THE CHANGE

Becky tuned in to the ways of healthy living 15 years ago, shortly after the birth of one of her children. "I gained a lot of weight during my pregnancy," she says. "I wanted to do something about it." So did her physician husband, John, who had put on 40 "sympathy" pounds. They made a commitment to themselves and to each other, and have never looked back. Except to notice how much slimmer their profiles became.

But it was not in Becky's nature to guard a good thing jealously. She knew that what she had learned could make many other people healthy—and happy. The first audience was her own family. With John already on board, the challenge was the children. But sons Gavin, 16, and Andy, 17, and daughter April, 20, proved her toughest critics even as they were growing up. So Becky made "a game" out of showing them that healthy food can taste as good as—or better than—the high-fat and fast-food alternatives. Part of the ploy was to tackle high-fat restaurant favorites, such as a salmon-and-black-bean burrito Becky remembered from a California trip: "I wanted to see if I could create the same flavors while cutting out a lot of the fat and carbohydrates." She did, substituting lower-fat versions of the sour cream and beans. The kids went for it big time and still ask for it often. April even makes it on her own while she's away at college. In fact, she's fully joined Mom's movement and asks for new recipes to be faxed to her all the time. Dorm food never had a chance.

SPREADING THE MESSAGE

Family came first, but the rest of the world beckoned, too. Seven years ago, Becky expanded her catering business to include volunteering for nonprofit organizations such as Ronald McDonald House and the local cancer center. As her reputation for preparing low-fat cuisine grew, she started writing "Becky's Bites," a monthly recipe column in the regional magazine *Accent West*, and began teaching low-fat cooking classes at health clubs and for local civic groups. She's also developing new cooking classes, including one just for children. And in her spare time, Becky is working on a meal-planner cookbook. "Healthful cooking obviously is an important part of my life," she says. "But it's part of all our lives."

FITTING IN FITNESS

Keeping busy isn't necessarily keeping fit, so Becky and her family also make a point of finding time to exercise—even though time has a way of vanishing. John sneaks in some stretching moves in the doctor's lounge while waiting to see patients. When he can't get to the health club, he uses a stairstepper and free weights at home. "Every day, I wake up with the intention to exercise," John says. "I'm not always up to it, but my wife inspires me."

Becky makes it to the club frequently, taking BodyPump classes and playing tennis with friends. But what she likes best is a good 45-minute walk around the neighborhood with John.

Weekends offer the best occasions to put everything together, and one of the McKinleys' preferred destinations is the rugged beauty of nearby Palo Duro Canyon. John and Becky pack a healthy lunch and kick their walking up a notch by traversing more than five miles of rocky terrain. "A lot of men don't walk with their wives because they think it's a sissy thing to do," Becky says, laughing about a recent trip. "I challenge them to come up here and walk in the canyon. It's not as easy as it looks." Which is what you'd expect from a person who makes challenges easy for everyone.   —*Melissa Ewey Johnson*

HINTS TO HEALTHY LIVING

Healthy living is no more complicated than eating delicious, well-balanced meals and getting some exercise. Becky McKinley's tips:

Keep it simple. Keep family meals as uncomplicated as possible. "I try to get everything organized in advance using recipes that don't require dozens of ingredients," she says. "It's easier than most people think."

Stay balanced. "What's the point of eating something if it doesn't taste good?" Becky asks. "When I learned how to cook low-fat, great-tasting meals, I felt healthier and didn't miss the fat at all. But keeping a balance is important, too." That's why, for example, she uses reduced-fat instead of fat-free products and thinks that for some flavors, there are no substitutes. "I like my real butter," she says. "I just use it in smaller amounts."

Find exercise that works for you. Stick with activities you enjoy. "It's easier for me to stick with an exercise routine because it's fun and uncomplicated. I love to walk, so it's not hard to get out and do it."

Part 3

Eat Smart
for Healthy
Weight Loss

Instead of fretting about what **not** to eat, focus on all
the fabulous foods you **can** eat—foods that will keep
you healthy as well as help you lose weight.

Chapter 11

The Power of Positive Eating

Just say "yes" to healthy foods and
"yum" to lifelong pleasures.

Tired of being told what not to eat? Join the club. In the national quest for good health, finger-pointers and fearmongers too often shout down the voices of moderation, hope, and plain old enjoyment.

We wonder whether to quit carbohydrates, shun sugar, flee from fat, or ban beef. And every other new book on the market contains its own special prescription or some hitherto undiscovered "secret" about which foods to omit.

Cooking Light has always offered one elegantly simple message: Choose a balanced diet in combination with sensible exercise. You'll have fun, you'll eat well, and you'll stay healthy.

Not from us, though. *Cooking Light* has always offered one elegantly simple message: Choose a balanced diet in combination with sensible exercise. You'll have fun, you'll eat well, and you'll stay healthy.

We think it's worth noting that there's been an important shift in proactive advice from five of the nation's leading health organizations: the American Academy of Pediatrics, The American Dietetic Association, the American Heart Association, the American Institute for Cancer Research, and the National Institutes of Health. Recently, all have endorsed a new dietary position that emphasizes what might be called the power of positive eating: concentrating on what foods are good for you, rather than worrying about the ones that aren't.

RESHAPING THE AMERICAN DIET

The positive-eating messages started in June 1999 with a call from the American Institute for Cancer Research (AICR) for "reshaping the American diet in a positive manner." The new strategy "is to encourage people to eat what makes them healthier." That doesn't mean browbeating the public about what to fear, but giving people sound and appealing suggestions about how to make the good stuff, especially plant-based foods, more appealing.

That position, with some modifications, got strong backup a few weeks later when the other four health groups issued a joint call for what they dubbed "Unified Dietary Guidelines." Instead of confusing people with a lot of different diets, the groups said, the best advice would be for everyone to follow a single, simple set of parameters known to enhance, if not prolong, human life. The unified approach would be a low-fat, low-cholesterol diet high in vegetables, fruits, cereals, and grains. The Unified Guidelines also shifted the focus to the benefits of healthy eating, instead of emphasizing the adverse effects of unhealthy eating. It also strongly suggested that fad diets, which typically vilify or extol one or two dietary components, are irrelevant. The good news is that we don't need one diet to prevent heart disease, another to decrease cancer risk, and yet another to prevent obesity and diabetes.

EAT YOUR VEGGIES

Sure, these "eat positive" messages might sound like just another way of getting you to finish your broccoli. But there's more to it. It's a good idea to learn to love veggies, fruits, grains, and cereals for their own sakes—rather than just as a substitute for fatty, deep-fried, and sugar-loaded foods.

In general, a healthy diet is crucial in maintaining good health. It's estimated that half of all breast cancers, three of every four cases of colon cancer, and up to one out of every three cases of lung cancer could be prevented with better eating habits. And eating more vegetables and fruits is the common prevention strategy for each of those cancers, as well as the way to reduce the risk of heart disease and diabetes. Powerful foods, on their own and combined in hundreds of tempting ways, can also be some of the tastiest things you've ever put in your mouth. This approach works. It works because people like it. We're positive.

—*Maureen Callahan and Rod Davis*

Chapter 12

Eat Five and Live Longer

Evidence mounts that diversity in your diet
pays off in a longer, healthier life.

In recent years, headlines have ballyhooed the health benefits of certain "wonder" foods. First it was bran, then oatmeal and broccoli. Regardless of whether you even liked the food, you may have felt obliged to eat it as often as possible. That was, until you grew tired of it or another study put the initial finding into question.

Now nutrition researchers have begun paying greater attention to the big picture, examining the health consequences of overall eating patterns rather than individual foods. "We're recognizing that people don't eat just one single food. They eat a mixture of foods, and that's what we should be looking at," says Ashima Kant, Ph.D., associate professor of nutrition at Queens College in New York City. Her research provides plenty of evidence of the benefits of a diet that's diverse.

The better balanced your diet, the more likely you are to receive a protective health benefit from food.

Kant looked at the eating patterns of more than 42,000 women and found that women who ate the most diverse diets were 30 percent less likely to die of cancer, heart disease, or stroke. These findings held up even when other factors such as weight, exercise, and smoking were taken into account.

THE WEEKLY TALLY

In the study, Kant examined the diet and mortality records of women who had taken part in a breast-cancer screening project. Each of the women (with an average age of 61) had filled out an extensive food frequency questionnaire. On that questionnaire, Kant identified 23 foods representing a healthy, balanced diet. Then each woman was assigned a recommended foods score (RFS) of zero to 23, based on how many of those 23 foods she had eaten at least once a week.

Six years later, Kant compared the women's scores to their death rates. Those with the highest RFSs were far less likely to have died than women with the lowest scores. The women with the higher scores were more physically active, more likely to take supplements on a regular basis, and less likely to smoke than those with the lower scores. But even when those factors were taken out of the equation, dietary variety still greatly determined mortality rates.

The study didn't consider the effect junk food—calorie-dense and nutrient-poor—had on women's health. But it stands to reason that the top-scoring women didn't eat a lot of junk food, if only because they ate so much healthy food. The researchers concluded that the better balanced your diet, the more likely you are to receive a protective health benefit from food.

TAKE FIVE

The average person eats only about 13 or 14 foods on a regular basis, compared to the 23 foods (see page 62 for these foods) in Kant's study. But there is nothing magical about those 23 foods. As long as the foods you eat every day represent all five of the major food groups—fruits, vegetables, lean meats and fish, whole grains, and low-fat dairy—you get the health benefits of a balanced diet.

It appears to be more important to have foods from all five groups than to have diversity within a food group. If you exclude a food group from your diet, you're going to miss some nutrients, and having more variety in another food group isn't going to make up for those deficiencies. For instance, if you regularly eat oatmeal, milk, and an orange for breakfast; a turkey, lettuce, and tomato sandwich on whole wheat bread for lunch; and salad with pasta or broiled chicken for dinner, your diet includes all the food groups, even if it's not particularly varied. The increased health risk occurs when entire food groups are left out of a diet. These omissions have serious health consequences, according to Kant. Her follow-up analysis revealed that those women who missed at least two of the five major food groups on a regular basis faced a 40 percent higher mortality rate than those women who commonly ate foods from all five groups.

Kant's study and similar research lend more validity than ever to the advice *Cooking Light* and most nutritionists have been giving all along—eat a balanced diet. You'll live to tell about it.

—*Madonna Behen*

FIVE FAITHFUL FOOD GROUPS: WHAT'S YOUR SCORE?

Here are the 23 foods that were included in calculating the food score. The list doesn't include every healthy food or how the food was prepared, but it's a great way to insure you're eating a diet that includes choices from every food group. Check off each food that you eat during one week, aiming for as high a score as possible (at least a 15). And remember, you get only one point for each food consumed; if you've eaten fish three times in one week, you'll still get only one point out of a possible 23.

Fruits
☐ apples or pears
☐ oranges
☐ cantaloupe
☐ orange or grapefruit juice
☐ grapefruit
☐ other fruit juices

Vegetables
☐ dried beans
☐ tomatoes
☐ broccoli
☐ spinach
☐ mustard, turnip, or collard greens
☐ carrots or mixed vegetables with carrots
☐ green salad
☐ sweet potatoes or yams
☐ other potatoes

Meats
☐ baked or stewed chicken or turkey
☐ baked or broiled fish

Whole Grains
☐ dark breads like whole wheat, rye, or pumpernickel
☐ corn bread, tortillas, or grits
☐ high-fiber cereals such as bran, granola, or shredded wheat
☐ cooked cereals

Low-Fat Dairy
☐ 2% milk or beverages made with 2% milk
☐ 1% or fat-free milk

Chapter 13

The Power of Phytochemicals

Science is discovering powerful health benefits that phytochemicals give to foods.

Y ou've always dreamed this day would come: Chocolate has been declared something of a "health food." It turns out that this indulgence is rich in flavonoids, the same antioxidants that make red wine good for you. But that doesn't necessarily mean it's time to whip out the Visa and decimate Godiva's inventory.

Each year, researchers find dozens of "new" health-promoting compounds in food. Most are in fruits, vegetables, and other healthy foods, but others show up in surprising places, like chocolate. Some are calling the discovery of these phytochemicals (literally, "chemicals from plants") nutrition's second golden age, because science is uncovering a wealth of plant compounds that—like vitamins and minerals—may slow down aging, boost immunity, and protect against chronic disease of all kinds.

NATURAL PROTECTION

So what exactly are these compounds? They're simply the substances that make watermelon red, cabbage smell up the kitchen when it's cooking, and wine full-bodied and flavorful. In nature, they protect plants from bacteria, fungus, and harmful bugs. Until recently, we just didn't realize how much protection they could provide for us as well.

There are already hundreds of studies on these chemicals in foods, and hundreds more are on the way. "There's so much we have yet to discover," says Mark Kantor, Ph.D., a food scientist at the University of Maryland. "We know for certain that foods are filled with healthy phytonutrients. And the more different kinds of brightly colored plant foods you eat, the better. But we don't know exactly how all the compounds work, or how they interact with one another."

THE FOOD PHARMACY

Here's a list of the top ten phytochemicals in food and where to find them.

	Food Sources	Healing Benefits	Suggested Amounts
Allium Compounds	Garlic, onions, leeks, shallots	May inhibit the growth of cancer cells, lower cholesterol, and protect against heart disease	One to two garlic cloves a day. For best effects, allow chopped garlic to sit for 10 minutes before heating
Anthocyanins	Blueberries, cherries, cranberries, grapes, raspberries, strawberries	May protect against heart disease and age-related mental decline; may lessen inflammation and pain of diseases like arthritis and gout	Large quantities (a pint of blueberries or about 20 tart cherries) are necessary for "medicinal effect," but including these fruits even in lesser amounts will likely provide long-term benefits
Catechins	Tea (both green and black), chocolate	Protect against heart disease, stroke, and perhaps cancer; may also lower cholesterol and protect arteries from plaque buildup	As little as 1 cup of tea a day provides significant benefits. Dark chocolate has four times tea's catechins, but eat in moderation because of its high calories and fat
Genistein and Daidzein	Soy foods such as tofu, soy beverages, soybeans	May prevent breast and prostate cancer and lower LDL cholesterol, helping prevent heart disease	About 4 ounces of tofu or 8 ounces of soy milk a day. Pregnant and nursing women and post menopausal women with high breast cancer risk should eat in moderation because of possible hormonal effects
Indoles and Isothiocyanates	Cruciferous vegetables—broccoli, cauliflower, cabbage— and dark leafy greens	Seem to boost the body's cancer-fighting enzymes	At least five servings of cruciferous vegetables or greens a week

	Food Sources	Healing Benefits	Suggested Amounts
Lignans	Whole-grain foods, flaxseed, flaxseed oil, soy foods, berries, legumes	Behave like weak estrogen compounds and may lower risks of heart disease and breast cancer	At least six servings of whole grain foods a day
Limonene	Citrus fruits (especially the membrane, pulp, and white pith beneath the skin)	May have potent tumor-fighting power; may also inhibit blood clots and have anti-inflammatory properties	Until specific amount is determined, experts advise eating some citrus most days
Lutein	Kale, collards, spinach, turnip greens	Filters the sun's UV rays and may protect against macular degeneration, a leading cause of age-related blindness	½ cup cooked greens or 2 cups raw, four to seven times a week
Lycopene	Tomatoes, tomato sauces, grapefruit, apricots, watermelon	May prevent certain cancers, particularly of the prostate, breast, and cervix	10 servings a week (heating releases lycopene; eating it with a little oil makes it easier to absorb)
Quercetin	Red wine, grape juice, red and yellow onions, apples, broccoli, tea	Seems to lower heart-disease risk, protect against cancer, and prevent clotting disorders	Until specific amount determined, include at least some of these foods in weekly diet

The key to reaping the benefits of phytochemicals, Kantor and other experts say, isn't in gorging on M&M's for medicinal purposes, living on broccoli salad, megadosing on the superfood of the moment, or popping their hidden healthy compounds in pill form. Rather, the secret lies in this common wisdom: Good health comes from enjoying a wide array of foods—especially fruits, vegetables, legumes, and whole grains.

"That is the best way to drastically reduce your risk of almost all chronic diseases," advises Suzanne Dixon, M.P.H., M.S., R.D., a former nutrition epidemiologist at the University of Michigan's Comprehensive Cancer Center. In a recent six-year study of 42,000 women, those following U.S. Food Guide Pyramid recommendations to eat mostly fruits, vegetables, grains, and lean protein reduced their risk of death from all causes by almost a third.

See the chart on pages 64-65 for 10 potent phytochemicals that have been making headlines, where you can find them, and the amounts that studies indicate are most beneficial. While there are undoubtedly more to be discovered, these star performers seem to be most prominent and promising today. Stay tuned, though, because you never know where healthful substances may lurk. Today, chocolate. Tomorrow, foie gras?

—*Selene Yeager*

CONFUSED ABOUT PHYTOCHEMICALS? TRY COLOR CODING

Break out of the monochrome habit: Add a healthy dose of color to your palette. Rather than worrying about keeping track of individual disease-fighting substances in foods, use a paint-by-numbers approach to shopping the produce aisle. By adding colors (especially red, yellow, orange, and green) to your diet, you add substances that protect your cells, fill you up with fewer calories, and provide healthy fiber.

The more variety of healthy foods in your shopping cart, the better stocked your arsenal of disease-fighting nutrients. So start coloring!

Chapter 14

Antioxidants: The Heart Connection

Eat foods rich in antioxidants and steer
your way to a healthy heart.

So you've heard of the word "antioxidant," but do you really know what it is? If you don't, you're not alone because although the majority of Americans are familiar with the term, most of us tune out once the chemistry lesson starts.

THE ANTIOXIDANT SECURITY FORCE

Simply put, antioxidants are chemicals that protect the body from the adverse effects of oxygen. Yes, our cells need oxygen to work, but the chemical process that takes place when the cells use oxygen creates unstable molecules called free radicals. Although free radicals are by-products of normal metabolism, they can cause damage to cells and tissues, and this damage can result in heart disease (as well as certain cancers and other diseases). So even though you can't completely stop free radicals from forming, you can decrease the damage they do by either slowing down their production or making them ineffective. And you can do this by eating —eating foods that are rich in antioxidants. (See the chart on page 70 for a list of foods that contain the most antioxidants.)

AVOID THE TRAFFIC JAM

Research indicates that antioxidants keep your heart healthy by helping arteries stay clear and free-flowing. Arteries are the superhighway system of our bodies, transferring blood to various organs and tissues. Heart disease is like a traffic jam on the highway, and the jam is usually due to the buildup of plaque (cholesterol, fat, and other substances) in the arteries. This buildup can result in a total arterial impasse, making it difficult or impossible for blood to flow. Eventually the heart has to work harder and harder to move the blood through arteries and this can lead to a heart attack.

The slowdown in the arteries because of plaque buildup can be caused by any one or a combination of a variety of factors: gender, body shape, genetics, post-menopausal state, the aging process, smoking, activity level, weight, stress levels, and diet. One of

> ## LDL cholesterol is one of the main causes of plaque buildup in the arteries. Antioxidants help prevent this buildup.

the primary traffic offenders is low-density lipopro-tein (LDL) cholesterol, or "bad" cholesterol. LDL cholesterol operates as a "cholesterol delivery truck" taking beneficial cholesterol to various places where the body needs it. But if there are too many delivery trucks and all the cholesterol that is needed has already been delivered, the LDLs drive around in the blood stream looking for a place to unload. And one of the favorite stops is an artery wall. There, stuck LDLs are oxidized and release their cholesterol load onto the artery wall where it builds up, resulting in smaller passageways.

Where do antioxidants come in? It appears that they prevent the LDLs from being oxidized. If the LDLs are not oxidized, they can't dump their load of cholesterol on the artery wall, so there is no buildup.

THE FOOD FACTOR

Antioxidants are a family of compounds, and the best source of these compounds is food, specifically, fruits and vegetables. Though there are many types of antioxidants, vitamin E, vitamin C, and carotenoids are the antioxidants with the most scientific evidence of heart disease prevention. While there are no official recommendations on how much you need daily, some nutrition groups advocate as many as nine daily servings of antioxidant-containing fruits and vegetables. A minimum would be five servings a day, the number of servings promoted by the national "Five-A-Day" campaign.

VITAMIN E

Most of the positive evidence for the healthful effect of vitamin E comes from observational studies where increased dietary intake of vitamin E-rich foods and supplements was associated with a decreased risk of heart disease. The American Heart Association and the National Heart, Lung, and Blood Institute have yet to recommend massive vitamin E supplementation, but both agencies do recommend a diet high in fruits and vegetables.

While safflower oil, corn oil, wheat germ, sunflower seeds, and nuts are rich sources of vitamin E, most people still don't achieve the necessary Recommended Dietary Allowance (RDA) of 15 milligrams a day.

VITAMIN C

Vitamin C-rich foods are oranges, orange juice, peppers, tomatoes, and broccoli, and it's fairly easy to achieve the RDA (75 milligrams for women; 90 milligrams for men) with a healthful diet. The RDA for vitamin C, however, is the amount a healthy person needs to prevent a deficiency disease such as scurvy. The Institute of Medicine's Food and Nutrition Board has different recommendations for nutrients called Dietary Reference Intakes (DRIs) that are established at levels that will support optimal body needs and prevent diseases. The DRI for vitamin C was increased in 2000 from 75 milligrams to 90 milligrams a day for adult men and women. Smokers are advised to increase their intake of vitamin C by an additional 35 milligrams a day because of the added stress smoking places on the body.

CAROTENOIDS

Carotenoids are pigment substances in plants that can form vitamin A, an antioxidant. Beta-carotene is the most active type of carotenoid, although there are about 500 known carotenoids. Foods high in carotenoids are carrots, cantaloupe, broccoli, spinach, collard greens, orange juice, tomatoes, and tomato products. Although there is no DRI for carotenoids, health experts have been able to identify approximate suggested levels of intake at about 3 to 6 milligrams a day of beta-carotene. This is equivalent to the amount found in five or more servings of fruits and vegetables. Do you see a trend emerging?

VITAMIN E MEASUREMENTS

Vitamin E is really a group of substances called tocopherals. It's usually measured in alpha-tocopherol equivalents because alpha-tocopheral is the most active form of the vitamin. Vitamin E is also measured in International Units (IU). 1 milligram alpha-tocopherol equivalent = 1.5 IU. The RDA is 15 milligrams of alpha-tocopheral or 22 IU.

TEAMWORK

Antioxidants seldom work independently, and in fact, probably are more efficient as a team. Combined, they compensate for each other's deficiencies. Many researchers have speculated that looking at just one antioxidant, not the group of them, may be the reason for inconsistent findings in supplement intervention studies. Two observational studies of men and women's health and dietary habits have shown that men and women who eat the largest amounts of fruits and vegetables have the lowest risk of heart disease. Hmm, what was that again about five servings of fruits and vegetables a day?   —*Tamara Schryver*

POTENT PRODUCE: HIGHEST IN ANTIOXIDANTS

Researchers at the Human Nutrition Research Center on Aging at Tufts University believe most of us should consume between 2,200 and 3,500 units of antioxidants (such as vitamins A, C, and E) daily to help counteract processes that can lead to disease. There's a measurement called the oxygen radical absorbance capacity (ORAC), which gauges the total antioxidant potency of foods and supplements. See the chart below for the foods with the highest ratings, but remember that eating any antioxidant-containing food will provide health benefits.

Food/Amount	ORAC Score
Prunes (½ cup)	5,770
Blueberries (⅔ cup)	2,400
Kale (1½ cups)	1,770
Spinach (3 cups)	1,260
Brussels sprouts (1 cup)	980
Broccoli (1 cup)	890
Beets (¾ cup)	840
Red grapes (1 cup)	739
Red bell pepper (⅔ cup)	710
Plum (1 fruit)	633
Orange (1½ fruit)	500
Pink grapefruit (½ fruit)	483

For recipes featuring high-antioxidant foods, turn to these chapters: Desserts (page 188), Salads (page 261), Side Dishes (page 274), and Soups and Sandwiches (page 288).

Chapter 15

Chock-Full of Folate

Oranges, green veggies, dried beans, and grains
are even better when you realize how much good one
of their key nutrients does for your body.

Does the word "folate" make your mouth water? We didn't think so, but what if we rephrase it as oranges, hot bean soups, or your favorite green veggies? Now we're talking—good, healthful, tasty stuff you eat all the time, and all of it chock-full of folate, a nutrient that is part of the B-vitamin family. If you're not already friendly with folate, you're missing some great eating—and shunning a powerful ally for your heart, pregnancies, resistance to disease, and maybe even your memory.

Getting enough folate should be easy—fruits, leafy vegetables, whole grains, and dried beans are all excellent sources—but you have to actually eat them to get the benefit. Studies show that potential mothers don't, and that may be a cause of some birth defects. So in 1998, the Food and Drug Administration (FDA) initiated a requirement that folic acid (folate in vitamin supplement form) be added to a variety of starchy foods such as rice, pasta, bread, and flour.

FOLATE FIGHTS HEART DISEASE

That FDA requirement was only the beginning of what has become a drumbeat for folate awareness. By lowering elevated levels of homocysteine (an amino acid, or protein building block) in the bloodstream, folate may significantly reduce the risk of heart attack. The American Heart Association notes that more studies are needed to prove that taking folate can reduce a person's risk of heart attack, but researchers say at this point the odds look good. If you give people folate, their homocysteine levels will go down, and there is a strong suggestion that lower homocysteine levels mean less risk of coronary disease.

FOLATE AND MEMORY LOSS

Other studies suggest possible links between increased folate consumption and decreased risks of colon cancer and certain types of memory loss in older people. It's too early to say whether folate might, say, help prevent the onset of Alzheimer's disease, but researchers at Tufts University are looking into that and other possibilities. They think that there is a relationship between diet and vascular changes in the brain with aging, and that one of the dietary factors is folate.

With all these benefits, and with the new folic acid enrichments in flours and cereals, you might expect folic acid supplements (the pill form) to become as popularly recommended as Viagra. Not so. The best way to get your vitamins is to eat a good diet.

Even though folic acid in supplements is absorbed better and is somewhat more potent than folate in foods, the foods that contain folate also contain a lot of other good micronutrients. So why take folic acid in a supplement when you can get the folate you need with a dose of food.   —*Bill Beuttler*

WHAT'S IN A NAME: FOLATE AND FOLIC ACID

Although folate and folic acid are both biochemical forms of the same B vitamin, they aren't exactly interchangeable. Studies show that the body absorbs folic acid, the form of the vitamin found in supplements, much more efficiently than folate, the form that's found in foods.

But not to worry. Dietary recommendations do take this factor into account. Daily requirements for adults are set at 400 micrograms of "dietary folate equivalents." (The "equivalent" term is used to describe a diet that includes a mixture of folate from foods and fortified foods.) Rather than agonizing over terminology, just assume that you'll be getting at least some of that supply via breads and cereals, because by law they must now be fortified with folic acid. And aim to secure the rest from foods rich in folate such as spinach, legumes, and oranges, all of which, by the way, contain a whole lot of other good-for-you nutrients and disease-fighting chemicals.

For recipes that are high in folate, try White Bean Salad with Asparagus and Artichokes (page 266), Seared Scallops and Fresh Orange Salad (page 269), or Lentil-Vegetable Soup (page 290).

Chapter 16

The Truth About Carbohydrates

Carbs aren't evil—but some are clearly better for you than others. Here's how to tell the difference.

Instead of recommending just any old low-fat carbohydrate such as pasta, pretzels, and bagels, nutritionists are asking Americans to zero in on the carbohydrates that have real value to your body—those that are rich in fiber, vitamins, and minerals.

It may sound innocuous, but this growing movement could shake up the very base of the Food Guide Pyramid, which encourages everyone to get 6 to 11 servings of breads, grains, and pasta a day. That generous-sounding recommendation, coupled with the popular notion that if a food is low-fat or fat-free you have free rein, has led to the belief that you can load up on carbohydrates with impunity. But you can't.

CARBS AND WEIGHT GAIN

The proof is in the statistics. In the last five years, the national waistline has inflated by 8 pounds, despite an enduring love affair with low-fat carbohydrates. No wonder that anticarb books have won over serial dieters and health faddists from coast to coast. Their thesis, in a nutshell: The more carbs you eat, the more insulin you produce; the more insulin you produce, the more those carbohydrates are stored as thigh-enhancing fat rather than energy-providing glycogen.

But there is little, if any, science to support the carbohydrate-as-villain theory, according to Richard Surwit, Ph.D., professor and vice chairman for research in the department of psychiatry and behavioral sciences at Duke University Medical Center. "The idea that sugar and other simple carbohydrates are bad for us because they produce insulin resistance, obesity, and behavioral problems is one of the greatest misconceptions to be found in lay literature."

Not only is it a misconception, it could be a health hazard if you replace most of the carbs in your diet with fatty cuts of meat, butter, and cream. It's well-known that cancer and heart-disease risks rise as consumption of saturated fat goes up. What's more, too much protein and too little carbohydrate can foster a metabolic state called ketosis, which can put increased stress on the kidneys and cause the body to use muscle and other body tissue for the energy carbohydrates normally provide. The problem is that many people have become so intent on eliminating all traces of fat from their diets that they've gone overboard on carbohydrates.

SIMPLE VS. COMPLEX

Even worse, all carbohydrates have mistakenly been lumped into one basket. Although the main mission of carbs is to provide energy for body and brain, each type does so in its own way. Simple carbohydrates are found in both naturally occurring sugars and concentrated sweets. They provide quick energy but no significant nutritional extras. Complex carbohydrates (starch and fiber), on the other hand, are a slower and more sustained source of energy, helping you avoid spikes and dips in blood sugar. There are two groups of complex carbs: (1) highly processed complex carbs such as white-flour bread products, and (2) "supercomplex" carbs such as vegetables and whole grain products.

CARB-CURBING

If you're finding it tough to lose weight on a high-carb, low-fat diet, don't cut out carbohydrates completely. First, go for high-fiber, high-nutrient complex carbs. Then make sure you have a handle on portion size.

For instance, one carbohydrate serving is 15 grams. So if you have a typical bakery bagel (about four servings of carbs) and a cup of raisin bran (three servings) for breakfast, you've already racked up seven servings. (To do the math yourself, find the Total Carbohydrate entry on a label, and divide by 15 for the number of carb servings.)

Also, be realistic about where you fall in the range of 6 to 11 servings recommended in the Food Guide Pyramid. Active people who exercise frequently have larger storage tanks in muscle cells for carbohydrates than their inactive counterparts, so they can eat more carbs and are less likely to put on weight. People who put in at least three or four 30-minute workouts a week can usually eat 10 to 11 servings; less active people should restrict their servings to the lower end of the spectrum.

The supercomplex carbs are beneficial because they have increased fiber and ample amounts of folate, carotenoids, chromium, and magnesium, which may lower the risk of heart disease and several types of cancer. Supercomplex carbs also tend to be the better choice for waistline-watchers—their higher fiber content can make you feel fuller quicker than low-fiber choices. Here are several simple ways to make your meals and snacks more complex.

Go au naturel. In general, anything that comes in nature's original package—whole grains that haven't been processed, like brans and old-fashioned oatmeal; raw fruits and vegetables; and dried beans—will contain the most fiber and complex carbohydrates.

Know the terms. Don't be misled by terms like "unbleached wheat flour" or "enriched wheat flour" on a product's ingredients list. The nutrients and fiber have been refined and processed out of them. For maximum fiber, look for "whole wheat flour" as the first ingredient on a bread label, or "rolled oats or whole grain" on a cereal label. Stone-ground whole grains may be even better: Some research indicates that the larger the particle size of a grain, the more it may reduce heart-disease risk.

Look on the ingredients list, too, for words ending in "-ose" (including fructose) and anything described as "syrup," as well as honey and molasses. They can indicate high amounts of sugar and calories.

Don't judge a bread by its color. Many darker breads and bagels get that way not because of added whole grains, but because of caramel color. If you're buying bread at a bakery, look for loaves that contain large grains or seeds rather than finely milled flour.

Be creative. Beef up the complex-carbohydrate levels of everyday dishes by marrying them with foods that, at first glance, may not seem to go together. Empty a can of kidney beans into chicken soup, for example, or sprinkle uncooked oatmeal on top of baked macaroni before putting it in the oven; add some bran flakes to a meat loaf or shredded carrots to spaghetti sauce. And little by little, you'll find yourself swinging the pendulum toward the supercomplex carbs instead of their less-desirable siblings.

—*Wayne Kalyn*

For recipes that are good sources of "super-complex carbs", try Blueberry-Bran Muffins (page 181), Buckwheat-Honey Pancakes (page 181), Whole Wheat Chapati (page 182), and Minnesota Wild Rice Pilaf (page 287).

Chapter 17

Sweet Smarts

Cut down on sugar? It depends on the source.

I f you're watching what you eat, chances are you pay attention to your fat intake. But what about sugar? Experts contend that Americans eat too much of it—and it's in more of your food than you may realize.

NATURAL SUGAR VS. ADDED SUGAR

One current theory, though, may have you looking for sugar in all the wrong places. Some diet books say that you should avoid foods with natural sugars, like carrots, corn, and beets, just as you would sugary treats like cakes, candies, and cookies because these foods provoke an "intense" secretion of insulin, thereby causing your body to store excess sugar as fat. So, according to this theory, the carbohydrate in a carrot is the same as the carbohydrate in a piece of hard candy.

However, the carrot also supplies fiber and important nutrients, including beta-carotene and potassium. As for the hard candy, it's empty calories and nothing more.

It's the added sugar, not the naturally occurring kind, that can wreak havoc on your waistline.

In reality, the amount of sugar naturally occurring in foods is not a weight-control issue. The real problem is sugar added not only to sweets but also to processed foods like frozen dinners and salad dressings. It's this added sugar, not the naturally occurring kind, that can wreak havoc on your waistline and your health.

Sugars such as fructose (the sugar found in fruit and honey), lactose (the sugar in milk), and sucrose (table sugar, which also occurs naturally in fruits and vegetables) are found not only in foods that taste sweet but also in foods that don't, such as potatoes. During digestion, these sugars break down into glucose, which provides energy to the body's cells. Added sugars may take the form of any number of sweeteners, one of the most common being high-fructose corn syrup.

The Nutrition Facts food label lists how many grams of sugar a food contains, but it doesn't distinguish between naturally occurring sugars and added sugars. The U.S. Food and Drug Administration, which oversees food labeling, has been petitioned to require food labels to make this distinction. In the meantime, the best way to determine if a food has added sugars is to look for the following ingredients on the label.

Brown sugar	Dextrin	Invert sugar
Cane sugar	Dextrose	Malt
Confectioners' sugar	Evaporated cane juice	Maple sugar
Corn sweetener	Fruit-juice concentrate	Molasses
Corn syrup	High-fructose corn syrup	Raw sugar
Crystallized cane sugar	Honey	Turbinado sugar

In terms of energy, your body makes no distinction between complex and simple or natural and refined sugars—they're all broken down into glucose. More important than the type of sugar you eat is how much you eat and whether it's taking the place of other nutrients in your diet.

EMPTY CALORIES

Foods with lots of added sugar may threaten your health for two reasons. First, they tend to be high in calories and can contribute to weight gain. Second, those calories are usually empty—that is, they don't come packaged with health-promoting nutrients like vitamins, minerals, and plant chemicals. And the more you fill up on empty calories, the fewer nutritious foods you're likely to eat.

This doesn't mean sugar is inherently bad for you. Unlike fat, sugar hasn't been linked to chronic diseases. That's why there's no standard recommendation for how much sugar you should eat. The U.S. Department of Agriculture (USDA) does, however, suggest limiting added sugars to 6 to 10 percent of your total calories. That's 6 teaspoons (24 grams) a day if you eat about 1,600 calories daily and 12 teaspoons (48 grams) if you consume 2,200 calories. (Food labels list sugar in grams; four grams is equivalent to one teaspoon, which contains 16 calories.)

Yet according to USDA data, Americans consume much more—an average of 20 teaspoons (80 grams), or more than one-third cup, of added sugar a day. The biggest contributor of added sugars to the American diet is carbonated soft drinks—one 12-ounce can of Coke, for example, contains 10 teaspoons (40 grams) of added sugar. The second biggest is pastries: cakes, cookies, pies, sweet rolls, and muffins. The third is fruit drinks (not juice), punches, and "ades." (A 12-ounce can of fruit drink can contain as much as one-fourth cup, 48 grams, of sugar.)

Again, the problem lies not in how much sugar a particular food contains, but how much of it you consume. Ketchup and teriyaki sauce, for example, list sugar (corn syrup) as the second ingredient—but you eat them by the tablespoon. Cookies, cakes, and ice cream, though, are typically eaten in larger potions. Therein lies the problem. The bottom line: Eat high-sugar foods in moderation, high-fat or not, and choose foods with no added sugar whenever possible.

SUGAR SHAKEDOWN

Compare the calories and the amount of sugar per serving in these sweet treats.

	Calories	Sugars (tsp)
Candies		
M&M's (1 package, 1.7 ounces)	240	7¾
Reese's Peanut Butter Cups (2 candies, 1.6 ounces)	250	5¼
Cereals		
Kellogg's Frosted Flakes (¾ cup)	120	3¼
Cookies (number closest to 1 ounce)		
Nabisco Oreos (3)	160	3¼
SnackWell's Creme Sandwich Cookies (2)	110	2½
Dairy products		
Breyers Fat Free Vanilla Ice Cream (8 ounces)	220	10½*
Dairy Queen Heath Breeze, medium (14 ounces)	710	25¾*
Fruit-flavored drinks (8 ounces)		
Gatorade, any flavor	50	3½
Tropicana Twister Orange Raspberry	120	6½
Pastries and cakes		
Cheesecake Factory Original Cheesecake (7 ounces)	710	12¼
Hostess Twinkies (1 snack cake, 1.5 ounces)	150	3½

*Includes natural milk sugar   tsp = teaspoons

Chapter 18

Stand By Your Bran

Eating high-fiber foods can be a powerful way to fight disease and fend off excess weight.

Despite a recent chorus of researchers claiming that the benefits of fiber in preventing cancer had been overstated, there are many well-respected studies showing otherwise. Fiber not only has a longstanding reputation for helping diminish the prevalence of certain cancers, but can also dramatically reduce the risk of cardiovascular disease and play a crucial role in weight management.

FIBER ACTION

So how does fiber work its magic? There are two types of fiber: insoluble (the kind found in vegetables, wheat, and cereals) and soluble (the kind generally found in fruits, oats, barley, and legumes). Insoluble fiber seems to fight cancer by binding to or diluting cancer-causing agents in the gut and speeding them through the colon. In addition, some studies show that it further blunts cancer risk by slowing the growth of cells in the colon.

And breast cancer? While some researchers may have been too quick to label fiber as a cancer cure, there are valid studies that back its role in fighting the disease. The latest research suggests that insoluble fiber binds to estrogen, an important breast-cancer risk factor, reducing blood levels of the hormone. A study published in the American Journal of Clinical Nutrition shows that women who doubled their fiber intake from 15 to 30 grams a day had significantly lower estrogen levels after two months.

Soluble fiber has its own part to play in keeping your body healthy: preventing heart disease. New studies show that the fiber forms a gel in the intestine that traps and ushers cholesterol out of the body. In addition, soluble fiber can help reduce insulin levels, which in turn lowers triglycerides (another major risk factor in heart disease). High-fiber diets slow down the rate of digestion, which lowers both blood sugar levels and the insulin needed to transport that blood sugar into the cells.

Eat More Fiber, Lose More Weight

As if that weren't enough to convince skeptics to forgo Pop-Tarts in favor of some prunes and bran, eating foods high in both types of fiber can also be a powerful way to keep off excess pounds. Fiber's role in insulin reduction is again important because high insulin levels can promote weight gain. One study suggests that fiber consumption (or the lack thereof) is even more crucial than fat consumption in gauging future weight gain, blood cholesterol levels, and other heart disease risk factors.

What's more, foods high in soluble fiber such as oatmeal and barley stay in your stomach longer than foods low in this fiber. The result is that you feel fuller longer and eat less at your next meal. In fact, people in a recent study who ate a diet high in soluble fiber lost, on average, about a half-pound a week.

How to Increase Your Fiber

Experts recommend a minimum of 25 grams of total fiber each day and would frankly rejoice if people started edging up to 35 grams daily, considering most Americans manage only 12 to 15 grams a day. That's one reason, perhaps, that the new edition of the federal government's Dietary Guidelines for Americans urges people to "choose a variety of grains daily, especially whole grains." Toward that end, here are some easy ways to elevate your fiber levels.

Choose heavyweights. To meet the 25- to 35-gram fiber quota, choose foods that provide the most fiber in a serving: whole grain bran cereals and legumes, then hearty whole grain breads, and finally fruits and vegetables. A cup-and-a-half of raisin bran, for instance, will net you 12 grams of fiber, a sandwich made with two slices of 100% whole wheat bread another 4 grams. Finish off your lunch with an apple (4 grams) and have a bowl of vegetarian chili for dinner (5 or 6 grams), and you'll easily cross the 25-gram finish line.

Focus on food. When you get fiber from foods, you're also tapping into vitamins, minerals, and phytochemicals that come along for the ride. Experts believe it's the synergy of all these nutrients, most of which aren't contained in fiber supplements, that confers the most dramatic health benefits.

Go natural. You'll get higher levels of fiber if you eat products that come in nature's original packaging. Consume fruits and vegetables in their skins, a good source of roughage. (Rule of thumb: With a few exceptions, if you can put your fingernail through the skin, leave it on.) Regarding grains, the coarser the grain—

in other words, the less it has been ground—the better it is for your blood sugar, which rises gently with such types of grains and slowly sinks back down.

—*Wayne Kalyn*

FOUNTS OF FIBER

Although you should get both soluble and insoluble fiber in your diet every day, most experts say there's no need to fixate on one type over another. Because most whole plant foods contain both types of fiber, just increasing your levels of foods high in roughage will get you beneficial amounts of both. Aim for 25 to 35 grams of fiber each day. Here are some fiber-filled standouts.

Food	Fiber (grams)
Grains, cereals, bread	
Wheat-bran cereal (½ cup)	11.0
Oatmeal (1 cup cooked)	4.0
Brown rice (1 cup cooked)	3.5
Barley (½ cup cooked)	3.0
Whole wheat bread (1 slice)	2.0
Vegetables	
Potato (baked with skin on)	5.0
Carrots (½ cup cooked)	3.0
Brussels sprouts (½ cup cooked)	2.5
Legumes	
Black-eyed peas (½ cup cooked)	8.0
Black beans (½ cup cooked)	7.5
Kidney beans (½ cup cooked)	6.5
Lima beans (½ cup cooked)	6.5
Fruits	
Apple (with skin on)	4.0
Pear (with skin on)	4.0
Raisins (⅔ cup seedless)	4.0
Raspberries (½ cup)	4.0
Orange (1 medium)	3.0

MORE FIBER, LESS TROUBLE

Boosting your fiber intake to the recommended 25 grams a day is definitely good for your health, but it can cause excess gas and be tough on your stomach. Here are four simple tips for increasing fiber without discomfort.

Go slowly. Instead of bulking up on fiber all at once, ramp up by about 5 grams a week. Giving yourself time to adapt to a new diet can lessen gas problems.

Think small. Scaled-down portions of potentially problematic foods such as beans, whole grains, and fruits that contain insoluble fiber (such as apples, apricots, pears, and peaches) are easier to digest.

Practice moderation. Some causes of gas may surprise you—such as soft drinks sweetened with high-fructose corn syrup or low-calorie goodies sweetened with sorbitol. The solution: Eat gas-producing foods in moderate amounts.

Don't count on pills. Over-the-counter anti-gas remedies haven't been studied extensively enough to prove their worth. If you still have stomach troubles after taking the measures outlined above, talk to your physician.

For recipes that are high in fiber, try Curried Kidney Bean Burritos (page 220), Three-Bean Vegetable Moussaka (page 223), Tabbouleh with Arugula and Chicken (page 271), Spiced Fruity Oatmeal (page 286), and North Woods Bean Soup (page 291).

Chapter 19

Where It's At with Fat

New research on fats could change the way you eat.

Over the past 20 years, we've heard the message that fat is bad. The media, diet-book authors, and even well-meaning nutrition experts like us have hammered so hard on fat's health dangers that we've created a nation of virtual fatphobics.

The reality is that dietary fat is not all bad. In fact, the deeper nutrition experts look into how fats work in the body, the more they know that all fats are not created equal. Fats contain saturated, polyunsaturated, monounsaturated, and trans fatty acids. Most fats are a mixture of these four, but are classified according to the one that is predominant. **Saturated fats** are found mostly in animal products (and also in palm kernel oil and coconut oil). These are the fats that raise the level of harmful cholesterol in your blood the most. **Polyunsaturated fats** are found primarily in plant sources such as nuts, sunflower seeds, and vegetable oils such as corn, safflower, and sunflower. These fats can lower blood levels of total cholesterol. **Monounsaturated fats** also come from plant foods such as avocados, nuts, olive oil, and peanut oil. These fats can lower total cholesterol and also increase the ratio of good cholesterol to bad. **Trans fats** form when vegetable oils are turned solid (hydrogenated) and are found in margarine and many commercial baked goods. In the last two decades, attention has zeroed in on the "bad" kind of fat: saturated fat. More recently, trans fatty acids have been under scrutiny. (See "Take That, Trans Fat!" on page 84.)

> The reality is that dietary fat is not all bad.

But new research is casting some other fats in a more positive light, suggesting that they aren't just OK, but that they're actually good for you—if consumed in the context of a healthy diet. You may have heard that monounsaturated olive oil is heart-healthy, but fats in nuts and fish may be just as beneficial, particularly if they replace less-healthy fats in your diet.

GOOD-FOR-YOU FATS?

The idea that fats should be part of a healthy diet may at first strike you as odd, given that *Cooking Light* has preached the low-fat message since the magazine's inception in 1987. And we will continue doing so, guided by the same solid scientific research used by The American Dietetic Association and the American Heart Association. We all agree with the federal government's newly revised Dietary Guidelines for Americans that still suggest that you limit your total fat intake to no more than 30 percent of daily calories.

This new research is an evolution, not a revolution, helping health-conscious people make better choices about the fats that comprise their 30 percent. And it's helping to reinforce our longstanding message of balance, moderation, and variety, because if you've stripped almost all fat out of your diet in the name of good health, you may be missing out on some important benefits.

BETTER THAN BUTTER

The first hint that some fat may be good for you emerged more than 40 years ago. Studies of people in Corfu and Crete, Greek islands located in the Mediterranean Sea, found low rates of heart disease despite the high amount of fat (40 percent) in

TAKE THAT, TRANS FAT!

The Food and Drug Administration has proposed that the amount of trans fatty acids, an unhealthy ingredient in margarine and many processed baked goods, be listed on the Nutrition Facts label. The reason? Trans fatty acids seem to raise levels of LDL cholesterol—the bad kind—while reducing the level of beneficial HDL cholesterol. The net effect may be even worse than that of saturated fat, according to a study in the New England Journal of Medicine.

The proposed FDA rule requires that trans fat be added to the nutrition label and limits the amount of trans fats a serving can contain if a product is to be touted as "reduced saturated fat," "low in cholesterol," or "lean."

Until trans fat values start showing up on food labels, you can check ingredient lists for "hydrogenated" or "partially hydrogenated" oils; they signal the presence of trans fats (although not the amount). Another tip: If the label lists the saturated, monounsaturated, and polyunsaturated fats per serving, just add them up and subtract the sum from the total amount of fat listed. The difference is approximately the amount of trans fats per serving.

their diets. But these Greeks weren't filling up on bacon cheeseburgers; they were dipping their pita bread in olive oil.

Subsequent studies found that olive oil seems to reduce total cholesterol levels without affecting HDL (good cholesterol). This yields a better ratio of HDL to LDL (bad cholesterol), a powerful indicator of heart health. Other kinds of fat, meanwhile, affect that ratio differently; saturated fat actually increases harmful LDL cholesterol, for instance.

> Healthy fats may help with weight control because it's easier to stick with a diet that includes some fat. Meals end up being more varied, appetizing, and satisfying.

Olive oil's protective effects may be mimicked by another source of monounsaturated fat: peanuts. One study showed that participants who followed a "peanut butter diet," which derived 36 percent of its calories from fat (half of it from peanuts and peanut butter), reduced their heart-disease risk by 21 percent. Others experienced a similarly encouraging result when olive oil accounted for just over a third of their daily fat calories.

Compare that to those who kept their total fat at 25 percent, with no admonition to emphasize monounsaturates. Their risk of heart disease did drop, but only by 12 percent. The bottom line: Don't just cut the fat in your diet without regard to the variety you're eating. You're better off replacing saturated fats and trans fatty acids with monounsaturated fats such as olive oil and peanut butter. And if your diet is heavy on healthier monounsaturated fats, you may not have to micromanage your meals as much. For example, if you substitute olive oil for butter in your pasta, you can probably use a little more because the oil is better for you.

OMEGA, OK?

Walnuts, flaxseed, and fish are also turning up on the healthier-fats list. They're rich in omega-3 fatty acids, a type of polyunsaturated fat that also seems to keep HDL (good cholesterol) high while reducing total cholesterol. A study in Lyon, France, showed heart-attack survivors had a much lower risk of recurrence when they ate a Mediterranean-style diet heavy on omega-3s than those eating American-style diets high in butter, cream, and fatty meats.

Other factors help make the Mediterranean diet healthy, of course, including its emphasis on vegetables and grains. But this take-home message still applies: You're better off eating more omega-3s and less saturated fat. Omega-3s appear to be better than other polyunsaturated fats, like corn and sunflower oils, that scientists call omega-6 fatty acids. Omega-6s seem to lower both good and bad cholesterol levels, resulting in little or no improvement in heart-disease risk. In addition, diets heavy in omega-6s may increase risk for inflammatory conditions such as arthritis, asthma, and allergies, while omega-3s seem to do the opposite.

Tipping the scales toward omega-3s and monounsaturated fats doesn't have to mean a culinary overhaul. Just eat fish a couple of times a week, and as often as possible, cook with peanut, olive, or canola (another monounsaturated fat) oil instead of using corn or sunflower oil, butter, margarine, or vegetable shortening.

A Diet You Can Stomach

We, like other experts, are concerned that spreading the healthy-fat message might backfire in a country where obesity has hit an all-time high. "If the same people eating more calories now start saying, 'Now I can have more fat,' we've got an even worse problem," says John Erdman, Ph.D., director of the division of Nutritional Sciences at the University of Illinois. But a diet including healthy fats may help with weight control because it's easier to stick with. A recent study bears witness: Researchers put 50 overweight men and women on a 35 percent-calories-from-fat diet and another 50 on a 20 percent-calories-from-fat diet. Both diets emphasized healthy fats such as fish oils, olive oil, and nut oils and butters, and their calories were the same.

After 18 months, those in the higher-fat group lost more weight than the lower-fat dieters—some of whom gained weight after the first year. In fact, only 10 of the ultralow-fat dieters made it through the whole study.

Study author Kathy McManus, M.S., R.D., director of the department of nutrition at Brigham and Women's Hospital in Boston, says that the participants in the higher-fat group said their meals ended up being more varied, appetizing, and satisfying. "They didn't feel like they were dieting," she adds.

McManus, too, says she's concerned that now some people may interpret this new good-fat message as "now I can go out and eat half a jar of peanut butter." The best foundation for a healthy diet is still plenty of fruits, vegetables, and grains, she says. But a spoonful of peanut butter is just fine—especially if it helps the celery go down.

—*Carole Sugarman*

WHERE TO FIND THE GOOD-FOR-YOU FATS

Want to make fat work in your favor? Tip your balance toward monounsaturated fats and omega-3 fatty acids (a type of polyunsaturated fat), and away from saturated fats and trans fatty acids. Here are how oils, spreads, nuts, and other sources of fat stack up. (Numbers are rounded to the nearest whole digit, so sums may be a bit off.) A ½-ounce portion of nuts is approximately the amount in a bag of airline peanuts.

Food	Amount	Total fat (grams)	Saturated (grams)	Monoun-saturated (grams)	Polyun-saturated (grams)
Olive oil	1 tbsp.	14	2	10	1
Safflower oil	1 tbsp.	14	1	10	2
Canola oil*	1 tbsp.	14	1	8	4
Peanut oil	1 tbsp.	14	2	6	4
Vegetable shortening**	1 tbsp.	13	3	6	3
Corn oil	1 tbsp.	14	2	3	8
Sunflower oil	1 tbsp.	14	1	3	9
Stick margarine**	1 tbsp.	11	2	5	4
Butter	1 tbsp.	12	7	3	0
Macadamia nuts***	½ oz.	11	2	8	0
Hazelnuts***	½ oz.	9	1	7	1
Pecans***	½ oz.	11	1	6	3
Almonds***	½ oz.	8	1	5	2
Cashews***	½ oz.	7	1	4	1
Peanuts ***	½ oz.	7	1	4	2
Pistachio nuts***	½ oz.	7	1	3	2
Walnuts*	½ oz.	9	1	1	7
Avocado	½ avocado	15	2	10	2
Peanut butter	2 tbsp.	16	3	8	4
Flaxseed*	1 tbsp.	4	0	1	3

*   Good source of omega-3 fatty acids
**   High in trans fatty acids
***   All figures for nuts pertain to dry-roasted nuts, except walnuts

Key
tbsp. = tablespoon
oz. = ounce

Low-Fat and Fat-Free Food: As Good as the Real Thing?

We asked some nutrition experts to name their picks for the best and worst low-fat foods on the market. All were happy to help—with one crucial caveat: Light foods aren't light if you double your helpings.

TOP PICKS

Milk, yogurt, and soft cheeses: You're almost halving calories when you switch from whole to fat-free milk, without losing the calcium that's critical to your bone health. And low-fat ricotta, cream cheese, cottage cheese, milk, and yogurt taste just as good as their higher-fat cousins.

Mayonnaise: The lighter varieties are an easy way to cut calories without sacrificing flavor.

Ground beef: Switching from ground chuck to lean ground beef lowers fat and calories by almost two-thirds without affecting flavor significantly.

Granola: Low-fat granolas contain about a third of the fat of regular granola.

Crackers: Most snack crackers have an equally good reduced-fat version, and you'll never miss the fat. And some give you fiber plus flavor.

THE DUDS

Chips: People tend to eat more because they're not satisfied or they think they're eating fewer calories. But one extra handful cancels any calories saved. Instead, try a good-tasting, naturally lower-fat chip like Cape Cod's Yukon Gold.

Light peanut butter: Light peanut butter offers little calorie advantage, in part because the light versions have added sugar to compensate for the missing fat.

Reduced-fat sweets: Many of these offerings may be lower in fat but not in calories—they're often loaded with sugar. And generally speaking, the flavor just doesn't compare to that of the real thing.

Light salad dressings: Good low-fat dressings are hard to come by. Try diluting a standard dressing with a little bit of water. It won't stick to the leaves as thickly, so you won't get as much. Or just use less full-fat dressing.

Light breads and pretzels: Breads and pretzels have little fat to begin with, so their lighter counterparts don't offer much savings. Just choose whole grain products for the high-fiber benefit.

Chapter 20

Go Lean with Protein

The power of protein to make you lean lies in the choices you make.

Many weight-loss prophets advocate high-protein, low-carbohydrate diets as the sure-fire way to shed pounds. And while protein is an absolute must in any health maintenance or weight-loss diet, the amount of protein in these diets versus more conventional diets seems to be fodder for debate.

PROTEIN BASICS

Before discussing how much protein should be included in any weight-loss regimen, it's important to understand protein's function in the body. On a fairly simple level, protein is necessary for growth, especially during periods of rapid growth such as pregnancy and childhood. Protein is a complex compound made up of amino acids and nitrogen that come both from foods and the human body to make a series of biological proteins involved in cell structure, hormones, enzymes, immunity, and muscle contraction. Protein helps to build the body and regulate its functions. Excess dietary protein is used either as a source of energy or converted to fat for storage.

The human body requires a total of 20 amino acids, nine of which it cannot make itself. These nine amino acids are called essential amino acids because the body cannot make them, so they need to come from the diet. Food sources of protein break down further into two categories. Animal proteins (beef, lamb, pork, poultry, fish, shellfish, eggs, milk, and milk products) provide complete proteins, where there are enough of the essential amino acids in the correct amounts for the human body. Incomplete proteins are predominantly plant-based proteins—grains, legumes, nuts, and seeds—that are missing one or more of the essential amino acids. The exception to this rule is soy protein, which is considered a complete plant protein.

For those who do not eat animal proteins, it's possible to eat combinations of plant-based proteins in the same meal or throughout the day and consume all the essential amino acids. The general rule of thumb for complementing proteins is to combine grains and legumes or combine legumes and nuts or seeds within a meal or the day to get a complete protein profile.

How Much Protein?

Just how much protein is essential to maintain the complex functions of the body? There are different ways of counting protein intake, but all equate to approximately the same amount. The USDA Food Guide Pyramid recommends 5 ounces of protein for people on a 1,600-calorie diet, or 6 ounces of protein for those on a 2,200-calorie diet. Nutrition professionals recommend that 10 to 15 percent of the overall calories in a diet originate from protein sources. This equates to 50 grams of protein a day for women and 63 grams of protein a day for men. Currently, American women eat about 63 to 66 grams of protein, while their male counterparts eat about 88 to 92 grams of protein. For most people simply aiming to maintain a healthful diet, the target is two servings of protein a day. (See the chart below for recommended servings sizes.)

Portion size is everything. Super-sized portions can lead to unintended weight gain. Reality check: A 3-ounce serving of meat is equivalent in size to a stack of playing cards or approximately the same size as a woman's palm—a far cry from the large portions usually served in restaurants today.

Serving Sizes for Common Sources of Protein

Here are the serving sizes for a variety of protein foods.

Food	Serving Size
Cooked lean meat, poultry, pork, or fish	2-3 ounces
Soy burger	2-3 ounces
Egg	1 whole
Egg whites	2
Legumes	½ cup
Peanut butter	2 tablespoons
Nuts	⅓ cup
Tofu or tempeh	4 ounces
Soy milk	1 cup

PROTEIN POWER

Here are some tips for keeping your protein lean.

- Trim all visible fat from beef and poultry, and remove the skin from poultry before preparing or eating.
- Bake, broil, roast, poach, steam, or microwave meat dishes instead of deep fat frying. To preserve the flavor and tenderness, baste with wine, citrus juice, or low-fat broth, or capture the moisture in foil.
- Experiment with herbs, spices, and low-calorie sauces such as picante sauce.
- When pan-frying or stir-frying, use small amounts of vegetable oils such as olive oil, canola oil, or safflower oil. Another option is to use spray oils.
- Choose kitchen equipment that is conducive to low-fat cooking such as pressure cookers, nonstick frying pans, or a grill pan.
- Cook meat on a rack so that the fat will drain off.
- Cook the meat a day in advance and refrigerate overnight. Before reheating, trim the fat that has separated from the meat during cooling.
- Substitute cholesterol-free egg substitute or two egg whites for one whole egg.
- Choose lean cuts of meat. Examples of these contain the word "loin" or "round" such as sirloin, tenderloin, top round, and ground round. Drain excess fat after browning meat.
- Limit liver, brains, chitterlings, kidney, heart, sweetbreads, and other organ meats.
- Be sure to include at least one, but preferably two servings a week of fish such as albacore tuna, salmon, lake trout, mackerel, herring, or sardines because these protein sources are high in omega-3 fatty acids.

HIGH-PROTEIN DIETS

How do high-protein, low-carbohydrate diets stack up to current health recommendations? High. In fact, too high. High-protein diets are often high-fat diets. While the protein levels may range from 25 to 65 percent of the total calories, the fat percentage may be anywhere from the lower, more acceptable level of 30 percent all the way up to 70 percent. And for many high-protein regimes, the source of that fat is primarily saturated fat, or fat from animal sources.

It is true that people can lose weight on these diets, primarily because the overall calorie content is reduced. In the initial stages of a high-protein diet, people often experience rapid weight loss. Part of this weight loss is due to carbohydrate restriction. When carbohydrates are limited, sodium, water, and glycogen (the stored form of energy) are depleted from the body and this is reflected as weight loss on the scale. However, the water weight is regained when the diet ends, unless the diet continues for a long enough time to actually affect fat stores.

It's not unusual to hear a high-protein enthusiast rave about feeling full and content. However, clinical research has been unable to confirm or deny this effect. The lower cholesterol, blood glucose, blood pressure, and insulin levels that are often seen as a result of a high-protein plan are probably due to the actual weight loss rather than the carbohydrate restriction. Weight loss, regardless of the method, most always results in better health parameters for diabetes and heart disease.

When carbohydrates are limited, sodium, water, and glycogen are depleted from the body and this is reflected as weight loss on the scale. The weight is regained when the diet ends, unless the diet continues for a long enough time to actually affect fat stores.

In addition to being high in fat and saturated fat, high-protein diets can also be low in other needed nutrients. By eliminating common carbohydrates such as fruits, vegetables, and grains, you eliminate vitamins, minerals, antioxidants, phytochemicals, and fiber. Though proponents of the high-protein diets recommend supplementation, some of the phytochemicals in fruits and vegetables aren't in the pills, nor does supplementation offer the right mix of nutrients that work together to provide health benefits. Both a high saturated fat diet and a low fruit and vegetable diet seem to be counterproductive in preventing heart disease and cancer.

—*Tamara Schryver*

Chapter 21

Calcium Does Every Body Good

Feast on these new reasons to get your fill of this important mineral.

Calcium should not be labeled a "chick mineral," even though it helps prevent osteoporosis, a bone-thinning disease that occurs predominately in women. Men need calcium, too, just as much as women. And not only because 2 million of the 10 million people with osteoporosis in the United States are male: A laundry list of newly-discovered health benefits beyond building and preserving bone makes calcium crucial for both genders. Recent studies have shown that the mineral can help reduce and prevent hypertension, may lower the risk of developing colon cancer, and may even be a strong ally in the battle against obesity.

CALCIUM AND HEALTH

"It seems that calcium does a body good on many levels," explains Gregory Miller, Ph.D., senior vice president of Nutrition and Scientific Affairs at the National Dairy Council. A recent National Institutes of Health (NIH) study suggests that a diet containing 1,200 milligrams or more of calcium daily, plus plenty of fruits and vegetables, relaxes the smooth muscle in arteries, widening the pathways and thereby lowering blood pressure, sometimes within as little as two weeks. In addition, University of Minnesota researchers found that about 2,000 milligrams of calcium a day reduces abnormal cell formation that can lead to cancer in the colons of high-risk men and women. Still another study suggested that those with the high intakes of calcium were three times less likely to get colon cancer than those who consumed low amounts of calcium.

CALCIUM AND WEIGHT LOSS

Calcium's role in weight loss is less understood, but it appears that calcium stokes the body's fat-burning furnace. In one study at Purdue University, women who consumed only 700 milligrams of calcium per day gained body fat, while those on the same diet who got 1,000 to 1,200 milligrams of calcium per day maintained or lost body fat.

"It's ironic that many people who try to lose weight throw out the baby with the bath water," says calcium researcher Robert Heaney, M.D., a professor at Creighton University in Omaha, Nebraska. "They eliminate entire food groups, especially dairy, a group of foods that might actually help them lose weight." Many people have the mistaken notion that dairy products will sabotage their health or are inordinately fattening, and they're unaware that calcium is also present in a variety of foods such as soy products and even specially fortified pastas.

> Calcium's role in weight loss is not fully understood, but it appears that calcium stokes the body's fat-burning furnace.

To raise your calcium consciousness, we caucused with top experts in the field to find out the best ways to strengthen your bones, lower your risk of disease, and lose weight at the same time.

Count on the cow. While it's true that calcium-fortified foods such as orange juice, pasta, and cereals are a convenient way to round out your daily total, milk, yogurt, and cheese are better nutritional bets. In addition to calcium, they also contain an impressive second string of vitamins (A, B12, D, niacin, riboflavin) and other minerals (phosphorus and potassium). When you opt for a calcium-fortified food, you aren't necessarily getting the same deluxe nutritional package you get in good old dairy products.

Aim low. The only thing lacking in low-fat milk or low-fat yogurt is artery-clogging saturated fat. When you cut the fat, you not only lower your risk of heart disease and extra poundage, you raise your calcium quotient slightly: One cup of skim milk contains about 10 more milligrams of calcium than a cup of whole milk (302 milligrams vs. 291 milligrams).

Divide your dose. To ensure your body fully absorbs what you consume, split up your 1,000 to 1,200 milligrams daily total into three or four doses. Do it the no-brainer way: Include a dairy product or a calcium-fortified food such as orange juice (300 milligrams per cup) with every meal.

Be savvy about supplements. If you're concerned that you might not be getting enough calcium from your diet, talk to your doctor about supplements.

Don't rely solely on fruits and vegetables. You'd have to eat pounds of produce to meet your daily calcium requirements. For instance, it takes three cups of cooked broccoli or two cups of cooked mustard greens to equal the calcium in a cup of milk. Spinach is a good source, but spinach also contains compounds called oxalates that bind the calcium and block its absorption. And fruit? Do you really want to devour six oranges (52 milligrams of calcium each) to reach only about one-third of your calcium RDA?

Even if you're not a big fat-free milk fan, you can still sneak in some easy sources of calcium: a glass of calcium-fortified orange juice, a PowerBar or yogurt as a snack, or a glass of chocolate milk with your kids. Minimal effort, maximum rewards. All nutritional investments should be so easy and provide such dividends.

—*Wayne Kalyn*

HOW MUCH CALCIUM?

How much calcium should a 35-year-old woman get? Does it vary among different age groups?

"About 1,000 milligrams a day is ideal," says Connie Weaver, Ph.D., professor and head of the foods and nutrition department at Purdue University. The Recommended Dietary Allowance (RDA) of calcium for women ages 25 to 50 is 1,000 milligrams, roughly the equivalent of 3 (8-ounce) glasses of milk. For people under 25 and over 50, the RDA is 1,200 to 1,500 milligrams.

Consuming more than the RDA isn't dangerous, but it's not clear if it will help you, even though some studies have shown that 2,000 milligrams a day might reduce the risk of colon cancer. The experts think that no more than 2,500 milligrams a day is a safe level.

For recipes that are high in calcium, try Mocha Cocoa (page 176), Mediterranean Lasagna (page 227), Sonora Grilled Cheese (page 294), and Spinach Calzone (page 296).

Calcium Counts

You can get your calcium quota without drinking milk or eating cheese. But who wants a peanut butter cookie without milk or a grilled cheese without the cheese? Your best bet is to combine natural calcium sources with some fortified ones.

Foods with naturally occurring calcium	One serving	Calcium (milligrams)
Baked beans	1 cup	127
Black-eyed peas	1 cup	211
Broccoli, boiled	1 cup	94
Collards, boiled	1 cup	226
Buttermilk	8 ounces	285
Cheddar cheese, reduced-fat	1 ounce	200
Cottage cheese, 2% milk fat	4 ounces	78
Kale, boiled	1 cup	94
Milk, fat-free	8 ounces	300
Molasses, blackstrap	1 tablespoon	172
Sardines, Atlantic, canned in oil, drained, with bone	1 can (3.75 ounces)	351
White beans, canned	1 cup	191
Yoplait Yogurt, Raspberry	6 ounces	200

Calcium-fortified foods*	One serving	Calcium (milligrams)
Aunt Jemima Complete Pancake and Waffle Mix, made with water	2 pancakes	150
Better 'n Eggs Egg Substitute	¼ cup	100
Betty Crocker Blueberry Muffin Mix, made with water	1 muffin	20
Cheerios cereal, dry	1 cup	100
Clif Luna Bar, Chocolate Pecan Pie	1 bar	350
Earthgrains IronKids Bread	2 slices	400
Eggo Buttermilk Waffles	2 waffles	100
General Mills Harmony cereal, dry	1¼ cups	600
Glenny's Low-Fat Soy Crisps, Barbecue	14 crisps	300

Calcium-fortified foods (continued)	One serving	Calcium (milligrams)
Hain Mini Munchies Rice Cakes	9 cakes	100
Hershey's Sweet Escapes Crunchy Peanut Butter Bar	1 bar	100
J.J. Nissen Calcium-Fortified Enriched Bread	2 slices	100
Keebler Grahams with Calcium	8 crackers	100
Kix cereal, dry	1⅓ cups	150
Minute Maid Fruit Punch Juice Box	6.75 ounces	100
Nabisco Cream of Wheat	3 tablespoons	100
Nabisco Kool Stuf Fruit and Graham Bars, Strawberry Seas	1 bar	200
Nasoya Firm Tofu, raw, prepared with calcium sulfate**	3 ounces	100
Nesquik Chocolate Milk Mix	2 tablespoons	100
Pepperidge Farm Giant Goldfish Crackers	14 crackers	100
Pepperidge Farm Sandwich Bread	2 slices	100
PowerBar, Peanut Butter	1 bar	300
Quaker Fruit and Oatmeal Bars, Iced Raspberry	1 bar	200
Quaker Instant Oatmeal, Regular	1 envelope	100
Quaker Instant Oatmeal Nutrition for Women	1 envelope	350
Soy Dream Original Enriched Non-Dairy Beverage**	8 ounces	300
Sunshine Cheez-It Juniors Crackers	44 crackers	200
Nestle's Fat-Free Hot Cocoa Mix	1 envelope	300
Tropicana Pure Premium Orange Juice with Calcium and Extra Vitamin C	8 ounces	350
Whole Grain Total cereal, dry	¾ cup	1,000

*These products are high in calcium because of fortification; other brands will provide different amounts of calcium.

**When purchasing soy products, make sure the kind you get is calcium-fortified—many of these products contain very little naturally occurring calcium.

Chapter 22

Meet Your Multivitamin Needs

The dos and don'ts of vitamin supplementation
when you're on a weight-loss plan

Shopping for a multivitamin used to be easy: If you were an adult, you took one formula; if you were a kid, you took a Flintstones. Today, it's a different story. There are multivitamin formulas tailored to gender, age, vegetarianism, athleticism, energy and stress level, mood—all these characteristics, and then some. Then there are "natural" supplements, time-release formulas, and sugarless pills. Choosing the right multivitamin is so complicated, it's enough to make you want to forget the whole thing. Which brings us to this question: With the abundance of year-round fresh produce and grocery-store shelves full of vitamin-fortified foods, are vitamins really necessary at all?

FOOD OR PHARMACY?

Your health and longevity reflect a complex combination of genetics, eating habits, lifestyle, and chance. You can't influence the first or the last much, but the middle two are up to you. If you're relatively healthy, don't smoke or drink alcohol excessively, and load your grocery cart with fruits, vegetables, grains, and low-fat sources of protein, it's less likely you need to take supplements. If you skip meals, eat lots of high-fat foods, few green vegetables, and too much sugar—or are sometimes less than diligent about your diet—a multivitamin/multimineral supplement can fill in some of the nutritional gaps. While The American Dietetic Association's (ADA) official position is to recommend multis only when dietary selection is limited—when

> First concentrate on your diet, and then consider a supplement as a stopgap measure.

you're on a severely restricted weight-loss diet, for instance—many dietitians encourage their clients to take them regardless of how they eat. "I recommend a multi to just about everybody," says Elizabeth Ward, M.S., R.D., a former ADA spokesperson. "Nobody eats an exemplary diet. A multivitamin is a cheap, harmless insurance policy."

According to the National Academy of Sciences (NAS), many people don't get enough of the currently recommended vitamins and minerals. Additionally, there's good reason to think that slightly higher levels of some of these nutrients may improve your odds for long-term wellness, prompting the NAS to release new recommendations aimed at preventing conditions such as heart disease and cancer. Even most of these elevated levels, though, can be attained through your diet if you're conscientious about what you eat. The advice is clear: First concentrate on your diet, and then consider a multivitamin/multimineral as a stopgap measure.

GO FOR 100%

A multivitamin is meant to enhance your diet, not replace foods—that's why it's called a supplement. Even the best multis won't give you a complete dose of all of the vitamins and minerals you need daily. The reason is simple: space. Minerals need more room than vitamins. A pill containing all the recommended vitamins is the size of an M&M's candy, but one that also has all of the necessary minerals would be the size of a large cherry—much too large to swallow. Look for a multi with levels of vitamins and minerals as close as possible to 100% of the Daily Value (DV).

FOR WOMEN ONLY

Women-specific supplements sometimes make compromises that don't make sense. A One-A-Day Women's formula, for example, provides a noble 450 milligrams of calcium. But to fit this in a single tablet, other important nutrients such as selenium and magnesium are nixed. It's wiser to take a more complete regular multivitamin (many of which contain around 160 milligrams of calcium, or 16% of the DV) and wash it down with a glass of calcium-fortified orange juice or skim milk, or take a separate calcium supplement. (See page 95 for more information on calcium supplements.)

Women's supplements might also contain extra iron, but most women don't need it. Unless you're anemic or have bleeding ulcers or extremely heavy menstrual flow, you'll get plenty of iron through foods and a basic multivitamin/multimineral supplement.

IRON STRENGTH

Because men and postmenopausal women typically get enough iron through their diets, don't lose blood on a regular basis, and tend to store more iron than younger women, they are in danger of getting too much iron. High iron levels may be toxic and have been associated with increased risk of heart disease. Men and postmenopausal women should opt for supplements that contain no more than 10 milligrams of iron, or 55 percent of the DV of 18 milligrams.

BABY AND YOU

Pregnant or breast-feeding women have increased needs for vitamins B1, B12, C, and folic acid, as well as iron and calcium. It's crucial to get these nutrients for the baby's health. For women who are trying to become pregnant, a daily multivitamin will ensure the 400 micrograms of folic acid needed to prevent neural-tube defects such as spina bifida. A basic multivitamin/multimineral should provide this level.

NEW DIETARY STANDARDS: AN UPDATE

The Food and Nutrition Board of the National Academy of Sciences' Institute of Medicine (IOM) is gradually introducing new standards called Dietary Reference Intakes (DRIs). The DRIs are more thorough than the current Daily Values because they not only offer recommended nutrient levels to stave off deficiency diseases, but they also offer suggestions for levels that scientific data conclude should benefit your health—amounts that seem to help fight cancer, cardiovascular disease, osteoporosis, and other conditions.

Researchers formulating the DRIs are recommending higher intakes of key vitamins and confirming reports that diet can help prevent some deadly diseases. For instance, they were responsible for increasing the daily recommendation for calcium from 800 to 1,000 milligrams to the current 1,000 to 1,200 milligrams for all men and for women over 50.

While you won't see DRIs on food or multivitamin labels yet, they will likely someday affect—or even replace—the DVs we use now. The board has already released DRIs for antioxidants, B vitamins, calcium, vitamins C, D, and E, folic acid, and selenium. More reports will follow. For details, visit the IOM Web site at www.iom.edu.

CALCIUM AND VITAMIN E

Calcium and vitamin E may be worthy of their own pills. Ask your doctor if you need to take either of these as single supplements. According to the latest NAS recommendations, women ages 25 to 50 and all men should get 1,000 milligrams of calcium daily; women over age 50 should get 1,200 milligrams. No multi will provide the full amount.

Vitamin E may protect you from heart attacks and some types of cancer. A new NAS report advises against vitamin E supplements for the general population, citing inconclusive scientific evidence for these benefits. Nevertheless, if you're at risk for heart disease, stroke, or prostate or colon cancer, your doctor may recommend a daily supplement of 200 to 400 international units (IU)—much higher than what you'd find in a typical multivitamin.

THE PRICE IS RIGHT

When it comes to vitamins, price doesn't dictate quality. Generic multis are just as good as name-brand, as long as they have close to 100 percent of the DV. Freshness can affect potency, though. Opt for brands with expiration dates. Other claims—such as time-release or sugar-, yeast-, starch-, coloring-, or flavoring-free— likely have little to do with the efficacy of the supplement. You certainly shouldn't pay more because of them.

HERBS, ETC.

Including herbs in a multivitamin could mean important time-tested nutrients are left out. The same goes for other substances such as garlic, red wine extract, and lutein. Even though garlic and red wine consumption have been associated with lower risk of heart disease, and lutein may help preserve eye health as you age, research doesn't support including them in a multivitamin over other more important ingredients for which there are established DVs.

STRESS FACTORS

Stress formulas usually contain higher amounts of the B vitamins, vitamin C, magnesium, and pantothenic acid. The idea that they may combat the effects of stress came from a government report in the 1950s that people who are stressed due to injury or illness suffer appetite loss and may need to replenish their vitamin stores. There's no evidence that these vitamins have any effect on psychological stress.   —Ed Blonz

THE TOP 25 VITAMINS AND MINERALS

It's hard to know what you're missing in a multivitamin/multimineral if you don't know what you need in the first place. Here are the 25 vitamins and minerals for which there are set Daily Values.

Nutrient	Daily Value
Vitamin A	5,000 IU
Vitamin B1 (thiamine)	1.5mg
Vitamin B2 (riboflavin)	1.7mg
Vitamin B6	2mg
Vitamin B12	6mcg
Biotin	300mcg
Vitamin C	60mg
Calcium	1,000mg*
Chloride	3,400mg
Chromium	120mcg
Copper	2mg
Vitamin D	400 IU
Vitamin E	30 IU
Folic acid	400mcg
Iodine	150mcg
Iron	18mg
Vitamin K	80mcg
Magnesium	400mg
Manganese	2mg
Molybdenum	75mcg
Niacin	20mg
Pantothenic acid	10mg
Phosphorous	1,000mg
Selenium	70mcg
Zinc	15mg

IU = international units
mg = milligrams
mcg = micrograms
*Women over age 50 should get 1,200mg calcium per day.

Part

4

Get Started on Your Weight-Loss Lifestyle

Begin your path to a healthy life by consciously
choosing the right foods and behaviors, and soon
those behaviors will become second nature.

Chapter 23

Day by Day

Who has the time to eat well, exercise, and relax?
You do! Stick with us for 24 hours, and this healthy
living stuff might just stick with you forever.

What makes a healthy day? No one component, for sure. What foods you eat, how you exercise, ways you cope with challenges, and whether you take time to relax—all these play important roles. There is no simple formula. But where do we strike the balance?

First, by recognizing the value of doing so. You already know what constitutes a healthy diet—embark on the path to a healthy life by giving it more than lip service. Skip the bacon and fried eggs in favor of a blueberry muffin and a strawberry smoothie because you know they will make your body run better. And you prefer the taste. That's basically the trick: Make conscious choices for healthy eating.

> When you eat light, nutritious foods and enjoy the way they make you feel, French fries and candy bars lose their appeal.

Sounds difficult? It isn't, really. When you eat light, nutritious foods and enjoy the way they make you feel, French fries and candy bars lose their appeal. Healthful food makes you feel vibrant, and, in turn, physical activity comes naturally. Exercise then motivates you to stick to nutritious fare such as fruits, vegetables, and pasta. In other words, one good practice feeds the other. Soon you realize that a healthy day is a result of good habits. You may start on your path to a healthy life by consciously choosing the right foods and behaviors, but soon those behaviors will become second nature. Staying the course will be easy.

Paying attention to your body's own signals helps maintain health. If you observe your pants tightening around your waist, well, you know what's up—your weight. If there's a spring in your step, you intuitively know you're on the right eating track. And, as we've been showing you in *Cooking Light* magazine for more than a decade, a healthful lifestyle doesn't mean deprivation.

In fact, you can make your entire day a healthy pleasure. Will it be perfect? That's up to you and your own schedules, needs, and preferences. But to put our theory into practice, we've come up with a model—24 hours of sensible exercise, balanced eating, and creative relaxation. Give it a try. You'll see that living a healthy life is no more difficult than imagining it.

6 a.m. You're out the door on schedule for a brisk before-work walk: three miles in about 45 minutes, enough of an aerobic charge to boost your energy for the day as well as burn some calories. It helped that you'd laid out your workout clothes the night before so you'd see them and haul yourself out of bed before the old excuses sent you burrowing back under the covers.

7:40 a.m. You've just exercised, showered, and dressed. Now it's time for breakfast. Don't mutter about "not being a morning person"—treat yourself. It's true what the experts say: This is the most important meal of the day. Studies have shown that children who skip breakfast perform poorly on school tests. The same could be true for adults. Because blood sugar levels are at their lowest when you wake up, eating in the a.m. perks you up and wakes up your taste buds, too.

Our suggestion: Have a Blueberry-Bran Muffin (page 181) and a Strawberry-Banana Soy Smoothie (page 174). The duo is both tasty and healthful. Soy milk contains isoflavones, disease-fighting chemicals that help ward off cancer, prevent some bone loss, and help alleviate symptoms of menopause. Blueberries are high in fiber and vitamin C, and they contain the antioxidant anthocyanin, which may help prevent cancer and slow the effects of aging.

9 a.m. At the office watering hole, go for the clear liquid rather than coffee. Not that coffee is bad for you, in moderation. But water is vital, second only to air in its importance to maintaining life. We recommend six to eight glasses a day. While you work, keep a glass of water—or fruit juice, which contains lots of water—on your desk.

Our suggestion: On days when the ties that bind you to the office remain firmly knotted, keep yourself as mobile as possible. Stretch your legs while you're on the phone; hop up frequently to file papers; take your hands off the keyboard and point them upward, rotating them both ways at the wrist; walk to a colleague's office instead of picking up the phone. Not only do these movements keep aches and pains at bay, but they also help the battle of the bulge. A study published recently in *Science* found that people who fidget burn substantially more calories in a day than nonfidgeters.

10 a.m. If by midmorning your stomach starts complaining of neglect, take heed and nosh. Snacking during the day can actually help you eat more moderately at lunch and dinner. In fact, many weight-loss experts say eating between meals is one of the healthiest things we can do; it keeps our bodies functioning and our metabolism burning.

Our suggestion: An apple or any fruit or raw vegetable. This helps ensure that you'll get two to four servings of fruit and three to five servings of vegetables per day, the number of servings recommended in the U.S. Dietary Guidelines.

10:30 a.m. An appointment a few blocks away presents a midmorning opportunity for fresh air and movement. This is not a full-fledged workout, but the 10-minute stroll each way lets you clear your head, loosen muscles, and get a little cardiovascular boost. Such lifestyle exercise, the incidental movement rather than an all-out push, plays a big role in keeping us active and healthy. A study conducted by the Cooper Institute for Aerobics Research found that those who do 30 minutes of walking, vacuuming, vigorous car-cleaning, and the like keep as fit as people who put in 30 minutes at a gym. The somewhat surprising difference: Lifestyle exercisers are more likely to maintain their fitness because activity is integrated into their daily routines.

12:30 p.m. Congratulating yourself for packing a tasty lunch, you head off to the nearby park for an alfresco hour. Or, if the weather is inclement, you know of a pleasant indoor spot nearby. By making your own lunch, you save money, avoid hassle, and dodge the pitfalls of fast food. And you can fill your lunchbox with nutrients. Forgo solitude and eat with a friend. Research has shown that strong friendships are linked to better physical health, stress reduction, and happiness. Even if your friend cancels, get out of the office. Go to a museum or a bookstore: Not only will this take your mind off work issues, but you'll also be engaging, or expanding, your interests. Your brain will feel less fatigued for the rest of the day because it's been "fed," too.

Our suggestion: A Roast Beef Sandwich with Horseradish Cream (page 298). For a boost of fiber, any time you make a sandwich, pile on the tomatoes and opt for whole grain bread instead of simple wheat bread, which can be just as refined as its white counterpart. (Most whole grain breads are clearly marked as such on the label.) We need between 25 to 35 grams of fiber each day, but most of us eat only half that amount. And instead of sipping a soft drink, which is sometimes your only choice at typical lunch joints, reach for a carton of low-fat milk. Though it has less fat than whole milk, it provides as much bone-benefiting calcium—something you already know you need.

> By making your own lunch, you save money, avoid hassle, and dodge the pitfalls of fast food.

3 p.m. Because your emotional well-being is important, too, you need to take a short break. Call your sister to plan a menu for your next family gathering, for instance, or try taking a quick walk with a friend. Such connections keep us healthy. The groundbreaking Alameda County (California) Study showed that people with strong social ties, whether with a spouse, other family members, or friends, were less likely to die early than their socially isolated counterparts.

3:55 p.m. For an energy boost that will stay with you until dinner and temper your appetite at that meal, take a moment for an afternoon treat. And no, not from the vending machine.

Our suggestion: Try a Chewy Coconut-Granola Bar (recipe on the next page). This grain-and-fruit-filled snack contains just enough sweetness to seem decadent. We loaded ours with dried fruits, which are high in fiber and iron.

5 p.m. If a morning workout just didn't fit into your schedule, the hour or so after work is a perfect time to give it a try. Gyms and running trails are full of proof that many people find afternoon activity a great de-stressing transition from work to home. A little sweat therapy is a great way to forget all the people in your office who make you crazy.

CHEWY COCONUT-GRANOLA BARS

Cooking spray
- 2 teaspoons all-purpose flour
- ⅔ cup all-purpose flour
- ⅓ cup whole wheat flour
- 1 teaspoon baking powder
- ½ teaspoon salt
- 1¼ cups packed brown sugar
- ¼ cup vegetable oil
- 2 tablespoons fat-free milk
- 2 large eggs
- 1½ cups low-fat granola without raisins
- ¾ cup chopped dried mixed fruit
- ½ cup flaked sweetened coconut

1. Preheat oven to 350°.

2. Coat a 13 x 9-inch baking pan with cooking spray; dust with 2 teaspoons all-purpose flour. Lightly spoon ⅔ cup all-purpose flour and whole wheat flour into dry measuring cups; level with a knife. Combine flours, baking powder, and salt. Combine sugar, oil, milk, and eggs; beat with a mixer at high speed until smooth. Add flour mixture, beating at low speed until blended. Fold in granola and fruit. Spoon batter into pan. Sprinkle with coconut. Bake at 350° for 20 minutes or until golden. Cool on a wire rack. Yield: 20 servings (serving size: 1 bar).

CALORIES 157 (27%from fat); FAT 4.7g (sat 1.6g, mono 1.2g, poly 1.5g); PROTEIN 2.1g; CARB 27.8g; FIBER 1.1g; CHOL 22mg; IRON 1mg; SODIUM 122mg; CALC 34mg EXCHANGES: 1 Starch, 1 Fruit, 1 Fat

6:30 p.m. A busy day can be draining, but instead of opting for takeout or cold cereal, think of cooking dinner as a way to rebuild your energy. Why? It's creative and relaxing; you'll feel better doing something like this than just sinking into lethargy. And cooking is thoroughly social: Get your family in on the act. You can catch up with everyone's day while building bonds through one of the most ancient of all forms of teamwork. Keep it fun, too, by trying new foods. Studies have shown that diets with the widest variety tend to be the most healthful. That's probably because you don't bore yourself into bad dining. Variety has other benefits. Your body needs 40 nutrients per day—but not the same ones every day. Eat eclectically. Spinach for iron today, for instance, and potatoes for potassium tomorrow.

Our suggestion: Artichoke-Spinach Pizza (page 228). It doesn't take much time to make, but it spices up the table in a yummy way. Tomorrow, go for Grilled Salmon Salad (page 270).

7:45 p.m. There's no need to shun the occasional dessert or early-evening snack, especially after a day of balanced eating. In fact, if you allow yourself such pleasures every once in a while, you're more likely to stick with good eating habits. Deprivation never lasts.

Our suggestion: An Ultradecadent Double-Chip Brownie (page 199) when that hankering hits. You won't believe it has only 3.3 grams of fat. You will believe eating it was a brilliant choice.

8 p.m. Time to slow down. You might exercise your creative spirit by drawing, painting, or writing for an hour. Or build brain cells by deciphering a challenging crossword puzzle or having a great conversation with your mate. Maybe you need to get lost in a book that transports you to another era. Turn on your CD player and dance—whatever you choose, resist the impulse to tidy up the house or veg out in front of the television. Tell your mate or family members that you need this time to yourself. If you're up-front about your need for privacy, they'll be less likely to intrude and may even take some personal time themselves.

9 p.m. The day's pretty much a done deal by now, and you're on the long, low glide to your nightly rest. Still, you might be storing a little tension, especially in your back, shoulders, neck, and hamstrings. This is why stretching was invented. You think it's trouble? Check out your dog or cat. They stretch like they were getting paid by the hour. Take 10 to 15 minutes to ease into muscle-friendly positions, such as those found in yoga, that your body finds most helpful. (See page 348 for details on stretching movements.) But that's not your only option. Take the dog for a walk. You can also relax with a warm bath. Or try meditation, one of the most effective of all de-stressing techniques. Whatever you choose, make it a habit. Evening rituals can help relax and clear your mind before you turn back the sheets.

10 p.m. Get horizontal. Resist staying up for the late show. Most people need 8 to 8½ hours of shuteye a night—yet more than a third of us don't get that. Sleep deprivation is serious; for the average person, sleeping 6½ to 7 hours a night leads to a 32 percent decrease in alertness the next day, which can result in car accidents, poor job performance, and plain old orneriness. After 15 minutes with a good book, you're down for the count. It's been a good day. Tomorrow promises more of the same, and you'll be ready.

—Kerri Westenberg

Chapter 24

Healthy Habits
A to Z

An alphabetical guide to help you build
a healthier body, mind, and spirit

Acclimate yourself to the cold so you'll be more likely to exercise outdoors. The snowman's secret: Wear a hat and scarf because you lose up to 70 percent of your body heat through your head. Peel off layers as you need to, choosing an outer shell of windproof nylon or Gore-Tex.

Blood sugar control will help you avoid that afternoon energy crisis. Keep your blood sugar levels even by eating five to seven small meals a day. That may also help keep you from developing a predisposition to diabetes.

Colds are what you think you'd catch by heading out into the frosty air. But exercise—even in winter—seems to boost immunity. Indeed, a group of women who walked briskly 40 to 45 minutes five days a week for more than 12 weeks called in sick half as much as a group of nonexercisers in a study at Appalachian State University in Boone, North Carolina.

D is perhaps the most unique vitamin because your body makes it when you're exposed to sunlight (about 15 minutes' worth daily does the trick). A study of 5,000 women at the Northern California Cancer Center in Union City, California, suggests that sun exposure and getting the recommended daily intake of vitamin D (200 to 400 international units) may lower your risk of breast cancer by 30 percent or more. Moreover, vitamin D can aid in the fight against osteoporosis by helping your body absorb calcium.

Early is the way to be. Vow to get to your destination 10 minutes ahead of time so your life won't be a perpetual race. Wouldn't you much rather be there waiting, calm and collected, than arrive frantic?

Fitness should be your goal, not thinness. "Deprioritize the scale and prioritize the tape measure," says Pamela Peeke, M.D., M.P.H., assistant clinical professor of medicine at the University of Maryland School of Medicine in Baltimore. "The fitter you are, the smaller your dress size, but not necessarily the lower your weight. Muscle weighs more than fat."

Grapefruit juice is a great source of vitamin C: Just 6 ounces fulfills your daily requirement of 60 milligrams. But check with your doctor if you're taking any medication because grapefruit juice can increase the potency of some prescription drugs.

Homocysteine is an amino acid by-product that you should control in order to have a healthy heart. Homocysteine may be more harmful to your heart than LDL cholesterol, says Kenneth H. Cooper, M.D., M.P.H., founder of The Cooper Institute for Aerobics Research in Dallas. Fortunately, just 400 micrograms of folate (found in legumes, green leafy vegetables, and fruits such as oranges) each day can keep homocysteine at healthy levels.

Ice is the best way to reduce initial swelling after a minor injury. Apply 20 to 25 minutes at a time for the first two days, then switch to heat to help increase blood flow and speed the healing.

Job satisfaction helps keep you healthy. A study of 3,020 Boeing aircraft workers, reported in the journal *Spine*, is testament: Those who "hardly ever" enjoyed their jobs were 2.5 times more likely to report a back injury than their more satisfied coworkers.

Kasha and other high-fiber grains such as oats, quinoa, barley, and brown rice help reduce your chances of heart disease and several cancers, including breast and colon cancer.

Let go of your negative emotions: You're best off forgiving and forgetting than blowing up or stewing. The risk of heart attack at least doubles following a bout of intense anger. Ire also batters your immunity, leading to colds and possibly other health problems, too. Take a deep breath and ask yourself, "Will this matter a year from now?" If it won't, chill out.

Memory—no matter what your age—can be enhanced with these simple tricks. Make notes as a reminder—but say things out loud before you write them down to reinforce recall. Use visualization—for example, if you're afraid you might forget your umbrella when you leave a restaurant, visualize it hanging from the doorknob of the exit. If you're picking up a few items at the grocery store, create a word from the first letter of each or invent a story using all of them.

Nuts can help lower your cholesterol. A recent study at the University of Otago in New Zealand found that men with high cholesterol who ate a low-fat diet rich in walnuts experienced a 10-point drop in total cholesterol and a 14-point drop in LDL cholesterol. Although nuts are high in calories, they're rich in monounsaturated fats, which are most likely responsible for their cholesterol-lowering power.

Overhaul your diet one item, or one day at a time. Choose one small goal—say, to drink half a cup of fruit juice each morning. Sometimes people take on too much change at once, and it's difficult. Change can be easier if you proceed slowly.

Papaya and other exotic fruits—such as star fruit, persimmons, kiwis, bergamots, boysenberries, and casabas—can make meeting your five-a-day fruit and vegetable quota fun. And don't forget veggies such as bok choy, rutabagas, turnips, and chard. No one food has every nutrient in it, so eat a large variety.

Quit while you're behind. You don't have to finish everything you start, says Beverly Hills psychiatrist Carole Lieberman, M.D. "We often stick with unnecessary projects until the very end to find the one part that justifies all the time we spent. You have to know when to stop."

Rest. Better rest is one of the perks of exercising. One study showed that people who walked briskly or did aerobics at least 30 minutes four times weekly fell asleep twice as fast—about 11.5 minutes faster—than those who didn't exercise. Their sleep also was deeper, reports Abby King, Ph.D., a health researcher at Stanford University School of Medicine.

Soy is surely a superfood. Just 2 tablespoons of soy powder daily lessened hot flashes and night sweats in women ages 45 to 60, according to research at Wake Forest University in Winston-Salem, North Carolina. Within the trial's six weeks, the subjects' cholesterol levels also fell 10 percent, and their blood pressure dropped, too. What's more, in another preliminary study at the University of Illinois, 66 postmenopausal women who consumed a diet high in soy regained an average of 2 percent of lost bone in their spines within six months.

Touch not only feels great, but the relaxation it affords may also help boost your brain power. Twenty-six men and women who had 15-minute back, neck, and arm massages twice weekly for five weeks were able to perform math problems in half the time—with half the errors—of those who didn't get massages, according to a study at the University of Miami's Touch Research Institute.

Urge yourself, your family, and your friends to use sunscreen year-round. And sign up for a once-yearly skin check with a dermatologist—it takes less than 15 minutes. With more than 1 million skin cancers diagnosed per year, "there are more skin cancers in America than all the other cancers combined," says Darrell S. Rigel, M.D., a New York City dermatologist and past president of the American Academy of Dermatology.

Vacation, even if it's only for 3 minutes, three times each day. You might close your eyes, breathe deeply, do a yoga pose, chat with a friend, or gaze out the window. You'll not only feel better, you may be healthier for it. Such mind-drifting increased virus-conquering immunity levels by an average of 48 percent, according to a study in the *Journal of Clinical Psychology*.

Weightlifting not only helps replace bone lost to aging, but it can also aid in weight loss. Tufts University researchers have found that women who watched what they ate and strength-trained twice a week for six months lost 13 pounds—or 44 percent more body fat than those who only dieted. "Once you become stronger, you find it much easier to be physically active," says Dr. Miriam Nelson, director for the Center for Physical Fitness at Tufts University. "So you do more—and burn more calories."

XX would be the rating of a national study of 8,145 women ages 18 to 49 that suggests exercise can improve your sex life. A total of 40 percent of the women who exercised three times weekly were more easily aroused, and 31 percent had sex more often than those who didn't work out. One explanation: Your levels of testosterone and feel-good endorphins are elevated for up to 1½ hours after you exercise, according to California-based sex therapist Linda De Villers, Ph.D.

Yogurt is a great source of bone-strengthening calcium. You'll get 450 milligrams of calcium in a cup of plain fat-free yogurt versus only 300 milligrams in a glass of milk or calcium-fortified orange juice. Getting the daily requirement of 1,000 milligrams of calcium (or up to 1,200 milligrams if you're pregnant, breast-feeding, or past menopause) will help ward off osteoporosis.

Zucchini is wonderful for upping your water intake to meet the recommended eight-glass-a-day quota. The vegetable is made up of at least 95 percent water, which helps flush out your organs and keep your skin glowing. In addition to eating water-dense fruits and vegetables, you should drink as much water as you can.

—*Michele Meyer*

Chapter 25

It's About Balance

The world tries to throw you off-kilter every day, but with these 10 tips, you can keep a steady balance.

From Confucius to Aristotle and Freud to the Dalai Lama, sages have long equated happiness and health with emotional stability and moderation in all things. The ancient Greeks used the term *sôphrosunê* to refer to tempered balance and wisdom; the Romans called the same virtue *temperantia*.

But achieving balance may be life's greatest challenge, because in this world it's easy to tip toward the extremes—to be too strict or too flexible, too thrifty or too extravagant, too softhearted or too hard. How to stay steady? Get a good grip on something solid (family, friends, career, religion), and heed this advice from veteran coaches on psychological surefootedness. Their tips will help you find your balance in 10 areas of life where you might often teeter.

1. Bend like bamboo. In balance: self-discipline. Out of balance: rigidity. The Chinese use a lot of bamboo in their drawings because it's symbolic. "Bamboo bends with the wind. The balanced person does the same," says Bernard Seif, Ed.D., a clinical psychologist and abbot of the Salesian Monastery in Brodheadsville, Pennsylvania. New York psychologist Albert Ellis adds that rigidity, unlike self-discipline, typically involves a certain arbitrariness. He offers the example of someone who decides to give up sugar or salt, and then finds himself in a situation where the only food available may contain some sugar or salt. "The self-disciplined person will realize that bending the rules slightly is not going to shatter his goals of healthier nutrition. The rigid one will eat nothing and suffer."

2. Spend less time in front of the mirror. In balance: beauty. Out of balance: vanity. The desire to look your best is normal. And there's certainly nothing wrong with making sure your accessories match before you leave the house or fixing your 'do before company arrives. But at what point does the attention you pay to your looks reach an unhealthy level? When you sacrifice comfort for a pair of 3-inch heels? When missing one workout sends you into a panic? When you spend so much time primping that you're late for work? According to Rita Freedman, Ph.D., a Harrison, New York-based psychologist and expert on body image, any of these may indicate it's time to downgrade the importance you're placing on your appearance. "Start by giving yourself a quota," Freedman says. "If you now spend 20 minutes a day in front of the mirror, try knocking that down to 15 minutes, then 10."

3. Pay attention to your health. In balance: health awareness. Out of balance: hypochondria. Your body is constantly sending you important signals about your health. A cough, for instance, might send a balanced person to the drugstore or even to the doctor. But he wouldn't be convinced he has TB. "About 9 percent of the patients seen by general practitioners have such an obsession with illness that they might be diagnosed as hypochondriacs," says Marc Feldman, M.D., medical director of the University of Alabama at Birmingham's Center for Psychiatric Medicine. If friends and family have begun to express annoyance at your preoccupation with health, that's a sign you may be going overboard.

4. Don't be too polite. In balance: polite. Out of balance: wimp. When someone asks you a nosy question you don't care to answer—such as "How old are you?" or "Why aren't you married?"—what do you do? The balanced person won't pop a cork, but neither will she be cowed into answering. "If you can, interject a little humor," advises Peggy Post, the latest member of Emily Post's family to assume the role of national etiquette maven. In response to the marriage question, you might say, "I'm waiting for Prince Charming, and he seems to be late."

If you can't think of anything comical, just respond with something straightforward, like "I'd rather not talk about it." In some situations, you may be tempted to lie for the sake of politeness, such as, for example, when Aunt Martha asks you how you like her new dress (you don't). "Find some small truth," Post suggests. "You might say, 'It's a nice color,' or 'My, it's very interesting.'"

5. Keep money in perspective. In balance: thrifty. Out of balance: cheap. Saving for a rainy day and making sure your cash flow doesn't become a trickle are signs of responsibility. A balanced person might have a balanced checkbook, but he won't be so consumed with controlling his finances that he ignores what should be more important life goals, such as maintaining good health and close relationships.

"There's little question that people who are overly tight with money have less fun in life," says Miriam Tatzel, Ph.D., professor of human development at the State University of New York's branch of Empire State College in New City and an expert on the psychology of money. Two signs you may be too tight, Tatzel says: Other people, especially family members, resent the way you handle money, such as your constant reluctance to pull out your wallet. (Unsure? Ask them.) And you find yourself doing a lot of "poor-mouthing"—representing yourself to others as poorer than you are. "If this describes you, you might remind yourself that you really can't take it with you," Tatzel says.

> Much of life is about taking chances. Calculate the risk and reward; don't gamble more than you can afford to lose.

6. Take a chance. In balance: risk-taking. Out of balance: recklessness. Much of life is about taking chances. "The smart risk-taker calculates both the risks and the rewards and never gambles more than he can afford to lose," says psychologist Carl Pickhardt, Ph.D., of Austin, Texas. "The reckless person doesn't consider the odds—or knows the odds but takes the risk anyway, perhaps for enjoyment's sake." Quitting a job you dislike can be a smart risk if, for example, you're moving directly into another job that promises to be better. But someone who bolts from a job without another lined up—plus having an empty bank account and heavy debts—is probably being reckless.

7. Stay optimistic. In balance: optimist. Out of balance: dreamer. "Optimists carry out their dreams, while dreamers only dream," says psychologist Michael Mercer, Ph.D. "The dreamer will see herself as hardy and fit, and so will the optimist, but only the optimist will cook light, eat right, and exercise. The dreamer will see herself in a glamorous career, and so will the optimist, but only the optimist will work hard to obtain the necessary career skills."

8. Cut back on the overtime. In balance: dedication. Out of balance: workaholism. It's not the number of hours that separates the hard worker from the workaholic. It's more a state of mind. If working long hours is necessary to achieve a goal, such as winning an election or putting a down payment on a house, that's not workaholism, he says. "Workaholics don't work to achieve goals—they work compulsively, needlessly, in the belief that the work will somehow make them noble." The cure? "It often comes in realizing that self-worth can't be measured in hours of overtime," psychologist Albert Ellis says.

9. Be assertive. In balance: assertiveness. Out of balance: aggression. Your neighbor's cat has been ripping up your flower garden. What to do? "The assertive person merely expresses her feelings and desires. The aggressive person tries to control the neighbor's behavior with an implied or expressed threat," Dr. Carl Pickhardt explains. So the assertive person might say, "I've put a lot of work into raising those flowers, and I'm not at all happy about their being destroyed." The aggressive person might say, "Keep your cat out of my flower garden, or I'll let my German shepherd loose." Neither mode of conduct is always right or always wrong, Pickhardt says. "But assertiveness is a more workable strategy in most life situations."

10. Help others. In balance: good Samaritan. Out of balance: sucker. We've all heard stories of people who get into dire trouble, and although there are many bystanders, no one offers aid. Are people today that much out of balance? Jack Levin, Ph.D., a sociologist at Northeastern University in Boston who has studied good Samaritanism, has concluded that the biggest reason people don't come forward is fear of embarrassment. "It's terribly embarrassing to come to someone's rescue and then not be wanted," he says. "But being a balanced person means you must draw the line on the side of chance, forget about your own image, and go to help that person. Yes, you may wind up looking like a sucker, but you might save a life, too." Psychologist Seif adds: "We're freest and healthiest when we can make conscious choices without worrying, 'What are others thinking of me?'"

—Russell Wild

Chapter 26

Forgive for Your Health

There's a powerful reason for cultivating goodwill toward others—and it may just help in the quest to lose weight.

Just as we now know that managing anger and hostility can benefit your health, researchers are discovering that forgiveness has powerful restorative effects. Frank Boehm, M.D., says he will never forget the way he learned first-hand how helpful forgiveness can be. A patient suffering abdominal pain, headaches, and high blood pressure revealed that she was estranged from her siblings because years earlier they had abandoned her in a time of need. She "lived daily with anger, frustration, and resentment," according to Boehm, director of Maternal/Fetal Medicine at Vanderbilt University Medical Center in Nashville, Tennessee. "I attributed her ailments to that estrangement and urged her to consider forgiving her family."

Later, he got a letter from her saying she had indeed taken his advice and that soon after, her physical troubles had abated. "She had found forgiveness, and from this, good health," Boehm says.

THE MIND-BODY CONNECTION

"Chronic anger, resentment, hostility, shame, and guilt all affect our physical well-being," agrees Robin Casarjian, founder and director of the Lionheart Foundation, which promotes forgiveness in prisons and schools. "If inner conflicts aren't resolved, the body suffers. In the last 10 years, more medical research has shown that these unforgiving emotions correlate significantly with physical breakdown."

The evidence is overwhelming. Research from HeartMath, a mind/body think tank in Boulder Creek, California, shows that chronic negativity alters nervous-system balance and function and suppresses the immune system. This can lead to health problems that include more frequent colds and flu, fatigue, hypertension, asthma, and migraines, says Howard Martin, HeartMath executive vice president.

What's more, a University of North Carolina study found that angry people are almost three times as likely to have a heart attack or sudden cardiac death as those without that propensity. The reason may be that the stress of negative emotions can damage arteries and cause irregular heartbeats.

THE HEALTHY POWER OF FORGIVENESS

Forgiveness "releases us from so much," says psychiatrist Gerald Jampolsky, M.D., founder of the Center for Attitudinal Healing in Sausalito, California. "When we make peace of mind our goal, we take responsibility for our own happiness. That's what heals us—the knowledge that we have the choice to change our thoughts."

The first step toward healing is an understanding of what forgiveness is—and what it is not. Robert Enright, Ph.D., professor of educational psychology at the University of Wisconsin-Madison and founder of the International Forgiveness Institute, explains that "forgiveness does not mean excusing, forgetting, denying, condoning, condemning, seeking justice, or blindly reconciling at all costs." Instead, it is a voluntary gift of mercy that can open a doorway to personal healing—a process that does not necessarily always end in reconciliation or restoration of trust.

"It can give you your life back, but not necessarily your relationships," Enright says. He cites the example of a young man whose father beat him as a child. He was plagued by a frothing anger that created nightmares for 22 years. The man's dreams of his father chasing him stopped after he truly forgave his father, but their relationship was never reestablished.

Enright, who began researching forgiveness and its ramifications 15 years ago, says scientific data show a clear connection between prolonged resentment and emotional problems such as depression and anxiety. His early work with incest survivors found that those who were able to forgive their abusers experienced marked reductions in anxiety and depression, and remarkable increases in self-esteem and hope. "We've been surprised at how strong forgiveness can be as a healing agent," he says. "You can actually change a person's well-being by helping them to forgive."

For Enright, "reframing" is a crucial step. This means learning to see offenders as human beings, considering what they might have gone through in the past as well as at the time they inflicted the hurt. Whether you might be coping with the infidelity of a spouse or betrayal by a friend, studies suggest that learning to empathize with a person who has caused you pain can lead to compassion and acceptance, even to seeing the process of forgiving as affirming and transformative.

"It's one of the more vital aspects to the good life," Enright says. "It's about knitting broken relationships, and it is also a way to make sure that the brokenness of this world becomes more whole."

Phyllis Mayberg can attest to the restorative powers of forgiveness. To cope with a messy divorce and the depression that followed, the Stanford University administrative assistant enrolled in a course called "The Art and Science of Forgiveness." Offered through the Stanford Forgiveness Project, the popular six-week classes emphasize behavioral and psychoemotional changes and incorporate stress-management techniques such as meditation, imaging, and breathing awareness to support the actual work of forgiveness.

"I felt betrayed and overwhelmed," Mayberg says, recalling the abrupt end to her four-year marriage and the 20 subsequent years she spent waiting for her ex-husband to apologize for leaving her. "Now, even though he never said 'I'm sorry,' I can accept who he is and the way things are. It's not easy to change, and it's impossible to forget what happened. But I'm more in control of how I react to things, less anxious, more self-reliant. I don't concentrate so much on the past.

"I can forgive myself as well as others, and that's healing." —*Beth Witrogen McLeod*

5 STEPS TO FORGIVENESS

Do you want to forgive but simply don't know how? Everett Worthington, Ph.D., who spearheads the Campaign for Forgiveness Research at Virginia Commonwealth University, suggests these five steps to forgiveness that can heal you, too.

1. Recall objectively the hurt or blame, without wallowing in victimization. (This may take some time.)
2. Empathize with the person who hurt you. Think through what might have been going on in that person's mind.
3. Recall times when you hurt or offended someone and how it felt to be forgiven. Ask yourself if you'd be willing to give that gift to the person who hurt you.
4. Speak aloud your commitment to forgive.
5. Remember forgiveness when doubt creeps in. It's normal to remember the pain, but that doesn't mean you haven't truly forgiven.

Chapter 27

Are You an Emotional Eater?

How you feel can affect how you eat.
Take this quiz to find out if you're feeding something
more than an empty stomach.

Think about all the times in life where feelings and food are intertwined—getting a cookie after a bad spill on your bike, having a pizza party after you won your soccer game, or eating a pint of mint chocolate chip ice cream after your boyfriend broke your heart. Putting feelings and food together isn't necessarily a bad thing. There *is* a certain serenity in sitting down with a bowl of chicken soup when you've got a cold or sharing a chocolate chip cookie with your eight-year-old after she's had a rough day at school. But when feeding your emotional hunger leads to overeating, especially eating too much of high-fat, high-calorie foods, your body starts to pay the price. "Emotions are a big factor not only in when you eat, but often in what you eat," says Janet Helm, M.D., R.D., a registered dietitian in New York. "People eat when they are stressed. They eat when they are depressed, bored, or lonely. They eat when they are celebrating. It's when this emotional eating leads to overeating or eating regrettably that problems begin."

Study after study has shown a connection between emotions, eating, and being overweight. A recent study looked at the eating habits of obese women and discovered that they tend to eat more when they're in a bad mood or a good mood than they do when emotions are relatively calm.

Clearly there are people who have serious issues with food and mood that can lead to destructive eating disorders. In these cases, seeking professional help is appropriate. But many of us simply don't pay attention to how our mood might affect what and how we eat.

So are you an emotional eater? Most of us are, to some extent, so don't be too hard on yourself. Take this lighthearted quiz and see if you recognize yourself in any of these familiar situations.

1. It's your best friend's 40th birthday. You surprise her with a birthday dinner at her favorite restaurant. Since it's such a festive occasion you decide you can splurge a little, so you . . .

    A. Order your favorite cheesy chicken dish and eat half (you'll have the rest at lunch tomorrow) and split a piece of birthday cheesecake with a couple of friends.

    B. Munch on an appetizer until dinner comes, polish off your entrée, and relish every morsel of birthday cake—after all, your friend is only 40 once!

2. You've been working on a project for two months and the final presentation is tomorrow. After a morning of getting last minute details together you decide to take a break, so you . . .

    A. Get outside and take a walk around the block. The fresh air always clears your mind.

    B. Make a beeline for the nearest vending machine. Chocolate is the only way to deal with this kind of pressure.

    C. Take a few minutes to chat with a friend about her trip to Hawaii. At least hearing about the tropics will relax you.

3. You and the hubby have been arguing all week about the amount of overtime he's been putting in lately. He calls to say he's going to be late again and the tension erupts into a huge fight. You slam the phone down and . . .

    A. Run to the bedroom and cry into your pillow.

    B. Grab a spoon and a pint of Rocky Road ice cream from the freezer and head to the couch to watch "When Harry Met Sally" for the 230th time.

    C. Take your tennis racket and a few balls outside and practice your back hand to work off your anger.

4. It's late evening and your mom just called to tell you that your favorite aunt died. Your first reaction is to . . .

    A. Grab your husband and sob on his shoulder.

    B. Finish off that chocolate cake in the fridge.

    C. Call your cousins and ask if there's anything you can do to help.

5. It's Friday night. The kids are going camping with friends and your husband is fishing with his buddies. You have a whole weekend to yourself and have decided to become a hermit for the next few days. Though most of the weekend is bliss, by Saturday night you start missing the sounds of life that usually fill your home. To fill the silence you decide to . . .

    A. Call your best friend and gab for a few uninterrupted hours.

    B. Rent a few movies, grab a six-pack of soft drinks, a supersize pack of M&M's, and some chips, and have a movie and munchie night all by yourself.

    C. Clean that downstairs bathroom. Last time you checked there was something growing in the toilet.

RESULTS

If you answered "**B**" to any of the above questions, it may be time to take a close look at yourself and discover the emotions that trigger your eating. Helm suggests keeping a food diary. "A diary is a great tool for people who tend to eat in response to their emotions," Helms says. Keeping a food diary is simple, just write down what you ate during the day and how you felt before and after eating. (See page 309 for details about keeping a food journal or diary.)

Once you discover your emotional triggers, make a conscious effort to railroad the desire to munch. If you typically eat when you're stressed, try doing some yoga or taking a walk instead of grabbing a doughnut. If you're lonely, call a friend. Sidetracking the urge to eat in response to your emotions can leave you feeling better in the long run and includes a bonus—you may just start losing weight and gaining more control over your body and mind.   *—Michele Mann*

5

Supermarket Savvy and Secrets
from the Test Kitchens

The editors of *Cooking Light* share the shopping strategies and flavor secrets that lead to weight loss.

Chapter 28

Buyer, Be Aware

Making wise choices at the grocery store puts
you on the road to healthy weight loss.

Healthful eating starts at the grocery store—that is, if you can figure out how to avoid the high-calorie, high-fat traps. Before you get started on a grocery shopping adventure, arm yourself with some travel tips for navigating the aisles of the supermarket. These tips will help you come out of the market with a supply of groceries that can help you stick with your weight-control plan.

TIPS FOR THE SAVVY SUPERMARKET TRAVELER

- Make a list. Plan ahead for meals and snacks for the week and make a list of what you need. When you have a list, it's a lot easier to avoid buying impulse items.
- Find your best shopping time. Instead of shopping at the end of a busy workday, find another time to shop when you are less likely to be tired and hungry. Shopping when you are hungry can lead to impulse buying of high-fat, high-sugar foods.
- Be coupon conscious. If you use coupons, be selective and only clip the ones for items that are a part of your healthy eating plan. Some foods with coupons aren't always the best bargain in terms of cost or nutrition.
- Shop the outside aisles. Most grocery stores are organized in basically the same way, with food such as fresh produce, dairy, meats, and poultry on the outside aisles. If you fill your cart with fresh, low-fat items first, you'll have less room for high-fat, high-sugar items.
- Beware of sale traps. Don't buy sweets and snacks just because they are featured in a sale special and displayed at the ends of aisles.
- Shop for convenience. If you know that fresh produce will go bad before you have a chance to use it, buy canned or frozen.

- Scan the top and bottom shelves. Stores frequently place sugary cereals and snack foods on the middle shelves—usually to attract the attention of children. So look up high or down low on the shelf to find the more nutritious foods in that section.
- Overcome your sweet tooth. If you cannot resist cookies and candy or snack foods, avoid those aisles altogether. Or buy an individual package of chips or cookies rather than a large, family-size bag.
- Don't be snared by the checkout trap. Once you make it by the cookie and chip aisles, there's yet another obstacle: the checkout lane. Move to a candy-free lane, or keep your mind occupied by reading the headlines of the magazines and tabloids.
- Read food labels. The information on the package label is a valuable roadmap that will help you make nutritious selections.

LABEL ABLE

When you see "fat-free" on a label, can you believe it? Yes. The U.S. Department of Agriculture (USDA) has strict labeling regulations that food manufacturers are required to follow. Here are some food label terms and what they mean.

- **Fat-free:** less than 0.5 grams of fat per serving
- **Low-fat:** 3 grams of fat (or less) per serving
- **Lean (on meat labels):** less than 10 grams of fat per serving, with 4.5 grams or less of saturated fat and 95 milligrams or less of cholesterol
- **Extra-lean (on meat labels):** less than 5 grams of fat per serving, with 2 grams or less of saturated fat and 95 milligrams or less of cholesterol
- **Less (fat, calories, cholesterol, or sodium):** contains 25 percent less (fat, calories, cholesterol, or sodium) than the food it is being compared to
- **Reduced:** a product that contains at least 25 percent fewer calories, sodium, or sugar than the regular version of the product
- **Lite (light):** contains one-third fewer calories or no more than one-half the fat of the higher-calorie, higher-fat version; or no more than one-half the sodium of the higher-sodium version
- **Cholesterol-free:** less than 2 milligrams of cholesterol and 2 grams or less of saturated fat per serving
- **Low-calorie:** fewer than 40 calories per serving

If you know how to decipher a food label, you can fit any food into a healthy eating plan. Here's a guide to help you understand the food label.

Nutrition Facts

Serving Size: ½ cup (114g) ❶
Servings Per Container: 4

Amounts Per Serving

Calories 90	❷ **Calories from Fat** 30

❸ % Daily Value

Total Fat 3g ❹	5%
Saturated Fat 0g ❺	0%
Cholesterol 30mg ❻	0%
Sodium 300mg ❼	13%
Total Carbohydrate 13g ❽	4%
Dietary Fiber 3g ❾	12%
Sugars 3g ❿	
Protein 3g	

Vitamin A	4%	Vitamin C	2%
Calcium	20% ⓫	Iron	4%

* Percent Daily Values are based on a 2,000 calorie diet. Your daily values may be higher or lower depending on your calorie needs:

	Calories	2,000	2,500
Total Fat	Less than	65g	80g
Sat Fat	Less than	20g	25g
Cholesterol	Less than	300mg	300mg
Sodium	Less than	2,400mg	2,400mg
Total Carbohydrate		300g	375g
Dietary Fiber		25g	30g

Calories per gram:
Fat 9 • Carbohydrate 4 • Protein 4

g = grams
mg = milligrams

❶ **Serving Size** Values are for one serving of the food. A portion may be more or less than what you expect, so pay attention to the amount given.

❷ **Calories from Fat** Choose foods with a big difference between total calories and calories from fat.

❸ **% Daily Value (DV)** This percentage indicates how much of your daily requirement for the nutrient you get from one serving of the food. For fat, saturated fat, cholesterol, and sodium, choose foods with a low % DV. For fiber, vitamins, and minerals, the goal is 100 percent each day.

❹ **Total Fat** Try to keep fat intake at 30 percent or less of total calories. If you're eating about 2,000 calories a day, that's 65 grams of fat per day (1 gram of fat = 9 calories).

❺ **Saturated Fat** The value for saturated fat is included in Total Fat. A high intake of saturated fat is associated with the risk of heart disease and certain cancers.

⑥ Cholesterol Try to keep cholesterol intake to less than 300 milligrams per day.

⑦ Sodium You call it salt, the label says sodium. Try to keep your sodium intake to no more than 2,400 milligrams per day.

⑧ Total Carbohydrate The value for total carbohydrate includes the starches, sugars, and dietary fiber in a serving. If you have diabetes, the total carbohydrate in your diet is an important part of blood sugar control.

⑨ Dietary Fiber This value is included in and listed under Total Carbohydrate. Try to eat at least 25 grams of fiber every day.

⑩ Sugars This value refers to both natural sugars and added sugar, but you need to look on the ingredients list panel to determine the type of sugar. The sugar value is included in Total Carbohydrate.

⑪ Vitamins and Minerals These are essential nutrients needed for disease prevention and to promote good health. The goal is 100 percent each day for each nutrient.

Navigating the Aisles

How do you figure out which foods are the best, and where do you go to find them? Use this guide to make wise choices in each section of the grocery store.

DAIRY

* Look for low-fat and fat-free products: milk, cheese, yogurt, and sour cream.
* Chocolate milk can be whole, 2 percent, 1 percent, or fat-free. It has added chocolate or cocoa and some type of sweetener.
* Check the sugar content of yogurt. Some low-fat and fat-free yogurts are sweetened with sugar, so they might be higher in calories than you think.
* If you don't like low-fat cheese, use high-flavored cheeses such as sharp Cheddar and Parmesan because you can get more flavor with less cheese.

MILKING IT

Nutritionally speaking, the difference between whole, reduced-fat, and fat-free milk is the fat and calorie content. Here's how they compare.

Milk (1 cup)	Calories	Fat (grams)
Whole	150	8.0
2% or reduced-fat	121	5.0
1%	102	3.0
Fat-free or skim milk	90	0.5

A CHEESE COURSE

How does your favorite cheese stack up in terms of fat?

Percent Calories from Fat	Type of Cheese
0 to 9%	• Fat-free cottage cheese • Fat-free cream cheese • Fat-free cheese slices
10 to 29%	• 1% low-fat cottage cheese • 2% low-fat cottage cheese
30 to 39%	• Low-fat American processed cheese slices • Low-fat Swiss processed cheese slices
40 to 49%	• Creamed small-curd cottage cheese • Lite ricotta cheese
50 to 59%	• Reduced-fat mild Cheddar • Reduced-fat sharp Cheddar • Reduced-fat colby • Reduced-fat Monterey Jack • Part-skim mozzarella • Parmesan • Part-skim ricotta
60 to 69%	• Process American cheese slices • Light cream cheese • Gouda • Mozzarella • Muenster • Provolone • Ricotta • Romano • Swiss
70 to 79%	• Blue • Brick • Brie • Camembert • Cheddar • Colby • Edam • Feta • Gruyère
80 to 90%	• Monterey Jack • Cream cheese • Neufchatel cheese

FRESH PRODUCE

It's hard to make a wrong turn in this section because fresh fruits and vegetables are low in calories and fat, and high in nutrients. Here are a few things to keep in mind.

- In general, the darker the color of the fruit or vegetable, the higher the nutrient content. For example, dark leafy greens such as spinach have more nutrients than pale green iceberg lettuce.
- For the best buy and the best flavor, stock up on in-season produce.
- If fresh is not available, frozen and canned are perfectly fine choices. The sodium in canned vegetables is higher than that of fresh or frozen, so if you're cutting back on sodium, look for low-sodium or no-added-salt canned vegetables.
- If you're buying bagged salads, get the ones that do not have dressing packets or discard the packet.
- To buy small amounts of chopped fruits or veggies, check out the salad bar.
- Since fresh produce does not come with labels (unless it's already packaged) keep in mind that most fruits have about 60 calories and 0 grams fat for a ½-cup serving, and most vegetables have only about 25 calories and 0 grams of fat for a ½-cup serving, cooked, or 1 cup raw.

FATS AND OILS

- Butter and margarine are the same in terms of total fat and calories. Butter contains mostly saturated fat while margarine is mostly polyunsaturated. However, margarine contains a kind of fat called trans fat, which is thought to be just as bad as saturated fat in terms of heart disease risk. So your best bet is to use smaller amounts of either butter *or* margarine.
- Look for margarine made with liquid oil rather than hydrogenated oil or vegetable shortening. When you see the word "hydrogenated," that means the product is high in saturated fat and trans fat.
- Whipped margarines and soft tub margarines usually have less fat per tablespoon than stick margarines or butter because air is whipped in to add volume.
- Low-fat and fat-free spreads are suitable for spreading, but not always suitable for baking. If a product contains less than 50 to 60 percent oil, you should not use it for baking.
- Butter-flavored sprays have a high water content and are suitable for adding flavor, but not for baking. These sprays contain negligible amounts of fat and no calories.

- All vegetable oils have the same amount of calories and all are cholesterol-free, but olive oil and canola oil are high in monounsaturated fat, a kind of fat that appears to be good for your heart.
- When you see the word "light" on a bottle of oil, it refers to the color and does not mean that the oil is lower in calories or fat.

NEED AN OIL CHANGE?

Compare the fatty acid content of a variety of fats and oils. The fats that are better for your heart are the ones with the highest percentage of monounsaturated fat, followed by the ones with a high percentage of polyunsaturated fat. So the top five "healthiest" fats (in bold below) are olive, canola, safflower, sunflower, and corn oil.

Type of Fat	Saturated (Fatty Acids)	Monounsaturated (Fatty Acids)	Polyunsaturated (Fatty Acids)
Butter	66%	30%	4%
Canola oil	7%	58%	35%
Coconut oil	87%	6%	2%
Corn oil	13%	25%	62%
Cottonseed oil	26%	18%	52%
Lard	41%	47%	12%
Margarine	19%	49%	32%
Olive oil	14%	77%	9%
Palm kernel oil	80%	10%	2%
Palm oil	49%	37%	9%
Peanut oil	18%	49%	33%
Safflower oil	10%	13%	77%
Sesame oil	18%	40%	40%
Soybean oil	15%	24%	61%
Sunflower oil	11%	20%	69%
Vegetable shortening	28%	44%	28%

Source: Composition of Foods, *Agricultural Handbook No. 8-4. Washington, D.C., USDA, 1990.*

MEAT, FISH, AND POULTRY
Meats
- For the leanest cuts of meat, buy beef with the words "round" or "loin" on the label. Buy pork or lamb with the words "loin" or "leg."
Some examples of lean cuts of meat are:

BEEF	VEAL	PORK	LAMB
eye of round	cutlet	tenderloin	leg
top round steak	blade or arm steak	top loin roast	loin chop
top round roast	rib roast	top loin chop	arm chop
sirloin steak	rib or loin chop	center loin chop	foreshanks
top loin steak		sirloin roast	
tenderloin steak		loin rib chop	
chuck arm pot roast			

- Choose leaner grades of meats. Beef cuts labeled "prime" have more marbled fat (the thin streaks of fat that run between the muscle) than cuts labeled "choice" or "select." Select cuts have the least amount of marbled fat.
- Buy well-trimmed meat with ⅛-inch fat trim or less.
- For ground meats, look for packages that have the greatest percent lean to fat ratio. For example, ground beef labeled 95 percent lean is a good choice. Percent lean refers to the weight of the meat, not the calories it contains.
- Avoid deli meats if you are trying to limit sodium. While deli meats can be very lean, they are also high in sodium.

Fish and Shellfish
- Fish usually has less fat than meat and poultry.
- In general, the lighter the color of the fish, the lower in fat it is. Fish that is firm and darker in color tends to have more fat.
- The fat in fish is the heart-healthy kind of fat called omega-3 fat.
- Avoid frozen fish products that have been breaded and fried.
- Buy canned fish such as tuna that is packed in water instead of oil.
- Although shrimp does have more cholesterol than other types of fish and shellfish, it's still very low in saturated fat. Four ounces of boiled shrimp has just 1.2 grams of total fat and 221 milligrams of cholesterol, which is still below the American Heart Association recommended amount of 300 milligrams of cholesterol per day.

Poultry

- Most of the fat in poultry is in the skin. Buy skinless poultry, or remove the fat before eating. It's fine to cook with the skin still on, just remove it before you eat.
- White meat (breast) is lower in fat than dark meat (thigh, wings, and drumsticks).
- For timesaving chicken, buy whole roasted chickens in the deli. These chickens are higher in sodium than fresh, and you need to remove the skin before eating.
- There is no legal definition of free-range chicken, and free-range chickens don't necessarily have less fat than factory farm chickens.
- Self-basting turkeys are injected with fat, so they're higher in fat than the regular turkeys.
- Check the labels of ground turkey so you'll know how much fat you're getting. Buy ground white meat for the least amount of fat. Regular ground turkey contains both white and dark meat (and sometimes skin and fat), so it's higher in fat than ground white meat. Turkey sausage is not always much lower in fat than pork and beef sausage because fat and skin is sometimes included.

PASTA, RICE, AND GRAINS

Grain products are excellent sources of complex carbohydrates, fiber, B vitamins, and minerals, and are generally low in fat. They can become high-fat when fats and oils are added during processing. Check the labels to make nutritious choices.

- Look for breads and baked goods with 3 grams of fat or less per serving.
- Choose cereals with at least 3 grams of fiber per serving.
- Check the ingredients list to see if the first thing listed is a whole grain such as whole wheat, oats, or millet. (Despite their dark color, rye and pumpernickel are not whole grain breads.)
- Watch out for granola-type cereals and breads. While they might seem to be the most nutritious choices, some are actually loaded with sugar and saturated fats. For any cereal, make sure the first ingredient is a grain and not a sugar or fat.
- Packaged rice and grain mixes can be low-fat if you prepare them without butter or oil, but they're often high in sodium because of the added seasonings. If there is a seasoning packet, you can omit it, or just use half of the packet.
- Choose brown and wild rice instead of white to get more fiber. Expand your world of grains to include high-fiber products such as barley, bulgur, kasha, and quinoa.
- Pasta is low in fat but can become a high-fat food when you add a rich, creamy sauce. To increase fiber, use whole wheat spaghetti, macaroni, or lasagna.

Chapter 29

The Ultimate Pantry

There's no need to pile on calories at the fast-food drive-thru if your pantry's prepared for dinner.

"**B**e prepared" is not only a motto for the scouts, it's also a weight-loss strategy. When you keep your pantry stocked with plenty of healthy items, you'll be less likely to yield to the temptation of high-fat fast food or calorie-laden snacks.

And, if you stock your pantry with the ingredients in our pantry list, you'll almost always be able to cook some of your favorite *Cooking Light* recipes. You'll figure out what you need to keep on hand so you're ready in a flash to get something good on the table—in fair weather and foul, without stopping at the store on the way home from work.

Our list is long, but fear not. You don't need to fill up your pantry in one fell swoop. There's an art to building a healthy, working pantry. Why not take your first lessons today?

On the next page, you'll find a list to help you build a healthy pantry. Use this list when you initially stock up and as you go to the grocery store to re-stock. We've organized the list in the following categories: Foundations and Extra Foundations (basic items that can be the building blocks for a variety of meals), Flavor Builders and Extra Flavor Builders (ingredients that give your recipes character), Assistants (ingredients that help round out the flavor of the foundation items), Sweet Returns (sugar and other sweeteners), and Cool Stuff (refrigerated and frozen items). You might want to re-order your list based on your supermarket's layout so that you can efficiently shop for items in the order that you move throughout the store.

The majority of these ingredients can be found at your local supermarket. For some of the more unusual items, though, you may need to find an Asian market or a gourmet grocery store.

The Healthy Pantry

Foundations
- ❏ canned beans: black, great Northern, pinto
- ❏ canned tuna
- ❏ pastas: couscous, penne, spaghetti
- ❏ white rice

Extra Foundations
- ❏ canned beans: cannellini, garbanzo
- ❏ canned salmon
- ❏ cornmeal, grits, semolina flour
- ❏ grains: barley, bulgar, millet, quinoa
- ❏ pasta: variety of shapes and sizes
- ❏ rice: Arborio, basmati, jasmine, sticky, sweet, wild

Flavor Builders
- ❏ capers
- ❏ chutneys
- ❏ dark sesame oil
- ❏ dried herbs
- ❏ extra-virgin olive oil
- ❏ fresh garlic
- ❏ low-sodium soy sauce
- ❏ mustards: Dijon, honey, stone-ground
- ❏ peanut butter
- ❏ salsa
- ❏ vinegars: balsamic, red wine, rice, sherry

Extra Flavor Builders
- ❏ anchovy, chili, and curry pastes
- ❏ bottled roasted red bell peppers
- ❏ chipotle chiles in adobo sauce
- ❏ fish sauce, hoisin sauce, oyster sauce
- ❏ golden raisins
- ❏ spirits: red and white wine, sherry
- ❏ sun-dried tomatoes

Assistants
- ❏ canned tomato products
- ❏ chicken and vegetable broths
- ❏ pasta sauce

Sweet Returns
- ❏ cocoa
- ❏ honey
- ❏ maple syrup
- ❏ molasses
- ❏ semisweet chocolate
- ❏ sugars: brown, granulated, powdered

Cool Stuff
- ❏ butter
- ❏ cheeses: blue, feta, mozzarella, Parmesan, Romano
- ❏ eggs, egg substitute
- ❏ fresh chiles: jalapeño, serrano
- ❏ fresh fish: catfish, salmon, shrimp
- ❏ fresh herbs
- ❏ fresh parsley
- ❏ frozen spinach
- ❏ jellies and preserves
- ❏ lemons, limes
- ❏ nuts: almonds, hazelnuts, pecans, pine nuts, walnuts
- ❏ olives: kalamata, niçoise
- ❏ reduced-fat salad dressings
- ❏ skinless, boneless chicken breasts
- ❏ tofu: firm, soft
- ❏ tubes of polenta

Chapter 30

On Hand and Easy

Our Top 10 list of easy-to-prepare foods
will help steer you toward healthier
habits and weight-loss success.

The road toward healthier living and lighter food has been paired with new products that, now taken for granted, were once true innovations. These ten items get our vote as the most important food products in helping to make healthier, low-fat eating a real choice for millions of people in terms of convenience, simplicity, flavor, and availability.

1. Skinless, Boneless Chicken Breasts It wasn't until the mid-1970s that this super-convenient food was first introduced, and not until the late '70s that it began to change the way we cook. Skinless, boneless chicken breasts are low-fat, as well as quick and easy to prepare.

2. Frozen Dinners Frozen dinners are the ultimate in convenience and, if selected wisely, in healthfulness. Today, healthy eaters can choose from an amazing array of products and can quickly assess each nutrient and every calorie due to labeling laws.

3. Yogurt Yogurt didn't really go mainstream in the United States until the 1970s, when everyone learned how good it tastes frozen. Now you can find yogurt (frozen and refrigerated) almost everywhere, in cartons, cups, bars, and soft-serve cones. It comes with and without sugar and in a wide variety of flavors.

4. Tortillas Corn tortillas have been around since ancient times, but the 20th century saw their use skyrocket. Corn tortillas are virtually fat-free if cooked without oil. And their flour cousins have only about 2.5 grams of fat each. Tortillas of either kind are incredibly versatile and easy to fill or top with healthy ingredients.

5. Tofu The popularity of this healthy and low-fat food has developed rapidly in the last decade. Tofu is made from soy milk curds that are pressed and drained in a process similar to cheesemaking.

6. Veggie Burgers These burgers were around as far back as the 1950s, but their flavor has improved since then. Today, companies such as Boca Burger and Gardenburger sell frozen burgers made from vegetables, grains, and soy.

7. Pasta Today there are hundreds of types and shapes of pasta and just as many ways to cook and serve them. Dried pasta stays fresh for a long time, is easy and quick to cook, and is low in fat.

8. Angel Food Cake This heavenly low-fat mixture of egg whites, sugar, flour, and air was created in the late 19th century. And just as it did in the past, angel food cake gives us a light and tasty option for dessert.

9. Low-Fat Snacks When they first came out, low-fat snacks proved so popular that other options followed quickly: chips, crackers, air-popped popcorn, cookies, cakes, and ice cream.

10. Cooking Spray These cans of propellant and vegetable oil have been on the market since 1959, but the 1990s brought a switch to canola oil and the introduction of flavored sprays such as butter, olive oil, lemon, and garlic.

—Jim Fobel

Chapter 31

Cook Light, Cook Right

Here are all the tips, techniques, and tools you'll need to master low-fat flavorful cooking.

Low-fat cooking is actually very simple—it's all about getting back to the basics. No fancy cooking techniques and complicated procedures are required. All you need are a few simple tips to get you started on a whole new way of cooking and eating.

THE SECRETS OF SUCCESS

Here's what the *Cooking Light* experts do to cook with flavor, not fat.

- Start with the freshest, leanest, and most colorful ingredients, especially when it comes to fresh produce. Great ingredients mean great food, and you usually don't have to do much to it for it to taste great.

- Cook chicken with the skin on to keep in moisture and flavor. Then just remove the skin before eating.

- Make soups and stews ahead of time and chill overnight. After the soup has chilled, you can skim the hardened fat off the top and throw it away. If there's no time to chill overnight, toss a couple of ice cubes into the warm liquid; the fat will cling to the ice cube. When the cube is coated with fat, remove it from the soup.

- Brown meat in a nonstick skillet, remove the meat and drain on paper towels. Wipe the skillet dry with paper towels if there is grease remaining in the pan.

- Coat baking dishes, pans, and skillets with cooking spray instead of oil or grease. For added flavor, use a flavored cooking spray. Another trick is to spray the food with cooking spray: This can give you some nice browning for baked goods and pan-seared meats and fish.

- Add flavor instead of fat to dishes by cooking with wine, herbs, spices, fruit juices, flavored vinegars, and fat-free broths. (See Chapter 32, "Low-Fat Flavor Secrets.")

- Use these low-fat, high-flavor condiments to add zest to your recipes:

Chutneys	Flavored vinegars	Soy sauce
Mustards	Reduced-fat salad dressings	Salsas

- Reserve a few tablespoons of the pasta cooking water when you're making a pasta dish. Add it back to the pasta when you add the sauce to help the pasta stay moist without having to add oil.

SEND IN THE SUBSTITUTES

Sometimes all you need for low-fat cooking are a few simple reduced-fat substitutions for the high-fat ingredients.

	If the recipe calls for:	You can use:
Fats and Oils	Butter	Light butter, reduced-calorie margarine
	Margarine	Reduced-calorie margarine
	Mayonnaise	Fat-free, light, or low-fat mayonnaise
	Oil	Polyunsaturated or monounsaturated oil in a reduced amount
	Salad dressing	Fat-free or reduced-fat salad dressing or vinaigrette
	Shortening	Polyunsaturated or monounsaturated oil in a reduced amount
Meats, Poultry, and Eggs	Bacon	Reduced-fat bacon; turkey bacon; lean ham; Canadian bacon
	Ground beef	Ground round; extra-lean ground beef; ground turkey
	Sausage	50%-less-fat pork sausage; turkey sausage
	Luncheon meat	Sliced turkey, chicken, lean roast beef, or lean ham
	Tuna packed in oil	Tuna packed in water
	Egg, whole	2 egg whites; ¼ cup egg substitute

- Cook rice and other grains in fat-free broth or juice instead of water to get more flavor without adding fat.
- Experiment with replacing some of the oil or shortening in baked goods with applesauce or another pureed fruit.
- Replace high-fat ingredients with their reduced-fat and fat-free counterparts. See the chart below for a list of substitutions.

	If the recipe calls for:	You can use:
Dairy Products	Sour cream	Fat-free or reduced-fat sour cream; fat-free or low-fat plain yogurt
	Cheddar, Swiss, Monterey Jack, mozzarella cheeses	Reduced-fat cheeses
	Cottage cheese	Fat-free or 1% low-fat cottage cheese
	Cream cheese	Fat-free or light cream cheese; Neufchâtel cheese
	Ricotta cheese	Part-skim ricotta or fat-free ricotta
	Whole milk	Fat-free or skim milk; 1% low-fat milk
	Evaporated milk	Fat-free evaporated milk
	Half-and-half	Fat-free half-and-half or fat-free evaporated milk
	Whipped cream	Fat-free or reduced-calorie frozen whipped topping
	Ice cream	Fat-free or low-fat ice cream; fat-free or low-fat frozen yogurt; sherbet; sorbet
Miscellaneous	Soups, canned	Low-fat, reduced-sodium soups
	Fudge sauce	Fat-free chocolate syrup
	Nuts	Use a reduced amount—one-third to one-half less
	Baking chocolate, 1 ounce	3 tablespoons unsweetened cocoa plus 1 tablespoon vegetable oil

10 Essential Tools

No cook should be without these pieces of kitchen equipment. They make low-fat cooking a snap.

1. **Measuring cups and spoons:** Successful recipes depend on accurate measuring. You also need measuring cups to check portion sizes.

2. **Nonstick skillets and saucepans:** With nonstick cookware, you can cook with little or no fat in the pan. Be sure to use wooden or plastic utensils so you won't scratch the nonstick surface.

3. **Set of sharp knives:** Chopping, dicing, and slicing is so much easier when you use high-quality knives and keep them sharp.

4. **Kitchen shears:** Kitchen scissors are handy for mincing herbs, chopping tomatoes in the can, trimming fat from meats and poultry, and many other uses.

5. **Steam basket or vegetable steamer:** Steaming vegetables is a quick and easy way to cook them because it preserves nutrients as well as flavor.

6. **Broiler pan/broiler rack:** When you broil, much of the fat drips away in the pan, so broiling is a quick and low-fat cooking method.

7. **Instant read thermometer:** A key kitchen safety factor is cooking foods to the proper temperature. Use a thermometer to take the temperature of eggs, meat, and poultry.

8. **Blender or food processor:** Either of these countertop appliances can help you with a multitude of tasks, but our editors use theirs most to whip up low-fat smoothies and milkshakes. They're also handy for blending soups, fruit and vegetable purees, and low-fat sauces and salad dressings.

9. **Cutting board:** Use plastic or wood, but wash either thoroughly to avoid food contamination.

10. **Stainless steel box grater:** When you use a grater, a little bit of cheese goes a long way. You can also use it for shredding vegetables such as carrots and onions and for grating citrus fruit to get rind.

Simple Steps to Great Recipes

It's not necessary to go to culinary school to use these simple low-fat cooking methods. You're probably already familiar with most of them.

Bake or Roast: to cook, covered or uncovered, with dry heat in the oven. (See Pepper-Crusted Tenderloin with Horseradish Sauce, page 238.)

Braise: to simmer over low heat in a small amount of liquid in a covered pot.

Broil: to cook with direct heat, usually under the heating element in the oven. The cooking temperature is regulated by the distance between the food and the heat. (See Feta Omelet with Breadcrumbs, page 219.)

Grill: to cook with direct or indirect heat over hot coals. (See Spicy Herb-Grilled Salmon Steaks, page 210.)

Oven-Fry: to cover pieces of food in some type of bread coating and either bake on a rack to give all sides equal exposure to the heat, or turn the pieces so that all sides get equally browned. (See Crisp-Crusted Catfish, page 204.)

Panbroil: to cook, uncovered, in a hot skillet without adding oil or water. (See Blackened Catfish, page 204.)

Poach: to cook gently in liquid just below the boiling point. No added fat is required, and the food retains its shape, flavor, and texture.

Sauté or Stir-Fry: to cook quickly in a small amount of either liquid or fat, stirring constantly so the food browns evenly. (See Pork, Kale, and Bok Choy Stir-Fry, page 243.)

Steam: to cook with steam heat over boiling water (not in the boiling water). You can steam foods in the microwave oven or in a steam basket in a saucepan on the stovetop. (See Holiday Green Beans, page 278.) Another method of steaming is to wrap food in foil or leaves and cook over boiling water or on a grill.

Stew: to cook in liquid in a tightly covered pot over low heat. (See Thai-Style Pork Stew, page 439.)

Chapter 32

Low-Fat
Flavor Secrets

Pump up the flavor and lose the fat with these secrets
from the *Cooking Light* Test Kitchens.

Low-fat equals no flavor, right? We beg to differ. Once you stop relying on fat for flavor and start experimenting with herbs and spices, oils, vinegars, and marinades, you'll find that there's a whole new world of taste sensations to savor.

According to consumer research, taste is the number one reason consumers buy one food over another. If the food doesn't taste good, it doesn't matter how good it is for you, you're not going to eat it. With these flavor tips from our kitchens, taste is the ticket, so get ready to take your taste buds on a ride.

NATURE'S BEST SEASONINGS

One of the easiest ways to give food more flavor without fat is with spices and herbs. People have been flavoring their foods with natural ingredients since ancient times—and with today's new spice blends and mixes, spicing things up is easier than ever.

There is a difference between an herb and a spice, although both are used for flavor and contain virtually zero calories, fat, or sodium. Spices come from the bark, buds, fruit, root, seeds, or stems of plants and trees and are usually dried. (Fresh garlic and gingerroot are two exceptions.) Herbs are the fragrant leaves of plants and are often used in both fresh and dried forms.

MARINADE MAGIC

When you soak a food in a seasoned liquid mixture before you cook it, the food absorbs the flavor of the marinade. If you are marinating a tough cut of meat, marinating also tenderizes.

Typical marinade ingredients include an acidic ingredient such as wine, vinegar, or fruit juice, plus herbs and spices. Some marinades contain a little oil or other fat, but the source of most of the flavor in marinades is from the other low-fat, high-flavor ingredients.

One of the easiest ways to marinate food is in a zip-top plastic bag. The bag doesn't take up much space in the refrigerator, and it's convenient to flip the bag over so that all of the food gets coated in the marinade. Use just enough marinade to cover the food, and after it's marinated, just throw the bag away.

To get started, try some of the marinades on pages 147 and 148.

VIVA LA VINEGAR

A splash of vinegar adds just the right zesty punch to recipes—and whether you want a slightly sweet flavor or a citrusy tang, vinegar does the trick without calories or fat. Look for flavored vinegars on the supermarket shelves next to the favorite standbys: cider, red wine, and balsamic vinegars. Balsamic vinegar is sweeter and more full-flavored than other vinegars because it's made from the reduced juice of sweet grapes and aged in wooden barrels to develop the flavor. True aged balsamic vinegar is expensive, but you can find a non-aged product that still has plenty of flavor with the other vinegars in the grocery store.

DISCOVER OIL

Current research shows that a little oil, especially heart-healthy monounsaturated oil, is good for you. So as long as you're going to use a little oil, why not use one with the most flavor and make a little go a long way in terms of taste? All oils contain about the same amount of fat and have the same number of calories per teaspoon. But you'll get a lot more flavor from 1 teaspoon of dark sesame oil than you will from a teaspoon of plain corn oil. Also check out the flavored oils such as chili oil and garlic oil.

Tips for Using Herbs and Spices

- Store dried herbs and spices in tightly covered containers and keep them in a cool, dark, dry place. Do not store them in the refrigerator, and don't keep your spice rack next to the stove or near a window because heat and bright light can destroy flavor.
- Use dried herbs and spices within a year of purchase. Even when they are stored properly, herbs and spices start losing their flavor after a year.
- See if your seasonings are fresh by rubbing a small amount between your fingers. If there's not much aroma, you probably need a fresh supply.
- To get the best herb flavor, go for the fresh. To keep fresh herbs fresh, snip the stem ends and stand them in a glass of water. Cover them with a plastic bag, and store in the refrigerator.
- Use this equivalent when substituting fresh herbs for dried:

1 tablespoon of fresh herb =
1 teaspoon dried herb.

Dried herbs are stronger than fresh in most cases, except for rosemary where you can use about the same amount of fresh and dried.
- Don't always double the herbs and spices when you're doubling a recipe. Most of the time it works to use 1½ times the amount called for in the original recipe.
- Add herbs and spices near the end of the cooking time for dishes such as stews that cook a long time. If you add the seasonings at the beginning, the flavor might cook out.
- Experiment with different flavors by using some of the spice blends on the market today: Cajun, Creole, Greek, Mexican, and Thai. Check the sodium content. Some seasoning blends are available in both regular and salt-free versions.
- Better yet, make your own flavorful seasoning blends and marinades using the recipes on these pages.

Mexican Seasoning Blend

- ½ cup chili powder
- ¼ cup paprika
- 2 tablespoons ground cumin
- 2 teaspoons garlic powder
- 1 teaspoon ground red pepper
- ½ teaspoon salt

1. Combine all ingredients. Store in an airtight container; shake well before each use. Use with chicken or turkey. Yield: 1 cup.

Per Tablespoon CALORIES 21; FAT 1.0g (sat 0.2g); PROTEIN 0.9 g; CARB 3.7g; CHOL 0mg; SODIUM 113mg
EXCHANGE: Free

CREOLE SEASONING BLEND

1½ tablespoons garlic powder
1½ tablespoons dried basil
1½ tablespoons dried parsley flakes
1 tablespoon onion powder
2½ teaspoons paprika
2 teaspoons dry mustard
1 teaspoon ground red pepper
½ teaspoon black pepper

1. Combine all ingredients. Store in an airtight container; shake well before each use. Use with chicken, fish, or vegetables. Yield: ½ cup.

Per Tablespoon CALORIES 16; FAT 0.4g (sat 0 g); PROTEIN 0.8g; CARB 3.0; CHOL 0mg; SODIUM 2 mg
EXCHANGE: Free

ITALIAN SEASONING BLEND

⅓ cup dried oregano
¼ cup dried basil
¼ cup dried parsley flakes
3 tablespoons rubbed sage
1 tablespoon garlic powder
1 teaspoon dried rosemary
½ teaspoon salt

1. Combine all ingredients. Store in an airtight container; shake well before each use. Use with chicken, vegetables, pizza, and bread. Yield: 1 cup.

Per Tablespoon CALORIES 11; FAT 0.3g (sat 0 g); PROTEIN 0.5g; CARB 2.3g; CHOL 0mg; SODIUM 75mg
EXCHANGE: Free

CITRUS MARINADE

1 teaspoon grated orange rind
½ cup fresh orange juice
⅓ cup fresh grapefruit juice
1 teaspoon grated lime rind
2 tablespoons fresh lime juice
2 tablespoons vegetable oil
2 tablespoons honey
1 tablespoon white wine vinegar
1 teaspoon white wine
Worcestershire sauce
½ teaspoon Dijon mustard
¼ teaspoon ground red pepper

1. Combine all ingredients. Use immediately or store in refrigerator. Use to marinate chicken, pork, lamb, or fish. Yield: 1⅓ cups.

Per Tablespoon CALORIES 20; FAT 1.2g (sat 0.2 g); PROTEIN 0.1g; CARB 2.5g; CHOL 0mg; SODIUM 5mg
EXCHANGE: Free

MAPLE-BOURBON MARINADE

1 cup plus 2 tablespoons maple syrup
⅔ cup bourbon
1 teaspoon black pepper
⅛ teaspoon ground red pepper

1. Combine ingredients. Use to marinate chicken, beef, or pork. Yield: 1¾ cups.

Per Tablespoon CALORIES 34; FAT 0g (sat 0g); PROTEIN 0g; CARB 8.6g; CHOL 0mg; SODIUM 1mg
EXCHANGE: ½ Starch

CURRY MARINADE

1/4 cup fat-free, less-sodium chicken broth

1/4 cup low-sodium soy sauce

1 tablespoon curry powder

1 tablespoon safflower oil

2 teaspoons sugar

1 garlic clove, minced

1. Combine all ingredients. Use to marinate chicken, beef, pork, or fish. Yield: 1/2 cup plus 2 tablespoons.

Per Tablespoon CALORIES 21; FAT 1.5g (sat 0.1g); PROTEIN 0.1g; CARB 1.3g; CHOL 0mg; SODIUM 156mg EXCHANGE: Free

THAI-STYLE MARINADE

1/2 cup packed brown sugar

1/2 cup finely chopped green onions

1/2 cup low-sodium soy sauce

2 tablespoons white wine vinegar

1 teaspoon dried crushed red pepper

1/2 teaspoon ground ginger

12 garlic cloves, halved

1. Combine all ingredients. Use to marinate beef or fish. Yield: 1 cup plus 1 tablespoon.

Per Tablespoon CALORIES 32; FAT 0g (sat 0g); PROTEIN 0.2g; CARB 7.3g; CHOL 0mg; SODIUM 187mg EXCHANGE: Free

FLAVOR-BOOSTING COOKING METHODS

Sometimes it's the way you cook the food that adds the flavor. Here are a few high-flavor, low-fat cooking methods.

- Toasting creates the most intense flavor as well as a great smelling kitchen. Toss whole spices and nuts into a dry skillet and cook them over medium-high heat for about a minute.
- Indoor grilling is the way to get smoky grilled flavor all year long. You can use a heavy-duty grill pan, or one of the indoor grilling machines with a nonstick surface.
- Roasting is a labor saver because you can be relaxing while your food is getting more flavorful by the minute. Roasting usually involves cooking at high heat (350° to 450°) for a long time, although some vegetables can be done in about 5 to 10 minutes.
- Braising, or long, slow cooking in liquid, is the ideal way to make inexpensive, leaner meats melt-in-your-mouth tender.
- Deglazing takes those browned morsels that stick to the bottom of the pan and turns them into a flavorful sauce. Just add wine or stock to the pan, scrape, and stir the mixture.

15 FLAVOR FACTS

Cooking experts know that sometimes the magic is in the details. So here are a few tidbits of information that will help you add a new dimension of flavor to your food.

1. Toasting seeds and nuts brings out extra flavor.
2. Stirring dried spices for a few minutes in a hot skillet (with or without oil) brings out a toasted, more pronounced flavor.
3. The darker the honey, the stronger the flavor.
4. Wash strawberries first, then cap. Rinsing strawberries after they're capped results in a loss of flavor.
5. The hottest chile peppers are generally the ones with the darkest green skins and pointed rather than blunt tips.
6. To keep the heat in fresh chile peppers, don't remove the seeds.
7. When wine, beer, liqueurs, or spirits are cooked, most of the alcohol and calories evaporate, leaving only the flavor behind.
8. Strongly flavored cheeses such as blue cheese or Parmesan provide intense flavor with a small amount of cheese.
9. A trick for adding flavor to breads and other baked goods is to sprinkle the most flavorful ingredient (seeds, herbs, or cheese) on the outside rather than stirring it into the dough or batter.
10. Pasta, rice, and other grains absorb the flavor of the cooking liquid, so cook in broth or juice instead of water.
11. Fat carries flavor in food, so sometimes just a small amount of fat will improve the flavor.
12. A few grains of salt can bring out the other flavors in food, even making some foods taste sweeter. Have you ever sprinkled salt on watermelon to bring out the sweetness? (Note: Don't start adding salt to your foods if you are on a sodium-restricted diet.)
13. The temperature of food affects the flavor, so serve food at the temperature that most enhances its flavor.
14. Foods taste best when they are at their peak of freshness. The fresher the better.
15. Taste buds are more vigorously stimulated when there are a variety of flavors at a single meal.

Chapter 33

Reader Recipe Makeovers

Our Top 10 favorite reader-requested recipe makeovers

There's no need to give up your family favorite recipes when you're changing your eating habits. With a few simple substitutions and quick tune-ups, you can transform your high-fat favorites into weight-loss wonders. We'll share how we lightened up 10 reader recipes, then you can give it a try on your own recipes. These are some of our favorites—we think they'll become your favorites, too.

Birthday Bonus

For one Oklahoma couple, Applesauce-Raisin Cake with Caramel Icing has reigned as the birthday cake of choice for 31 years. But when a family history of heart disease caught up with the husband, he knew they needed to either give up the cake, or make some changes in the recipe. The solution was a simple process of elimination. By reducing the amounts of shortening and nuts by more than half, we were able to cut out an almost unbelievable 1,896 calories and 240 grams of fat from the total recipe without sacrificing any of the sweet and sinful appeal. The end result: a cake with 67 percent fewer calories and 33 percent less fat than the original. Now the couple is counting the days until the next birthday.

Before

Calories per serving	494
Fat	17.6g
Percent of calories from fat	32%
Sodium	320mg

After

Calories per serving	333
Fat	6g
Percent of calories from fat	16%
Sodium	267mg

150 Supermarket Savvy and Secrets

APPLESAUCE-RAISIN CAKE WITH CARAMEL ICING

Even though the icing starts out with the consistency of a glaze, it sets up as it cools.

CAKE:

    1   cup granulated sugar
    1   cup packed brown sugar
    1/3 cup vegetable shortening
    2   cups applesauce
    3   cups all-purpose flour
    4   teaspoons unsweetened cocoa
    2   teaspoons baking soda
    2   teaspoons ground cinnamon
    2   teaspoons ground nutmeg
    1/2 teaspoon salt
    1/2 cup raisins
    1/4 cup chopped pecans
    1   teaspoon vanilla extract
    Cooking spray

ICING:

    1   cup packed dark brown sugar
    1/2 cup 1% low-fat milk
    2   tablespoons butter or margarine
    1/4 teaspoon salt
    1 1/2 cups powdered sugar
    1   teaspoon vanilla extract

1. Preheat oven to 350°.

2. To prepare cake, beat first 3 ingredients with a mixer at low speed until well blended (about 5 minutes). Add applesauce; beat well. Lightly spoon flour into dry measuring cups, and level with a knife. Combine flour and next 5 ingredients, stirring well with a whisk. Add flour mixture to applesauce mixture; beat just until moist. Stir in raisins, pecans, and 1 teaspoon vanilla.

3. Spoon batter into 2 (9-inch) round cake pans coated with cooking spray. Bake at 350° for 35 minutes or until a wooden pick inserted in center comes out clean. Cool in pans 10 minutes on a wire rack; remove from pans. Cool completely on a wire rack.

4. To prepare icing, combine 1 cup brown sugar, milk, butter, and 1/4 teaspoon salt in a medium saucepan; bring to a boil over medium-high heat, stirring constantly. Reduce heat, and simmer until slightly thick (about 5 minutes), stirring occasionally. Remove from heat. Add powdered sugar and 1 teaspoon vanilla; beat with a mixer at medium speed until smooth and slightly warm. Cool 5 minutes (icing will thicken as it cools).

5. Place 1 cake layer on a plate; working quickly, spread with 1/3 cup icing, and top with remaining layer. Spread remaining icing over top and sides of cake. Store loosely covered in refrigerator. Yield: 18 servings (serving size: 1 slice).

CALORIES 333 (16% from fat); FAT 6g (sat 1.7g, mono 2.3g, poly 1.6g); PROTEIN 2.9g; CARB 68.5g; FIBER 1.3g; CHOL 4mg; IRON 1.8mg; SODIUM 267mg; CALC 43mg EXCHANGES: 4 Starch, 1 Fat

The Big Dip

One *Cooking Light* reader had perfected her recipe for Spinach-and-Artichoke Dip, but she knew it had too much fat. And she was right. A switch from marinated artichokes to canned artichoke hearts got rid of 15 percent of the fat. Our next move was to substitute reduced-fat sour cream and cheeses for the full-fat varieties used in the original. When we totaled it up, we'd created a new 148-calorie-per-serving dip, compared to 223 in the old version. We all but banished the fat, dropping it to 5 grams per serving, a nearly two-thirds reduction. The verdict? Two chips up!

Before

Calories per serving	223
Fat	14.1g
Percent of calories from fat	57%
Sodium	379mg

After

Calories per serving	148
Fat	5g
Percent of calories from fat	30%
Sodium	318mg

SPINACH-AND-ARTICHOKE DIP

2   cups (8 ounces) shredded part-skim mozzarella cheese, divided

½   cup fat-free sour cream

¼   cup (1 ounce) grated fresh Parmesan cheese, divided

¼   teaspoon black pepper

3   garlic cloves, crushed

1   (14-ounce) can artichoke hearts, drained and chopped

1   (8-ounce) block ⅓-less-fat cream cheese, softened

1   (8-ounce) block fat-free cream cheese, softened

½   (10-ounce) package frozen chopped spinach, thawed, drained, and squeezed dry

1   (13.5-ounce) package baked tortilla chips (about 16 cups)

1. Preheat oven to 350°.

2. Combine 1½ cups mozzarella, sour cream, 2 tablespoons Parmesan, and next 6 ingredients in a large bowl, and stir until well blended. Spoon mixture into a 1½-quart baking dish. Sprinkle with ½ cup mozzarella and 2 tablespoons Parmesan. Bake at 350° for 30 minutes or until bubbly and golden brown. Serve with tortilla chips. Yield: 5½ cups (serving size: ¼ cup dip and about 6 chips).

CALORIES 148 (30% from fat); FAT 5g (sat 2.9g, mono 1.5g, poly 0.5g); PROTEIN 7.7g; CARB 18.3g; FIBER 1.5g; CHOL 17mg; IRON 0.6mg; SODIUM 318mg; CALC 164mg EXCHANGES: 1 Starch, 1 Vegetable, 1 Fat

Breakfast Bounty

This luscious, high-fat breakfast dish (with a dozen eggs, cream cheese, and whipping cream) is especially tempting because it's so easy to make, and can be made ahead and refrigerated. If only it had less fat! We did a little juggling with the ingredients by replacing whipping cream with a mixture of 2% reduced-fat milk and half-and-half, cutting out four eggs, and switching to ⅓-less-fat cream cheese. That makes for 127 fewer calories and almost 60 percent less fat, and the taste is still irresistible!

Before	
Calories per serving	473
Fat	27.9g
Percent of calories from fat	53%
Sodium	297mg
After	
Calories per serving	346
Fat	11.5g
Percent of calories from fat	30%
Sodium	169mg

FRENCH TOAST SOUFFLÉ

A firm white bread produces the best texture in this make-ahead breakfast casserole.

10 cups (1-inch) cubed sturdy white bread (such as Pepperidge Farm Hearty White, about 16 [1-ounce] slices)
Cooking spray
1 (8-ounce) block ⅓-less-fat cream cheese, softened
8 large eggs
1½ cups 2% reduced-fat milk
⅔ cup half-and-half
½ cup maple syrup
½ teaspoon vanilla extract
2 tablespoons powdered sugar
¾ cup maple syrup

1. Place bread cubes in a 13 x 9-inch baking dish coated with cooking spray. Beat cream cheese with a mixer at medium speed until smooth. Add eggs, 1 at a time, mixing well after each addition. Add milk, half-and-half, ½ cup maple syrup, and vanilla, and mix until smooth. Pour cream cheese mixture over top of bread; cover and refrigerate overnight.

2. Preheat oven to 375°.

3. Remove bread mixture from refrigerator; let stand on counter for 30 minutes. Bake at 375° for 50 minutes or until set. Sprinkle soufflé with powdered sugar, and serve with maple syrup. Yield: 12 servings (serving size: 1 slice of soufflé and 1 tablespoon maple syrup).

CALORIES 346 (30% from fat); FAT 11.5g (sat 5.5g, mono 3.8g, poly 1g); PROTEIN 11.6g; CARB 51.7g; FIBER 2.7g; CHOL 169mg; IRON 1.9mg; SODIUM 396mg; CALC 131mg EXCHANGES: 3½ Starch, 2 Fat

Granny's Cake

A reader realized that her grandmother's Poppyseed Cake recipe had just a "skosh" too much fat. We subtracted two eggs, half the butter, and all the sour cream; then we switched regular cream cheese in the icing for fat-free. The bottom line: We trimmed more than a third of the calories from each serving, and almost 10 grams of fat. We think grandmom will love it.

Before

Calories per serving	460
Fat	28g
Percent of calories from fat	55%
Cholesterol	138mg

After

Calories per serving	278
Fat	9.4g
Percent of calories from fat	30%
Cholesterol	63mg

POPPY-SEED CAKE

CAKE:

2	cups all-purpose flour
1½	teaspoons baking powder
⅛	teaspoon salt
1½	cups granulated sugar
¾	cup (6 ounces) block-style fat-free cream cheese
½	cup butter or margarine, softened
3	large eggs
¼	cup poppy seeds
1	tablespoon grated lemon rind
1½	teaspoons vanilla extract
	Cooking spray

FROSTING:

¼	cup (2 ounces) block-style fat-free cream cheese, chilled
2	tablespoons butter or margarine, chilled
1	teaspoon grated lemon rind
1½	cups powdered sugar

1. Preheat oven to 325°.

2. To prepare cake, lightly spoon flour into dry measuring cups, and level with a knife. Combine flour, baking powder, and salt in a bowl, stirring well with a whisk. Beat 1½ cups granulated sugar, ¾ cup cream cheese, and ½ cup softened butter with a mixer at medium speed until well blended. Add eggs, 1 at a time, beating mixture well after each addition. Add flour mixture, and beat at low speed just until blended. Stir in poppy seeds, 1 tablespoon lemon rind, and vanilla.

3. Spoon batter into a 9-inch tube pan coated with cooking spray. Bake at 325° for 40 minutes or until a wooden pick inserted near center comes out clean. Cool in pan 10 minutes on a wire rack; remove cake from pan. Cool completely on wire rack.

4. To prepare frosting, beat ¼ cup fat-free cream cheese, 2 tablespoons butter, and

1 teaspoon lemon rind until mixture is fluffy. Gradually add powdered sugar, beating just until blended (do not over-beat). Spread frosting over top of cake. Yield: 16 servings (serving size: 1 slice).
Note: The cake can be made using a 10-inch tube pan; bake at 325° for 30 minutes or until a wooden pick inserted

near center of cake comes out clean. You can also bake the cake in a 9 x 5-inch loaf pan; bake at 325° for 1 hour or until a wooden pick inserted near center comes out clean.

CALORIES 278 (30% from fat); FAT 9.4g (sat 4.9g, mono 2.6g, poly 1.2g); PROTEIN 5.3g; CARB 43.5g; FIBER 0.6g; CHOL 63mg; IRON 1.2mg; SODIUM 236mg; CALC 107mg EXCHANGES: 3 Starch, 1 Fat

A Texas-Size Cake

From California to Virginia, households across America are battling an addiction to a decadent chocolate confection known as Texas Sheet Cake. But our readers' passions were exceeded only by their alarm at the untamed levels of fat and calories. We cut the butter in the cake by half, and then took more butter out of the icing, along with some of the sugar and some of the pecans. In the end, we lowered the fat by more than half and dropped 157 calories per serving without diminishing the great taste.

Before	
Calories per serving	455
Fat	25.6g
Percent of calories from fat	50%
After	
Calories per serving	298
Fat	10g
Percent of calories from fat	30%

TEXAS SHEET CAKE

CAKE:

Cooking spray
2 teaspoons all-purpose flour
2 cups all-purpose flour
2 cups granulated sugar
1 teaspoon baking soda
1 teaspoon ground cinnamon
¼ teaspoon salt
¾ cup water
½ cup butter or margarine
¼ cup unsweetened cocoa

½ cup low-fat buttermilk
1 teaspoon vanilla extract
2 large eggs

ICING:

6 tablespoons butter or margarine
⅓ cup fat-free milk
¼ cup unsweetened cocoa
3 cups powdered sugar
¼ cup chopped pecans, toasted
2 teaspoons vanilla extract

(continued on next page)

(Texas Sheet Cake, continued from page 155)

1. Preheat oven to 375°.

2. To prepare cake, coat a 15 x 10-inch jelly roll pan with cooking spray, and dust with 2 teaspoons flour. Set aside.

3. Lightly spoon flour into dry measuring cups; level with a knife. Combine 2 cups flour and next 4 ingredients in a large bowl; stir well with a whisk. Combine water, ½ cup butter, and ¼ cup cocoa in a small saucepan; bring to a boil, stirring frequently. Remove from heat; pour into flour mixture. Beat with a mixer at medium speed until well blended. Add buttermilk, 1 teaspoon vanilla, and eggs; beat well. Pour batter into prepared pan; bake at 375° for 17 minutes or until a wooden pick inserted in center comes out clean. Place on a wire rack.

4. To prepare icing, combine 6 tablespoons butter, milk, and ¼ cup cocoa in a medium saucepan; bring to a boil, stirring constantly. Remove from heat, and gradually stir in powdered sugar, pecans, and 2 teaspoons vanilla. Spread over hot cake. Cool completely on wire rack.

Yield: 20 servings (serving size: 1 slice).

Note: You can also make this recipe in a 13 x 9-inch baking pan. Bake at 375° for 22 minutes.

CALORIES 298 (30% from fat); FAT 10g (sat 5.5g, mono 3.2g, poly 0.7g); PROTEIN 3.1g; CARB 49.8g; FIBER 0.5g; CHOL 44mg; IRON 1.1mg; SODIUM 188mg; CALC 25mg
EXCHANGES: 3 Starch, 2 Fat

Flying High

This cake recipe was submitted by a flight attendant who knew that, because of the fat and calories in this cake, it would never soar. By cutting out almost a cup of butter and switching to reduced-fat cream cheese, we were able to slash more than 1,600 calories and 187 grams of fat from the total recipe. Additionally, we replaced whipping cream—which had contributed a quarter of the fat—with fat-free whipped topping that's just as tasty.

Before

Calories per serving	470
Fat	28.9g
Percent of calories from fat	55%

After

Calories per serving	322
Fat	10.6g
Percent of calories from fat	30%

STRAWBERRY CREAM CAKE

CAKE:

Cooking spray
- ³/₄ cup sliced strawberries
- 2 cups granulated sugar
- 6 tablespoons butter, softened
- 1 (3-ounce) package strawberry-flavored gelatin
- 3 large eggs
- 2¼ cups all-purpose flour
- 2½ teaspoons baking powder
- 1¼ cups 1% low-fat milk
- 1 teaspoon vanilla extract

FILLING:

- 1½ cups frozen fat-free whipped topping, thawed
- 2 tablespoons granulated sugar
- ½ teaspoon vanilla extract

FROSTING:

- 1 (8-ounce) block ⅓-less-fat cream cheese
- ¼ cup butter, softened
- ¼ teaspoon vanilla extract
- 1 cup powdered sugar

REMAINING INGREDIENTS:

- ³/₄ cup sliced strawberries
- 1½ cups quartered strawberries

1. Preheat oven to 350°.

2. Coat 2 (9-inch) round cake pans with cooking spray; line pans with wax paper. Coat wax paper with cooking spray.

3. Place ³/₄ cup sliced strawberries in a blender; process until smooth.

4. Place 2 cups granulated sugar, butter, and gelatin in a bowl; beat with a mixer at medium speed until blended. Add eggs, 1 at a time, beating well after each addition.

5. Spoon flour into dry measuring cups; level with a knife. Combine flour and baking powder; stir well. Add flour mixture to sugar mixture alternately with milk, beginning and ending with flour. Stir in pureed strawberries and 1 teaspoon vanilla.

6. Pour batter into pans; tap pans once on counter to remove air bubbles. Bake at 350° for 45 minutes or until a pick inserted in center comes out clean. Cool in pans 10 minutes on a wire rack; remove from pans. Peel off wax paper; cool completely.

7. Combine whipped topping, 2 tablespoons granulated sugar, and ½ teaspoon vanilla.

8. Beat cream cheese, ¼ cup butter, and ¼ teaspoon vanilla in a medium bowl with a mixer at low speed just until well blended. Gradually add powdered sugar, and beat just until well blended.

9. Place 1 cake layer on a plate; spread with ³/₄ cup filling. Arrange ³/₄ cup sliced strawberries over filling; top with remaining cake layer. Spread remaining filling over top of cake. Spread frosting over sides of cake. Arrange quartered strawberries on top of cake. Store cake in refrigerator. Yield: 18 servings (serving: 1 slice).

CALORIES 322 (30% from fat); FAT 10.6g (sat 6.3g, mono 3.1g, poly 5.1g) PROTEIN 5.1g; CARB 51.6g; FIBER 1g; CHOL 64mg; IRON 1.1mg; SODIUM 255mg; CALC 80mg EXCHANGES: 3 Starch, 2 Fat

Momma, Mia!

This fat-laden pasta dish had been a family favorite for many years, but momma got concerned about the amount of fat and asked if *Cooking Light* could help. We switched from ground beef to lean ground round and halved the amount of beef. We also deleted some of the Cheddar cheese and the full-fat versions of sour cream and cream cheese, replacing each with lower-fat versions. We cut nearly 40 grams of fat, 100 milligrams of cholesterol, and 347 calories from each serving.

Before	
Calories per serving	755
Fat	53.4g
Percent of calories from fat	62%
Cholesterol	167mg
Sodium	1263mg

After	
Calories per serving	408
Fat	13.7g
Percent of calories from fat	30%
Cholesterol	67mg
Sodium	849mg

SPAGHETTI PIE

- 1 pound ground round
- ¼ teaspoon salt
- ¼ teaspoon black pepper
- 2 (8-ounce) cans tomato sauce with garlic
- 1½ cups low-fat sour cream
- ½ cup chopped green onions
- ¼ cup (2 ounces) ⅓-less-fat cream cheese, softened
- 4 cups hot cooked spaghetti (about 8 ounces uncooked pasta)
- Cooking spray
- 1⅓ cups (about 5 ounces) shredded reduced-fat extra-sharp Cheddar cheese

1. Preheat oven to 350°.

2. Cook meat in a large nonstick skillet over medium heat until browned, stirring to crumble. Drain well, and return meat to pan. Stir in salt, pepper, and tomato sauce. Bring to a boil; reduce heat, and simmer 20 minutes.

3. Combine sour cream, onions, and cream cheese in a small bowl, and set aside.

4. Place spaghetti in a 2-quart casserole coated with cooking spray. Spread sour cream mixture over spaghetti. Top with meat mixture. Sprinkle with Cheddar cheese. Cover and bake at 350° for 25 minutes. Uncover; bake an additional 5 minutes or until cheese is bubbly. Yield: 6 servings.

CALORIES 408 (30% from fat); FAT 13.7g (sat 7.3g, mono 4.2g, poly 0.8g); PROTEIN 28.4g; CARB 39.9g; FIBER 2.9g; CHOL 67mg; IRON 3.4mg; SODIUM 849mg; CALC 376mg
EXCHANGES: 3 Starch, 3 Lean Meat

Using Your Noodles

The original recipe for this crunchy salad wins big points for ease and flavor, but loses when it comes to fat and calories. We cut the butter and oil in the dressing by more than half without reducing the flavor. Ramen noodles contributed a lot of fat to the original salad because they're deep-fried. So we decided to use Japanese noodles and soak them in the lower-fat dressing so they wouldn't be too crunchy. Because of these two changes, we cut the calories from 249 per serving to 183. (The Japanese curly noodles can be found in Asian markets or in the Asian section of most large grocery stores.)

Before	
Calories per serving	249
Fat	19.4g
Percent of calories from fat	70%
After	
Calories per serving	183
Fat	6.1g
Percent of calories from fat	30%

ORIENTAL SALAD

- ⅓ cup rice or cider vinegar
- ¼ cup sugar
- 2½ tablespoons vegetable oil
- 2 tablespoons honey
- 2 tablespoons low-sodium soy sauce
- 1 tablespoon butter or margarine
- ¼ cup slivered almonds, toasted
- 2 tablespoons sunflower seed kernels
- 2 (5-ounce) packages Japanese curly noodles (chucka soba), crumbled
- 8 cups shredded napa (Chinese) cabbage
- 2 cups shredded carrot
- 1 cup thinly sliced green onions

1. Combine first 5 ingredients in a small saucepan. Bring to a boil, and cook 1 minute, stirring constantly. Spoon mixture into a bowl; cover and chill.

2. Melt butter in a large nonstick skillet over medium-high heat. Add almonds, sunflower kernels, and noodles; cook 3 minutes or until lightly toasted, tossing occasionally. Spoon mixture into a large bowl; cover and chill.

3. Add vinegar mixture to noodle mixture; let stand 15 minutes. Add cabbage, carrot, and onions, tossing to coat.

Yield: 12 servings (serving size: ¾ cup).

CALORIES 183 (30% from fat); FAT 6.1g
(sat 1.4g, mono 2g, poly 2.4g); PROTEIN 4.4g;
CARB 29g; FIBER 2g; CHOL 3mg; IRON 1.1mg;
SODIUM 259mg; CALC 68mg
EXCHANGES: 2 Starch, 1 Fat

Tex-Mex Magic

We nursed this favorite south-of-the-border recipe back to health. By substituting reduced-fat extra-sharp Cheddar for some of the milder Monterey Jack, we could use less cheese and keep the flavor. By replacing whipping cream with 2% milk, we cut 63 grams of fat and 529 calories. Instead of frying the tortillas in oil, we softened them in simmering water—slashing an additional 27 grams of fat and 241 calories. Fat-free sour cream further lowered the fat. In all, we reduced the total fat for the whole recipe by 185 grams and the calories by 1,586—without sacrificing creaminess or flavor.

Before
Calories per serving 899
Fat...............................62.8g
Percent of calories from fat 63%

After
Calories per serving 502
Fat...............................16.6g
Percent of calories from fat 30%

CHICKEN ENCHILADAS
FILLING:

- 3 cups water
- ¼ teaspoon salt
- 8 black peppercorns
- 1 onion, quartered
- 1 bay leaf
- 1 pound skinless chicken breast halves
- ¾ cup (3 ounces) shredded Monterey Jack cheese, divided
- ¾ cup (3 ounces) shredded reduced-fat extra-sharp Cheddar cheese, divided
- ½ cup chopped onion

SAUCE:

- ⅔ cup 2% reduced-fat milk
- ¼ cup chopped fresh cilantro
- ¼ cup egg substitute
- ⅛ teaspoon salt
- 1 (11-ounce) can tomatillos, drained

- 1 (4.5-ounce) can chopped green chiles, undrained

REMAINING INGREDIENTS:

- 8 (6-inch) corn tortillas
- ⅔ cup fat-free sour cream

1. Place first 6 ingredients in a Dutch oven; bring to a boil. Cover, reduce heat, and simmer 45 minutes. Remove chicken from cooking liquid; cool. Remove chicken from bones; shred with 2 forks. Discard bones. Reserve broth for another use.

2. Preheat oven to 375°.

3. Combine chicken, ½ cup each Monterey Jack and Cheddar cheeses, and ½ cup onion; set aside.

4. Place milk and next 5 ingredients in a food processor; process until smooth.

5. Fill a skillet with 1 inch of water; bring to a simmer. Dip 1 tortilla in water

using tongs. Spoon ½ cup filling in center of tortilla; roll tightly, and place in an 11 x 7-inch baking dish. Repeat procedure with remaining tortillas and filling.
6. Pour sauce over enchiladas. Cover and bake at 375° for 20 minutes. Uncover; sprinkle with ¼ cup each

Monterey Jack and Cheddar. Bake 5 minutes. Top with sour cream. Yield: 4 servings (serving size: 2 enchiladas and about 2½ tablespoons sour cream).

CALORIES 502 (30% from fat); FAT 16.6g (sat 8.4g, mono 3.7g, poly 2g); PROTEIN 47.6g; CARB 40g; FIBER 4.6g; CHOL 114mg; IRON 3mg; SODIUM 725mg; CALC 598mg EXCHANGES: 2½ Starch, 6 Lean Meat

Comfort Food

"Aw Maw" is a grandma who has served this potato dish to her family for years. Her daughter called us to lighten this ultimate comfort food. By substituting fat-free milk for half-and-half, using reduced-fat cheese, and cutting nearly two-thirds of the butter and a third of the salt, we stripped 152 calories, 17.8 grams of fat, and 310 milligrams of sodium from the original.

Before	
Calories per serving	365
Fat	24.8g
Percent of calories from fat	61%
Sodium	851mg
After	
Calories per serving	213
Fat	7g
Percent of calories from fat	30%
Sodium	541mg

AW MAW'S POTATOES

4 pounds unpeeled baking potatoes
Cooking spray
⅓ cup butter
3 cups fat-free milk
1 cup (4 ounces) shredded reduced-fat sharp Cheddar cheese, divided
2 teaspoons salt
¼ teaspoon black pepper

1. Place potatoes in a Dutch oven, and cover with water. Bring to a boil; reduce heat, and simmer 20 minutes. Drain. Cover and chill.

2. Preheat oven to 350°.
3. Peel and shred potatoes, and place in a 13 x 9-inch baking dish coated with cooking spray. Melt butter in a saucepan over medium heat. Stir in milk, ½ cup cheese, salt, and pepper. Cook 8 minutes or until cheese melts, stirring occasionally. Pour over potatoes; stir. Bake at 350° for 45 minutes. Sprinkle with ½ cup cheese. Bake 15 minutes. Yield: 12 servings (serving size: ⅔ cup).

CALORIES 213 (30% from fat); FAT 7g (sat 4.5g, mono 1.9g, poly 0.3g); PROTEIN 8g; CARB 30.2g; FIBER 2.4g; CHOL 20mg; IRON 1.2mg; SODIUM 541mg; CALC 174mg EXCHANGES: 2 Starch, 1 Fat

Part
6

No-Diet, No-Denial Recipes

With appealing appetizers, easy entrées, and decadent desserts, we prove that eating well can lead to weight loss.

Chapter 34

Eat More of All Things Good for You

See how you can eat more instead of less and lose weight.

It's not as ancient as the Four Food Groups guide that you might remember from elementary school health class, but it's still a fairly familiar symbol in the modern nutrition world: the Food Guide Pyramid. (See the diagram on page 164.) Developed by the U.S. Department of Agriculture (USDA) as a visual guide to good nutrition, the pyramid offers a framework for healthy eating that allows flexibility for individual preferences and eating styles.

The idea is to eat more of the foods at the base of the pyramid and fewer of the foods at the tip. All food groups make up the pyramid, meaning that you need a variety of foods to have a healthy diet. Eating a variety of foods is especially important when you are trying to lose weight because you must make sure that you are getting adequate nutrition on fewer calories.

JOURNEY INTO THE PYRAMID

The base of the pyramid is the block with the Bread, Cereal, Rice, and Pasta Group, and the recommended number of servings is six to eleven per day. The foods in this group provide complex carbohydrates, fiber, iron, and B vitamins. The next two sections of the pyramid are the Vegetable and Fruit Groups—good low-fat sources of fiber, vitamins, and minerals. The recommended number of daily servings for these groups are three to five vegetables, and two to four fruits. When you fill up on low-fat, high-fiber grain products, vegetables, and fruits, you'll have less room for high-fat, high-calorie foods.

The Meats and Milk Groups are in the middle; Fats, Oils, and Sweets are at the tip, indicating that you need less of those foods. When you're trying to lose weight, it's wise to aim for the lower number of servings when a range is listed.

The minimum number of servings from each group provides about 1,600 calories; the maximum number provides 2,800 calories. In addition to the basic pyramid, there are other versions that accomodate particular eating styles: the Mediterranean Diet Food Pyramid, the Vegetarian Pyramid, and the Soul Food Pyramid.

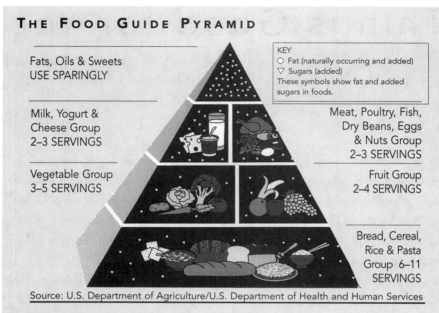

THE FOOD GUIDE PYRAMID

Fats, Oils & Sweets
USE SPARINGLY

KEY
○ Fat (naturally occurring and added)
▽ Sugars (added)
These symbols show fat and added sugars in foods.

Milk, Yogurt & Cheese Group
2–3 SERVINGS

Meat, Poultry, Fish, Dry Beans, Eggs & Nuts Group
2–3 SERVINGS

Vegetable Group
3–5 SERVINGS

Fruit Group
2–4 SERVINGS

Bread, Cereal, Rice & Pasta Group 6–11 SERVINGS

Source: U.S. Department of Agriculture/U.S. Department of Health and Human Services

Standard serving sizes for the Food Guide Pyramid

Bread, Cereal, Rice, and Pasta

- 1 slice bread (approximately 1 ounce)
- 1 ounce ready-to-eat cereal
- ½ cup cooked cereal, rice, or pasta

Milk, Yogurt, and Cheese

- 1 cup milk or yogurt
- 1½ ounces natural cheese
- 2 ounces processed cheese

Vegetable and Fruit

- 1 cup raw leafy vegetables or other raw vegetables
- ½ cup cooked vegetables
- ½ cup vegetable juice
- 1 medium apple, banana, or orange
- ½ cup chopped, cooked, or canned fruit
- ½ cup fruit juice

Meat, Poultry, Fish, Dry Beans, Eggs, and Nuts

- 2 to 3 ounces cooked lean meat, poultry, or fish
- ½ cup cooked dry beans
- 1 large egg = 1 ounce lean meat
- 2 tablespoons peanut butter = 1 ounce meat
- ⅓ cup nuts = 1 ounce meat

PYRAMID PRESSURE

Recently, the pyramid has come under fire from some nutrition experts who believe that the guide is oversimplified and does not offer advice for making wise selections from each of the food groups. Critics say, for example, that all starches are not created equal and that the current pyramid does not distinguish between refined starches and whole grain products, which are higher in nutrients and fiber than their refined counterparts. Other critics have a problem with fruits and vegetables not forming the base of the pyramid, as they say that you "can never eat too many fruits and vegetables."

Having fats at the tip of the pyramid (indicating that you should only eat a few items from this group) is contrary to current research showing that a healthy diet contains plenty of heart-healthy monounsaturated fats and oils such as olive oil and nuts.

But it always comes back to choice. The beauty of the pyramid is its simplicity, but it's important to make good choices in each group if you plan to use the pyramid to take off the pounds.

EAT MORE TO LOSE

If you make good choices from all food groups, you *can* eat more food and lose weight, especially if you choose *Cooking Light* recipes. There's no reason to feel deprived.

According to Sandra Lira, a *Cooking Light* reader who has lost 30 pounds, "*Cooking Light*'s low-fat, low-calorie recipes appeal to me. I didn't feel as though I was denying myself anything. The taste is still there, just without the fat and calories."

JeAnne Swinley, another reader who is 195 pounds lighter, says, "*Cooking Light* introduced me to new flavors and foods—and accurate portions."

Turn the page and start experiencing the flavor and the satisfaction that these two women (and millions of other *Cooking Light* readers) are getting from our no-diet, no-denial recipes.

Chapter 35

Appetizers and Beverages

Snack and sip your way to health and weight loss with these savory bites and nutrient-packed drinks.

CAJUN TORTILLA CHIPS

Take these low-fat chips to your next Super Bowl party. Whether you eat them plain or use them to scoop up a low-fat dip, they're a sure way to minimize the munchies.

CAJUN SEASONING:

1½ teaspoons paprika
1 teaspoon dried thyme
½ teaspoon garlic powder
½ teaspoon onion powder
½ teaspoon black pepper
¼ teaspoon salt
¼ teaspoon sugar
¼ teaspoon ground red pepper

CHIPS:

10 (7-inch) flour tortillas, cut into 8 wedges
Cooking spray

1. Preheat oven to 375°.

2. To prepare Cajun seasoning, combine first 8 ingredients in a small bowl.

3. To prepare chips, arrange tortilla wedges on 2 baking sheets coated with cooking spray. Coat wedges with cooking spray. Sprinkle 2 teaspoons Cajun seasoning over wedges. Bake chips at 375° for 6 minutes or until crisp. Yield: 80 chips (serving size: 4 chips).

Note: Store remaining Cajun seasoning in an airtight container.

CALORIES 63 (20% from fat); FAT 1.4g (sat 0.2g, mono 0.6g, poly 0.5g); PROTEIN 1.7g; CARB 10.8g; FIBER 0.6g; CHOL 0mg; IRON 0.7mg; SODIUM 104mg; CALC 25mg EXCHANGE: 1 Starch

ITALIAN BAGUETTE CHIPS

Instead of high-fat chips and crackers, try these savory chips with your favorite low-fat dip. We like them with the Creamy Feta-Spinach Dip on page 169.

ITALIAN SEASONING:

¼ cup grated Parmesan cheese
1 teaspoon dried oregano
1 teaspoon dried basil
¼ teaspoon salt
¼ teaspoon garlic powder
¼ teaspoon black pepper

CHIPS:

40 (¼-inch-thick) slices diagonally cut French bread baguette
Cooking spray

1. Preheat oven to 375°.
2. To prepare Italian seasoning, combine first 6 ingredients in a small bowl.
3. To prepare chips, arrange bread slices on 2 baking sheets coated with cooking spray. Coat bread with cooking spray. Sprinkle 4 teaspoons Italian seasoning over bread. Bake at 375° for 8 minutes or until crisp. Yield: 40 chips (serving size: 4 chips).
Note: Store remaining Italian seasoning in an airtight container in the refrigerator.

CALORIES 89 (12% from fat); FAT 1.2g (sat 0.3g, mono 0.4g, poly 0.2g); PROTEIN 3g; CARB 16.3g; FIBER 0.9g; CHOL 0mg; IRON 0.8mg; SODIUM 216mg; CALC 32mg EXCHANGE: 1 Starch

CURRIED POPCORN

For an even speedier low-fat snack, combine the first four spices and add to a bag of popped low-fat microwave popcorn.

2 teaspoons curry powder
1 teaspoon salt
1 teaspoon ground cumin
⅛ teaspoon ground red pepper
1 tablespoon canola oil
½ cup unpopped corn kernels

1. Combine first 4 ingredients in a heavy-duty zip-top plastic bag, shaking well. Set aside.
2. Heat oil in a large Dutch oven over medium-high heat. Add popcorn, stirring to coat. Reduce heat to medium; cover and cook, shaking constantly, until popping sound stops.
3. Add popcorn to spice mixture, and shake thoroughly. Yield: 6 servings (serving size: 1½ cups).

CALORIES 84 (33% from fat); FAT 3.3g (sat 0.2g, mono 1.4g, poly 0.7g); PROTEIN 2.2g; CARB 12.6g; FIBER 2.4g; CHOL 0mg; IRON 0.7mg; SODIUM 389mg; CALC 6mg EXCHANGES: 1 Starch, ½ Fat

ASIAN PARTY MIX

Add crunch and fire to an old favorite with sesame rice crackers and wasabi peas. Look for dried green peas coated with wasabi in the bulk foods department of the supermarket. Look for rice crackers in the snack or Asian section of your grocery store.

    2   cups crispy corn cereal squares
        (such as Corn Chex)
    2   cups crispy rice cereal squares
        (such as Rice Chex)
    2   cups sesame rice crackers, broken
    1   cup tiny fat-free pretzel twists
    ¾   cup wasabi peas
    ¼   cup lightly salted, dry-roasted
        peanuts
    3   tablespoons unsalted butter
    1   tablespoon sugar
    1   tablespoon curry powder
    1   tablespoon low-sodium soy sauce
    1   teaspoon Worcestershire sauce
    ½   teaspoon garlic powder
    ½   teaspoon ground cumin
    ¼   teaspoon salt
    ¼   teaspoon ground red pepper
    Cooking spray

1. Preheat oven to 200°.
2. Combine first 6 ingredients in a large bowl; set aside. Melt butter in a small saucepan over medium heat. Add sugar and next 7 ingredients, stirring with a whisk. Pour butter mixture over cereal mixture, tossing gently to coat. Spread the mixture onto a jelly roll pan coated with cooking spray. Bake at 200° for 45 minutes, stirring occasionally. Cool completely before serving. Yield: 8 cups (serving size: ½ cup).

CALORIES 116 (29% from fat); FAT 3.7g (sat 1.6g, mono 1.3g, poly 0.6g); PROTEIN 2.9g; CARB 18.6g; FIBER 1.2g; CHOL 6mg; IRON 2.8mg; SODIUM 269mg; CALC 38mg EXCHANGES: 1 Starch, 1 Fat

FRESH MANGO SALSA

Not only is this fruity salsa good with low-fat chips for snacking, it's a fresh, tangy topping for grilled fish and chicken.

    1½   cups chopped peeled mango
    1½   cups chopped tomato
     2   tablespoons minced fresh cilantro
     2   tablespoons fresh lime juice
     1   tablespoon finely chopped
         seeded jalapeño pepper
     1   teaspoon minced peeled fresh
         ginger

1. Combine all ingredients in a medium bowl; cover, and chill. Yield: 3 cups (serving size: ½ cup).

CALORIES 39 (7% from fat); FAT 0.3g (sat 0.1g, mono 0.1g, poly 0.1g); PROTEIN 0.7g; CARB 9.8g; FIBER 1.2g; CHOL 0mg; IRON 0.4mg; SODIUM 6mg; CALC 9mg EXCHANGE: ½ Fruit

ANTIPASTO SALSA

Plain salsa may never hold the same allure once you've sampled this Italian-style version. And it's a great example of how to eat the heart-healthy Mediterranean way: with fresh vegetables, herbs, vinegar, and olive oil.

1	cup diced tomato
1	cup diced zucchini
½	cup chopped drained canned artichoke hearts
½	cup chopped fresh basil
⅓	cup diced bottled roasted red bell peppers
¼	cup minced onion
2	tablespoons chopped pitted kalamata olives
1	tablespoon balsamic vinegar
2	teaspoons olive oil

1. Combine all ingredients in a medium bowl; cover and chill. Yield: 3 cups (serving size: ½ cup).

CALORIES 39 (46% from fat); FAT 2g (sat 0.3g, mono 1.4g, poly 0.3g); PROTEIN 1.3g; CARB 5.2g; FIBER 0.8g; CHOL 0mg; IRON 0.6mg; SODIUM 80mg; CALC 22mg EXCHANGE: 1 Vegetable

CREAMY FETA-SPINACH DIP

This low-fat party food contains a good bit of calcium, thanks to the spinach and the low-fat dairy products.

1	(8-ounce) carton plain low-fat yogurt
¾	cup (3 ounces) crumbled feta cheese
¼	cup (2 ounces) ⅓-less-fat cream cheese, softened
¼	cup low-fat sour cream
1	garlic clove, crushed
1½	cups finely chopped spinach
1	tablespoon minced fresh or 1 teaspoon dried dill
⅛	teaspoon black pepper

1. Spoon yogurt onto several layers of heavy-duty paper towels; spread to ½-inch thickness. Cover with additional paper towels, and let stand 5 minutes.
2. Scrape yogurt into the bowl of a food processor using a rubber spatula. Add cheeses, sour cream, and garlic, and process until smooth, scraping sides of bowl once. Spoon yogurt mixture into a bowl, and stir in spinach, minced dill, and pepper. Cover and chill. Yield: 2 cups (serving size: ¼ cup).

CALORIES 78 (62% from fat); FAT 5.4g (sat 3.4g, mono 1.4g, poly 0.2g); PROTEIN 4.2g; CARB 3.6g; FIBER 0.4g; CHOL 20mg; IRON 0.4mg; SODIUM 178mg; CALC 130mg EXCHANGES: 1 Vegetable, 1 Fat

Layered Chili, Cheese, and Roasted-Corn Dip

One of our editors gets asked to bring this dip to every party, and she always comes home with an empty dish.

2   (16-ounce) cans pinto beans, drained, rinsed, and divided
½   teaspoon ground cumin
¼   teaspoon hot sauce
⅛   teaspoon black pepper
1   (8-ounce) block fat-free cream cheese
Cooking spray
1   (11-ounce) can no-salt-added whole-kernel corn, drained
2   garlic cloves, minced
2   cups cooked basmati or other long-grain rice
½   cup minced fresh cilantro
1   (4.5-ounce) can chopped green chiles
1   cup bottled salsa
½   cup (2 ounces) reduced-fat shredded sharp Cheddar cheese
8   cups baked tortilla chips (about 8 ounces)

1. Preheat oven to 375°.
2. Combine 2 cups beans, cumin, hot sauce, black pepper, and cream cheese in a food processor; process until smooth. Place bean mixture in a medium bowl; stir in remaining beans. Set aside.
3. Place a medium nonstick skillet coated with cooking spray over medium-high heat. Add corn and garlic, and sauté for 3 minutes or until lightly browned. Remove from heat, and stir in rice, cilantro, and chiles.
4. Spread half of bean mixture in bottom of a shallow 2-quart baking dish coated with cooking spray. Spread half of salsa over bean mixture. Spread rice mixture over salsa. Top with remaining salsa and bean mixture, and sprinkle with cheese. Cover and bake at 375° for 30 minutes or until thoroughly heated. Serve with chips. Yield: 16 servings (serving size: ½ cup dip and ½ cup chips).

CALORIES 174 (10% from fat); FAT 1.9g (sat 0.6g, mono 0.6g, poly 0.6g); PROTEIN 8.5g; CARB 31.8g; FIBER 3g; CHOL 5mg; IRON 1.5mg; SODIUM 446mg; CALC 120mg
EXCHANGES: 2 Starch

Yogurt-Tahini Dip

Serve this creamy dip at your next party with these low-fat dippers: baby carrots, celery sticks, broccoli florets, pita wedges, or crisp breadsticks.

1   cup plain low-fat yogurt
3   tablespoons tahini (sesame-seed paste)
2   tablespoons fresh lemon juice
1   tablespoon chopped fresh flat-leaf parsley
½   teaspoon salt
1   garlic clove, crushed

1. Combine all ingredients in a large bowl; cover and refrigerate 30 minutes. Yield: 1 cup (serving size: 1 tablespoon).

CALORIES 27 (60% from fat); FAT 1.8g (sat 0.4g, mono 0.6g, poly 0.6g); PROTEIN 1.3g; CARB 1.9g; FIBER 0.3g; CHOL 1mg; IRON 0.3mg; SODIUM 87mg; CALC 41mg EXCHANGE: Free (up to 3 tablespoons)

SHRIMP-AND-BLACK BEAN NACHOS

When you're making nachos, use baked low-fat tortilla chips—they have 83 percent less fat than regular tortilla chips.

SHRIMP SALSA:

- ¾ cup chopped fresh cilantro
- ½ cup diced red onion
- 2 tablespoons fresh lime juice
- 1 tablespoon minced seeded serrano chile
- 1 tablespoon extra-virgin olive oil
- 1 teaspoon Worcestershire sauce
- ½ teaspoon salt
- ¼ teaspoon black pepper
- ¾ pound medium shrimp, cooked, peeled, and chopped
- 2 cups diced tomato
- ½ cup diced peeled avocado

REMAINING INGREDIENTS:

- 1 cup drained canned black beans
- ½ teaspoon ground cumin
- 30 baked tortilla chips

1. To prepare shrimp salsa, combine first 9 ingredients in a large bowl; toss well. Cover and refrigerate 30 minutes. Stir in tomato and avocado.

2. Place beans and cumin in a food processor or blender, and process 30 seconds or until smooth. Spread each chip with 1 teaspoon black-bean mixture. Top with 1 tablespoon shrimp salsa. Serve immediately. Yield: 15 servings (serving size: 2 nachos).

CALORIES 83 (26% from fat); FAT 2.4g (sat 0.4g, mono 1.4g, poly 0.4g); PROTEIN 5.4g; CARB 10.7g; FIBER 1.6g; CHOL 26mg; IRON 1.2mg; SODIUM 187mg; CALC 29mg EXCHANGE: 1 Starch

QUICK-FIX SNACKS

Here are some low-fat, low-calorie snacks to serve when you don't have time to prepare a recipe.

- Baked tortilla chips and bottled chunky salsa
- Fruit-flavored light cream cheese and gingersnaps
- Reduced-fat Cheddar cheese, apple wedges, and grapes
- Baby carrots, broccoli florets, and light ranch dressing
- Reduced-fat snack mix
- Pretzels

DEVILED EGGS

Because of the mixture of fat-free yogurt and low-fat mayonnaise, these eggs have less than half the fat of traditional deviled eggs and are a great addition to summer picnics.

12 large eggs
⅓ cup plain fat-free yogurt
3 tablespoons low-fat mayonnaise
1 tablespoon Dijon mustard
1 to 2 teaspoons hot pepper sauce
⅛ teaspoon salt
⅛ teaspoon paprika
⅛ teaspoon black pepper

1. Place eggs in a large saucepan. Cover with water to 1 inch above eggs; bring just to a boil. Remove from heat; cover and let stand 15 minutes. Drain and rinse with cold running water until cool. Slice eggs in half lengthwise, and remove yolks. Discard 3 yolks.
2. Combine yogurt and next 4 ingredients in a medium bowl. Add remaining yolks; beat with a mixer at high speed until smooth. Spoon about 1 tablespoon yolk mixture into each egg white half. Cover and chill 1 hour. Sprinkle with paprika and black pepper. Yield: 24 servings (serving size: 1 egg half).

CALORIES 38 (50% from fat); FAT 2.1g (sat 0.6g, mono 0.7g, poly 0.3g); PROTEIN 3.1g; CARB 1.3g; FIBER 0g; CHOL 80mg; IRON 0.3mg; SODIUM 82mg; CALC 21mg
EXCHANGE: ½ Medium-Fat Meat

PESTO CROSTINI WITH ROASTED PEPPER AND GOAT CHEESE

Use roasted red peppers in a jar for an easy way to add a rich, distinctive flavor to recipes. Not only are they low-fat, red bell peppers are also a good source of disease-fighting vitamin C.

12 (½-inch-thick) slices diagonally cut French bread baguette
2 tablespoons commercial pesto, divided
1 cup bottled roasted red bell peppers, drained and thinly sliced
¼ cup (1 ounce) crumbled goat cheese

1. Preheat oven to 400°.
2. Place bread on an ungreased baking sheet; bake at 400° for 7 minutes, turning once.
3. Preheat broiler.
4. Spread each slice with ½ teaspoon pesto. Top evenly with roasted pepper and goat cheese. Broil 3 minutes or until lightly browned. Yield: 12 servings (serving size: 1 crostino).

CALORIES 68 (46% from fat); FAT 3.5g (sat 1.2g, mono 1.1g, poly 0.3g); PROTEIN 2.6g; CARB 6.7g; FIBER 0.6g; CHOL 3.5mg; IRON 0.6mg; SODIUM 161mg; CALC 53mg
EXCHANGES: ½ Starch, ½ Fat

MINI FRITTATAS WITH HAM AND CHEESE

Using egg whites and only one whole egg instead of all whole eggs keeps the fat low in these snack-sized frittatas.

Cooking spray
½ cup finely chopped onion
⅔ cup chopped reduced-fat ham (about 2 ounces)
⅓ cup (about 1½ ounces) reduced-fat shredded sharp Cheddar cheese
2 tablespoons chopped fresh chives
⅛ teaspoon dried thyme
⅛ teaspoon black pepper
4 large egg whites
1 large egg

1. Preheat oven to 350°.
2. Heat a large nonstick skillet coated with cooking spray over medium-high heat. Add onion; sauté 2 minutes or until crisp-tender. Add ham; sauté 3 minutes. Remove from heat; cool 5 minutes. Combine cheese and remaining 5 ingredients in a large bowl; stir with a whisk. Add ham mixture, stirring with a whisk. Spoon ham mixture into 24 miniature muffin cups coated with cooking spray. Bake at 350° for 20 minutes or until set. Yield: 8 servings (serving size: 3 frittatas).

CALORIES 39 (30% from fat); FAT 1.3g (sat 0.5g, mono 0.2g, poly 0.1g); PROTEIN 4.4g; CARB 2.3g; FIBER 0.4g; CHOL 32mg; IRON 0.2mg; SODIUM 121mg; CALC 80mg EXCHANGE: 1 Very Lean Meat

BAKED ITALIAN OYSTERS

1½ (1-ounce) slices white bread
Cooking spray
⅓ cup sliced green onions
¼ cup chopped fresh parsley
2 garlic cloves, minced
¼ cup Italian-seasoned breadcrumbs
¼ cup (1 ounce) grated fresh Parmesan cheese
1 teaspoon fresh lemon juice
⅛ teaspoon ground red pepper
⅛ teaspoon black pepper
24 oysters on the half shell
8 lemon wedges

1. Preheat oven to 450°.
2. Place bread in a food processor, and pulse 10 times or until coarse crumbs form to measure ¾ cup.
3. Heat a nonstick skillet coated with cooking spray over medium heat. Add onions, parsley, and garlic; sauté 5 minutes. Remove from heat; stir in fresh breadcrumbs, Italian breadcrumbs, and next 4 ingredients. Place oysters on a jelly roll pan. Sprinkle oysters evenly with breadcrumb mixture. Bake at 450° for 7 minutes or until edges of oysters curl. Serve with lemon wedges. Yield: 8 servings (serving size: 3 oysters).

CALORIES 76 (30% from fat); FAT 2.5g (sat 1g, mono 0.5g, poly 0.5g); PROTEIN 5.4g; CARB 7.7g; FIBER 0.4g; CHOL 26mg; IRON 3.3mg; SODIUM 234mg; CALC 77mg EXCHANGES: ½ Starch, ½ Medium-Fat Meat

BANANA-MANGO SMOOTHIE

For breakfast in a hurry, you can't beat a super smoothie with protein, calcium, and vitamin C—all in one glass!

1	cup cubed peeled ripe mango
³/₄	cup sliced ripe banana (about 1 medium)
²/₃	cup fat-free milk
1	tablespoon nonfat dry milk (optional)
1	teaspoon honey
¼	teaspoon vanilla extract

1. Arrange mango cubes in a single layer on a baking sheet; freeze until firm (about 1 hour). Place frozen mango and remaining ingredients in a blender. Process until smooth. Yield: 2 servings (serving size: 1 cup).

Note: Freeze the cubed mango overnight in an airtight container so it will be a snap to throw the smoothie together in the morning.

CALORIES 160 (4% from fat); FAT 0.7g (sat 0.3g, mono 0.2g, poly 0.1g); PROTEIN 5.1g; CARB 36.1g; FIBER 2.6g; CHOL 2mg; IRON 0.3mg; SODIUM 65mg; CALC 160mg EXCHANGES: 2 Fruit, ½ Skim Milk

STRAWBERRY-BANANA SOY SMOOTHIE

Soy products are excellent sources of isoflavones, which may help prevent breast cancer and heart disease. Make sure to select a soy milk that is calcium-fortified. For more information on soy, see page 64.

2	cups hulled strawberries, halved (about 10 strawberries)
1½	cups vanilla low-fat soy milk
1½	tablespoons honey
½	teaspoon vanilla extract
1	banana, sliced
1	cup frozen fat-free whipped topping, thawed

1. Combine first 5 ingredients in a blender, and process until smooth. Top each serving with ¼ cup whipped topping. Serve immediately. Yield: 4 servings (serving size: 1 cup).

CALORIES 147 (7% from fat); FAT 1.2g (sat 0.1g, mono 0.3g, poly 0.6g); PROTEIN 2.3g; CARB 32.4g; FIBER 2.5g; CHOL 0mg; IRON 0.4mg; SODIUM 47mg; CALC 43mg EXCHANGES: 1 Starch, 1 Fruit

Passion Potion

Instead of filling up on sugary sodas, quench your thirst with a sweet and fruity vitamin-packed drink.

    2   cups cubed peeled ripe mango
    1   cup cubed pineapple
 1½   cups orange juice, chilled
    ½   cup passionfruit nectar, chilled

1. Arrange mango and pineapple cubes in a single layer on a baking sheet; freeze until firm (about 1 hour).

2. Remove from freezer; let stand 10 minutes.

3. Combine mango, juice, and nectar in a blender, and process until smooth. With blender on, add pineapple; process until smooth. Serve immediately. Yield: 4 servings (serving size: 1 cup).

Note: Substitute apricot or papaya nectar if you can't find passionfruit nectar.

CALORIES 134 (3% from fat); FAT 0.4g (sat 0.1g, mono 0.1g, poly 0.1g); PROTEIN 1.2g; CARB 33.7g; FIBER 1.9g; CHOL 0mg; IRON 0.4mg; SODIUM 3mg; CALC 19mg EXCHANGES: 2 Fruit

Mulled Cranberry-Orange Cider

This cider is perfect for holiday sipping and guaranteed not to cause seasonal weight gain.

    4   whole cloves
    4   whole allspice
    2   star anise
    1   (3-inch) cinnamon stick, broken
         in half
    5   cups apple cider
    3   cups cranberry juice cocktail
    ¼   cup packed brown sugar
    4   orange slices
    8   small orange slices (optional)

1. Place first 4 ingredients on a cheesecloth square. Gather edges of cheesecloth together; tie securely. Combine spice bag, cider, cranberry juice, sugar, and 4 orange slices in a Dutch oven. Bring to a boil. Reduce heat; simmer, partially covered, 10 minutes.

2. Remove from heat; let stand 30 minutes. Discard spice bag and orange slices. Serve with additional orange slices, if desired. Yield: 8 servings (serving size: 1 cup).

CALORIES 155 (1% from fat); FAT 0.1g (sat 0g, mono 0g, poly 0.1g); PROTEIN 0.6g; CARB 38.5g; FIBER 0.1g; CHOL 0mg; IRON 0.3mg; SODIUM 20mg; CALC 21mg EXCHANGES: 1 Starch, 1½ Fruit

Mocha Cocoa

Don't skimp on milk and other dairy products when you're trying to lose weight. New research suggests that eating low-fat calcium-containing foods may actually help you burn fat. See page 94 for more details about calcium and weight loss.

1 cup 1% low-fat milk
1 tablespoon unsweetened cocoa
1 tablespoon sugar
½ teaspoon instant espresso granules (or 1 teaspoon instant coffee granules)

1. Pour milk into a microwave-safe container, and microwave at HIGH 1 to 2 minutes or until milk is hot, but not boiling.
2. Place cocoa, sugar, and coffee granules in a blender. Add milk, and process until blended. Pour into mug, and serve immediately. Yield: 1 serving (serving size: 1 cup).

CALORIES 165 (17% from fat); FAT 3.3g (sat 2.1g, mono 1g, poly 0.1g); PROTEIN 9.2g; CARB 27.4g; FIBER 1.8g; CHOL 9.8mg; IRON 0.9mg; SODIUM 125mg; CALC 308mg
EXCHANGES: 1 Starch, 1 Skim Milk

Chocolate-Caramel Café au Lait

Using fat-free flavored syrups is a great way to curb a craving for sweets.

¾ cup 2% reduced-fat milk
2 tablespoons fat-free caramel-flavored syrup
2 tablespoons chocolate-flavored syrup
½ teaspoon vanilla extract
3 cups hot strong brewed coffee

1. Combine first 3 ingredients in a small saucepan. Bring to a simmer over medium heat, stirring constantly. Remove from heat; stir in vanilla.
2. Pour ¾ cup brewed coffee into each mug. Add ¼ cup milk mixture to each mug, stirring well. Serve warm. Yield: 4 servings (serving size: 1 cup).

CALORIES 80 (11% from fat); FAT 1g (sat 0.6g, mono 0.3g, poly 0g); PROTEIN 2g; CARB 15.2g; FIBER 0g; CHOL 4mg; IRON 0.3mg; SODIUM 50mg; CALC 66mg
EXCHANGE: 1 Starch

Chapter 36

Breads

Eat bread and lose weight? Sure—if you choose low-fat, high-fiber and whole grain breads.

GREEK BREAD

Pump up the flavor of French bread with a creamy olive topping.

1   (8-ounce) loaf French bread
4   ounces ⅓-less-fat cream cheese
1   tablespoon low-fat mayonnaise
1   teaspoon Greek seasoning
½   cup (2 ounces) crumbled feta cheese
2   tablespoons chopped kalamata olives
¼   cup chopped pepperoncini peppers

1. Preheat oven to 375°.
2. Slice loaf in half horizontally. Combine cream cheese, mayonnaise, and seasoning; spread over cut sides of bread. Sprinkle bread halves evenly with feta cheese, olives, and peppers. Bake at 375° for 10 minutes. Yield: 8 servings (serving size: 1 slice).

CALORIES 143 (37% from fat); FAT 5.9g (sat 3.3g, mono 0.9g, poly 0.3g); PROTEIN 5.2g; CARB 16.5g; FIBER 1g; CHOL 16mg; IRON 0.9mg; SODIUM 469mg; CALC 89mg EXCHANGES: 1 Starch, 1 Fat

JACK CHEESE BREADSTICKS

Use refrigerated breadstick dough for a quick and easy low-fat bread.

¼   cup (1 ounce) finely shredded Monterey Jack cheese with jalapeño peppers
½   teaspoon ground cumin
1   (11-ounce) can refrigerated breadstick dough
Cooking spray

1. Preheat oven to 375°.
2. Combine cheese and cumin. Cut dough along perforations to form 12 breadsticks; sprinkle cheese mixture over dough, gently pressing into dough. Twist each breadstick, and place on a baking sheet coated with cooking spray.
3. Bake at 375° for 13 minutes or until lightly browned. Yield: 1 dozen (serving size: 1 breadstick).

CALORIES 83 (23% from fat); FAT 2.1g (sat 0.5g, mono 0.5g, poly 0.6g); PROTEIN 2.6g; CARB 12.7g; FIBER 0g; CHOL 3mg; IRON 0.8mg; SODIUM 209mg; CALC 18mg EXCHANGE: 1 Starch

MEDITERRANEAN PINWHEELS

Turn pizza dough into pinwheels with a low-fat, high-flavor filling.

- ½ cup boiling water
- 12 sun-dried tomatoes
- 16 chopped pitted kalamata olives
- ½ cup chopped fresh parsley
- 2 teaspoons dried basil
- 2 teaspoons dried oregano
- 1 garlic clove, minced
- 1 (10-ounce) can refrigerated pizza dough

1. Preheat oven to 425°.
2. Combine boiling water and tomatoes in a bowl; let stand 10 minutes or until soft. Drain and chop.
3. Stir together olives and next 4 ingredients. Add reserved tomato.
4. Roll dough into a 12 x 8-inch rectangle; spread evenly with olive mixture. Roll up dough, starting at long side and pressing firmly to eliminate air pockets; pinch seam to seal. Place on an ungreased baking sheet. Bake at 425° for 15 minutes or until lightly browned. Let stand 5 minutes. Cut into diagonal slices, using a serrated knife. Serve immediately. Yield: 16 servings (serving size: 1 slice).

CALORIES 64 (24% from fat); FAT 1.7g (sat 0.1g, mono 0.8g, poly 0.2g); PROTEIN 2g; CARB 10.1g; FIBER 0.7g; CHOL 0mg; IRON 0.9mg; SODIUM 218mg; CALC 12mg EXCHANGE: 1 Starch

CHEDDAR-HERB ROLLS

Brush rolls with an egg white mixture and sprinkle with minced onion before baking. You'll get onion flavor with every bite, making it easier to skip the butter.

- ½ (25-ounce) package homestyle roll dough
- 1 teaspoon dried thyme
- 1 teaspoon dried basil
- 1 teaspoon dried oregano
- ½ cup (2 ounces) reduced-fat shredded sharp Cheddar cheese
  Cooking spray
- 1 large egg white
- 1 tablespoon water
- 1 tablespoon instant minced onion

1. Thaw dough according to package directions.
2. Combine thyme, basil, and oregano.
3. Divide dough into 12 equal portions. Working with one portion at a time (cover remaining portions to keep dough from drying out), sprinkle ¼ teaspoon herb mixture and 2 teaspoons cheese over dough. Knead dough to incorporate herbs and cheese. Shape each portion of dough into a ball. Place in a muffin cup or on a baking sheet coated with cooking spray. Repeat procedure with remaining dough, herbs, and cheese. Let rise according to package directions.

4. Preheat oven to 350°.

5. Combine egg white and water in a bowl; stir well with a whisk. Brush rolls with egg white mixture; sprinkle evenly with minced onion. Bake at 350° for 13 minutes or until golden. Yield: 1 dozen (serving size: 1 roll).

CALORIES 100 (21% from fat); FAT 2.4g (sat 0.7g, mono 0g, poly 0g); PROTEIN 4.6g; CARB 15.7g; FIBER 1.1g; CHOL 3mg; IRON 1.3mg; SODIUM 210mg; CALC 47mg EXCHANGES: 1 Starch, ½ Fat

ONION BISCUITS

Making dough in the food processor is a breeze, but if you don't have one, you can make it by hand, using a pastry blender or two knives to cut in the shortening.

    Cooking spray
    1   cup minced fresh onion
    ½   teaspoon sugar
    2   cups all-purpose flour
    2   teaspoons baking powder
    ½   teaspoon baking soda
    ½   teaspoon salt
    3   tablespoons vegetable shortening
    ¾   cup low-fat buttermilk (1%)
    1   large egg, lightly beaten
    2   teaspoons water

1. Preheat oven to 450°.

2. Heat a small nonstick skillet coated with cooking spray over medium-high heat. Add onion and sugar; sauté 8 minutes or until onion is golden. Cool.

3. Lightly spoon flour into dry measuring cups; level with a knife. Place flour, baking powder, baking soda, and salt in a food processor; pulse 2 times or until blended. Add shortening, and pulse 2 times or until combined. Sprinkle onion mixture over flour mixture. With processor on, slowly add buttermilk through food chute; process until dough forms a ball.

4. Turn dough out onto a floured surface, and knead lightly 4 to 5 times. Pat dough into an 8 x 6-inch rectangle; cut into 12 squares. Place on a baking sheet. Combine egg and water, and brush over biscuits. Bake at 450° for 11 minutes or until golden. Yield: 1 dozen (serving size: 1 biscuit).

CALORIES 114 (25% from fat); FAT 3.2g (sat 0.7g, mono 1.1g, poly 1.1g); PROTEIN 2.9g; CARB 18.3g; FIBER 0.8g; CHOL 0mg; IRON 1.1mg; SODIUM 252mg; CALC 70mg EXCHANGES: 1 Starch, 1 Fat

SWEET POTATO BISCUITS

Mashed sweet potato adds a touch of sweetness (not to mention antioxidant vitamin A) to these tender, reduced-fat biscuits. For more information on antioxidants, see page 67.

2 cups all-purpose flour
1/3 cup yellow cornmeal
2 1/2 teaspoons baking powder
1/2 teaspoon salt
1/3 cup chilled butter or stick margarine, cut into small pieces
1 cup mashed cooked sweet potato
1/2 cup fat-free milk
2 tablespoons honey

1. Preheat oven to 400°.
2. Lightly spoon flour into dry measuring cups; level with a knife. Combine flour, cornmeal, baking powder, and salt in a bowl; cut in butter with a pastry blender or 2 knives until mixture resembles coarse meal. Add sweet potato, milk, and honey; stir just until moist.
3. Turn dough out onto a heavily floured surface; knead lightly 5 times. Pat dough into a 9-inch square; cut into 16 squares. Place biscuits on a baking sheet. Bake at 400° for 20 minutes or until golden. Yield: 16 biscuits (serving size: 1 biscuit).

CALORIES 134 (28% from fat); FAT 4.1g (sat 2.4g, mono 1.1g, poly 0.3g); PROTEIN 2.5g; CARB 21.9g; FIBER 1.2g; CHOL 11mg; IRON 1.1mg; SODIUM 196mg; CALC 60mg EXCHANGES: 1 Starch, 1 Fat

BANANA-BRAN SOY MUFFINS

1 cup wheat bran
1 cup mashed ripe banana
2/3 cup soy milk
1/4 cup packed brown sugar
2 tablespoons prune baby food
1 large egg, lightly beaten
1 1/4 cups all-purpose flour
1/4 cup soy flour
1/4 cup finely chopped pecans
2 teaspoons baking powder
1 teaspoon ground cinnamon
1/2 teaspoon salt
Cooking spray

1. Preheat oven to 375°.
2. Combine first 3 ingredients in a medium bowl; let stand 5 minutes. Stir in sugar, prunes, and egg.
3. Lightly spoon flours into dry measuring cups; level with a knife. Combine flours and next 4 ingredients in a bowl; make a well in center of mixture. Add bran mixture to flour mixture, stirring just until moist. Spoon batter into 12 muffin cups coated with cooking spray. Bake at 375° for 20 minutes or until muffins spring back when touched lightly in center. Remove muffins from pans immediately; cool on a wire rack. Yield: 1 dozen (serving size: 1 muffin).

CALORIES 134 (21% from fat); FAT 3.2g (sat 0.5g, mono 1.4g, poly 1g); PROTEIN 4.3g; CARB 24.7g; FIBER 3.5g; CHOL 18mg; IRON 1.9mg; SODIUM 193mg; CALC 76mg EXCHANGES: 1 1/2 Starch, 1/2 Fat

BLUEBERRY-BRAN MUFFINS

Blueberries are a good source of anthocyanins, which may help reduce the risk of cancer and heart disease.

1½ cups shreds of wheat bran cereal
1¼ cups 1% low-fat milk
½ cup sugar
3 tablespoons vegetable oil
1 large egg
1 cup all-purpose flour
1 tablespoon baking powder
½ teaspoon salt
1 cup blueberries

1. Preheat oven to 400°.
2. Combine cereal and milk, stirring well. Let stand 10 minutes.
3. Stir sugar, oil, and egg into cereal.
4. Lightly spoon flour into a dry measuring cup; level with a knife. Combine flour, baking powder, and salt; add to cereal mixture, stirring just until moist. Gently fold in blueberries.
5. Place 12 paper muffin cup liners in muffin cups; spoon batter into cups. Bake at 400° for 18 to 20 minutes or until muffins spring back when touched lightly in center. Remove muffins from pans immediately; cool on a wire rack. Yield: 1 dozen (serving size: 1 muffin).

CALORIES 145 (26% from fat); FAT 4.5g (sat 0.6g, mono 2.3g, poly 1.3g); PROTEIN 3.5g; CARB 25.5g; FIBER 3.1g; CHOL 19mg; IRON 1.9mg; SODIUM 254mg; CALC 131mg EXCHANGES: 1½ Starch, 1 Fat

BUCKWHEAT-HONEY PANCAKES

Buckwheat flour adds a nutty flavor and extra fiber.

⅔ cup buckwheat flour
½ cup all-purpose flour
1 teaspoon baking powder
¼ teaspoon baking soda
¼ teaspoon salt
⅛ teaspoon ground nutmeg
¾ cup plain fat-free yogurt
¼ cup honey
¼ cup fat-free milk
2 tablespoons vegetable oil
¾ teaspoon vanilla extract
3 large eggs, lightly beaten

1. Lightly spoon flours into dry measuring cups; level with a knife. Combine flours and next 4 ingredients. Combine yogurt and remaining ingredients; add to flour mixture, stirring until smooth.
2. For each pancake, spoon about ¼ cup batter onto a hot nonstick griddle or a nonstick skillet. Turn pancakes when tops are covered with bubbles and edges look cooked. Yield: 1 dozen (serving size: 1 pancake).
Note: Store buckwheat flour in your refrigerator or freezer so it won't spoil.

CALORIES 117 (29% from fat); FAT 3.8g (sat 0.9g, mono 1.2g, poly 1.3g); PROTEIN 4.3g; CARB 16.9g; FIBER 0.5g; CHOL 56mg; IRON 0.8mg; SODIUM 148mg; CALC 68mg EXCHANGES: 1 Starch, 1 Fat

Sweet Potato-Pecan Pancakes

Sweet potatoes are one of the best sources of beta-carotene—a substance in food that the body converts to vitamin A. Because it is an antioxidant, vitamin A appears to help reduce the risk of developing heart disease and lung cancer. See page 69 for more information.

1¼ cups all-purpose flour
¼ cup chopped pecans, toasted and divided
2¼ teaspoons baking powder
1 teaspoon pumpkin-pie spice
¼ teaspoon salt
1 cup fat-free milk
¼ cup packed dark brown sugar
1 tablespoon vegetable oil
1 teaspoon vanilla extract
2 large eggs, lightly beaten
1 (16-ounce) can sweet potatoes or yams, drained and mashed

1. Lightly spoon flour into dry measuring cups; level with a knife. Combine flour, 2 tablespoons pecans, baking powder, pumpkin-pie spice, and salt in a large bowl. Combine milk and next 4 ingredients; add to flour mixture, stirring until smooth. Stir in sweet potatoes.
2. For each pancake, spoon about ¼ cup batter onto a hot nonstick griddle or large nonstick skillet. Turn pancakes when tops are covered with bubbles and edges look cooked. Sprinkle pancakes evenly with remaining 2 tablespoons pecans. Yield: 1 dozen (serving size: 1 pancake).

CALORIES 135 (27% from fat); FAT 4.0g (sat 0.7g, mono 1.8g, poly 1.2g); PROTEIN 3.7g; CARB 21.3g; FIBER 1.2g; CHOL 37mg; IRON 1.1mg; SODIUM 167mg; CALC 93mg EXCHANGES: 1 Starch, 1 Fat

Whole Wheat Chapati

A northern Indian flatbread, chapati is traditionally made with just two ingredients—flour and water—so it has almost no fat at all. Its mild flavor complements spicy Indian dishes.

¾ cup all-purpose flour
¾ cup whole wheat flour
½ cup water

1. Lightly spoon flours into dry measuring cups; level with a knife. Combine flours and water in a large bowl. Press mixture together using a rubber spatula or your hands (mixture is dry but will stay together).
2. Turn dough out onto a lightly floured surface. Knead 3 minutes. Cover and let rest 15 minutes.
3. Divide dough into 12 equal portions, shaping each into a ball. Roll 1 ball into a 5-inch circle (circles will be very thin) on a lightly floured surface. Cover the remaining dough while working to prevent it from drying out.

4. Heat a large nonstick skillet over medium-high heat until very hot. Place 1 dough round in pan, and cook 30 seconds or until brown spots appear, turning after about 15 seconds. Place bread on a cooling rack over the eye of a gas burner. Hold bread over flame with tongs, turning until both sides of bread are puffed and brown spots appear (some chapatis will puff more than others). Repeat procedure with remaining dough. Yield: 6 servings (serving size: 2 flatbreads).

CALORIES 108 (3% from fat); FAT 0.4g (sat 0.1g, mono 0.1g, poly 0.2g); PROTEIN 3.7g; CARB 22.8g; FIBER 2.3g; CHOL 0mg; IRON 1.3mg; SODIUM 1mg; CALC 7mg EXCHANGES: 1½ Starch

OLIVE BREAD

Capitalize on the convenience of frozen bread dough, filling it with a flavorful olive paste. Serve the savory bread with soup or a salad for a light lunch.

    1   (1-pound) loaf frozen white
        bread dough
  ½   cup pitted kalamata olives
    3   tablespoons capers
    3   tablespoons fresh lemon juice
    1   teaspoon dried thyme
    4   canned anchovy fillets
    2   garlic cloves, peeled
Cooking spray

1. Thaw dough in refrigerator 12 hours.

2. Combine olives and next 5 ingredients in a food processor; process until well blended.

3. Roll dough into a 12 x 8-inch rectangle on a lightly floured surface. Spread olive mixture onto dough, leaving a ½-inch border. Beginning at short side, roll up dough tightly, jelly roll fashion; pinch seam and ends to seal. Place roll, seam side down, in an 8 x 4-inch loaf pan coated with cooking spray. Cover and let rise in a warm place (85°), free from drafts, 2½ hours or until doubled in size. (Press two fingers into dough. If indentation remains, the dough has risen enough.)

4. Preheat oven to 375°.

5. Bake at 375° for 25 minutes or until lightly browned. Cool in pan 10 minutes on a wire rack; remove from pan. Cool completely on wire rack. Yield: 1 loaf, 12 slices (serving size: 1 slice).

CALORIES 163 (17% from fat); FAT 3g (sat 0.5g, mono 1g, poly 1.3g); PROTEIN 5.7g; CARB 28.4g; FIBER 1.1g; CHOL 1mg; IRON 1.7mg; SODIUM 423mg; CALC 46mg EXCHANGES: 2 Starch

SPINACH-FETA BREAD

This bread is packed with high-calcium ingredients: spinach and cheese.

1   (1-pound) loaf frozen white bread dough
1   cup (4 ounces) crumbled feta cheese
1/3 cup (3 ounces) 1/3-less-fat cream cheese
1/2 teaspoon dried oregano
1/4 teaspoon salt
1   (14-ounce) can artichoke hearts, drained and chopped
1   (10-ounce) package frozen chopped spinach, thawed, drained, and squeezed dry
3   garlic cloves, minced
1   large egg white
Cooking spray
2   tablespoons grated fresh Parmesan cheese

1. Thaw dough in refrigerator 12 hours.
2. Combine feta and next 7 ingredients.
3. Roll dough into a 16 x 10-inch rectangle on a lightly floured surface. Spread spinach mixture over dough, leaving a 1/2-inch border. Beginning at long side, roll up dough tightly, jelly roll fashion; pinch seam and ends to seal. Place roll, seam side down, on a baking sheet coated with cooking spray. Cut diagonal slits into top of roll using a sharp knife. Cover and let rise in a warm place (85°),
1 hour or until doubled in size.
4. Preheat oven to 350°.
5. Sprinkle top of roll with Parmesan cheese. Bake at 350° for 45 minutes or until golden. Yield: 1 loaf, 16 slices (serving size: 1 slice).

CALORIES 143 (23% from fat); FAT 3.7g (sat 2.2g, mono 1g, poly 0.3g); PROTEIN 6.4g; CARB 21.7g; FIBER 1.2g; CHOL 14mg; IRON 1.7mg; SODIUM 461mg; CALC 99mg EXCHANGES: 1 1/2 Starch, 1/2 Fat

BANANA-OAT QUICK BREAD

Oats provide soluble fiber, which helps control blood sugar levels.

1 1/2 cups all-purpose flour
1   cup quick-cooking oats
3/4   cup packed brown sugar
2 1/2 teaspoons baking powder
1/4   teaspoon salt
1   cup mashed ripe banana
1/2   cup low-fat buttermilk (1%)
1/4   cup vegetable oil
1/4   cup egg substitute
Cooking spray
1/4   cup quick-cooking oats
2   tablespoons coarsely chopped walnuts
2   tablespoons brown sugar
2   teaspoons butter or margarine

1. Preheat oven to 350°.
2. Lightly spoon flour into dry measuring cups; level with a knife. Combine flour

and next 4 ingredients; make a well in center of mixture. Combine mashed banana, buttermilk, oil, and egg substitute; add to flour mixture. Stir just until moist. Spoon batter into an 8 x 4-inch loaf pan coated with cooking spray.

3. Combine ¼ cup oats, walnuts, 2 tablespoons brown sugar, and butter; sprinkle over batter. Bake at 350° for 1 hour or until a wooden pick inserted in center comes out clean. Cool 5 minutes in pan on a wire rack; remove from pan. Cool completely on wire rack. Yield: 16 servings (serving size: 1 slice).

CALORIES 170 (28% from fat); FAT 5.2g (sat 1.1g, mono 1.4g, poly 2.2g); PROTEIN 3.3g; CARB 28.4g; FIBER 1.4g; CHOL 1mg; IRON 1.3mg; SODIUM 132mg; CALC 69mg EXCHANGES: 1 Starch, 1 Fruit, 1 Fat

DATE BREAD

The dates soak overnight, so you need to start making this bread a day ahead.

2	cups chopped pitted dates
2	cups boiling water
2	teaspoons baking soda
	Cooking spray
4	teaspoons all-purpose flour
1	cup sugar
1	tablespoon butter, melted
1	teaspoon vanilla extract
1	large egg, lightly beaten
2¼	cups all-purpose flour
½	teaspoon salt

1. Combine first 3 ingredients in a large bowl; cover date mixture, and let stand 24 hours.

2. Preheat oven to 325°.

3. Coat 2 (8 x 4-inch) loaf pans with cooking spray, and dust each pan with 2 teaspoons flour. Add sugar, butter, vanilla, and egg to date mixture. Lightly spoon 2¼ cups flour into dry measuring cups; level with a knife. Add flour and salt to date mixture, stirring just until blended. Divide batter evenly between prepared pans.

4. Bake at 325° for 45 minutes or until a wooden pick inserted in center comes out clean. Cool loaves 10 minutes in pans on a wire rack. Remove loaves from pans, and cool completely on wire rack. Yield: 2 loaves, 16 servings per loaf (serving size: 1 slice).

CALORIES 94 (7% from fat); FAT 0.7g (sat 0.3g, mono 0.2g, poly 0.1g); PROTEIN 1.4g; CARB 21.4g; FIBER 1.1g; CHOL 8mg; IRON 0.6mg; SODIUM 122mg; CALC 6mg EXCHANGE: 1 Starch

HONEY WHEAT BREAD

This recipe makes three loaves, so freeze two of them to use later. Place each baked loaf in an airtight container or wrap in heavy-duty plastic wrap or foil. Seal and freeze up to 1 month.

     2   packages dry yeast (about 1½ tablespoons)
    ⅓   cup honey
     1   cup warm water (100° to 110°)
     1   cup half-and-half
     4   large eggs, lightly beaten
    4¾   cups bread flour
    1½   cups whole wheat flour
    1½   teaspoons salt
         Cooking spray

1. Dissolve yeast and honey in warm water in a large mixing bowl; let stand 5 minutes. Add half-and-half and eggs; beat with a heavy-duty stand mixer at medium speed until well blended. Lightly spoon flours into dry measuring cups; level with a knife. Add whole wheat flour and salt to bowl, beating well. Gradually stir in enough bread flour, ½ cup at a time, to form a soft dough.
2. Turn dough out onto a well floured surface. Knead until smooth and elastic (about 5 minutes). Place dough in a large bowl coated with cooking spray, turning to coat top. Cover and let rise in a warm place (85°), free from drafts, 45 minutes or until doubled in size.

3. Punch dough down; turn dough onto a lightly floured surface, and knead lightly 4 to 5 times. Divide dough into 3 equal portions. Working with one portion at a time (cover remaining dough to keep it from drying out), roll each portion into a 12 x 8-inch rectangle on a lightly floured surface. Beginning at short side, roll up each rectangle tightly, pressing firmly to eliminate air pockets; pinch seam and ends to seal. Place each roll of dough, seam side down, in an 8 x 4-inch loaf pan coated with cooking spray.
4. Cover and let rise 30 minutes or until doubled in size.
5. Preheat oven to 375°.
6. Bake at 375° for 20 minutes or until loaves sound hollow when tapped. Remove bread from pans immediately, and cool on wire racks. Yield: 3 loaves, 48 servings (serving size: 1 [½-inch] slice).

Note: You may use a dough hook and a heavy-duty stand mixer for kneading, if desired.

CALORIES 72 (16% from fat); FAT 1.3g (sat 0.5g, mono 0.4g, poly 0.1g); PROTEIN 2.6g; CARB 12.8g; FIBER 0.6g; CHOL 20mg; IRON 0.7mg; SODIUM 81mg; CALC 11mg EXCHANGE: 1 Starch

Sweet Potato Bread with Flaxseed and Honey

Flaxseed is one of the "new" wonder foods, even though it's been around for centuries. This seed is rich in both omega-3 and omega-6 fatty acids, fiber, and phytoestrogens, so it can help reduce the risk of heart disease and colon cancer, reduce cholesterol, and lessen the discomfort of menopause.

⅓   cup flaxseed
2   cups all-purpose flour
1   teaspoon baking powder
½   teaspoon baking soda
¼   teaspoon salt
¼   cup (2 ounces) ⅓-less-fat
        cream cheese, softened
3   tablespoons butter, softened
½   cup packed brown sugar
¼   cup honey
1   large egg
1   large egg white
1   cup mashed cooked sweet potato
Cooking spray

1. Preheat oven to 350°.
2. Place flaxseed in a clean coffee grinder or blender; process until coarsely ground. Lightly spoon flour into dry measuring cups; level with a knife. Combine flaxseed, flour, baking powder, baking soda, and salt in a large bowl; make a well in center of mixture. Beat cream cheese and next 5 ingredients; stir in sweet potato. Add to flour mixture, stirring just until moist.

3. Spoon batter into an 8 x 4-inch loaf pan coated with cooking spray. Bake at 350° for 50 minutes or until a wooden pick inserted in center comes out clean. Cool 10 minutes in pan on a wire rack; remove from pan. Cool completely on wire rack. Yield: 16 servings (serving size: 1 [½-inch] slice).

CALORIES 171 (27% from fat); FAT 5.1g (sat 2.1g, mono 1.3g, poly 1.4g); PROTEIN 3.6g; CARB 29g; FIBER 1.8g; CHOL 22mg; IRON 1.4mg; SODIUM 157mg; CALC 44mg EXCHANGES: 2 Starch, 1 Fat

Super Foods

In addition to flaxseed, there are several other items making the list of foods with the power to prevent disease.

- Beans
- Citrus fruits
- Cruciferous vegetables (such as broccoli, cabbage, and cauliflower)
- Dark leafy greens
- Flaxseed
- Olive oil
- Orange vegetables
- Soy products
- Tomatoes
- Wine

See page 63 for more information on the healing powers of food.

Chapter 37

Desserts

Indulge in decadent desserts so you'll never
feel deprived while you're losing weight.

MACERATED RASPBERRIES WITH NECTARINES

Macerating is similar to marinating, but it's a term generally used when a fruit is soaked in liquid such as wine, liquor, or a syrup to infuse the fruit with flavor.

1   cup dry red wine
1/3 cup sugar
8   whole cloves
2   (3-inch) cinnamon sticks
2   cups fresh or frozen raspberries, thawed
1/2 teaspoon vanilla extract
3   cups sliced unpeeled nectarine (about 4 nectarines)

1. Combine first 4 ingredients in a saucepan. Bring to a boil over high heat; cook, uncovered, 8 to 10 minutes or until sauce is reduced to 1/3 cup. Remove from heat.
2. Place raspberries in a bowl. Pour sauce through a wire-mesh strainer over berries; let stand 30 minutes or until cool. Stir in vanilla.

3. Place 3/4 cup nectarine slices in each of 4 dessert dishes; spoon 1/4 cup raspberry mixture over each serving. Yield: 4 servings.

CALORIES 158 (27% from fat); FAT 0.9g (sat 0.1g, mono 0g, poly 0.2g); PROTEIN 1.6g; CARB 38.7g; FIBER 6.5g; CHOL 0mg; IRON 0.8mg; SODIUM 5mg; CALC 23mg EXCHANGES: 1 Starch, 1½ Fruit

CRUNCHY PEAR-BERRY GRANOLA CRISP

This fruity dessert gives you a little extra fiber because the crisp topping is made with granola cereal.

4   cups sliced peeled pear (about 3 pears)
1/2 cup dried cranberries
3   tablespoons dark brown sugar
1   tablespoon cornstarch
1   tablespoon lemon juice
1/2 teaspoon vanilla extract
Butter-flavored cooking spray
2   cups low-fat granola cereal without raisins (such as Healthy Choice)

1. Preheat oven to 400°.

2. Combine first 6 ingredients in a large bowl; toss well. Spoon mixture into a 9-inch pie plate coated with cooking spray.

3. Top fruit mixture with granola; coat granola generously with cooking spray. Bake at 400° or until fruit is tender and topping is lightly browned. Yield: 8 servings (serving size: ½ cup).

CALORIES 184 (10% from fat); FAT 2.1g (sat 0.3g, mono 0.3g, poly 0.9g); PROTEIN 2.3g; CARB 41.3g; FIBER 3.5g; CHOL 0mg; IRON 1.2mg; SODIUM 62mg; CALC 23mg EXCHANGES: 1 Starch, 2 Fruit

BERRIES JUBILEE

This is a berry version of the traditional flaming cherries jubilee.

    2   tablespoons sugar
    1   tablespoon cornstarch
    ⅛   teaspoon salt
    ½   teaspoon grated orange rind
    1¼ cups orange juice
    1½ cups fresh blueberries
    1½ cups fresh raspberries
    ¼   cup brandy
    4   cups vanilla low-fat ice cream

1. Combine first 3 ingredients in a large skillet. Stir in rind and juice; bring to a boil. Cook 1 minute or until slightly thick.

2. Add berries; cook 3 minutes or until thoroughly heated. Pour brandy into one side of pan. Ignite brandy with a long match; let flames die down. Spoon berry sauce over ice cream. Yield: 8 servings (serving size: ½ cup ice cream and ⅓ cup sauce).

CALORIES 152 (18% from fat); FAT 3.1g (sat 1.8g, mono 0.8g, poly 0.2g); PROTEIN 3.2g; CARB 29.8g; FIBER 2.4g; CHOL 9mg; IRON 0.3mg; SODIUM 95mg; CALC 102mg EXCHANGES: 1 Starch, 1 Fruit, ½ Fat

STRAWBERRIES ROMANOFF SUNDAES

Use ¼ cup orange juice instead of triple sec, if you prefer.

    2   cups quartered strawberries
    ¼   cup triple sec (orange-flavored liqueur)
    3   tablespoons sugar
    1¼   cups sliced strawberries
    3   cups vanilla low-fat ice cream
    2   tablespoons chopped pistachios, toasted

1. Combine first 3 ingredients in a blender, and process until smooth. Combine strawberry puree and sliced strawberries in a bowl; cover and chill.

2. Serve strawberry mixture over ice cream. Sprinkle with nuts. Yield: 6 servings (serving size: ½ cup ice cream, ⅓ cup strawberry sauce, and 1 teaspoon nuts).

CALORIES 195 (23% from fat); FAT 5g (sat 2g, mono 2.1g, poly 0.6g); PROTEIN 3.8g; CARB 30.9g; FIBER 2.3g; CHOL 9mg; IRON 0.6mg; SODIUM 57mg; CALC 109mg EXCHANGES: 1 Starch, 1 Fruit, 1 Fat

CHUNKY PLUM-AND-GINGER ICE CREAM

Gingersnaps are good cookies to keep on hand when you crave a little something sweet. One cookie has only about 1 gram of fat and 30 calories.

4   cups vanilla low-fat ice cream, softened
1   cup diced plum (about 3 plums)
1   tablespoon finely chopped crystallized ginger
6   gingersnaps

1. Combine first 3 ingredients in a freezer-safe container. Cover and freeze until firm.
2. Spoon ice cream into 6 small bowls, and crumble 1 gingersnap over each serving. Yield: 6 servings (serving size: ⅔ cup ice cream and 1 gingersnap).

CALORIES 177 (27% from fat); FAT 5.3g (sat 2.7g, mono 1.8g, poly 0.5g); PROTEIN 4.1g; CARB 29.8g; FIBER 0.6g; CHOL 15mg; IRON 0.7mg; SODIUM 86mg; CALC 139mg EXCHANGES: 1 Starch, 1 Fruit, 1 Fat

CAPPUCCINO GRANITA

Start with double-strength brewed coffee in this icy treat to heighten the coffee flavor.

½   cup ground coffee beans
1¾   cups water
⅓   cup sugar
⅓   cup water
1   teaspoon vanilla extract
¼   teaspoon ground cinnamon
½   cup 1% low-fat milk

1. Assemble drip coffee maker according to manufacturer's directions. Place ground coffee in coffee filter or filter basket. Add 1¾ cups water to coffee maker and brew; set coffee aside.
2. Combine sugar and ⅓ cup water in a small saucepan. Bring to a boil; cook 1 minute or until sugar dissolves. Stir in vanilla and cinnamon. Remove from heat; stir in brewed coffee and milk.
3. Cool coffee mixture completely; pour into an 8-inch square baking dish. Cover and freeze at least 8 hours or until firm. Remove coffee mixture from freezer; scrape entire mixture with a fork until fluffy. Spoon into a freezer-safe container; cover and freeze up to 1 month. Yield: 6 servings (serving size: ⅔ cup).

CALORIES 56 (3% from fat); FAT 0.2g (sat 0.1g, mono 0.1g, poly 0g); PROTEIN 0.7g; CARB 12.3g; FIBER 0g; CHOL 1mg; IRON 0.1mg; SODIUM 10mg; CALC 26mg EXCHANGE: 1 Starch

MANGO FREEZE

Increase your calcium and vitamin intake with this fruity frozen treat.

4 cups peeled ripe mango, cut into 1-inch pieces (about 4 large)
¾ cup powdered sugar
½ cup mashed ripe banana
1 tablespoon fresh lime juice
1 (8-ounce) carton vanilla low-fat yogurt

1. Place mango pieces on a baking sheet lined with plastic wrap; freeze at least 4 hours. Remove from freezer; let stand 10 minutes.
2. Place mango pieces in a food processor or blender; process until smooth, scraping sides of bowl occasionally. Add sugar, banana, and lime juice. With food processor on, slowly spoon yogurt through food chute; process until smooth, scraping sides of bowl once. Spoon mixture into a freezer-safe container; cover and freeze 3 hours or until firm. Yield: 10 servings (serving size: ½ cup).
Note: Let the Mango Freeze soften a little before serving.

CALORIES 108 (4% from fat); FAT 0.5g (sat 0.2g, mono 0.2g, poly 0.1g); PROTEIN 1.6g; CARB 26.1g; FIBER 1.3g; CHOL 1mg; IRON 0.1mg; SODIUM 17mg; CALC 46mg EXCHANGES: 2 Fruit

WATERMELON-CANTALOUPE SORBET

Cool and refreshing, this melon sorbet has practically no fat and is a great alternative to premium ice cream.

½ cup sugar
⅓ cup water
1½ cups cubed peeled cantaloupe
1½ cups cubed seeded watermelon
3 tablespoons fresh lime juice

1. Combine sugar and water in a small saucepan. Bring to a boil; cook 1 minute or until sugar dissolves. Cool completely. Place cantaloupe and watermelon in a blender or food processor, and process until smooth.
2. Combine sugar syrup, melon mixture, and lime juice. Pour mixture into freezer can of an ice-cream freezer, and freeze according to manufacturer's instructions. Spoon sorbet into a freezer-safe container; cover and freeze 1 hour or until firm. Yield: 3 cups (serving size: ½ cup).

CALORIES 93 (3% from fat); FAT 0.3g (sat 0.1g, mono 0g, poly 0.1g); PROTEIN 0.6g; CARB 23.4g; FIBER 0.5g; CHOL 0mg; IRON 0.2mg; SODIUM 5mg; CALC 8mg EXCHANGES: 1½ Fruit

PINEAPPLE-BROWN SUGAR FROZEN YOGURT

This recipe makes 9 cups but can easily be halved if you don't need that much.

1½ cups packed light brown sugar
2 (15¼-ounce) cans crushed pineapple in juice, undrained
4 cups vanilla low-fat yogurt
2 teaspoons vanilla extract

1. Combine sugar and pineapple in a medium saucepan over medium heat, and cook until sugar dissolves, stirring occasionally. Remove from heat, and cool slightly. Chill.
2. Combine pineapple mixture, yogurt, and vanilla in a large bowl. Pour mixture into freezer can of an ice-cream freezer, and freeze according to manufacturer's instructions. Spoon yogurt into a freezer-safe container; cover and freeze 1 hour or until firm. Yield: 9 cups (serving size: ½ cup).

CALORIES 142 (4% from fat); FAT 0.7g (sat 0.4g, mono 0.2g, poly 0.1g); PROTEIN 2.7g; CARB 32.4g; FIBER 0.4g; CHOL 3mg; IRON 0.5mg; SODIUM 41mg; CALC 109mg EXCHANGES: 1 Starch, 1 Fruit

FROZEN CHOCOLATE DECADENCE BROWNIES

Start with a low-fat brownie mix and end up with a double-chocolate fruity frozen fantasy with only 3 grams of fat per serving.

1 (20.5-ounce) package low-fat brownie mix (such as Betty Crocker Sweet Rewards)
⅔ cup water
Cooking spray
1 (2.25-ounce) package sliced almonds
¾ cup seedless raspberry spread
2 (1-pound) cans dark cherries in heavy syrup
4 cups chocolate low-fat ice cream, softened
1½ teaspoons instant coffee granules
1 (12-ounce) container frozen fat-free whipped topping, thawed

1. Preheat oven to 350°.
2. Stir together brownie mix and water. Pour batter into a 13 x 9-inch pan coated with cooking spray. Bake at 350° for 20 to 25 minutes or until a wooden pick inserted in center comes out clean. Toast almonds on rack below brownies during last 5 minutes of baking. Cool brownies and almonds completely on a wire rack.
3. Place raspberry spread in a bowl; stir with a whisk until smooth. Drain cherries, reserving 2 tablespoons juice; set juice

aside. Rinse cherries; drain well. Add cherries to raspberry spread, stirring to coat.

4. Spread ice cream over brownies; spoon cherry mixture over ice cream.

5. Combine reserved cherry juice and coffee granules, stirring until coffee dissolves. Fold in whipped topping; spread over cherry mixture. Sprinkle with almonds. Cover and freeze at least 8 hours. Yield: 24 servings (serving size: 1 square).

CALORIES 226 (12% from fat); FAT 3g (sat 0.4g, mono 0.6g, poly 0.2g); PROTEIN 3.6g; CARB 44.8g; FIBER 1.3g; CHOL 0mg; IRON 1.3mg; SODIUM 110mg; CALC 34mg EXCHANGES: 3 Starch, ½ Fat

MINI MOCHA-TOFFEE CRUNCH CHEESECAKES

Phyllo shells are a crispy low-fat alternative to high-fat piecrusts.

36	commercial prebaked miniature phyllo dough shells
1½	teaspoons instant coffee granules
1	teaspoon hot water
1	teaspoon Kahlúa (coffee-flavored liqueur)
½	cup sugar
½	cup (4 ounces) ⅓-less-fat cream cheese
½	cup (4 ounces) block-style fat-free cream cheese
1	tablespoon all-purpose flour
¼	teaspoon vanilla extract
1	large egg
3	tablespoons toffee bits

1. Preheat oven to 350°.

2. Place 1 phyllo shell into each of 36 miniature muffin cups.

3. Combine coffee granules, hot water, and Kahlúa in a small bowl. Place coffee mixture, sugar, and next 5 ingredients in a food processor; process until smooth. Spoon about 1 tablespoon cheese mixture into each shell; discard remaining filling. Sprinkle cheesecakes evenly with toffee bits.

4. Bake at 350° for 15 minutes or until set. Remove from pans, and cool on a wire rack. Yield: 3 dozen (serving size: 1 mini cheesecake).

Note: Look for phyllo dough shells in the freezer section of the supermarket. There are usually 15 shells per package.

CALORIES 55 (38% from fat); FAT 2.3g (sat 0.8g, mono 0.9g, poly 0.6g); PROTEIN 1.5g; CARB 6.5g; FIBER 0g; CHOL 10mg; IRON 0.1mg; SODIUM 47mg; CALC 10mg EXCHANGE: ½ Starch

ALCOHOL SUBSTITUTIONS

If you don't want to use liqueurs in dessert recipes, here are some simple substitutions.

- **2 tablespoons Kahlúa:**
  2 tablespoons brewed coffee plus 1 teaspoon sugar
- **2 tablespoons Grand Marnier:**
  2 tablespoons orange juice
- **2 tablespoons amaretto:**
  ½ teaspoon almond extract

Peanut Butter-Chocolate Cheesecake Squares

Be sure to use the stick form of light butter instead of a reduced-calorie tub margarine. Tub margarine has added water and air, so it doesn't produce the best crust.

$1/3$ cup all-purpose flour
2 tablespoons brown sugar
2 tablespoons chilled light butter
Cooking spray
$1/2$ cup fat-free hot fudge topping
1 (8-ounce) block fat-free cream cheese
$1/2$ cup sugar
1 large egg
$1/2$ cup reduced-fat creamy peanut butter
1 tablespoon fat-free milk
1 teaspoon vanilla extract

1. Preheat oven to 350°.
2. Combine flour and brown sugar; stir well. Cut in small pieces of butter with a pastry blender or 2 knives until mixture resembles coarse meal. Press mixture firmly into bottom of an 8-inch square baking pan coated with cooking spray. Bake at 350° for 8 minutes. Remove from oven.
3. Place fudge topping in a small microwave-safe bowl. Microwave at HIGH 1 minute or until thoroughly heated, stirring after 30 seconds.
4. Beat cream cheese with a mixer at medium speed until smooth. Gradually add sugar, beating well. Add egg and next 3 ingredients, beating well. Pour batter over prepared crust. Drizzle fudge topping over batter. Using the tip of a knife, swirl fudge into batter. Bake at 350° for 20 minutes or until set. Cool completely in pan on a wire rack. Yield: 16 servings (serving size: 1 square).

CALORIES 135 (27% from fat); FAT 4.1g (sat 1.2g, mono 1.6, poly 0.9g); PROTEIN 5g; CARB 19.4g; FIBER 0.8g; CHOL 19mg; IRON 0.4mg; SODIUM 195mg; CALC 49mg EXCHANGES: 1½ Starch, 1 Fat

Lemon-Flaxseed Loaf Cake

Flaxseed adds a pleasant, nutty flavor to this cake, and it also protects against cancer and heart disease.

Cooking spray
1 tablespoon granulated sugar
$1/4$ cup flaxseed
1 cup granulated sugar
2 large eggs
2 cups all-purpose flour
$1 1/2$ teaspoons baking powder
$1/2$ teaspoon baking soda
$1/2$ teaspoon salt
$3/4$ cup low-fat buttermilk (1%)
$1/4$ cup vegetable oil
2 teaspoons grated lemon rind
1 teaspoon vanilla extract
$1/2$ cup powdered sugar
1 tablespoon fresh lemon juice

1. Preheat oven to 350°.

2. Coat an 8 x 4-inch loaf pan with cooking spray; sprinkle with 1 table-spoon granulated sugar. Set pan aside. Place flaxseed in a blender or clean coffee grinder, and process until ground to measure about 6 tablespoons flaxseed meal; set aside.

3. Combine 1 cup granulated sugar and eggs in a large bowl; beat with a mixer at high speed 3 minutes or until mixture is thick and pale. Lightly spoon flour into dry measuring cups; level with a knife. Combine flaxseed meal, flour, baking powder, baking soda, and salt; stir well with a whisk. Combine butter-milk, oil, rind, and vanilla. Add flour mixture to egg mixture alternately with buttermilk mixture, beginning and ending with flour mixture.

4. Spoon batter into prepared pan. Bake at 350° for 55 minutes or until a wooden pick inserted in center comes out clean. Cool in pan 5 minutes on a wire rack; remove from pan. Cool completely on wire rack.

5. Combine powdered sugar and lemon juice; drizzle over top of loaf. Yield: 12 servings (serving size: 1 slice).

CALORIES 242 (28% from fat); FAT 7.4g (sat 1.4g, mono 2.1g, poly 3.5g); PROTEIN 4.5g; CARB 40.7g; FIBER 1.4g; CHOL 37mg; IRON 4.6mg; SODIUM 232mg; CALC 70mg EXCHANGES: 2½ Starch, 1 Fat

PECAN-CHOCOLATE CHIP SNACK CAKE

Pecans add crunch and provide heart-healthy monounsaturated fat.

½ cup all-purpose flour
¼ teaspoon baking soda
¼ teaspoon salt
¾ cup packed brown sugar
1 teaspoon vanilla extract
2 large egg whites
⅓ cup chopped pecans
¼ cup semisweet chocolate chips
Cooking spray
2 teaspoons powdered sugar

1. Preheat oven to 350°.

2. Spoon flour into a dry measuring cup; level with a knife. Combine flour, baking soda, and salt, stirring with a whisk.

3. Combine brown sugar, vanilla, and egg whites; beat with a mixer at high speed for 1 minute. Add flour mixture, beating just until combined. Stir in pecans and chocolate chips. Spread batter into an 8-inch square baking pan coated with cooking spray. Bake bars at 350° for 18 minutes or until golden and crusty on top. Cool in pan 10 minutes. Sprinkle with powdered sugar. Yield: 16 servings (serving size: 1 square).

CALORIES 87 (27% from fat); FAT 2.6g (sat 0.6g, mono 1.3g, poly 0.6g); PROTEIN 1.2g; CARB 15.4g; FIBER 0.5g; CHOL 0mg; IRON 0.5mg; SODIUM 68mg; CALC 12mg EXCHANGE: 1 Starch

LEMON PUDDING CAKE

Butter and margarine both have the same amount of calories and total fat, and either works well in this recipe.

3 large egg whites
⅔ cup sugar, divided
¼ cup all-purpose flour
1½ cups 1% low-fat milk
2 large egg yolks
4 teaspoons grated lemon rind
¼ cup fresh lemon juice
1 tablespoon butter or margarine, melted and cooled slightly
1 teaspoon vanilla extract
   Cooking spray
2 tablespoons sifted powdered sugar

1. Preheat oven to 325°.
2. In a large bowl, beat egg whites with a mixer at high speed until foamy. Gradually add ¼ cup sugar, 1 tablespoon at a time, beating until stiff peaks form. Set aside.
3. Lightly spoon flour into a dry measuring cup; level with a knife. Combine flour and remaining sugar in a medium bowl; add milk, egg yolks, and lemon rind, stirring with a whisk until smooth. Stir in lemon juice, butter, and vanilla (batter will be very thin). Add about one-fourth batter to beaten egg whites, stirring well. Stir remaining batter into egg white mixture.
4. Pour mixture into an 8-inch square baking dish coated with cooking spray.

Place dish in a 13 x 9-inch baking pan; add hot water to pan to a depth of 1 inch. Bake at 325° for 45 minutes or until lightly browned and sides begin to pull away from pan. Let stand in pan 5 minutes. Remove dish from pan; cool 15 minutes. Sprinkle top with powdered sugar; serve warm. Yield: 6 servings.

CALORIES 192 (21% from fat); FAT 4.5g (sat 2.2g, mono 1.4g, poly 0.4g); PROTEIN 5.2g; CARB 33g; FIBER 0.2g; CHOL 80mg; IRON 0.5mg; SODIUM 78mg; CALC 86mg EXCHANGES: 2 Starch, 1 Fat

CRANBERRY-CHOCOLATE CHIP BISCOTTI

Serve these crisp cookies with coffee for a great low-fat ending to a holiday dinner.

2¾ cups all-purpose flour
1 cup sugar
½ cup dried cranberries
⅓ cup semisweet chocolate chips
2 teaspoons baking powder
⅛ teaspoon salt
1 tablespoon vegetable oil
1 teaspoon almond extract
1 teaspoon vanilla extract
3 large eggs
   Cooking spray

1. Preheat oven to 350°.
2. Lightly spoon flour into dry measuring cups, and level with a knife. Combine flour and next 5 ingredients in

a large bowl. Combine oil, extracts, and eggs; add to flour mixture, stirring until well blended (dough will be dry and crumbly). Turn dough out onto a lightly floured surface; knead lightly 7 to 8 times. Divide dough in half. Shape each portion into an 8-inch-long roll. Place rolls 6 inches apart on a baking sheet coated with cooking spray; flatten each roll to 1-inch thickness.

3. Bake at 350° for 35 minutes. Remove rolls from baking sheet; cool 10 minutes on a wire rack.

4. Cut each roll diagonally into 15 (½-inch) slices. Place slices, cut sides down, on baking sheet. Reduce oven temperature to 325°, and bake for 10 minutes. Turn cookies over; bake an additional 10 minutes (cookies will be slightly soft in center but will harden as they cool). Remove from baking sheet; cool completely on wire rack. Yield: 2½ dozen (serving size: 1 biscotto).

CALORIES 98 (17% from fat); FAT 1.8g (sat 0.7g, mono 0.6g, poly 0.4g); PROTEIN 2g; CARB 18.6g; FIBER 0.4g; CHOL 22mg; IRON 0.7mg; SODIUM 50mg; CALC 24mg EXCHANGE: 1 Starch

ESPRESSO MERINGUE COOKIES

4 large egg whites
¼ teaspoon cream of tartar
¼ teaspoon salt
1 cup sugar
1½ tablespoons instant espresso granules
1 teaspoon vanilla extract
36 whole coffee beans
1 teaspoon unsweetened cocoa

1. Adjust oven racks to divide oven into even thirds and preheat oven to 250°.

2. Beat egg whites, cream of tartar, and salt with a mixer at high speed until foamy. Add sugar, 1 tablespoon at a time, beating until stiff peaks form. Add espresso granules and vanilla; beat until well blended.

3. Cover 2 baking sheets with parchment paper; secure with masking tape. Drop batter by level tablespoons onto baking sheets. Top each with 1 coffee bean. Sprinkle evenly with cocoa. Bake at 250° for 2 hours or until dry. Turn oven off, and partially open oven door; leave meringues in oven 1 hour. Remove from oven; carefully remove from paper. Cool completely on wire racks. Store at room temperature in an airtight container. Yield: 3 dozen (serving size: 1 cookie).

CALORIES 24 (0% from fat); FAT 0g (sat 0g, mono 0g, poly 0g); PROTEIN 0.4g; CARB 5.7g; FIBER 0g; CHOL 0mg; IRON 0mg; SODIUM 22mg; CALC 1mg EXCHANGE: ½ Starch

Spicy Oatmeal Crisps

Pepper may sound like an odd ingredient for a cookie, but it complements the other spices well in this flavorful, reduced-fat cookie.

- ¾ cup all-purpose flour
- 1 teaspoon ground cinnamon
- ½ teaspoon baking soda
- ½ teaspoon ground allspice
- ½ teaspoon grated whole nutmeg
- ¼ teaspoon salt
- ¼ teaspoon ground cloves
- ¼ teaspoon freshly ground black pepper (optional)
- 1 cup packed brown sugar
- 5 tablespoons butter or stick margarine, softened
- 1 teaspoon vanilla extract
- 1 large egg
- ½ cup regular oats
- Cooking spray

1. Preheat oven to 350°.

2. Lightly spoon flour into dry measuring cups; level with a knife. Combine flour and next 6 ingredients, and pepper, if desired, in a medium bowl. Beat sugar, butter, and vanilla in a large bowl with a mixer at medium speed until light and fluffy. Add egg; beat well. Stir in flour mixture and oats.

3. Drop by level tablespoons 2 inches apart onto baking sheets coated with cooking spray. Bake at 350° for 12 minutes or until crisp. Cool on pan 2 to 3 minutes or until firm. Remove cookies from pan; cool on wire racks. Yield: 2 dozen (serving size: 1 cookie).

CALORIES 81 (34% from fat); FAT 3.1g (sat 1.7g, mono 0.9g, poly 0.3g); PROTEIN 1.5g; CARB 12.2g; FIBER 0.7g; CHOL 15mg; IRON 0.6mg; SODIUM 71mg; CALC 12mg EXCHANGE: 1 Starch

Puffed-Up Chocolate-Chip Cookies

These chocolate-chip cookies are low in fat because some of the fat normally used is replaced with applesauce.

- 1¼ cups all-purpose flour
- 1½ teaspoons baking powder
- ¾ teaspoon salt
- ½ cup applesauce
- 1 cup packed brown sugar
- ¼ cup butter, softened
- 1 tablespoon vanilla extract
- 1 large egg
- 1 cup semisweet chocolate chips
- Cooking spray

1. Preheat oven to 375°.

2. Lightly spoon flour into dry measuring cups; level with a knife. Combine flour, baking powder, and salt in a small bowl; stir well with a whisk.

3. Spoon applesauce into a fine sieve over a bowl; let stand 15 minutes.

4. Discard liquid. Scrape drained applesauce into a large bowl. Add sugar and butter; beat with a mixer at medium speed until light and fluffy (about 2 minutes). Beat in vanilla and egg. Add flour mixture; beat at low speed until well blended. Fold in chips.

5. Drop by level tablespoons 2 inches apart onto baking sheets coated with cooking spray. Bake at 375° for 10 minutes or until almost set. Cool on pan 2 to 3 minutes or until firm. Remove cookies from pan; cool on wire racks. Yield: 3 dozen (serving size: 1 cookie).

CALORIES 78 (33% from fat); FAT 2.9g (sat 1.7g, mono 0.9g, poly 0.2g); PROTEIN 0.8g; CARB 12.8g; FIBER 0.2g; CHOL 10mg; IRON 0.5mg; SODIUM 87mg; CALC 20mg EXCHANGE: 1 Starch

ULTRADECADENT DOUBLE-CHIP BROWNIES

Using drained applesauce instead of oil or butter in this recipe produces a surprisingly rich, moist brownie.

1¼	cups applesauce
2½	cups sugar
2	teaspoons vanilla extract
2	large eggs, lightly beaten
2	large egg whites, lightly beaten
1½	cups all-purpose flour
1	cup unsweetened cocoa
¾	teaspoon salt
½	cup semisweet chocolate minichips
½	cup vanilla-flavored baking chips
	Cooking spray

1. Preheat oven to 350°.

2. Spoon applesauce into a fine sieve over a bowl; let stand 15 minutes.

3. Discard liquid. Scrape drained applesauce into a large bowl. Add sugar, vanilla, eggs, and egg whites; stir well.

4. Lightly spoon flour into dry measuring cups; level with a knife. Combine flour, cocoa, and salt, stirring well with a whisk. Add to applesauce mixture; stir just until moist. Fold in chips.

5. Spoon batter into a 13 x 9-inch baking pan coated with cooking spray, and bake at 350° for 45 minutes. Cool on a wire rack. Yield: 2 dozen (serving size: 1 brownie).

CALORIES 175 (17% from fat); FAT 3.3g (sat 1.8g, mono 1.1g, poly 0.2g); PROTEIN 3.1g; CARB 34.4g; FIBER 0.4g; CHOL 19mg; IRON 1.2mg; SODIUM 89mg; CALC 18mg EXCHANGES: 2 Starch, ½ Fat

FAT REPLACERS

Fat has unique characteristics that are important for taste and texture in baked goods.

Carbohydrate-based fat replacers such as applesauce, pureed prunes, and commercial fruit-based butter and oil substitutes, can be used successfully in baked products because they add flavor and approximate the "mouth-feel" of fat. These fat replacers work because the pectin in fruit helps hold moisture in the product and creates a texture in baked goods that is similar to that provided by butter or margarine.

Individual Chocolate Soufflés

Here's an elegant chocolate indulgence for a special occasion.

Cooking spray
4 teaspoons granulated sugar
1 cup water
½ cup powdered sugar
¼ cup unsweetened cocoa
¼ cup 1% low-fat milk
1 tablespoon all-purpose flour
2 large egg yolks
¼ teaspoon vanilla extract
2 large egg whites
¼ teaspoon cream of tartar
2 tablespoons granulated sugar
4 teaspoons powdered sugar

1. Preheat oven to 350°.
2. Coat 4 (8-ounce) ramekins with cooking spray, and sprinkle with 4 teaspoons granulated sugar. Place ramekins on a baking sheet; set aside.
3. Combine water and next 5 ingredients in the top of a double boiler. Cook over simmering water until thick (about 10 minutes), stirring constantly with a whisk. Remove from heat; add vanilla.
4. Beat egg whites and cream of tartar with a mixer at high speed until soft peaks form. Gradually add 2 tablespoons granulated sugar, beating until stiff peaks form. Fold one-fourth of egg white mixture into chocolate mixture;

gently fold in remaining egg white mixture. Spoon evenly into prepared ramekins. Bake at 350° for 20 minutes or until puffy and set. Sprinkle each soufflé with 1 teaspoon powdered sugar. Serve immediately. Yield: 4 servings.

Note: For a romantic dinner, just half this recipe and make two soufflés. See the recipe for two on page 456.

CALORIES 188 (19% from fat); FAT 3.9g (sat 1.4g, mono 1.4g, poly 0.6g); PROTEIN 5.4g; CARB 33g; FIBER 0g; CHOL 110mg; IRON 1.4mg; SODIUM 41mg; CALC 40mg EXCHANGES: 2 Starch, ½ Fat

Simple Strawberry Mousse

2 cups quartered strawberries
3 tablespoons sugar
½ cup low-fat sour cream
1½ cups frozen reduced-calorie whipped topping, thawed

1. Combine strawberries and sugar in a blender; process until smooth. Combine strawberry puree and sour cream in a large bowl, stirring well with a whisk. Fold topping into strawberry mixture.
2. Spoon into 6 (6-ounce) custard cups. Cover and freeze 4 hours or until firm. Yield: 6 servings.

CALORIES 102 (41% from fat); FAT 4.7g (sat 3.6g, mono 0.7g, poly 0.2g); PROTEIN 1.4g; CARB 14.5g; FIBER 1.2g; CHOL 8mg; IRON 0.2mg; SODIUM 20mg; CALC 40mg EXCHANGES: 1 Fruit, 1 Fat

CHOCOLATE BREAD PUDDING

Chocolate contains flavenoids, which may help reduce the risk of heart disease. For more information on flavenoids, see page 64.

1⅔ cups fat-free milk, divided
3 tablespoons semisweet chocolate chips
1 (1-ounce) square unsweetened chocolate, chopped
½ cup sugar
½ teaspoon vanilla extract
2 large eggs, lightly beaten
4 cups (1-inch) cubes stale French bread (about 4 ounces)
Cooking spray

1. Preheat oven to 350°.
2. Combine 1 cup milk and chocolates in a large microwave-safe bowl. Microwave at HIGH 3 minutes or until chocolate melts, stirring every minute.
3. Add remaining ⅔ cup milk, sugar, vanilla, and eggs; stir well. Add bread cubes; toss well to coat. Let stand 10 minutes. Spoon mixture into an 8-inch square baking dish coated with cooking spray. Bake at 350° for 25 minutes or until set. Yield: 9 servings.

CALORIES 145 (29% from fat); FAT 4.4g (sat 2.1g, mono 1.6g, poly 0.3g); PROTEIN 4.6g; CARB 23.3g; FIBER 0.5g; CHOL 48mg; IRON 0.8mg; SODIUM 121mg; CALC 75mg EXCHANGES: 1½ Starch, 1 Fat

APRICOT-CRANBERRY TARTS

1 (15-ounce) package refrigerated pie dough (such as Pillsbury)
1 cup chopped dried apricots
1 cup golden raisins
½ cup sweetened dried cranberries
½ cup dark rum
½ cup pineapple juice
3 tablespoons honey
1 tablespoon butter
¼ teaspoon ground cinnamon
⅛ teaspoon salt

1. Preheat oven to 425°.
2. Roll each dough portion into a 12-inch circle on a floured surface. Cut into 36 circles with a 2½-inch round cutter. Press 1 dough circle into each of 36 miniature muffin cups. Press into bottoms and up sides of cups. Bake at 425° for 7 minutes. Remove from pans; cool on wire racks.
3. Combine apricots and next 4 ingredients in a saucepan; bring to a boil. Reduce heat; simmer 10 minutes or until liquid is absorbed. Stir in honey and remaining ingredients. Cool. Spoon about 2 teaspoons apricot mixture into each shell. Yield: 3 dozen (serving size: 1 tart).

CALORIES 94 (38% from fat); FAT 4g (sat 1.1g, mono 1.7g, poly 1g); PROTEIN 1g; CARB 14.2g; FIBER 1.1g; CHOL 1mg; IRON 0.6mg; SODIUM 69mg; CALC 7mg EXCHANGES: ½ Starch, ½ Fruit, 1 Fat

CHOCOLATE-CREAM PIE

Here's a pie you can "wow" your friends and family with when you're asked to bring dessert. They'll never guess it's not a full-fat cream pie (which has about 360 calories and 22 grams of fat per slice).

CRUST:
- 40 graham crackers (10 full sheets)
- 2 tablespoons sugar
- 2 tablespoons butter or margarine, melted
- 1 large egg white

Cooking spray

FILLING:
- 2 cups fat-free milk, divided
- 2/3 cup sugar
- 1/3 cup unsweetened cocoa
- 3 tablespoons cornstarch
- 1/8 teaspoon salt
- 1 large egg
- 2 ounces semisweet chocolate, chopped
- 1 teaspoon vanilla extract
- 1 1/2 cups frozen reduced-calorie whipped topping, thawed
- 3/4 teaspoon grated semisweet chocolate

1. Preheat oven to 350°.

2. To prepare crust, place crackers in a food processor; process until crumbly. Add 2 tablespoons sugar, butter, and egg white; pulse 6 times or just until moist. Press mixture into a 9-inch pie plate coated with cooking spray. Bake at 350° for 8 minutes; cool on a wire rack 15 minutes.

3. To prepare filling, combine 1/2 cup milk, 2/3 cup sugar, and next 4 ingredients in a large bowl, stirring with a whisk. Heat 1 1/2 cups milk in a heavy saucepan over medium-high heat to 180° or until tiny bubbles form around edges (do not boil). Remove from heat. Gradually add hot milk to sugar mixture, stirring constantly with a whisk. Return milk mixture to pan. Add chopped chocolate; cook over medium heat until thick and bubbly (about 5 minutes), stirring constantly. Reduce heat to low; cook 2 minutes, stirring constantly. Remove from heat; stir in vanilla. Pour into prepared crust; cover surface of filling with plastic wrap. Chill 3 hours or until cold. Remove plastic wrap; spread whipped topping evenly over filling. Sprinkle with grated chocolate. Yield: 10 servings (serving size: 1 wedge).

CALORIES 242 (30% from fat); FAT 8g (sat 4.6g, mono 2.1g, poly 0.8g); PROTEIN 5g; CARB 38.5g; FIBER 0.1g; CHOL 30mg; IRON 1.4mg; SODIUM 189mg; CALC 83mg
EXCHANGES: 2 Starch, 2 Fat

FROZEN BUTTERFINGER PIE

At last, a reduced-fat pie for candy bar lovers. It uses only 1 candy bar, but it tastes like it's full of them.

40	chocolate graham crackers (10 full sheets)
1½	tablespoons butter or margarine, melted
1	large egg white
	Cooking spray
4	cups vanilla fat-free frozen yogurt
3	tablespoons light-colored corn syrup
3	tablespoons creamy peanut butter
1	tablespoon fat-free milk
1	(2.1-ounce) chocolate-covered crispy peanut-buttery candy bar (such as Butterfinger), chopped

1. Preheat oven to 350°.

2. Place graham crackers in a food processor; pulse until crumbly. Add butter and egg white; pulse until moist. Press crumb mixture into a 9-inch pie plate coated with cooking spray. Bake at 350° for 8 minutes; cool on a wire rack 15 minutes. Freeze 15 minutes.

3. Remove yogurt from freezer, and let stand at room temperature for 15 minutes to soften. Spoon half of yogurt into prepared crust.

4. Combine corn syrup, peanut butter, and milk in a small bowl, stirring until smooth. Drizzle half of peanut butter mixture over yogurt in crust. Sprinkle with half of chopped candy bar. Repeat procedure with remaining yogurt, peanut butter mixture, and candy bar. Cover with plastic wrap, and freeze 3 hours or until firm. Yield: 9 servings (serving size: 1 wedge).

CALORIES 230 (30% from fat); FAT 7.6g (sat 2.5g, mono 2.8g, poly 1.1g); PROTEIN 6.1g; CARB 36.6g; FIBER 1g; CHOL 5mg; IRON 1.4mg; SODIUM 221mg; CALC 104mg EXCHANGES: 2 Starch, 1½ Fat

MAXIMIZE THE FLAVOR

Candy bars in a weight-loss book? Absolutely.

It's only one candy bar, but a small amount of intense flavor can go a long way in providing eating pleasure and satisfaction.

In our test kitchens, we've learned that you can "get more for your money" in terms of taste and texture when you use a small amount of a high-flavor ingredient instead of larger amounts of less flavorful items.

And, in case you're still worried about that candy bar, it's only adding 33 calories and 1.3 grams of fat to each serving of this pie.

Chapter 38

Fish and Shellfish

Eat more fish to lose weight and to
reduce the risk of heart disease.

CRISP-CRUSTED CATFISH

This tastes just like fried catfish, but
has about 69 percent less fat.

2 tablespoons light ranch dressing

2 large egg whites

6 tablespoons yellow cornmeal

¼ cup (1 ounce) grated fresh
Parmesan cheese

2 tablespoons all-purpose flour

¼ teaspoon ground red pepper

⅛ teaspoon salt

4 (6-ounce) farm-raised catfish
fillets

Cooking spray

4 lemon wedges

1. Preheat oven to 425°.
2. Combine dressing and egg whites in
a bowl, and stir with a whisk. Combine
cornmeal, cheese, flour, pepper, and salt
in a shallow dish. Dip fish in egg white
mixture; dredge in cornmeal mixture.
3. Place fish on a baking sheet coated
with cooking spray; bake at 425° for

12 minutes on each side or until lightly
browned and fish flakes easily when
tested with a fork. Serve with lemon
wedges. Yield: 4 servings.

CALORIES 313 (26% from fat); FAT 9.1g
(sat 2.8g, mono 3.6g, poly 3.3g);
PROTEIN 32.9g; CARB 14.3g; FIBER 1.1g;
CHOL 87mg; IRON 1.2mg; SODIUM 348mg;
CALC 101mg
EXCHANGES: 1 Starch, 4 Lean Meat

BLACKENED CATFISH

Double or triple this fat-free, high-flavor
spice mix and save the extra to use with
other seafood (such as shrimp), chicken,
pork, or even potatoes.

2 tablespoons paprika

1 tablespoon dried oregano

½ teaspoon salt

½ teaspoon freshly ground black
pepper

¼ teaspoon ground red pepper

4 (6-ounce) farm-raised catfish
fillets

2 teaspoons olive oil

1. Combine first 5 ingredients in a small bowl. Sprinkle both sides of fish with paprika mixture.

2. Heat oil in a large cast iron skillet over high heat. Add fish; cook 4 minutes on each side or until fish flakes easily with a fork. Yield: 4 servings.

CALORIES 232 (39% from fat); FAT 10.1g (sat 2.1g, mono 4.5g, poly 2.3g); PROTEIN 31.6g; CARB 2.9g; FIBER 1g; CHOL 99mg; IRON 3.1mg; SODIUM 402mg; CALC 93mg
EXCHANGES: 4 Lean Meat

ASIAN FLOUNDER

Steaming in the microwave cooks the fish quickly and keeps it moist. The unusual method of folding and arranging the fish is necessary because the food toward the edge of the dish cooks more rapidly than the food in the center.

8	green onions
1/4	cup minced fresh cilantro
1	tablespoon minced peeled fresh ginger
2	teaspoons dark sesame oil, divided
4	(6-ounce) flounder fillets, skinned
2	teaspoons rice vinegar
2	teaspoons low-sodium soy sauce
1/8	teaspoon salt
4	lemon slices

1. Remove green tops from onions; slice onion tops into 1-inch pieces to measure 1/4 cup; set aside. Reserve remaining onion tops for another use. Cut white portions of onions into 2-inch pieces.

2. Combine cilantro, ginger, and 1 teaspoon oil in a 9-inch pie plate. Fold each fillet in half crosswise. Arrange fish spokelike with thinnest portions pointing toward center of dish. Arrange white onion portions between each fillet. Combine 1/4 cup green onion tops, 1 teaspoon oil, vinegar, soy sauce, and salt; pour over fish. Cover with heavy-duty plastic wrap. Microwave at HIGH 4 minutes or until fish flakes easily when tested with a fork. Garnish each fillet with a lemon slice. Yield: 4 servings.

CALORIES 188 (21% from fat); FAT 4.4g (sat 0.8g, mono 1.3g, poly 1.5g); PROTEIN 32.8g; CARB 2.7g; FIBER 0.9g; CHOL 82mg; IRON 1.3mg; SODIUM 299mg; CALC 57mg
EXCHANGES: 4 Very Lean Meat

EAT MORE FISH

Because fish is so low in fat and offers protection against heart disease, most of the recipes in this chapter call for 6 ounces of fish per serving instead of the 4-ounce portions used for beef, pork, and poultry recipes.

Baked Grouper with Two-Pepper Relish

The low-fat pepper relish on this fish is packed with vitamin C, a vitamin that helps prevent heart disease.

1/3 cup chopped pitted kalamata olives
2 tablespoons minced fresh parsley
1 tablespoon extra-virgin olive oil
2 teaspoons red wine vinegar
1 1/2 teaspoons minced fresh or 1/2 teaspoon dried thyme
1/4 teaspoon salt
1 yellow bell pepper, roasted, peeled, and chopped
1 red bell pepper, roasted, peeled, and chopped
1 garlic clove, minced
6 (6-ounce) grouper fillets
1/4 teaspoon salt
1/4 teaspoon black pepper
Cooking spray
1/3 cup dry white wine
Thyme sprigs (optional)

1. Preheat oven to 375°.
2. Combine first 9 ingredients in a bowl.
3. Sprinkle fish with 1/4 teaspoon salt and black pepper. Place fish in a 13 x 9-inch baking dish coated with cooking spray. Add wine to baking dish. Bake at 375° for 24 minutes or until fish flakes easily when tested with a fork. Serve with pepper relish. Garnish with thyme sprigs, if desired. Yield: 6 servings (serving size: 1 fillet and about 1/4 cup relish).

CALORIES 225 (29% from fat); FAT 7.2g (sat 1g, mono 3.4g, poly 1.8g); PROTEIN 35.8g; CARB 2.4g; FIBER 0.7g; CHOL 80mg; IRON 2.2mg; SODIUM 355mg; CALC 96mg
EXCHANGES: 1 Vegetable, 5 Very Lean Meat

Hoisin Halibut

Update your pantry with a few flavorful low-fat ingredients such as hoisin sauce, rice vinegar, and chile paste with garlic. They'll come in handy for many other Asian-style dishes.

8 ounces uncooked rice sticks (rice-flour noodles) or 3/4 pound vermicelli
1/4 cup hoisin sauce, divided
1 cup sliced green onions
1/2 cup fat-free, less-sodium chicken broth
3 tablespoons rice vinegar
3 tablespoons low-sodium soy sauce
1 tablespoon vegetable oil
1 tablespoon grated peeled fresh ginger
1 teaspoon chile paste with garlic
1/8 teaspoon freshly ground black pepper
8 (6-ounce) halibut steaks (about 1 inch thick)
Cooking spray

1. Preheat broiler.
2. Cook noodles according to package

directions. Combine cooked noodles, 2 tablespoons hoisin sauce, and next 8 ingredients in a large bowl; keep warm.

3. Rub fish with 2 tablespoons hoisin sauce. Place fish on a broiler pan coated with cooking spray; broil 4 minutes on each side or until fish flakes easily when tested with a fork. Serve over noodles. Yield: 8 servings (serving size: 1 halibut steak and ¾ cup noodles).

CALORIES 323 (17% from fat); FAT 6.3g (sat 0.9g, mono 1.9g, poly 2.3g); PROTEIN 37.5g; CARB 27.6g; FIBER 0.5g; CHOL 53mg; IRON 1.9mg; SODIUM 455mg; CALC 109mg
EXCHANGES: 2 Starch, 4 Very Lean Meat

CAESAR MAHIMAHI

Award yourself double health points for grilling fish: Fish is a heart-healthy low-fat food, and grilling is an easy low-fat cooking method.

- ¼ cup plain fat-free yogurt
- 2 tablespoons grated Parmesan cheese
- 2 tablespoons fresh lemon juice
- 2 tablespoons low-fat buttermilk
- 1 tablespoon Dijon mustard
- 2 teaspoons Worcestershire sauce
- 2 teaspoons anchovy paste
- ¼ teaspoon black pepper
- 6 garlic cloves, crushed
- 4 (6-ounce) mahimahi or other firm white fish fillets

Cooking spray

1. Combine first 9 ingredients, and stir well with a whisk. Pour yogurt mixture into a large zip-top plastic bag, and add fish to bag. Seal and marinate in refrigerator 20 minutes.

2. Prepare grill or broiler.

3. Remove fish from bag, reserving marinade. Place fish on grill rack or broiler pan coated with cooking spray, and cook 3 minutes on each side or until fish flakes easily when tested with a fork, basting frequently with reserved marinade. Yield: 4 servings.

CALORIES 193 (14% from fat); FAT 3g (sat 0.8g, mono 0.4g, poly 0.3g); PROTEIN 34.7g; CARB 4.7g; FIBER 0.1g; CHOL 127mg; IRON 2.1mg; SODIUM 728mg; CALC 84mg
EXCHANGES: ½ Starch, 4 Very Lean Meat

FISHING FOR HAPPINESS

The dietary path to happiness may begin at the fish market. Scientists say that depression rates are lowest in nations where seafood is a staple. And there is evidence that fish oil can give people with mental illness a boost. One study showed that patients with manic depression had fewer episodes of mania and depression if they took fish oil capsules.

Mahimahi with Balsamic-Wine Sauce

Balsamic vinegar adds a slightly sweet, rich flavor to the wine sauce, and, like other vinegars, has essentially no calories and zero grams of fat.

4   (6-ounce) mahimahi fillets
¼   teaspoon salt
⅛   teaspoon black pepper
2   teaspoons olive oil
¼   cup finely chopped red onion
1   cup dry white wine
¼   cup balsamic vinegar
1   tablespoon capers
1   tablespoon chopped fresh parsley

1. Sprinkle fish with salt and pepper.
2. Heat olive oil in a large nonstick skillet over medium-high heat. Add fish and onion; cook 3 minutes. Turn fish over. Stir in wine, vinegar, and capers; cook 3 minutes. Remove fish from pan. Cook wine mixture 3 minutes or until reduced to ½ cup. Serve sauce with fish; sprinkle with parsley. Yield: 4 servings (serving size: 1 fillet and 2 tablespoons sauce).

CALORIES 182 (17% from fat); FAT 3.5g (sat 0.6g, mono 1.9g, poly 0.5g); PROTEIN 31.8g; CARB 4.2g; FIBER 0.3g; CHOL 124mg; IRON 2.4mg; SODIUM 369mg; CALC 39mg
EXCHANGES: 1 Vegetable, 4 Very Lean Meat

Lemon-Dill Pollock

The tangy low-fat marinade on this fish works well on any mild-flavored white fish such as flounder, sole, or orange roughy.

⅓   cup minced fresh dill
¼   cup fresh lemon juice
1   tablespoon olive oil
4   teaspoons Dijon mustard
¼   teaspoon salt
¼   teaspoon sugar
¼   teaspoon black pepper
1   garlic clove, minced
4   (6-ounce) pollock or other firm white fish fillets
Cooking spray

1. Combine all ingredients except cooking spray in a large zip-top plastic bag; seal and marinate in refrigerator 20 minutes. Remove fish from bag; discard marinade.
2. Prepare grill or broiler.
3. Place fish on grill rack or broiler pan coated with cooking spray. Cook 4 minutes on each side or until fish flakes easily when tested with a fork. Yield: 4 servings.

CALORIES 180 (19% from fat); FAT 3.7g (sat 0.5g, mono 1.5g, poly 1g); PROTEIN 33.2g; CARB 1.4g; FIBER 0.1g; CHOL 121mg; IRON 1.1mg; SODIUM 292mg; CALC 114mg
EXCHANGES: 4 Very Lean Meat

Baked Snapper with Tomato-Orange Sauce

This fish dish is full of disease-fighting vitamin C from both the tomatoes and the orange juice.

3   cups chopped red tomato
2   cups chopped yellow tomato
½   cup chopped onion
¼   cup dry white wine
1   teaspoon grated orange rind
¼   cup fresh orange juice
⅛   teaspoon ground turmeric
2   garlic cloves, minced
4   (6-ounce) red snapper, grouper, or other firm white fish fillets
1   teaspoon olive oil
¼   teaspoon salt
⅛   teaspoon black pepper

1. Preheat oven to 400°.
2. Combine first 8 ingredients in an 11 x 7-inch baking dish. Bake at 400° for 20 minutes. Arrange fish on top of tomato mixture. Drizzle with oil; sprinkle with salt and pepper. Cover with foil; bake 20 minutes or until fish flakes easily when tested with a fork. Yield: 4 servings (serving size: 1 fillet and 1 cup sauce).

CALORIES 246 (15% from fat); FAT 4.2g
(sat 0.7g, mono 1.4g, poly 1.2g);
PROTEIN 37.3g; CARB 14.9g; FIBER 2.9g;
CHOL 63mg; IRON 1.5mg; SODIUM 278mg;
CALC 77mg
EXCHANGES: 3 Vegetable, 5 Very Lean Meat

Potato-Crusted Snapper

Instant potato flakes make an amazingly crispy coating for fish and chicken.

½   cup low-fat buttermilk
¼   teaspoon salt
¼   teaspoon black pepper
2   garlic cloves, minced
¾   cup instant potato flakes (not granules)
4   (6-ounce) red snapper or mahimahi fillets
1   tablespoon butter or margarine
4   lemon wedges

1. Combine first 4 ingredients in a shallow dish. Place potato flakes in another shallow dish. Dip fillets in buttermilk mixture; dredge in potato flakes.
2. Melt butter in a large nonstick skillet over medium-high heat. Add fish; cook 3 minutes on each side or until golden and fish flakes easily when tested with a fork. Serve with lemon wedges. Yield: 4 servings.

CALORIES 244 (21% from fat); FAT 5.7g
(sat 1.4g, mono 1.8g, poly 1.7g);
PROTEIN 36.9g; CARB 9.2g; FIBER 0.4g;
CHOL 63mg; IRON 0.5mg; SODIUM 316mg;
CALC 101mg
EXCHANGES: 1 Starch, 5 Very Lean Meat

VERACRUZ SNAPPER

Canned and bottled tomato products such as diced tomatoes and salsa are high in lycopene, a substance that appears to help prevent prostate cancer.

 4   (6-ounce) red snapper fillets
Cooking spray
 ½   teaspoon ground cumin
 ¼   teaspoon salt
 ¼   teaspoon ground red pepper
 ¼   cup chopped fresh cilantro
 ¼   cup chopped pitted green olives
 ¼   cup bottled salsa
 1   (16-ounce) can pinto beans, drained
 1   (14.5-ounce) can diced tomatoes, drained

1. Preheat broiler.
2. Coat both sides of fish with cooking spray. Sprinkle fish with cumin, salt, and pepper. Place fish on a broiler pan coated with cooking spray; cook 5 minutes on each side or until fish flakes easily when tested with a fork.
3. Combine cilantro and remaining ingredients. Serve fish with salsa mixture. Yield: 4 servings (serving size: 1 fillet and ½ cup salsa).

CALORIES 202 (14% from fat); FAT 3.2g
(sat 0.5g, mono 1g, poly 1.2g); PROTEIN 28.2g;
CARB 14.6g; FIBER 5.2g; CHOL 42mg;
IRON 1.9mg; SODIUM 571mg; CALC 94mg
EXCHANGES: 1 Starch, 4 Very Lean Meat

SPICY HERB-GRILLED SALMON STEAKS

There's no need for added fat in this recipe. The flavor comes from the lightly charred, smoky-rich salmon and a lively sauce of fresh herbs, ginger, and chile peppers.

 ½   cup basil leaves
 ⅓   cup mint leaves
 3   tablespoons minced seeded jalapeño pepper
 2   tablespoons white vinegar
 2½ teaspoons minced peeled fresh ginger
 1   teaspoon sugar
 2   teaspoons fish sauce
 2   garlic cloves, chopped
 4   (6-ounce) salmon steaks (about 1 inch thick)
 ½   teaspoon salt
 ⅛   teaspoon black pepper
Cooking spray
 ¼   cup finely chopped fresh basil
 4   lime wedges

1. Prepare grill.
2. Combine first 8 ingredients in a blender or food processor, and process until smooth. Set aside.
3. Sprinkle fish with salt and black pepper. Place fish on grill rack coated with cooking spray, and grill 5 minutes on each side or until fish flakes easily when tested with a fork. Spoon sauce

over fish, and garnish with chopped basil and lime wedges. Yield: 4 servings (serving size: 1 steak and 2 tablespoons sauce).

CALORIES 293 (44% from fat); FAT 14.2g
(sat 2.5g, mono 6.8g, poly 3.2g);
PROTEIN 35.5g; CARB 3.7g; FIBER 0.3g;
CHOL 111mg; IRON 0.9mg; SODIUM 596mg;
CALC 27mg
EXCHANGES: 5 Lean Meat

INDIAN-SPICED ROAST SALMON

Salmon is packed with good-for-your-heart fatty acids, so when you eat salmon you can reduce your risk of developing heart disease.

1	teaspoon ground cumin
1	teaspoon ground coriander
½	teaspoon ground turmeric
½	teaspoon dried thyme
½	teaspoon fennel seeds, crushed
½	teaspoon black pepper
¼	teaspoon ground cinnamon
⅛	teaspoon ground cloves
4	(6-ounce) salmon fillets (about 1¼ inches thick)
½	teaspoon salt
1	teaspoon olive oil
¼	cup plain fat-free yogurt
4	lemon wedges

1. Heat oven to 400°.
2. Combine first 8 ingredients in a shallow dish. Sprinkle fillets with salt; dredge fillets in spice mixture. Heat oil in a large skillet over medium-high heat. Add fillets, skin sides up; cook 5 minutes or until bottoms are golden. Turn fillets over. Wrap handle of pan with foil; bake at 400° for 10 minutes or until fish flakes easily when tested with a fork. Remove skin from fillets; discard skin. Serve with yogurt and lemon wedges. Yield: 4 servings (serving size: 1 fillet, 1 tablespoon yogurt, and 1 lemon wedge).

CALORIES 301 (46% from fat); FAT 15.4g
(sat 2.7g, mono 7.7g, poly 3.2g);
PROTEIN 35.9g; CARB 2.6g; FIBER 0.3g;
CHOL 111mg; IRON 1.6mg; SODIUM 390mg;
CALC 54mg
EXCHANGES: 5 Lean Meat

HEART-HEALTHY FISH

The omega-3 fatty acids found in fish can help the heart in the following ways.
- maintain normal heart rhythm
- lower levels of triglycerides (blood fats linked to heart disease)
- act as a lubricant for the arteries so clots are less likely to form

TUNA-NOODLE CASSEROLE

A high-fat family favorite gets a makeover with the use of reduced-fat milk, reduced-fat soup, and water-packed tuna.

1	tablespoon butter or margarine
¾	cup diced onion
1	cup 2% reduced-fat milk
1	(10.5-ounce) can condensed reduced-fat cream of mushroom soup with cracked pepper and herbs, undiluted
3	cups cooked egg noodles (about 6 ounces uncooked pasta)
1¼	cups frozen green peas, thawed
1	tablespoon lemon juice
¼	teaspoon salt
¼	teaspoon black pepper
2	(6-ounce) cans low-sodium tuna in water, drained and flaked
1	(2-ounce) jar diced pimiento, drained
⅓	cup fresh breadcrumbs
2	tablespoons grated Parmesan cheese

1. Preheat oven to 450°.

2. Melt butter in a saucepan over medium-high heat. Add onion; sauté 3 minutes. Add milk and soup. Cook 3 minutes; stir constantly with a whisk. Combine soup mixture, noodles, and next 6 ingredients in a 2-quart casserole. Combine breadcrumbs and cheese; sprinkle over top. Bake at 450° for 15 minutes or until bubbly. Yield: 4 servings (serving size: 1¼ cups).

CALORIES 402 (17% from fat); FAT 7.7g (sat 2.2g, mono 2.4g, poly 1.5g); PROTEIN 28.8g; CARB 52.5g; FIBER 5.2g; CHOL 84mg; IRON 3.4mg; SODIUM 795mg; CALC 144mg
EXCHANGES: 3 Starch, 1 Vegetable, 2 Medium-Fat Meat

GRILLED TUNA STEAKS WITH GARLIC AND OREGANO

If you eat a 6-ounce tuna steak instead of the same size filet mignon, you'll save about 250 calories and 33 grams of fat.

⅓	cup dry white wine
1	tablespoon olive oil
2	teaspoons dried oregano
1	teaspoon salt
½	teaspoon freshly ground black pepper
2	garlic cloves, minced
6	(6-ounce) tuna steaks (about 1 inch thick)

Cooking spray

1. Combine first 6 ingredients in a large zip-top plastic bag, and add tuna steaks to bag. Seal bag, and marinate steaks in refrigerator 30 minutes or up to 2 hours. Remove tuna from bag, reserving marinade.

2. Prepare grill or broiler.

3. Place marinated fish on grill rack or broiler pan coated with cooking spray, and cook 4 minutes on each side or until fish is desired degree of doneness, basting frequently with reserved marinade. Yield: 6 servings (serving size: 1 tuna steak).

CALORIES 278 (35% from fat); FAT 10.8g (sat 2.5g, mono 4g, poly 3.1g); PROTEIN 39.8g; CARB 0.8g; FIBER 0.1g; CHOL 65mg; IRON 2.1mg; SODIUM 458mg; CALC 12mg EXCHANGES: 5 Lean Meat

PROVENÇALE GRILLED TUNA

Herbes de Provence is a blend of dried herbs commonly used in southern France. It usually contains basil, fennel, lavender, marjoram, rosemary, and sage.

1½	cups chopped seeded tomato (about 1½ pounds)
¾	cup chopped fresh parsley
¼	cup chopped pitted niçoise olives
1	tablespoon white wine vinegar
¼	teaspoon dried tarragon
¼	teaspoon salt
2	garlic cloves, minced
4	(6-ounce) tuna steaks (about ¾ inch thick)
1½	teaspoons dried herbes de Provence
¼	teaspoon salt
	Cooking spray
	Fresh chives (optional)

1. Combine first 7 ingredients in a medium bowl. Cover and chill 20 minutes.
2. Prepare grill.
3. Sprinkle fish with herbes de Provence and ¼ teaspoon salt. Place fish on grill rack coated with cooking spray; cook 3 minutes on each side or until fish is medium-rare or desired degree of doneness. Serve fish with tomato mixture. Garnish with chives, if desired. Yield: 4 servings (serving size: 1 tuna steak and ½ cup tomato mixture).

CALORIES 278 (31% from fat); FAT 9.7g (sat 2.4g, mono 3.1g, poly 3.1g); PROTEIN 40.8g; CARB 5g; FIBER 1.6g; CHOL 65mg; IRON 3.2mg; SODIUM 447mg; CALC 31mg EXCHANGES: 1 Vegetable, 5 Very Lean Meat

FISH SAFETY

Because of the mercury levels in certain types of fish, women who are considering pregnancy, or who are pregnant or nursing, should avoid the following fish: halibut, king mackerel, largemouth bass, marlin, pike, sea bass, shark, swordfish, tilefish, tuna steaks, walleye, white croaker, oysters from the Gulf of Mexico, and sport fish caught from waterways with fish advisories.

LINGUINE WITH CLAM SAUCE

Top your pasta with this low-fat tomato-based sauce rather than a high-fat cream sauce.

1 tablespoon olive oil
1 cup chopped Vidalia or other sweet onion
4 garlic cloves, minced
2 cups chopped seeded plum tomato
1 tablespoon chopped fresh parsley
1/4 teaspoon crushed red pepper
2 tablespoons water
36 littleneck clams or quahogs
1/8 teaspoon salt
4 cups hot cooked linguine (about 8 ounces uncooked pasta)

1. Heat olive oil in a medium nonstick skillet over medium-high heat. Add onion and garlic, and sauté 2 minutes. Add tomato, parsley, and crushed red pepper; cook 3 minutes, and set aside.
2. Add water and clams to a large Dutch oven over medium-high heat; cover and cook 4 minutes or until shells open. Remove clams from pan, and reserve 3/4 cup cooking liquid. Discard any unopened shells. Cool clams. Remove meat from shells.
3. Place cooking liquid in pan over medium-high heat until reduced to

1/2 cup (about 5 minutes). Add clams, cooking liquid, and salt to tomato mixture. Serve clam sauce over pasta. Yield: 4 servings (serving size: 1 cup pasta and 1/2 cup sauce).

CALORIES 312 (15% from fat); FAT 5.1g (sat 0.7g, mono 2.7g, poly 0.9g); PROTEIN 14.2g; CARB 52.4g; FIBER 3.3g; CHOL 14mg; IRON 8.8mg; SODIUM 111mg; CALC 50mg
EXCHANGES: 3 Starch, 1 Vegetable, 1 Very Lean Meat

CRAB CAKES

Instead of filling up on crab cakes for an appetizer, make larger patties and have them for your main dish.

1 pound lump crabmeat, shell pieces removed
1/2 cup crushed saltine crackers (about 12 crackers)
1/3 cup chopped fresh parsley
1/3 cup chopped bottled roasted red bell peppers
2 tablespoons plain low-fat yogurt
1 tablespoon water
1 tablespoon fresh lime juice
1/4 teaspoon hot sauce
1/4 teaspoon salt
1 large egg white, lightly beaten
1 tablespoon vegetable oil, divided

1. Combine all ingredients except oil in a large bowl. Divide crab mixture into 6 equal portions, shaping each into a 1-inch-thick patty.

2. Heat 1 1/2 teaspoons oil in a large nonstick skillet over medium-high heat. Add 3 patties; cook 4 minutes. Carefully turn patties over; cook 3 minutes or until golden. Repeat procedure with 1 1/2 teaspoons oil and remaining patties. Yield: 6 servings.

CALORIES 137 (30% from fat); FAT 4.6g
(sat 0.9g, mono 1.4g, poly 1.7g);
PROTEIN 16.9g; CARB 6.2g; FIBER 0.4g;
CHOL 76mg; IRON 1.3mg; SODIUM 457mg;
CALC 106mg
EXCHANGES: 1/2 Starch, 2 Lean Meat

PAN-SEARED SCALLOPS WITH GINGER-ORANGE SPINACH

Most of the alcohol and calories cook out of the vodka and vermouth, leaving only the flavor behind.

1	tablespoon julienne-cut peeled fresh ginger
1	tablespoon sliced green onions
4	garlic cloves, minced
20	sea scallops (about 1 1/2 pounds)
1/2	cup vodka
1/4	cup dry vermouth
1	teaspoon butter or margarine
1	teaspoon grated orange rind
1/3	cup fresh orange juice
1 1/2	pounds chopped spinach
1/2	teaspoon salt
1/8	teaspoon black pepper
	Cooking spray

1. Combine first 3 ingredients in a bowl.

2. Place scallops in a shallow dish. Add vodka, vermouth, and half of ginger mixture; toss gently. Cover and marinate in refrigerator 30 minutes.

3. Melt butter in a large skillet over high heat. Add remaining ginger mixture, and sauté 30 seconds. Add orange rind and juice, and bring to a boil. Stir in spinach, salt, and pepper; cook 2 minutes or until spinach wilts. Remove from pan, and keep warm.

4. Remove scallops from marinade, reserving marinade. Place pan coated with cooking spray over high heat until hot. Add scallops; cook 1 1/2 minutes on each side or until golden brown. Remove from pan; keep warm. Add reserved marinade to pan. Bring to a boil; cook until sauce is reduced to 1/4 cup (about 5 minutes).

5. Arrange scallops over spinach mixture; drizzle with sauce. Yield: 4 servings (serving size: 5 scallops, 3/4 cup spinach mixture, and 1 tablespoon sauce).

CALORIES 233 (13% from fat); FAT 3.3g
(sat 0.5g, mono 0.5g, poly 1g); PROTEIN 36.2g;
CARB 17.1g; FIBER 10.2g; CHOL 56mg;
IRON 7.5mg; SODIUM 799mg; CALC 302mg
EXCHANGES: 1 Starch, 5 Very Lean Meat

Portuguese-Style Scallops

Scallops are very low in fat with about 2 grams of fat per 5-ounce serving.

1½ pounds sea scallops
½ teaspoon salt
¼ teaspoon black pepper
1 tablespoon olive oil, divided
⅓ cup sweet red wine
2 tablespoons fresh lemon juice
¼ cup chopped fresh parsley
5 garlic cloves, minced
2 cups hot cooked long-grain rice

1. Sprinkle scallops with salt and pepper. Heat 1½ teaspoons oil in a 10-inch cast iron skillet over high heat until very hot (about 3 minutes). Add half of scallops; cook 2 minutes on each side. Remove scallops from pan; keep warm. Repeat with 1½ teaspoons oil and remaining scallops. Remove scallops from pan.
2. Stir in wine and lemon juice, scraping pan to loosen browned bits. Add scallops, 3 tablespoons parsley, and garlic; sauté 30 seconds. Serve over rice. Sprinkle with remaining 1 tablespoon parsley. Yield: 4 servings (serving size: 5 ounces scallops and ½ cup rice).

CALORIES 241 (15% from fat); FAT 3.9g
(sat 0.5g, mono 2.1g, poly 0.6g);
PROTEIN 24.8g; CARB 25g; FIBER 0.6g;
CHOL 45mg; IRON 1.4mg; SODIUM 456mg;
CALC 52mg
EXCHANGES: 2 Starch, 3 Very Lean Meat

Pasta Primavera with Shrimp

3 cups uncooked cavatappi (spiral tube-shaped pasta) or other short tube-shaped pasta
2 cups sugar snap peas, trimmed
1 tablespoon olive oil
1 pound medium shrimp, peeled and deveined
1 tablespoon chopped fresh oregano
¼ teaspoon salt
¼ teaspoon black pepper
2 garlic cloves, minced
4 cups torn spinach
1½ cups cherry tomatoes, halved
1 cup (4 ounces) crumbled feta cheese

1. Cook pasta in boiling water 6 minutes, omitting salt and fat. Add peas, and cook 2 minutes; drain.
2. Heat oil in a medium nonstick skillet over medium-high heat. Add shrimp, oregano, salt, pepper, and garlic; sauté 3 minutes or until shrimp are done. Combine pasta mixture, shrimp mixture, and remaining ingredients in a large bowl; toss well. Yield: 6 servings (serving size: about 1½ cups).

CALORIES 329 (23% from fat); FAT 8.5g
(sat 3.5g, mono 2.8g, poly 1.2g);
PROTEIN 25.6g; CARB 36.9g; FIBER 4.1g;
CHOL 131mg; IRON 5.7mg; SODIUM 458mg;
CALC 204mg
EXCHANGES: 2 Starch, 1 Vegetable, 3 Lean Meat

SOFT SHRIMP TACOS WITH TROPICAL SALSA

Here's a different taco twist: a spicy shrimp filling and fruity sweet salsa—all wrapped up in a low-fat flour tortilla.

SALSA:

- ¼ cup chopped green onions
- 1 tablespoon chopped fresh cilantro
- 1 tablespoon canned chopped green chiles
- 1 tablespoon lemon juice
- 1 (11-ounce) can mandarin oranges in light syrup, drained
- 1 (8-ounce) can pineapple tidbits in juice, drained

TACOS:

- Cooking spray
- 1 cup yellow bell pepper strips
- 1 cup vertically sliced red onion
- 1 garlic clove, minced
- 1½ pounds medium shrimp, peeled and deveined
- 1 cup chopped tomato
- ½ teaspoon ground cumin
- ½ teaspoon chili powder
- 2 tablespoons chopped fresh cilantro
- 8 (6-inch) flour tortillas
- 1¼ cups (5 ounces) shredded reduced-fat Monterey Jack cheese

1. To prepare salsa, combine first 6 ingredients in a bowl. Cover and chill.

2. To prepare tacos, place a large nonstick skillet coated with cooking spray over medium-high heat until hot. Add bell pepper, onion, and garlic; sauté 2 minutes. Add shrimp, tomato, cumin, and chili powder; sauté 3 minutes or until shrimp are done. Stir in cilantro. Spoon ½ cup shrimp mixture over one half of each tortilla, and top with about 3 tablespoons cheese and 2 tablespoons salsa; fold tortillas in half. Yield: 8 servings (serving size: 1 taco).

CALORIES 276 (24% from fat); FAT 7.3g (sat 2.6g, mono 2.2g, poly 1.7g); PROTEIN 22g; CARB 30.4g; FIBER 2.3g; CHOL 109mg; IRON 3.4mg; SODIUM 395mg; CALC 233mg EXCHANGES: 1 Starch, 1 Fruit, 3 Lean Meat

HEALTHY SHRIMP

Although shrimp is a little higher in cholesterol and sodium than many other types of seafood, it's still a terrific protein source with only 1 gram of fat per 3-ounce portion.

BARBECUE SHRIMP

This signature Creole-Sicilian favorite from New Orleans is reborn with a low-fat shortcut or two.

½ cup fat-free Caesar dressing
⅓ cup Worcestershire sauce
2 tablespoons butter or margarine
1 tablespoon dried oregano
1 tablespoon paprika
1 tablespoon dried rosemary
1 tablespoon dried thyme
1½ teaspoons black pepper
1 teaspoon hot pepper sauce
5 bay leaves
3 garlic cloves, minced
2 pounds large shrimp
⅓ cup dry white wine
10 (1-ounce) slices French bread baguette
10 lemon wedges

1. Combine first 11 ingredients in a large nonstick skillet; bring to a boil. Add shrimp, and cook 7 minutes, stirring occasionally. Add wine, and cook 1 minute or until shrimp are done. Serve with bread and lemon wedges. Yield: 5 servings (serving size: 5 ounces shrimp with sauce and 2 bread slices).

CALORIES 403 (20% from fat); FAT 9.1g
(sat 3.8g, mono 2.4g, poly 1.7g);
PROTEIN 34.4g; CARB 41.7g; FIBER 2.8g;
CHOL 219mg; IRON 7mg; SODIUM 1,021mg;
CALC 211mg
EXCHANGES: 3 Starch, 3 Lean Meat

SHRIMP AND FETA WITH ANGEL HAIR

Save yourself a little time and buy shrimp that has already been peeled and deveined from the seafood market or supermarket.

Cooking spray
2 pounds medium shrimp, peeled and deveined
2 cups chopped plum tomato (about ¾ pound)
1½ cups sliced green onions
½ cup sliced ripe olives
2 teaspoons dried dill
1 garlic clove, minced
4 cups hot cooked angel hair (about 8 ounces uncooked pasta)
1 cup (4 ounces) crumbled feta cheese

1. Heat a large nonstick skillet coated with cooking spray over medium-high heat. Add shrimp; cook 5 minutes, stirring frequently. Stir in tomato and next 4 ingredients; cook 4 minutes or until thoroughly heated. Combine shrimp mixture, pasta, and cheese in a large bowl; toss well. Yield: 6 servings (serving size: 1⅓ cups).

CALORIES 346 (21% from fat); FAT 8.2g
(sat 3.5g, mono 2.2g, poly 1.4g);
PROTEIN 31.7g; CARB 35.7g; FIBER 2.6g;
CHOL 189mg; IRON 5.5mg; SODIUM 490mg;
CALC 197mg
EXCHANGES: 2 Starch, 1 Vegetable, 3 Lean Meat

Chapter 39

Meatless Main Dishes

Fill up on hearty dishes packed with vegetables, grains, pastas, and soy-based products. Whether you're a vegetarian or simply cutting back on meat, these recipes are sure to satisfy.

FETA OMELET WITH BREADCRUMBS

Instead of using all whole eggs, this reduced-fat omelet has 4 whole eggs plus 4 egg whites. The yolk is the part of the egg that has the fat.

> 5 tablespoons water
> ¼ teaspoon salt
> 4 large eggs
> 4 large egg whites
> 1 tablespoon olive oil
> ¾ cup dry breadcrumbs
> ½ cup (2 ounces) crumbled feta cheese
> ¼ cup thinly sliced green onions
> 2 tablespoons chopped fresh parsley
> 1 tablespoon chopped fresh or 1 teaspoon dried oregano

1. Preheat broiler.

2. Combine first 4 ingredients in a bowl; stir well with a whisk. Heat oil in a 9-inch cast iron skillet over medium heat. Add breadcrumbs; cook 1 minute or until lightly browned. Spread egg mixture evenly in pan; top with cheese. Broil 15 minutes or until omelet is firm. Sprinkle with onions, parsley, and oregano. Cut into wedges. Yield: 6 servings (serving size: 1 wedge).

CALORIES 163 (47% from fat); FAT 8.5g (sat 3g, mono 3.8g, poly 0.9g); PROTEIN 9.7g; CARB 11.4g; FIBER 0.5g; CHOL 156mg; IRON 1.6mg; SODIUM 400mg; CALC 104mg EXCHANGES: 1 Starch, 1 High-Fat Meat

CHARD-BEAN FRITTATA

Beans and Swiss chard give you fiber, folate, B-vitamins, iron, and protein.

    7   large egg whites, lightly beaten
    2   large eggs, lightly beaten
  1/2   teaspoon salt
  1/4   teaspoon black pepper
    1   tablespoon finely chopped
        jalapeño pepper
    4   chopped pitted kalamata olives
    1   (16-ounce) can cannellini beans,
        rinsed and drained
    1   teaspoon olive oil
    2   cups torn Swiss chard or spinach
 1 1/2 cups chopped onion

1. Preheat broiler.

2. Combine egg whites, eggs, salt, and black pepper; stir with a whisk. Stir in jalapeño, olives, and beans.

3. Heat oil in a large nonstick skillet over medium-high heat. Add chard and onion; sauté 3 minutes. Pour egg mixture into pan; reduce heat to medium-low, and cook 10 minutes or until almost set.

4. Wrap handle of pan with foil. Broil egg mixture 4 minutes or until golden brown. Yield: 4 servings (serving size: 1 wedge).

CALORIES 193 (21% from fat); FAT 4.6g
(sat 1.2g, mono 2.2g, poly 0.7g);
PROTEIN 16.3g; CARB 22.6g; FIBER 4g;
CHOL 110mg; IRON 2.5mg; SODIUM 637mg;
CALC 90mg
EXCHANGES: 1 Starch, 1 Vegetable,
2 Lean Meat

CURRIED KIDNEY BEAN BURRITOS

This high-fiber "meal-in-a-tortilla" can be ready in under 30 minutes.

    1   tablespoon olive oil
 1 1/2 cups finely chopped onion
    1   tablespoon chopped jalapeño
        pepper
    1   teaspoon sugar
  1/2   teaspoon curry powder
    2   (14.5-ounce) cans diced
        tomatoes, drained
    2   (15-ounce) cans kidney beans,
        drained
    1   tablespoon minced fresh cilantro
    4   (8-inch) flour tortillas

1. Heat oil in a large nonstick skillet over medium-high heat. Add onion; sauté 6 minutes or until lightly browned. Add jalapeño, sugar, curry, and tomatoes; cover, reduce heat, and simmer 10 minutes. Add beans; cover and cook 3 minutes or until thoroughly heated; stir occasionally. Remove from heat; stir in cilantro.

2. Warm tortillas according to package directions. Spoon 1 1/4 cups bean mixture down center of each tortilla, and roll up. Yield: 4 servings (serving size: 1 burrito).

CALORIES 414 (17% from fat); FAT 8g (sat 1.6g,
mono 3.1g, poly 2.7g); PROTEIN 18.4g;
CARB 70.3g; FIBER 9.2g; CHOL 0mg;
IRON 6.4mg; SODIUM 710mg; CALC 182mg
EXCHANGES: 4 Starch, 2 Vegetable, 1 Fat

Black Bean Burgers with Spicy Cucumber and Red Pepper Relish

Here's a meat-free option for summer cookouts. Even burger lovers will devour these hearty, high-flavor patties.

RELISH:
²⁄₃ cup finely chopped peeled
    cucumber
½ cup finely chopped red bell
    pepper
¼ cup finely chopped red onion
1 tablespoon fresh lime juice
1 tablespoon honey
1 teaspoon finely chopped dill
⅛ teaspoon salt
Dash of ground red pepper

BURGERS:
1 (15-ounce) can black beans,
    rinsed and drained
½ cup dry breadcrumbs
¼ cup minced red onion
½ teaspoon dried oregano
¼ teaspoon ground cumin
⅛ teaspoon black pepper
1 large egg
Cooking spray
¼ cup light mayonnaise
4 (1½-ounce) hamburger buns

1. To prepare relish, combine first 8 ingredients in a medium bowl. Cover and chill 2 hours.

2. To prepare burgers, place beans in a large bowl; partially mash with a fork. Stir in breadcrumbs and next 5 ingredients. Divide bean mixture into 4 equal portions, shaping each into a ½-inch-thick patty.

3. Prepare grill.

4. Place patties on grill rack coated with cooking spray; grill 5 minutes on each side or until thoroughly heated. Spread 1 tablespoon mayonnaise on bottom half of each bun; top each with a patty, ¼ cup relish, and top half of bun. Yield: 4 servings (serving size: 1 burger).

CALORIES 375 (23% from fat); FAT 9.5g
(sat 1.9g, mono 2.4g, poly 3.7g);
PROTEIN 14.6g; CARB 59.2g; FIBER 5.7g;
CHOL 60mg; IRON 4.7mg; SODIUM 767mg;
CALC 136mg
EXCHANGES: 4 Starch, 1 Fat

MEAT-FREE MYTH

Meat-free does not always mean fat-free. A vegetarian-style diet is usually low in fat because of the emphasis on fruits, vegetables, and grains.

But this kind of diet can become high in fat and calories if large portions of high-fat cheese, whole milk, fried foods, and sweets are included.

Navy Bean-and-Artichoke Casserole with Goat Cheese

Boost your meatless meals with beans. Beans have no fat and are packed with protein, vitamins, and minerals. Plus, they're full of fiber, so they help you feel full and satisfied.

2   (1-ounce) slices whole wheat bread
2   (15-ounce) cans navy beans, undrained
2   teaspoons chopped fresh or ½ teaspoon dried thyme
2   teaspoons chopped fresh or ½ teaspoon dried rubbed sage
¼   teaspoon black pepper
4   garlic cloves, minced and divided
2   tablespoons olive oil, divided
3   cups chopped leek (about 3 large)
2   teaspoons chopped fresh or ½ teaspoon dried rosemary
⅛   teaspoon salt
1   (14-ounce) can artichoke bottoms, drained and each cut into 8 wedges
    Olive oil-flavored cooking spray
1¼ cups (5 ounces) crumbled goat cheese

1. Place bread in a food processor; pulse 10 times or until coarse crumbs form to measure 1 cup.

2. Preheat oven to 400°.

3. Drain beans in a colander over a bowl, reserving liquid. Add enough water to liquid to measure 1 cup. Combine beans, thyme, sage, pepper, and 1 garlic clove.

4. Heat 1 tablespoon oil in a large nonstick skillet over medium-high heat. Add 3 garlic cloves, leek, rosemary, salt, and artichokes; sauté 4 minutes. Stir in bean liquid mixture. Cover, reduce heat, and simmer 10 minutes, stirring occasionally. Remove from heat.

5. Spread half of bean mixture in an 11 x 7-inch baking dish coated with cooking spray, and top with half of goat cheese. Spread artichoke mixture over goat cheese; top with remaining bean mixture and remaining goat cheese. Combine breadcrumbs and 1 tablespoon oil; sprinkle over goat cheese. Bake at 400° for 25 minutes or until lightly browned. Yield: 6 servings (serving size: about 1 cup).

CALORIES 349 (28% from fat); FAT 10.8g (sat 4.4g, mono 4.7g, poly 1.1g); PROTEIN 17.3g; CARB 47.2g; FIBER 8.7g; CHOL 21mg; IRON 5.1mg; SODIUM 926mg; CALC 252mg
EXCHANGES: 3 Starch, 1 Medium-Fat Meat, 1 Fat

THREE-BEAN VEGETABLE MOUSSAKA

This meatless version of the traditional Greek dish offers all of the rich flavor, but much less fat because it has beans instead of lamb, and a marinara sauce instead of a high-fat white sauce.

1   cup (4 ounces) crumbled feta cheese
1   tablespoon chopped fresh or 1 teaspoon dried oregano
½   teaspoon ground cinnamon
2   (12.3-ounce) packages reduced-fat firm tofu, drained
1   (10-ounce) package frozen chopped spinach, thawed, drained, and squeezed dry
1   (8-ounce) container part-skim ricotta cheese
3   garlic cloves, minced
1   (1¼-pound) eggplant, cut lengthwise into ¼-inch-thick slices
Cooking spray
1   (25.5-ounce) jar fat-free marinara sauce
1   (16-ounce) can cannellini beans or other white beans, drained
1   (16-ounce) can kidney beans, drained
1   (15-ounce) can black beans, drained
2   cups (8 ounces) shredded part-skim mozzarella cheese

1. Preheat oven to 450°.

2. Combine first 7 ingredients in a bowl; stir until well blended. Set aside. Arrange eggplant on a baking sheet coated with cooking spray. Bake at 450° for 15 minutes or until lightly browned. Reduce oven temperature to 375°.

3. Spread 1 cup marinara sauce in bottom of a 13 x 9-inch baking dish coated with cooking spray. Arrange 5 eggplant slices over marinara, and top with 1⅔ cups spinach mixture and cannellini beans. Repeat layers, alternating remaining beans with each layer. Bake at 375° for 20 minutes. Top with cheese; bake 20 minutes or until cheese is browned. Yield: 8 servings.

CALORIES 390 (28% from fat); FAT 12.1g (sat 6.7g, mono 3g, poly 1.5g); PROTEIN 30.5g; CARB 41g; FIBER 7.3g; CHOL 38mg; IRON 5mg; SODIUM 817mg; CALC 478mg EXCHANGES: 2 Starch, 2 Vegetable, 3 Lean Meat

TOFU FOR YOU

Because it contains estrogen-like isoflavones, tofu may help reduce the risk of heart disease and certain cancers, strengthen bones, and ease menopausal hot flashes.

Tofu is low in saturated fat and sodium and has no cholesterol. Three ounces of regular tofu has 5 grams of fat; reduced-fat tofu has 1 gram. It's an excellent source of high-quality protein and contains vitamin E. Tofu does not naturally contain calcium, but many brands are fortified with calcium.

Garden Vegetable Stir-Fry with Tofu and Brown Rice

Brown rice has twice the fiber of white rice. Not only do you get more vitamins, the extra fiber in brown rice helps you feel full.

2   tablespoons water
1½ tablespoons cornstarch
1   cup vegetable broth
2   tablespoons oyster sauce
2   tablespoons low-sodium soy sauce
1   tablespoon rice vinegar
1   teaspoon sugar
1   teaspoon dark sesame oil
½   teaspoon crushed red pepper
3   teaspoons vegetable oil, divided
1   (12.3-ounce) package reduced-fat firm tofu, drained and cut into ½-inch cubes
1   cup thinly sliced onion
1   cup red bell pepper strips
3   cups sliced zucchini (about ¾ pound)
1   cup snow peas, trimmed
½   cup diagonally sliced carrot
1   (8-ounce) can sliced water chestnuts, drained
1   cup cilantro sprigs
3   cups hot cooked long-grain brown rice

1. Combine water and cornstarch in a bowl; stir with a whisk. Stir in broth and next 6 ingredients.

2. Heat 2 teaspoons vegetable oil in a large nonstick skillet over medium-high heat. Add tofu; stir-fry 8 minutes or until golden brown, stirring occasionally. Remove tofu from pan. Place tofu on several layers of paper towels.

3. Add 1 teaspoon vegetable oil to pan. Add onion and bell pepper, and stir-fry 2 minutes. Add zucchini, snow peas, carrot, and water chestnuts; stir-fry 1 minute. Add tofu and broth mixture. Bring to a boil, and cook 2 minutes. Stir in cilantro. Serve with rice. Yield: 4 servings (serving size: 1¼ cups stir-fry and ¾ cup rice).

CALORIES 365 (18% from fat); FAT 7.4g (sat 1.3g, mono 2.2g, poly 3.2g); PROTEIN 15.1g; CARB 60.8g; FIBER 6.3g; CHOL 0mg; IRON 4.3mg; SODIUM 827mg; CALC 129mg
EXCHANGES: 3 Starch, 3 Vegetable, 1 Fat

FRIED RICE WITH PINEAPPLE AND TOFU

Tofu, made from drained, pressed soybean curds, contains hormone-like compounds called isoflavones, which appear to help minimize the symptoms of menopause, reduce the risk of certain cancers, and help decrease levels of "bad" or LDL cholesterol.

1   (14-ounce) package firm tofu, drained and cut into ½-inch cubes
2   tablespoons peanut oil, divided
¼   teaspoon salt
1   cup (½-inch) pieces red bell pepper
¾   cup thinly sliced green onions
1   cup shelled green peas
¼   pound snow peas, trimmed and cut lengthwise into thin strips
4   cups cooked long-grain brown rice, chilled
¼   cup chopped fresh cilantro, divided
1   (15.25-ounce) can pineapple chunks in juice, drained
¼   cup low-sodium soy sauce
1   tablespoon chopped unsalted, dry-roasted peanuts

1. Place tofu between paper towels until barely moist. Heat 1 tablespoon oil in a large nonstick skillet or stir-fry pan over medium-high heat. Add tofu, and cook 8 minutes or until golden. Sprinkle with salt. Remove tofu from pan.

2. Heat 1 tablespoon oil in pan over medium-high heat. Add bell pepper and onions, and sauté 2 minutes. Add peas, and sauté 30 seconds. Stir in rice, and cook 2 minutes. Add tofu, 2 tablespoons cilantro, and pineapple; cook 1 minute, stirring gently. Remove from heat. Stir in soy sauce and peanuts. Sprinkle with 2 tablespoons cilantro.

Yield: 7 servings (serving size: 1 cup).

CALORIES 256 (30% from fat); FAT 8.5g (sat 1.4g, mono 3.1g, poly 3.4g); PROTEIN 10.3g; CARB 36.5g; FIBER 4.5g; CHOL 0mg; IRON 4.9mg; SODIUM 375mg; CALC 102mg
EXCHANGES: 2 Starch, 1 Vegetable, 1 High-Fat Meat

TYPES OF TOFU

Look for tofu in the fresh produce section of the grocery store or in Asian markets. It's usually either packed in water or vacuum packed.

There are several varieties of tofu, so be sure and use the type called for in the recipe.

Soft or silken: Use either one of these as a substitute for creamy ingredients in beverages, dips, puddings, and soups.

Firm or extra-firm: Cut this type into cubes, slice it, or crumble it, then use it in salads, stir-fries, and pasta dishes.

POLENTA WITH CORN AND GREEN CHILES

You can get the same nutritional benefits from canned and frozen vegetables that you get from fresh. The main difference is that the canned versions usually have more sodium.

POLENTA:

1¼ cups yellow cornmeal
2 garlic cloves, crushed
4 cups fat-free milk
¼ cup (1 ounce) preshredded fresh Parmesan cheese
1 tablespoon butter or margarine

VEGETABLES:

2 teaspoons olive oil
⅔ cup diced red bell pepper
1 (14.5-ounce) can diced tomatoes, undrained
1½ cups frozen whole-kernel corn, thawed
¼ cup chopped fresh cilantro
¼ teaspoon freshly ground black pepper
1 (4.5-ounce) can chopped green chiles

1. To prepare polenta, combine cornmeal and garlic in a large saucepan. Gradually add milk, stirring constantly with a whisk. Bring to a boil; reduce heat to medium, and cook 8 minutes, stirring frequently. Stir in cheese and butter.

2. To prepare vegetables, heat oil in a large nonstick skillet over medium heat. Add bell pepper and tomatoes; cook 8 minutes or until bell pepper is tender. Stir in corn and remaining ingredients; cook 2 minutes. Serve with polenta. Yield: 4 servings (serving size: 1 cup polenta and ¾ cup vegetables).

CALORIES 403 (19% from fat); FAT 8.7g (sat 3.8g, mono 3.5g, poly 1g); PROTEIN 17.9g; CARB 65.6g; FIBER 5.4g; CHOL 17mg; IRON 3.5g; SODIUM 778mg; CALC 430mg EXCHANGES: 4 Starch, 1 Vegetable, 1 Fat

FRESH VS. FROZEN

Don't worry if your favorite vegetable is not in season and you can't buy it fresh. Frozen and canned vegetables are just as good for you, and, in fact, might actually have more nutrients than fresh.

Why? Because produce picked to be canned or frozen is usually picked at its peak and packaged immediately. The fresh might be picked, transported, and stored a while before you get it, and nutrients can be lost during that time.

The difference is negligible, however, and the important thing is to eat more fruits and veggies in the version you prefer.

Pay attention to the labels of canned and frozen products to check on sodium and sugar content.

MEDITERRANEAN LASAGNA

Cheesy, hearty lasagna is not off-limits when it's layered with low-fat ingredients such as leeks, artichokes, bell peppers, beans, and spinach.

Cooking spray
2 cups chopped leek
1½ cups chopped onion
1 teaspoon dried mint flakes
½ teaspoon fennel seeds
3 garlic cloves, minced
1 (14-ounce) can artichoke hearts, drained and coarsely chopped
1 (7-ounce) bottle roasted red bell peppers, drained and chopped
1 cup drained canned cannellini beans
1½ tablespoons butter
2 tablespoons all-purpose flour
1½ cups fat-free milk
1 (4-ounce) package crumbled feta cheese
3 tablespoons grated fresh Parmesan cheese, divided
6 no-boil lasagna noodles (such as Barilla or Vigo)
1 (10-ounce) package frozen chopped spinach, thawed, drained, and squeezed dry
¾ cup (3 ounces) shredded part-skim mozzarella cheese, divided

1. Preheat oven to 375°.

2. Heat a large nonstick skillet coated with cooking spray over medium-high heat. Add leek and next 4 ingredients, and sauté 5 minutes. Add artichokes and bell pepper, and sauté 3 minutes. Stir in beans, and remove from heat.

3. Melt butter in a medium saucepan over medium heat. Add flour, and cook 2 minutes, stirring constantly with a whisk. Gradually add milk, stirring with a whisk until blended, and cook until slightly thick (about 4 minutes). Remove from heat. Add feta and 2 tablespoons Parmesan; stir until cheese melts.

4. Spread ¼ cup cheese sauce in bottom of an 8-inch square baking dish coated with cooking spray. Arrange 2 noodles over cheese sauce; top with half of leek mixture, half of spinach, ¼ cup mozzarella, and ½ cup cheese sauce. Repeat layers, ending with noodles. Pour remaining cheese sauce over noodles, and sprinkle with ¼ cup mozzarella and 1 tablespoon Parmesan. Cover and bake at 375° for 35 minutes. Uncover and bake 15 minutes or until top is golden. Let stand 5 minutes. Yield: 6 servings.

CALORIES 341 (31% from fat); FAT 11.9g
(sat 6.9g, mono 2.8g, poly 0.9g);
PROTEIN 18.8g; CARB 42.6g; FIBER 4.4g;
CHOL 53mg; IRON 4.1mg; SODIUM 548mg;
CALC 410mg
EXCHANGES: 3 Starch, 1 High-Fat Meat

ARTICHOKE-SPINACH PIZZA

One serving of this pizza provides about one-third of your daily calcium requirement. For more information on calcium, see page 93.

- 1 cup part-skim ricotta cheese
- ¼ cup thinly sliced green onions
- ¼ teaspoon bottled minced garlic
- ¼ teaspoon dried oregano
- ⅛ teaspoon black pepper
- 1 (10-ounce) package frozen chopped spinach, thawed, drained, and squeezed dry
- 1 (1-pound) Italian cheese-flavored pizza crust
- 1 (14-ounce) can quartered artichoke hearts, drained
- ⅔ cup (2½ ounces) grated sharp provolone or shredded part-skim mozzarella cheese

1. Preheat oven to 450°.
2. Combine first 5 ingredients in a medium bowl. Stir in spinach. Place pizza crust on a baking sheet. Spread spinach mixture over pizza crust, leaving a ½-inch border; top with artichokes and cheese.
3. Bake at 450° for 13 minutes or until cheese melts. Yield: 8 servings (serving size: 1 slice).

CALORIES 252 (29% from fat); FAT 8.4g
(sat 4.1g, mono 0.7g, poly 0.1g);
PROTEIN 13.8g; CARB 30.6g; FIBER 2.8g;
CHOL 18mg; IRON 2.4mg; SODIUM 648mg;
CALC 340mg
EXCHANGES: 2 Starch, 1 High-Fat Meat

PEPPER PESTO PIZZA

- 1 large garlic clove, peeled
- 1 cup basil leaves
- ¼ cup (1 ounce) grated fresh Parmesan cheese
- 2 tablespoons tomato paste
- 1½ tablespoons water
- 1 teaspoon sugar
- 1 teaspoon extra-virgin olive oil
- 1 (7-ounce) bottle roasted red bell peppers, drained
- 1 (1-pound) Italian cheese-flavored pizza crust
- ¾ cup (3 ounces) shredded part-skim mozzarella cheese
- 3 plum tomatoes, thinly sliced
- ½ teaspoon dried oregano

1. Preheat oven to 450°.
2. Drop garlic through food chute with food processor on; process until minced. Add basil and next 6 ingredients; process until smooth.
3. Place crust on a baking sheet. Spread pepper mixture over crust, leaving a ½-inch border; sprinkle with mozzarella. Arrange tomato on cheese. Bake at 450° for 10 minutes. Sprinkle with oregano. Yield: 6 servings (serving size: 1 slice).

CALORIES 285 (28% from fat); FAT 8.7g
(sat 3.9g, mono 3.4g, poly 0.9g);
PROTEIN 14.2g; CARB 37.2g; FIBER 1g;
CHOL 12mg; IRON 2.7mg; SODIUM 611mg;
CALC 376mg
EXCHANGES: 2 Starch, 1 Vegetable,
1 High-Fat Meat

Cabbage-and-Yukon Gold Potato Casserole

Yukon gold potatoes have a rich and buttery taste but don't have one bit more fat than regular baking potatoes.

- 3 cups sliced peeled Yukon Gold or baking potato (about 1 pound)
- 8 cups (1-inch-thick) sliced green cabbage (about 1½ pounds)
- 1 tablespoon butter
- 2 tablespoons chopped fresh or 2 teaspoons dried rubbed sage
- 1 garlic clove, chopped
- 1 teaspoon salt
- ¼ teaspoon black pepper
- Cooking spray
- ⅓ cup all-purpose flour
- 1⅓ cups 1% low-fat milk
- ½ cup (2 ounces) shredded part-skim mozzarella cheese
- ¼ cup (1 ounce) grated fresh Parmesan cheese
- 2 large eggs
- 1 large egg white

1. Preheat oven to 350°.
2. Place potato in a large Dutch oven, and cover with water. Bring potato to a boil, and cook 6 minutes or until tender. Remove potato with a slotted spoon, reserving cooking liquid in pan. Place potato in a large bowl, and set aside. Add cabbage to cooking liquid in pan, and cook 5 minutes. Drain well.

Add cabbage to potato.
3. Melt butter in a small skillet over medium heat; add sage and garlic. Sauté 1 minute. Stir chopped sage mixture, salt, and pepper into potato mixture. Spoon potato mixture into a 2½-quart casserole dish coated with cooking spray.
4. Lightly spoon flour into a dry measuring cup; level with a knife. Combine flour, milk, and remaining ingredients, and stir with a whisk. Pour milk mixture over potato mixture (do not stir). Bake at 350° for 50 minutes or until casserole is lightly browned. Yield: 6 servings (serving size: about 1½ cups).

CALORIES 225 (30% from fat); FAT 7.4g (sat 3.9g, mono 2.2g, poly 0.6g); PROTEIN 12.2g; CARB 28.5g; FIBER 4.2g; CHOL 90mg; IRON 1.9mg; SODIUM 613mg; CALC 256mg
EXCHANGES: 2 Starch, 1 Medium-Fat Meat

One Potato, Two Potato...

Eliminating starchy foods such as potatoes, rice, and pasta is a popular trend in the weight-loss world. There is no real evidence that starchy foods alone cause insulin resistance and obesity. Starchy foods can contribute to weight gain if portion sizes are huge and loaded with butter or high-fat sauces. So if you want to include potatoes, pasta, and rice in your meals, keep the serving sizes in check and use low-fat toppings and sauces.

Strudel Verde

In traditional phyllo dishes, you generously brush each layer of the phyllo dough with butter, but in this version, you use cooking spray. It's easier, and the fat savings are tremendous.

2 teaspoons olive oil
1 cup chopped onion
½ cup (½-inch) sliced asparagus
½ cup diced red bell pepper
½ cup sliced mushrooms
1 cup cooked long-grain brown rice
1 cup drained canned chickpeas (garbanzo beans), mashed
¼ cup frozen chopped spinach, thawed, drained, and squeezed dry
¼ cup frozen green peas, thawed
½ cup (2 ounces) crumbled feta cheese
¼ cup chopped fresh dill
½ teaspoon salt
¼ teaspoon black pepper
5 sheets frozen phyllo dough, thawed
Cooking spray
1 tablespoon sesame seeds

1. Preheat oven to 350°.

2. Heat oil in a large nonstick skillet over medium-high heat. Add onion, asparagus, bell pepper, and mushrooms; sauté 2 minutes. Stir in rice, chickpeas, spinach, and green peas. Remove from heat; cool to room temperature. Stir in feta, dill, salt, and black pepper.

3. Place 1 phyllo sheet on work surface; lightly coat with cooking spray. Working with 1 phyllo sheet at a time, coat remaining 4 phyllo sheets with cooking spray; place one on top of the other. Place a sheet of plastic wrap over phyllo; press gently to seal sheets together. Discard plastic wrap. Remove vegetable mixture from pan with a slotted spoon. Spoon vegetable mixture along 1 long edge of phyllo, leaving a 3-inch border. Fold over the short edges of phyllo to cover 2 inches of vegetable mixture on each end.

4. Starting at long edge with 2-inch border, roll up jelly roll fashion (do not roll tightly, or strudel may split). Place, seam side down, on a jelly roll pan coated with cooking spray. Lightly coat strudel with cooking spray; sprinkle with sesame seeds. Bake at 350° for 40 minutes or until golden brown. Yield: 4 servings (serving size: 1 [3-inch] piece).

CALORIES 321 (27% from fat); FAT 9.6g (sat 3g, mono 3.4g, poly 2.3g); PROTEIN 12.8g; CARB 48.1g; FIBER 6.2g; CHOL 13mg; IRON 5.8mg; SODIUM 637mg; CALC 242mg EXCHANGES: 3 Starch, 1 Vegetable, 2 Fat

Tortilla Casserole with Swiss Chard

Slightly stale corn tortillas work best for this casserole. If yours are fresh, spread them out on a counter and leave them uncovered for an hour or two. They should feel dry, but not hard or crisp.

    2   teaspoons vegetable oil
    2   cups thinly sliced onion, divided
    3   garlic cloves, finely chopped
    ½   teaspoon salt
    2   (8-ounce) packages button
        mushrooms, sliced
    2   jalapeño peppers, seeded and
        chopped
    4   cups finely chopped Swiss chard
        (about 1 bunch)
    ¼   cup chopped fresh parsley,
        divided
    ¼   cup water
    1   (14.5-ounce) can diced tomatoes,
        undrained
   12   (6-inch) corn tortillas, quartered
    1   cup (4 ounces) reduced-fat
        shredded sharp Cheddar cheese
    ¼   cup low-fat sour cream

1. Preheat oven to 375°.

2. Heat oil in a large nonstick skillet over medium-high heat. Add 1 cup onion and garlic, and sauté 1 minute. Stir in salt, mushrooms, and jalapeño peppers. Arrange chard over mushroom mixture. Cover, reduce heat, and cook 15 minutes or until tender. Stir in 2 tablespoons parsley.

3. Combine 1 cup onion, water, and tomatoes in a blender, and process until smooth. Pour tomato mixture into a saucepan. Bring to a boil; cook 4 minutes or until slightly thick.

4. Arrange 16 tortilla quarters in a single layer in a 13 x 9-inch baking dish. Spread about 1 cup mushroom mixture over tortilla pieces. Top with ½ cup tomato mixture. Sprinkle with ⅓ cup cheese. Repeat layers twice, ending with ⅓ cup cheese. Bake at 375° for 20 minutes or until cheese melts. Top servings evenly with sour cream and 2 tablespoons parsley. Yield: 6 servings (serving size: 1 [4½-inch] square, 2 teaspoons sour cream, and 1 teaspoon parsley).

CALORIES 251 (29% from fat); FAT 8.1g (sat 3.4g, mono 2.2g, poly 1.7g); PROTEIN 12g; CARB 36.1g; FIBER 5.2g; CHOL 16mg; IRON 2.8mg; SODIUM 585mg; CALC 314mg EXCHANGES: 2 Starch, 1 Vegetable, 1 High-Fat Meat

BARBECUED TEMPEH SANDWICHES SMOTHERED WITH PEPPERS AND ONIONS

Tempeh is a soybean cake with a slightly nutty flavor that pairs well with the sweet and spicy barbecue sauce. And, like other members of the soy food family, tempeh may help strengthen bones, ease menopausal symptoms, and reduce the risk of heart disease and some forms of cancer.

1/3	cup ketchup
1	tablespoon brown sugar
1 1/2	teaspoons vegetable oil
1 1/2	teaspoons cider vinegar
1	teaspoon Dijon mustard
1/4	teaspoon chili powder
1/4	teaspoon low-sodium soy sauce
1/4	teaspoon hot sauce
1	garlic clove, minced
1	(8-ounce) package tempeh
1	red bell pepper, cut in half
1	yellow bell pepper, cut in half
1	red onion, cut into 1/2-inch-thick slices

Cooking spray

4	(1 1/2-ounce) hamburger buns

1. Prepare grill.

2. Combine first 9 ingredients in a small bowl, stirring with a whisk.

3. Cut tempeh in half lengthwise; cut slices in half. Brush tempeh slices, bell peppers, and onion with ketchup mixture. Place on grill rack coated with cooking spray; grill 4 minutes on each side or until tempeh is thoroughly heated. Remove tempeh, bell peppers, and onion from grill. Cut bell peppers into 1/2-inch-wide strips; separate onions into rings.

4. Place 1 tempeh slice on bottom half of each bun. Top each tempeh slice with one-fourth of bell peppers, one-fourth of onion, and top half of bun. Yield: 4 servings (serving size: 1 sandwich).

CALORIES 309 (25% from fat); FAT 8.7g (sat 1.5g, mono 1.9g, poly 4.5g); PROTEIN 15.6g; CARB 45.2g; FIBER 3g; CHOL 0mg; IRON 3.6mg; SODIUM 531mg; CALC 130mg
EXCHANGES: 3 Starch, 1 High-Fat Meat

Chapter 40

Meats

There's no need to give up meat when you're giving up the extra pounds. These recipes show you how succulent and savory lean cuts of beef, lamb, and pork can be.

HEALTHY PICADILLO

Ground round has 15 percent fat compared to 27 percent for ground beef.

2	pounds ground round
1	tablespoon olive oil
1½	cups thinly sliced onion
1	garlic clove, minced
1½	cups chopped yellow bell pepper
1½	cups chopped red bell pepper
1	cup finely chopped carrot
¾	cup golden raisins
½	cup dry white wine
¼	cup sliced pimiento-stuffed green olives (about 15 olives)
2	tablespoons balsamic vinegar
1½	teaspoons salt
⅛	teaspoon black pepper
2	bay leaves
1	(14.5-ounce) can no-salt-added stewed tomatoes, undrained
1	(8-ounce) can no-salt-added tomato sauce

1. Cook beef in a large nonstick skillet over medium-high heat until browned; stir to crumble. Remove from pan; drain well.

2. Add oil to pan. Add onion and garlic; sauté 3 minutes. Add bell peppers and carrot; sauté 3 minutes. Return beef to pan. Stir in raisins and remaining ingredients; bring to a boil. Reduce heat; simmer 15 minutes, stirring occasionally. Discard bay leaves. Yield: 8 servings (serving size: 1 cup).

CALORIES 280 (29% from fat); FAT 9.1g (sat 2.8g, mono 4.4g, poly 0.6g); PROTEIN 26.4g; CARB 24g; FIBER 2.2g; CHOL 70mg; IRON 3.8mg; SODIUM 557mg; CALC 46mg
EXCHANGES: 1 Starch, 2 Vegetable, 3 Lean Meat

SHORTCUT LASAGNA

This quick-fix lasagna has less than half the fat of traditional lasagna.

8   ounces uncooked egg noodles
1¼   cups fat-free ricotta cheese
1½   cups (6 ounces) shredded sharp
     provolone cheese, divided
1   teaspoon dried basil
½   teaspoon dried oregano
¼   teaspoon salt
¼   teaspoon black pepper
1   pound ground round
2   cups tomato sauce
Cooking spray

1. Preheat oven to 375°.
2. Cook noodles in boiling water 5 minutes, omitting salt and fat.
3. Combine ricotta, 1 cup provolone, basil, oregano, salt, and pepper. Cook beef in a large nonstick skillet over medium-high heat until browned, stirring to crumble. Stir in tomato sauce.
4. Drain noodles. Combine noodles and meat. Place 3 cups mixture in an 11 x 7-inch baking dish coated with cooking spray. Spread ricotta mixture over noodle mixture. Top with remaining noodle mixture and ½ cup provolone. Bake at 375° for 15 minutes. Yield: 6 servings.

CALORIES 416 (30% from fat); FAT 14g
(sat 6.8g, mono 4.5g, poly 0.9g); PROTEIN 37g;
CARB 37.2g; FIBER 2.3g; CHOL 107mg;
IRON 4.1mg; SODIUM 912mg; CALC 333mg
EXCHANGES: 2 Starch, 1 Vegetable,
4 Lean Meat

GARLIC-HERB MEAT LOAF

This reduced-fat meat loaf has a mixture of ground sirloin and ground turkey, plus added fiber from the oats.

7   tablespoons ketchup, divided
1   cup quick-cooking oats
½   cup finely chopped onion
2   tablespoons dried parsley
1   tablespoon dried basil
¾   teaspoon salt
½   teaspoon black pepper
1   pound ground sirloin
1   pound ground turkey
2   large eggs, lightly beaten
2   large egg whites, lightly beaten
2   garlic cloves, minced
Cooking spray

1. Preheat oven to 375°.
2. Combine 3 tablespoons ketchup, oats, and next 10 ingredients.
3. Shape mixture into a 9 x 5-inch loaf on a broiler pan coated with cooking spray. Spoon 4 tablespoons ketchup over loaf. Insert a meat thermometer into loaf. Bake at 375° for 1 hour and 10 minutes or until thermometer registers 160°. Let stand 10 minutes. Remove meat loaf from pan; cut into slices. Yield: 8 servings.

CALORIES 230 (25% from fat); FAT 6.5g
(sat 2.1g, mono 2.3g, poly 1g); PROTEIN 29.5g;
CARB 12.3g; FIBER 1.6g; CHOL 125mg;
IRON 3.2mg; SODIUM 479mg; CALC 38mg
Exchanges: 1 Starch, 4 Very Lean Meat

OPEN-FACED BURGERS WITH ONION-MUSHROOM TOPPING

Instead of the usual hamburger buns, place these patties on English muffin halves and top with a savory low-fat mushroom-onion topping.

2	teaspoons olive oil
1	sweet onion, sliced and separated into rings
2	(8-ounce) packages presliced mushrooms
½	teaspoon salt
2	teaspoons balsamic vinegar
1½	tablespoons paprika
½	teaspoon salt
½	teaspoon dried thyme
¼	teaspoon ground red pepper
¼	teaspoon freshly ground black pepper
1	pound ground round
2	English muffins, split and toasted

1. Preheat grill.

2. Heat oil in a large nonstick skillet over medium-high heat. Add onion, and sauté 5 minutes or until golden. Add mushrooms and salt; sauté 5 minutes. Add vinegar; remove mixture from pan. Set aside.

3. Combine paprika and next 4 ingredients. Divide meat into 4 equal portions, shaping each into a ½-inch-thick patty.

Coat patties with spice mixture. Grill patties 4 minutes on each side or until done. Place patties on muffin halves, and top each with ¼ cup onion mixture. Yield: 4 servings (serving size: 1 sandwich).

CALORIES 320 (30% from fat); FAT 10.5g (sat 3g, mono 4.8g, poly 1.2g); PROTEIN 29.4g; CARB 27.3g; FIBER 4.6g; CHOL 70mg; IRON 5.1mg; SODIUM 813mg; CALC 82mg EXCHANGES: 2 Starch, 3 Lean Meat

MEAT SAFETY

For food safety reasons, be sure to cook meats to the proper internal temperature. This will ensure that any bacteria present in the raw meat will be destroyed.

To check the temperature, use a meat thermometer or an instant-read thermometer.

Meat	Internal Cooked Temperature (°F)
Ground Beef	160 or until no longer pink and juices run clear
Steak and Roasts	145 (medium-rare) 160 (medium) 170 (well done)
Pork, all cuts including ground	160 (medium) 170 (well done)

MEATBALLS AND PEPPERS

One red bell pepper has more vitamin C than a cup of orange juice—and eating foods with vitamin C may help reduce the risk of heart disease.

1	cup sliced green bell pepper
1	cup sliced red bell pepper
1	cup sliced yellow bell pepper
1⅓	cups water
1	(10½-ounce) can beef consommé
1	bay leaf
1	(1-ounce) slice whole wheat bread
1	pound ground round
1	tablespoon finely chopped onion
½	teaspoon dried oregano
½	teaspoon salt
½	teaspoon black pepper
1	large egg white
1	garlic clove, crushed
2	teaspoons olive oil
2	tablespoons all-purpose flour
¼	cup water
⅓	cup chopped fresh basil
2	teaspoons white wine vinegar

1. Combine first 6 ingredients in a large saucepan. Bring to a boil; cover, reduce heat, and simmer 20 minutes.
2. Place bread in a food processor; pulse 10 times or until coarse crumbs form to measure ½ cup. Combine breadcrumbs, beef, and next 6 ingredients in a bowl, shaping mixture into 36 (1-inch) meatballs. Heat oil in a large nonstick skillet over medium-high heat. Add meatballs; cook 10 minutes, browning on all sides.
3. Combine flour and ¼ cup water in a small bowl; stir with a whisk. Add to bell pepper mixture in pan. Add meatballs; cook 3 minutes, stirring constantly. Stir in basil and vinegar. Remove bay leaf.
Yield: 4 servings (serving size: 1 cup bell pepper mixture and 9 meatballs).

CALORIES 263 (34% from fat); FAT 9.8g (sat 2.9g, mono 4.7g, poly 0.8g); PROTEIN 30.2g; CARB 12.4g; FIBER 1.9g; CHOL 70mg; IRON 4.3mg; SODIUM 788mg; CALC 34mg
EXCHANGES: 2 Vegetable, 4 Very Lean Meat

SIZZLING STEAK WITH ROASTED VEGETABLES

A hot skillet allows you to control the degree of doneness more precisely, and the intense heat seals in flavor.

MARINADE:

⅓	cup dry red wine
¼	cup beef broth
2	tablespoons balsamic vinegar
1	tablespoon brown sugar
¼	teaspoon coarsely ground black pepper
3	garlic cloves, minced
4	(4-ounce) beef tenderloin steaks (1 inch thick)

ROASTED VEGETABLES:

- 1 cup (1-inch) pieces red bell pepper
- 1 cup (1-inch) pieces yellow bell pepper
- 2 teaspoons vegetable oil
- 12 small red potatoes, quartered (about 1½ pounds)
- 3 shallots, halved
- ¼ teaspoon salt

REMAINING INGREDIENTS:

- 2 teaspoons coarsely ground black pepper
- ½ teaspoon salt
- 1 teaspoon vegetable oil
- 1 teaspoon prepared horseradish

1. To prepare marinade, combine first 6 ingredients in a large zip-top plastic bag. Add steaks to bag, and seal. Marinate in refrigerator 2 hours, turning occasionally.

2. Preheat oven to 400°.

3. To prepare roasted vegetables, combine bell peppers, 2 teaspoons oil, potatoes, shallots, and salt in a 13 x 9-inch baking dish. Bake at 400° for 45 minutes or until potatoes are tender, stirring occasionally.

4. Remove steaks from bag, reserving marinade. Sprinkle 2 teaspoons black pepper and salt over each side of steaks. Heat 1 teaspoon oil in a large nonstick skillet over medium-high heat. Add steaks, and sauté 3 minutes on each side or until steaks are at the desired degree of doneness. Remove steaks from pan. Add reserved marinade to skillet, and boil 1 minute, scraping skillet to loosen browned bits. Stir in horseradish. Pour sauce over steaks and vegetables. Yield: 4 servings (serving size: 1 steak, 1 cup vegetables, and 2 tablespoons sauce).

CALORIES 379 (27% from fat); FAT 11.4g (sat 3.7g, mono 3.9g, poly 2.3g); PROTEIN 29g; CARB 37.4g; FIBER 4.7g; CHOL 73mg; IRON 7.1mg; SODIUM 620mg; CALC 49mg EXCHANGES: 2 Starch, 1 Vegetable, 3 Lean Meat

MARINADE SAFETY

When a marinade has been in contact with raw meat, you need to boil the marinade for at least 1 minute before using it as a basting sauce.

Boiling will kill any bacteria that might have been transferred from the raw meat to the marinade.

Pepper-Crusted Beef Tenderloin with Horseradish Sauce

Roasting is an ideal low-fat cooking method because the excess fat in the meat drips out of the meat and into the roasting pan.

1   (4-pound) beef tenderloin
1½ teaspoons olive oil
3   tablespoons dry breadcrumbs
3   tablespoons minced fresh parsley
1½ teaspoons coarsely ground black pepper
¾   teaspoon kosher salt, divided
Cooking spray
1   cup fat-free sour cream
2   tablespoons prepared horseradish
1   teaspoon grated lemon rind
½   teaspoon Worcestershire sauce
¼   teaspoon hot pepper sauce

1. Preheat oven to 400°.
2. Trim fat from tenderloin; fold under 3 inches of small end. Rub tenderloin with oil. Combine breadcrumbs, parsley, pepper, and ½ teaspoon salt. Rub tenderloin with crumb mixture; coat with cooking spray. Place tenderloin on rack of a broiler pan or roasting pan. Insert a meat thermometer into thickest portion of tenderloin. Bake at 400° for 30 minutes. Increase oven temperature to 425° (do not remove meat from oven). Bake

an additional 10 minutes or until thermometer registers 145° (medium-rare) to 160° (medium). Place tenderloin on a platter, and cover with foil. Let stand 10 minutes for meat to reabsorb juices.
3. Combine ¼ teaspoon salt, sour cream, and remaining ingredients. Serve with meat. Yield: 16 servings (serving size: 3 ounces meat and 1 tablespoon horseradish sauce).

CALORIES 195 (39% from fat); FAT 8.4g
(sat 3.2g, mono 3.4g, poly 0.4g);
PROTEIN 25.3g; CARB 2.4g; FIBER 0.2g;
CHOL 71mg; IRON 3.2mg; SODIUM 193mg;
CALC 12mg
EXCHANGES: 3 Lean Meat

Lamb Curry with Apples

This fruited lamb dish gets its flavor from an aromatic blend of curry, ginger, red pepper, and garlic.

1   pound lean lamb stew meat
1   tablespoon all-purpose flour
1   teaspoon vegetable oil
3   cups vertically sliced onion
2   teaspoons curry powder
1   teaspoon ground ginger
¼   teaspoon ground red pepper
1½ cups chopped peeled Golden Delicious apple
2   teaspoons bottled minced garlic
1   (14.5-ounce) can diced tomatoes, undrained
1   (14.5-ounce) can low-salt beef broth

1. Place lamb in a medium bowl. Sprinkle with flour, tossing to coat.
2. Heat oil in a large nonstick skillet over medium-high heat. Add lamb; cook 4 minutes or until browned, stirring frequently. Stir in onion, curry, ginger, and pepper; cook 5 minutes or until onion is tender. Stir in apple, garlic, tomatoes, and broth. Bring to a boil; cover, reduce heat, and simmer 15 minutes. Yield: 4 servings (serving size: 1½ cups).

CALORIES 265 (26% from fat); FAT 7.8g (sat 2.5g, mono 2.9g, poly 1.3g); PROTEIN 25.7g; CARB 22.2g; FIBER 3.6g; CHOL 74mg; IRON 3.4mg; SODIUM 248mg; CALC 67mg
EXCHANGES: ½ Starch, 1 Fruit, 3 Lean Meat

LAMB SHISH KEBABS

Marinating in a wine and herb mixture is a good way to infuse food with flavor without adding a lot of fat.

¼	cup dry red wine
1½	tablespoons dried oregano
1½	tablespoons dried mint flakes
2	tablespoons lemon juice
2	teaspoons olive oil
4	garlic cloves, minced
1½	pounds lean cubed boned leg of lamb
12	(1-inch) squares green bell pepper
12	cherry tomatoes
1	large onion, cut into 12 wedges
Cooking spray	

1. Combine first 6 ingredients in a large heavy-duty zip-top plastic bag; add lamb, and seal bag. Marinate in refrigerator 12 to 24 hours.
2. Prepare grill.
3. Remove lamb from bag, reserving marinade. Place marinade in a saucepan. Bring to a boil; remove from heat. Thread lamb, pepper, tomatoes, and onion alternately onto 12 (10-inch) skewers. Coat grill rack with cooking spray; place on grill over medium-hot coals (350° to 400°). Place kebabs on rack; grill, covered, 5 minutes on each side or until lamb is desired degree of doneness, turning and basting kebabs frequently with marinade. Yield: 6 servings (serving size: 2 kebabs).

CALORIES 215 (36% from fat); FAT 8.7g (sat 2.7g; mono 3.9g; poly 0.9g); PROTEIN 25.1g; CARB 9.1g; FIBER 2.3g; CHOL 75mg; IRON 3.6mg; SODIUM 86mg; CALC 52mg
EXCHANGES: 2 Vegetable, 3 Lean Meat

LEAN LAMB

To get the leanest cuts of lamb, look for those with the words "loin" or "leg" on the label. Some lean cuts of lamb include leg, loin chop, arm chop, and foreshanks.

SICILIAN VEAL CUTLETS

Flattening the veal tenderizes the meat and allows it to cook quickly.

8 (1½-ounce) veal leg cutlets
2 tablespoons all-purpose flour
½ teaspoon black pepper
2 teaspoons vegetable oil, divided
1 garlic clove, minced
1 cup dry white wine
1½ cups chopped seeded plum tomato (about 4)
6 pitted kalamata olives, chopped
1 (6-ounce) jar marinated artichoke hearts, drained and chopped
2 cups hot cooked angel hair (about 4 ounces uncooked pasta)

1. Trim fat from veal. Place each cutlet between 2 sheets of heavy-duty plastic wrap; flatten to ⅛-inch thickness using a meat mallet. Combine flour and pepper. Dredge veal in flour mixture; shake off excess flour.
2. Heat 1 teaspoon oil in a skillet over high heat. Add half of cutlets to pan. Cook 2 minutes on each side or until browned. Repeat with 1 teaspoon oil and remaining veal. Remove from pan.
3. Add garlic, and sauté 30 seconds. Add wine, scraping pan to loosen browned bits. Reduce heat to medium-high; boil wine mixture 3 minutes. Return veal to pan. Add tomato, olives,

and artichokes; cover and simmer 1 minute or until thoroughly heated. Serve with pasta. Yield: 4 servings (serving size: 2 pieces veal, ½ cup artichoke mixture, and ½ cup pasta).

CALORIES 293 (25% from fat); FAT 8.2g (sat 1.6g, mono 2.3g, poly 2.1g); PROTEIN 23g; CARB 32g; FIBER 1.8g; CHOL 68mg; IRON 3.1mg; SODIUM 316mg; CALC 49mg EXCHANGES: 2 Starch, 1 Vegetable, 2 Lean Meat

GLAZED VEAL CHOPS WITH GRAPES

The skins of red grapes contain a substance called resveratrol, which may help prevent heart disease and cancer.

4 (6-ounce) veal loin chops, trimmed
½ teaspoon salt
⅛ teaspoon pepper
1 teaspoon olive oil
¼ cup fresh orange juice
¼ cup balsamic vinegar
1 cup seedless red grapes, halved

1. Sprinkle veal with salt and pepper.
2. Heat oil in a large nonstick skillet over medium-high heat. Add veal; cook 7 minutes on each side or until done. Remove veal from pan; keep warm.
3. Add juice and vinegar to drippings; cook over medium heat 2 to 3 minutes, scraping pan to loosen browned bits. Return veal to pan; add grapes, and

cook 1 minute, turning veal to coat with sauce. Place veal on a serving platter. Pour sauce over veal. Yield: 4 servings (serving size: 1 chop and ¼ cup sauce).

CALORIES 258 (34% from fat); FAT 9.6g (sat 2.5g; mono 4g; poly 0.7g); PROTEIN 30.5g CARB 11.1g; FIBER 0.5g; CHOL 112mg; IRON 1.3mg; SODIUM 371mg; CALC 40mg EXCHANGES: 1 Fruit, 4 Lean Meat

CHEDDAR-ASPARAGUS PIE

Instead of a high-fat pastry crust, this potpie has a low-fat phyllo crust.

    4   cups (1-inch) sliced asparagus
    2   cups (½-inch) diced red potato
    ½   cup all-purpose flour
 1½   teaspoons paprika
    ¾   teaspoon salt
    ⅛   teaspoon ground red pepper
    1   garlic clove, minced
 2½   cups fat-free milk
    1   cup (4 ounces) shredded
        reduced-fat sharp Cheddar
        cheese
    ¾   cup (½-inch) diced lean smoked
        ham
    ½   cup sliced green onions
Cooking spray
    4   sheets frozen phyllo dough,
        thawed
    1   tablespoon butter or margarine,
        melted

1. Preheat oven to 350°.

2. Cook asparagus in boiling water 2 minutes or until crisp-tender. Remove from pan with a slotted spoon. Place asparagus in a bowl; set aside. Add potato to pan; cook in boiling water 5 minutes or until tender. Drain. Add to asparagus.

3. Lightly spoon flour into a dry measuring cup; level with a knife. Place flour and next 4 ingredients in a large saucepan. Add milk, stirring with a whisk until blended. Cook over medium heat until thick (about 10 minutes), stirring constantly. Add cheese, stirring until cheese melts. Remove from heat; stir in asparagus, potato, ham, and onions. Spoon into an 11 x 7-inch baking dish coated with cooking spray.

4. Place 1 phyllo sheet on a cutting board (cover remaining dough to keep from drying out), and gently brush 1 side of phyllo with about 1 teaspoon melted butter. Fold phyllo in half crosswise, and place over filling. Repeat procedure with remaining phyllo and butter. Trim excess phyllo from edges of dish, and discard. Lightly coat phyllo with cooking spray. Bake at 350° for 25 minutes or until golden brown and bubbly around edges. Let stand 10 minutes. Yield: 6 servings.

CALORIES 266 (25% from fat); FAT 7.3g (sat 3.6g, mono 2.1g, poly 1g); PROTEIN 18g; CARB 33.5g; FIBER 3.4g; CHOL 27mg; IRON 2.8mg; SODIUM 827mg; CALC 331mg EXCHANGES: 2 Starch, 1 Vegetable, 1 High-Fat Meat

PORK CUTLETS WITH CREAMY MUSTARD SAUCE

If you can't find pork cutlets, buy 4-ounce boneless loin pork chops and pound to about ¼-inch thickness.

4	(4-ounce) pork cutlets
¾	cup breadcrumbs
¼	cup chopped pecans
¼	cup reduced-fat sour cream
1	tablespoon fat-free milk
1	tablespoon Dijon mustard

1. Preheat oven to 400°.

2. Combine pork cutlets, breadcrumbs, and pecans in a heavy-duty zip-top plastic bag; shake to coat. Bake at 400° for 25 minutes, turning once.

3. Combine sour cream, milk, and mustard in a saucepan; cook over medium heat 2 to 3 minutes or until thoroughly heated, stirring constantly. Spoon sauce over pork. Yield: 4 servings (serving size: 1 pork cutlet and about 1 tablespoon sauce).

CALORIES 279 (45% from fat); FAT 13.8g (sat 3.8g, mono 5.9g, poly 2.4g); PROTEIN 27.8g; CARB 10.4g; FIBER 1g; CHOL 70mg; IRON 1.6mg; SODIUM 157mg; CALC 66mg
EXCHANGES: 1 Starch, 3 Lean Meat, 1 Fat

BARBECUED PORK CHOPS

Basting with this fat-free barbecue sauce helps keep the chops juicy and tender.

SAUCE:

¼	cup packed brown sugar
¼	cup ketchup
1	tablespoon Worcestershire sauce
1	tablespoon low-sodium soy sauce

REMAINING INGREDIENTS:

6	(6-ounce) bone-in center-cut pork chops (about ½ inch thick)
1	teaspoon dried thyme
1	teaspoon garlic salt
¼	teaspoon ground red pepper
	Cooking spray

1. Prepare grill or broiler.

2. To prepare sauce, combine first 4 ingredients in a small bowl. Place ¼ cup sauce in a small bowl, and set aside.

3. Trim fat from pork. Combine thyme, garlic salt, and pepper; sprinkle over pork. Place pork on grill rack or broiler pan coated with cooking spray; cook 6 minutes on each side, basting with remaining sauce. Serve pork chops with reserved ¼ cup sauce. Yield: 6 servings (serving size: 1 pork chop and 1½ tablespoons sauce).

CALORIES 244 (42% from fat); FAT 11.3g (sat 3.9g, mono 5g, poly 1.4g); PROTEIN 24.6g; CARB 9.9g; FIBER 0.2g; CHOL 77mg; IRON 1.5mg; SODIUM 649mg; CALC 22mg
EXCHANGES: 1 Starch, 3 Lean Meat

PORK, KALE, AND BOK CHOY STIR-FRY

Look for "loin" and "leg" on meat package labels when you're trying to pick out the leanest cuts of pork.

1	(³/₄-pound) pork tenderloin
3	tablespoons low-sodium soy sauce, divided
2	tablespoons minced garlic, divided
2	teaspoons minced peeled fresh ginger, divided
¹/₂	cup fat-free, less-sodium chicken broth
3	tablespoons hoisin sauce
1	teaspoon cornstarch
1	tablespoon vegetable oil
¹/₄	teaspoon crushed red pepper
2	cups sliced shiitake mushroom caps
1¹/₂	cups sliced green onions
4	cups sliced kale
4	cups sliced bok choy
5	cups hot cooked rice

1. Trim fat from pork; cut pork into 2 x ¹/₄-inch-wide strips. Combine pork, 2 tablespoons soy sauce, 2 teaspoons garlic, and 1 teaspoon ginger in a shallow bowl. Cover and marinate in refrigerator 2 hours.

2. Combine 1 tablespoon soy sauce, 2 teaspoons garlic, 1 teaspoon ginger, broth, hoisin sauce, and cornstarch; stir with a whisk. Heat oil in a large non-stick skillet over medium-high heat. Add 2 teaspoons garlic and crushed red pepper; stir-fry 30 seconds. Add mushrooms and onions; stir-fry 3 minutes. Add pork mixture and kale; stir-fry 3 minutes. Add broth mixture and bok choy; bring to a boil. Cook 1 minute or until mixture is thick. Serve over rice.

Yield: 5 servings (serving size: 1 cup stir-fry and 1 cup rice).

CALORIES 407 (13% from fat); FAT 5.8g (sat 1.2g, mono 1.9g, poly 1.9g); PROTEIN 23.4g; CARB 66.1g; FIBER 3.6g; CHOL 44mg; IRON 5.2mg; SODIUM 543mg; CALC 189mg
EXCHANGES: 4 Starch, 1 Vegetable, 1 Medium-Fat Meat

SKINNY PORK

Here are some examples of lean cuts of pork.
• pork tenderloin
• top loin roast
• sirloin roast
• top loin chop
• center loin chop
• loin rib chop
• shoulder blade steak

PORK MEDALLIONS WITH ORANGE-ROSEMARY SAUCE

Compared to the pork of 20 years ago, today's pork has 77 percent less fat.

1	pound pork tenderloin
½	teaspoon black pepper
¼	teaspoon salt
2	teaspoons olive oil, divided
Cooking spray	
1	tablespoon bottled minced garlic
½	cup dry red wine
½	teaspoon dried rosemary, crumbled
2	tablespoons tomato paste
¾	cup fat-free, less-sodium chicken broth
¼	cup orange juice

1. Trim fat from pork, and cut pork crosswise into 1-inch-thick pieces. Place each piece between 2 sheets of heavy-duty plastic wrap; flatten each piece to ½-inch thickness. Sprinkle both sides of pork with pepper and salt.
2. Heat 1 teaspoon oil in a 9-inch cast iron skillet coated with cooking spray over medium-high heat. Add pork; cook 3 minutes on each side or until done. Remove pork from pan; set aside.
3. Heat 1 teaspoon oil in pan. Add garlic; sauté 45 seconds. Stir in wine and rosemary, scraping pan to loosen browned bits. Add tomato paste; cook 2 minutes. Stir in broth and orange juice; cook until thick (about 6 minutes). Serve pork with sauce. Yield: 4 servings (serving size: 3 ounces pork and ¼ cup sauce).

CALORIES 195 (25% from fat); FAT 5.4g (sat 1.3g, mono 3g, poly 0.6g); PROTEIN 25.2g; CARB 5.4g; FIBER 0.6g; CHOL 74mg; IRON 2.2mg; SODIUM 302mg; CALC 27mg EXCHANGES: ½ Starch, 3 Lean Meat

FENNEL-CRUSTED PORK TENDERLOIN

Butterflying the pork allows the spice mixture to coat more surface area and infuse more of the meat with flavor.

2	tablespoons fennel seeds
1	tablespoon coriander seeds
6	tablespoons fat-free, less-sodium chicken broth, divided
1	tablespoon Worcestershire sauce
1	teaspoon bottled minced garlic
¼	teaspoon salt
⅛	teaspoon black pepper
1	(1-pound) pork tenderloin
2	teaspoons olive oil

1. Place fennel and coriander in a spice grinder; process until coarsely ground. Place in a blender. Add 2 tablespoons broth, Worcestershire sauce, garlic, salt, and pepper; process until blended.
2. Slice pork horizontally into 2 equal pieces. Slice each piece lengthwise, cutting to, but not through, other side; open flat. Rub spice mixture over pork.

3. Heat olive oil in a large nonstick skillet over medium heat. Add pork; cook 5 minutes on each side. Remove pork from pan; keep warm. Add ¼ cup broth to pan, and cook until liquid almost evaporates, scraping pan to loosen browned bits. Pour over pork. Yield: 4 servings (serving size: 3 ounces pork with pan juices).

CALORIES 168 (30% from fat); FAT 5.7g
(sat 1.3g, mono 3.4g, poly 0.6g);
PROTEIN 24.9g; CARB 3.5g; FIBER 0.9g;
CHOL 74mg; IRON 2.3mg; SODIUM 288mg;
CALC 58mg
EXCHANGES: 3 Lean Meat

ROAST PORK WITH DRIED FRUITS AND SQUASH

Serve this savory and sweet pork at your next holiday meal.

½	cup dried apricots
½	cup pitted prunes
2	cups hot water
½	teaspoon ground cinnamon
1	(5-pound) bone-in pork loin roast
1	tablespoon sugar
1	teaspoon grated peeled fresh ginger
¾	teaspoon salt
¼	teaspoon black pepper
5	cups cubed peeled butternut or acorn squash (about 1½ pounds)

1. Combine first 3 ingredients; cover and let stand 30 minutes or until soft. Drain in a colander over a bowl; reserve liquid. Combine fruit and cinnamon; set aside.
2. Preheat oven to 425°.
3. Trim fat from pork. Cut a 1½-inch-wide horizontal slit through center of pork to form a pocket using a long, thin knife. Stuff apricot mixture into pocket using handle of a wooden spoon to help push apricot mixture to center of pork.
4. Place pork on a broiler pan; insert meat thermometer into thickest portion of pork. Combine sugar, ginger, salt, and pepper. Pour ½ cup reserved liquid over pork; sprinkle with sugar mixture. Bake at 425° for 20 minutes. Reduce oven temperature to 325° (do not remove pork from oven); bake at 325° for 25 minutes. Arrange squash around pork. Bake at 325° an additional 45 minutes or until thermometer registers 160° (slightly pink), basting pork with remaining liquid every 15 minutes. Place pork on a serving platter; cover with foil. Let stand 15 minutes before slicing. Yield: 6 servings (serving size: 3 ounces pork and ⅓ cup squash).

CALORIES 336 (33% from fat); FAT 12.5g
(sat 4.1g, mono 5.3g, poly 1.5g);
PROTEIN 24.5g; CARB 33.3g; FIBER 2.1g;
CHOL 77mg; IRON 2.8mg; SODIUM 373mg;
CALC 63mg
EXCHANGES: 2 Starch, 3 Lean Meat

French-Bread Pizza with Sausage, Clams, and Mushrooms

You need to use only a small amount of Parmesan cheese to get an intense cheese flavor.

1	(4-ounce) link sweet Italian sausage
2	tablespoons all-purpose flour
1½	cups sliced mushrooms
½	cup 1% low-fat milk
½	teaspoon dried oregano
⅛	teaspoon black pepper
1	(6.5-ounce) can chopped clams, undrained
¾	cup (3 ounces) grated fresh Parmesan cheese, divided
1	(16-ounce) loaf French bread, cut in half horizontally
2	tablespoons chopped fresh parsley

1. Preheat oven to 400°.

2. Remove casing from sausage. Cook sausage in a large nonstick skillet over medium heat until browned, stirring to crumble. Add flour, and cook 2 minutes, stirring frequently. Add mushrooms, milk, oregano, pepper, and clams; bring to a boil, stirring constantly. Reduce heat; simmer 5 minutes or until thick. Remove from heat. Stir in ½ cup cheese.

3. Place bread halves on a baking sheet; spread clam mixture evenly over cut sides of bread. Sprinkle with ¼ cup cheese and parsley. Bake at 400° for 12 minutes or until golden brown. Cut each half into 3 pieces. Yield: 6 servings (serving size: 1 piece).

CALORIES 363 (28% from fat); FAT 11.3g (sat 4.7g, mono 4.4g, poly 1.3g); PROTEIN 19.3g; CARB 44.8g; FIBER 2.7g; CHOL 35mg; IRON 4mg; SODIUM 1,048mg; CALC 276mg
EXCHANGES: 3 Starch, 1 Medium-Fat Meat, 1 Fat

Don't Take Out Pizza

There's no reason to take pizza out of your diet when you're trying to lose weight.

With the right kinds of toppings and a low-fat crust, a slice of pizza can provide the nutrients you need to stay healthy and lose weight.

Choose fresh veggie toppings to get fiber, vitamins A and C, and folate. Top your pizza with a low-fat cheese (or a small amount of sharp-flavored cheese) to get calcium. Low-fat meat toppings give you protein and iron. A thin crust or French bread crust provides less fat and calories than a thick crust.

Chapter 41

Poultry

Add big variety to your meals with chicken and turkey. They're versatile, low-fat, and easy to prepare, as you'll see with the recipe selections in this chapter.

CHICKEN-MUSHROOM-RICE TOSS

Keep packages of cooked diced chicken in your freezer so you'll always have the start for a quick and easy low-fat meal.

2	(14½-ounce) cans fat-free, less-sodium chicken broth
1	(3½-ounce) bag boil-in-bag long-grain rice
1	tablespoon sesame oil
⅓	cup chopped green onions
1	tablespoon rice vinegar
2	teaspoons bottled minced garlic
1	teaspoon bottled minced ginger
2	cups thinly sliced shiitake or button mushroom caps (about 4½ ounces)
1½	cups chopped cooked chicken breast (about 9 ounces)

1. Bring broth to a boil in a medium saucepan. Add rice; cook, uncovered, 10 minutes. Drain rice in a colander over a bowl, reserving ¼ cup broth; set rice and broth aside.

2. Heat sesame oil in a large skillet over medium-high heat. Add green onions, vinegar, garlic, and ginger; sauté 1 minute. Add mushrooms; sauté 2 minutes. Stir in rice, reserved broth, and chicken. Cook 3 minutes or until liquid almost evaporates, stirring frequently. Yield: 3 servings (serving size: 1½ cups).

CALORIES 395 (16% from fat); FAT 7.2g (sat 1.4g, mono 2.7g, poly 2.5g); PROTEIN 29.9g; CARB 48g; FIBER 1.7g; CHOL 59.5mg; IRON 3.5mg; SODIUM 568mg; CALC 23mg
EXCHANGES: 3 Starch, 3 Lean Meat

ENCHILADAS VERDES

Use a prepackaged rotisserie chicken for this recipe, and be sure to remove the skin and any excess fat.

SALSA VERDE:

1   pound tomatillos (about 15)
1¼   cups fat-free, less-sodium chicken broth
¼   teaspoon salt
1   jalapeño pepper, seeded and chopped

FILLING:

2½   cups shredded chicken (about 12 ounces)
½   cup (2 ounces) shredded Asiago cheese
⅓   cup finely chopped onion
⅓   cup minced fresh cilantro
⅓   cup fat-free, less-sodium chicken broth
⅓   cup fat-free sour cream
1   tablespoon fresh lime juice
½   teaspoon ground cumin
¼   teaspoon salt
⅛   teaspoon black pepper

REMAINING INGREDIENTS:

Cooking spray
8   (6-inch) corn tortillas
¼   cup fat-free sour cream
Sliced jalapeño pepper (optional)

1. To prepare salsa verde, discard husks and stems from tomatillos; cut into quarters. Combine tomatillos, 1¼ cups broth, ¼ teaspoon salt, and chopped jalapeño in a saucepan over medium heat. Bring to a boil; reduce heat, and simmer 15 minutes or until tomatillos are tender. Cool slightly. Place salsa verde in a blender or food processor, and process until smooth or mash with a potato masher. Place a large nonstick skillet over medium-high heat until hot. Add salsa verde; cook until reduced to 2 cups (about 1 minute).

2. Preheat oven to 400°.

3. To prepare enchilada filling, combine chicken and next 9 ingredients in a large bowl. Spread ½ cup salsa verde in bottom of a 13 x 9-inch baking dish coated with cooking spray. Warm tortillas according to package directions. Spoon about ⅓ cup chicken mixture down center of each tortilla; roll up. Arrange enchiladas, seam sides down, crosswise in dish. Pour remaining salsa verde evenly over enchiladas. Cover and bake at 400° for 10 minutes or until thoroughly heated. Serve with sour cream, and garnish with sliced jalapeño, if desired. Yield: 4 servings (serving size: 2 enchiladas and 1 tablespoon sour cream).

CALORIES 386 (27% from fat); FAT 11.5g (sat 3.9g, mono 3.4g, poly 2.3g); PROTEIN 36.5g; CARB 38.9g; FIBER 4.8g; CHOL 86mg; IRON 2.9mg; SODIUM 841mg; CALC 205mg
EXCHANGES: 2 Starch, 1 Vegetable, 4 Lean Meat

Chicken Tetrazzini with Broccoli

We pumped up the fiber in this familiar dish by adding broccoli.

4	cups broccoli florets
12	ounces uncooked spaghetti
2	tablespoons butter or margarine
3	cups sliced mushrooms
1	teaspoon dried oregano
1	teaspoon dried basil
2	garlic cloves, crushed
½	cup all-purpose flour
3	cups fat-free, less-salt chicken broth
1	cup 2% reduced-fat milk
¾	cup (3 ounces) shredded sharp provolone cheese
2	tablespoons dry sherry
¾	teaspoon salt
⅛	teaspoon black pepper
4	cups chopped cooked chicken
	Cooking spray
¼	cup dry breadcrumbs

1. Cook broccoli in boiling water 5 minutes or until tender; remove broccoli with a slotted spoon, and drain. Return water to a boil; add spaghetti. Cook pasta according to package directions, omitting salt and fat. Drain; set aside.

2. Preheat oven to 450°.

3. Melt butter in a large nonstick skillet over medium-high heat. Add mushrooms, oregano, basil, and garlic; sauté 4 minutes.

Lightly spoon flour into a dry measuring cup; level with a knife. Stir flour into mushroom mixture. Gradually add chicken broth and milk; stir well with a whisk. Bring to a boil, and cook 5 minutes or until thick, stirring occasionally. Add cheese, sherry, salt, and pepper; stir well. Remove from heat, and stir in chicken.

4. Arrange 3 cups spaghetti in a 13 x 9-inch baking dish coated with cooking spray. Top with 2 cups broccoli and half of chicken mixture. Repeat layers. Sprinkle with breadcrumbs. Bake at 450° for 15 minutes or until golden brown. Yield: 8 servings.

CALORIES 422 (26% from fat); FAT 12.3g (sat 5.5g, mono 3.7g, poly 1.8g); PROTEIN 30.8g; CARB 46.2g; FIBER 3.1g; CHOL 74mg; IRON 3.9mg; SODIUM 604mg; CALC 175mg
EXCHANGES: 3 Starch, 3 Lean Meat, 1 Fat

Quick Chicken

To get 4 cups of chopped cooked chicken (if you don't have leftover chicken), place 5 (4-ounce) skinless, boneless chicken breasts on a jelly roll pan; bake at 450° for 10 to 15 minutes or until done. Or use one of the following items.

- deli-roasted chicken, skinned
- 2 (10-ounce) refrigerated packages grilled chicken strips
- 1 (20-ounce) package diced cooked chicken

Chicken-and-Sweet Pepper Fajitas

These fajitas are lower in calories and fat than traditional ones because they're filled with chicken instead of flank steak and have light cream cheese inside instead of sour cream and guacamole.

2   teaspoons vegetable oil, divided
2   cups vertically sliced onion
1   cup yellow bell pepper strips
1   cup red bell pepper strips
1   cup green bell pepper strips
¼   cup thinly sliced seeded jalapeño pepper (about 2 peppers)
⅓   cup chopped fresh cilantro
¼   teaspoon salt
⅛   teaspoon black pepper
12 ounces skinless, boneless chicken breast, cut into 2 x ¼-inch strips
4   (8-inch) flour tortillas
2   tablespoons light cream cheese with garlic and spices

1. Heat 1 teaspoon oil in a large non-stick skillet over medium-high heat. Add onion, bell peppers, and jalapeño; sauté 12 minutes or until crisp-tender. Remove bell pepper mixture from pan; stir in cilantro, salt, and black pepper. **2.** Heat 1 teaspoon oil in pan over medium-high heat. Add chicken; sauté 3 minutes or until done. Return pepper mixture to pan; cook 1 minute.

3. Heat tortillas according to package directions. Spread 1½ teaspoons cream cheese over each tortilla. Divide chicken mixture evenly among tortillas; roll up. Yield: 4 fajitas (serving size: 1 fajita).

CALORIES 334 (25% from fat); FAT 9.4g (sat 2.8g, mono 2.3g, poly 2.9g); PROTEIN 25.8g; CARB 36.6g; FIBER 4.1g; CHOL 57mg; IRON 3.7mg; SODIUM 480mg; CALC 98mg
EXCHANGES: 2 Starch, 1 Vegetable, 2 Lean Meat, 1 Fat

Oven "Fried" Chicken

Soaking the chicken breasts in low-fat buttermilk gives them great flavor, and dredging them in crushed cornflakes makes them crispy.

6   (4-ounce) skinless, boneless chicken breast halves
½   cup low-fat buttermilk
½   cup coarsely crushed cornflakes
¼   cup seasoned breadcrumbs
1   tablespoon instant minced onion
1   teaspoon paprika
¼   teaspoon dried thyme
¼   teaspoon freshly ground black pepper
1   tablespoon vegetable oil

1. Preheat oven to 400°. **2.** Combine chicken and buttermilk in a shallow dish; cover and chill 15 minutes. Drain chicken, discarding liquid. **3.** Combine cornflakes and next 5 ingredients in a large zip-top plastic bag; add

3 chicken pieces to bag. Seal and shake to coat chicken. Repeat with remaining chicken.

4. Spread oil in a jelly roll pan; arrange chicken in a single layer. Bake at 400° for 20 minutes or until chicken is done. Yield: 6 servings (serving size: 1 chicken breast half).

CALORIES 203 (18% from fat); FAT 4.1g (sat 0.7g, mono 1.8g, poly 1.1g); PROTEIN 21.6g; CARB 16g; FIBER 0.3g; CHOL 67mg; IRON 3mg; SODIUM 308mg; CALC 43mg
EXCHANGES: 1 Starch, 3 Very Lean Meat

FAST-FOOD CHICKEN

Don't be fooled into thinking that chicken is always a good low-fat choice at fast-food restaurants.

Many chicken items are coated with batter and deep-fried in oil. The batter acts as a sponge and absorbs a lot of the oil during the frying process. If the chicken is fried with the skin on, the skin adds fat, too.

One extra-crispy fried chicken breast from a fast-food restaurant chain has about 28 grams of fat and 470 calories.

Compare that to the Oven "Fried" Chicken above with only 4.1 grams of fat and 203 calories per serving.

BALSAMIC CHICKEN

This is the dish to make when you need dinner in a hurry. You can keep all the ingredients in either the pantry or freezer, and stir in any fresh veggies you happen to have on hand: spinach, zucchini, all kinds of mushrooms, or green onions.

1   teaspoon olive oil
3/4   cup coarsely chopped onion
4   garlic cloves, sliced
2   (4-ounce) skinless, boneless chicken breast halves
1   cup sliced green bell pepper
1/2   cup balsamic vinegar
1/4   cup sliced mushrooms
1   teaspoon dried Italian seasoning
1   (14 1/2-ounce) can diced tomatoes, undrained
1   cup hot cooked long-grain rice

1. Heat oil in a large skillet over medium-high heat. Add onion and garlic; sauté 3 minutes. Add chicken; cook 4 minutes on each side or until browned. Add bell pepper and next 4 ingredients. Reduce heat to medium-low; cook 20 minutes or until chicken is done. Serve over rice. Yield: 2 servings (serving size: 1 chicken breast half, 1 cup bell pepper mixture, and 1/2 cup rice).

CALORIES 376 (10% from fat); FAT 4.3g (sat 0.8g, mono 2.1g, poly 0.7g); PROTEIN 32g; CARB 52.3g; FIBER 6g; CHOL 66mg; IRON 3.8mg; SODIUM 355mg; CALC 110mg
EXCHANGES: 3 Starch, 1 Vegetable, 3 Very Lean Meat

Spicy Chicken Breasts with Caramelized Onion-Red Pepper Relish

Caramelizing the onion and peppers brings out their natural sweetness.

1½	teaspoons olive oil
1	teaspoon ground coriander
1	teaspoon chili powder
½	teaspoon salt
½	teaspoon garlic powder
½	teaspoon ground cinnamon
¼	teaspoon ground red pepper
4	(4-ounce) skinless, boneless chicken breast halves
2	cups sliced sweet onion
2	red bell peppers, each cut into 4 wedges
¼	cup chopped fresh basil
2	tablespoons pine nuts, toasted
1	tablespoon balsamic vinegar

1. Preheat oven to 450°.

2. Combine first 7 ingredients. Rub both sides of chicken with spice mixture. Arrange onion and peppers in a 13 x 9-inch baking dish; top with chicken. Bake at 450° for 20 minutes. Reduce temperature to 375° (do not remove chicken from oven), and bake 15 minutes or until chicken is done. Remove chicken from dish; keep warm.

3. Remove onion mixture from dish, and chop. Combine onion mixture, peppers, basil, nuts, and vinegar. Serve with chicken. Yield: 4 servings (serving size: 1 chicken breast half and about ½ cup relish).

CALORIES 212 (26% from fat); FAT 6.1g (sat 1.1g, mono 2.6g, poly 1.7g); PROTEIN 28.9g; CARB 11.1g; FIBER 2.7g; CHOL 66mg; IRON 2.2mg; SODIUM 377mg; CALC 45mg
EXCHANGES: 2 Vegetable, 3 Lean Meat

Herb-Oat Crusted Chicken

Oats have soluble fiber, which can help reduce the risk of heart disease.

1	cup regular oats
½	teaspoon salt
¼	teaspoon dried rubbed sage
¼	teaspoon dried summer savory or parsley
¼	teaspoon dried thyme
¼	teaspoon black pepper
⅓	cup egg substitute
6	(4-ounce) skinless, boneless chicken breast halves
	Cooking spray
2	tablespoons butter or margarine, melted

1. Preheat oven to 400°.

2. Arrange oats in a single layer on a jelly roll pan; bake at 400° for 5 minutes or until golden.

3. Combine oats, salt, and next 4 ingredients in a food processor; process until finely chopped. Place oat mixture in a shallow dish; place egg substitute in a medium bowl. Dip chicken in egg substitute, and dredge in oat mixture. Place chicken on a baking sheet coated with cooking spray; drizzle butter over chicken. Bake at 400° for 20 minutes or until done. Yield: 6 servings (serving size: 1 chicken breast half).

CALORIES 219 (25% from fat); FAT 6.2g (sat 2.9g, mono 1.7g, poly 0.8g); PROTEIN 29.7g; CARB 9.4g; FIBER 1.5g; CHOL 76mg; IRON 1.8mg; SODIUM 329mg; CALC 28mg
EXCHANGES: 1 Starch, 4 Very Lean Meat

GREEK CHICKEN WITH CAPERS AND RAISINS IN FETA SAUCE

Ingredients such as garlic, oregano, lemon, and capers add a big kick of flavor without adding fat.

```
4   (4-ounce) skinless, boneless
    chicken breast halves
2   tablespoons all-purpose flour
1   teaspoon dried oregano
1   tablespoon olive oil
1   cup thinly sliced onion
3   garlic cloves, minced
1½  cups fat-free, less-sodium
    chicken broth
⅓   cup golden raisins
2   tablespoons lemon juice
2   tablespoons capers
¼   cup (1 ounce) crumbled feta
    cheese
4   thin lemon slices
```

1. Place each chicken breast half between 2 sheets of heavy-duty plastic wrap; flatten to ¼-inch thickness. Combine flour and oregano in a shallow dish; dredge chicken in flour mixture.
2. Heat oil in a large nonstick skillet over medium-high heat. Add chicken; cook 5 minutes on each side. Remove chicken from pan; keep warm. Add onion and garlic to pan; sauté 2 minutes. Stir in broth, raisins, and lemon juice; cook 3 minutes, scraping pan to loosen browned bits. Return chicken to pan. Cover, reduce heat, and simmer 10 minutes or until chicken is done. Remove chicken from pan; keep warm. Add capers and cheese to pan, stirring with a whisk; top each chicken breast with ¼ cup sauce and 1 lemon slice. Yield: 4 servings.

CALORIES 256 (23% from fat); FAT 6.5g (sat 1.9g, mono 3.2g, poly 0.7g); PROTEIN 30g; CARB 19g; FIBER 1.3g; CHOL 72mg; IRON 1.6mg; SODIUM 671mg; CALC 71mg
EXCHANGES: 1 Fruit, 4 Very Lean Meat, 1 Fat

CHICKEN WITH EGGPLANT-PEPPER SAUCE

Microwaving is a great low-fat cooking method for vegetables because you don't need to add any fat.

- 1 eggplant (about ½ pound)
- 2 red bell peppers (about 1 pound)
- ¾ teaspoon salt, divided
- ¼ teaspoon ground ginger
- ¼ teaspoon garlic powder
- ¼ teaspoon ground red pepper, divided
- 4 (4-ounce) skinless, boneless chicken breast halves
- 2 teaspoons olive oil, divided
- 1 teaspoon paprika
- 4 teaspoons lemon juice

1. Slice eggplant in half lengthwise, and pierce skin with a fork. Cut tops off bell peppers; discard tops, seeds, and membranes. Place eggplant and bell peppers on a microwave-safe plate. Microwave at HIGH 8 minutes or until tender.

2. Combine ¼ teaspoon salt, ginger, garlic powder, and ⅛ teaspoon ground red pepper; sprinkle chicken with ginger mixture. Heat 1 teaspoon olive oil in a large nonstick skillet over medium-high heat. Add chicken, and cook 6 minutes on each side or until chicken is done.

3. Combine eggplant and bell peppers in a blender or food processor. Add ½ teaspoon salt, ⅛ teaspoon ground red

pepper, 1 teaspoon oil, paprika, and juice; process until smooth. Serve chicken with sauce. Yield: 4 servings (serving size: 1 chicken breast half and about ⅓ cup sauce).

CALORIES 194 (19% from fat); FAT 4.1g (sat 0.7g, mono 2g, poly 0.7g); PROTEIN 27.9g; CARB 11.8g; FIBER 3.9g; CHOL 66mg; IRON 1.7mg; SODIUM 518mg; CALC 29mg EXCHANGES: 2 Vegetable, 3 Very Lean Meat

HOISIN BARBECUED CHICKEN

Hoisin sauce forms the base of this simple fat-free barbecue sauce. It's good with chicken as well as lean pork.

BARBECUE SAUCE:
- ⅔ cup hoisin sauce
- 3 tablespoons rice wine or sake
- 3 tablespoons low-sodium soy sauce
- 3 tablespoons ketchup
- 2 tablespoons brown sugar
- 1 tablespoon minced garlic

REMAINING INGREDIENTS:
- 8 skinless chicken drumsticks, (about 2 pounds)
- 8 skinless chicken thighs, (about 2 pounds)
- Cooking spray

1. To prepare barbecue sauce, combine first 6 ingredients in a medium bowl. Place ¾ cup sauce in a large bowl; cover and chill remaining barbecue sauce.

2. Add chicken to barbecue sauce in a

large bowl; toss to coat. Cover and marinate in refrigerator 8 hours or overnight.

3. Preheat oven to 375°.

4. Remove chicken from bowl; reserve marinade. Place chicken on a broiler pan coated with cooking spray. Bake at 375° for 30 minutes. Turn chicken; baste with reserved marinade. Bake an additional 20 minutes or until done. Discard marinade.

5. Bring remaining ¾ cup barbecue sauce to a boil in a small saucepan; reduce heat, and cook until slightly thick and reduced to about ½ cup (about 5 minutes). Drizzle chicken with sauce. Yield: 8 servings (serving size: 1 drumstick, 1 thigh, and about 1 tablespoon sauce).

CALORIES 241 (23% from fat); FAT 6.1g
(sat 1.5g, mono 1.9g, poly 1.8g);
PROTEIN 26.6g; CARB 17.8g; FIBER 0.7g;
CHOL 97mg; IRON 1.7mg; SODIUM 727mg;
CALC 26mg
EXCHANGES: 1 Starch, 3 Lean Meat

SAUCE IT UP

Hoisin sauce is a thick, sweet sauce often used in Asian cooking. You can find it in most grocery stores along with the other condiments and sauces, or in Asian markets.

CHINESE-STYLE GLAZED CHICKEN BREASTS

Use preserves or fruit spreads to add flavor without fat.

¼ cup fat-free, less-sodium chicken broth
2 tablespoons hoisin sauce
1 tablespoon apricot preserves or fruit spread
4 (4-ounce) skinless, boneless chicken breast halves
½ teaspoon salt
⅛ teaspoon black pepper
1 tablespoon vegetable oil

1. Combine first 3 ingredients.

2. Place each chicken breast half between 2 sheets of heavy-duty plastic wrap; pound to ¼-inch thickness. Sprinkle chicken with salt and pepper.

3. Heat vegetable oil in a large skillet over medium-high heat. Add chicken, and sauté 3 minutes on each side. Remove chicken from pan. Reduce heat; carefully stir in broth mixture. Return chicken to pan; cook 3 minutes or until done, turning to coat. Yield: 4 servings (serving size: 1 chicken breast half and 1 tablespoon sauce).

CALORIES 186 (25% from fat); FAT 5.1g
(sat 0.9g, mono 1.3g, poly 2.5g);
PROTEIN 26.7g; CARB 6.9g; FIBER 0.3g;
CHOL 66mg; IRON 0.9mg; SODIUM 526mg;
CALC 17mg
EXCHANGES: ½ Starch, 3 Lean Meat

MOROCCAN CHICKEN

The flavor of the dark meat chicken complements the bold Moroccan spices.

8   (4-ounce) chicken thighs, skinned
4   teaspoons salt-free Moroccan seasoning
½   teaspoon salt
1   tablespoon olive oil
1   (15-ounce) can chickpeas, drained
1   (14.5-ounce) can no-salt-added diced tomatoes, drained
2   cups (¼-inch) sliced zucchini
½   cup fat-free, less-sodium chicken broth
1   tablespoon fresh lemon juice

1. Rub chicken with seasoning and salt.
2. Heat oil in a nonstick skillet over medium-high heat. Add chicken; sauté 3 minutes on each side. Add chickpeas and tomatoes; cook 5 minutes. Add zucchini and broth; bring to a boil. Cover, reduce heat, and simmer 10 minutes. Stir in lemon juice. Yield: 4 servings (serving size: 2 thighs and ½ cup chickpea mixture).

CALORIES 338 (29% from fat); FAT 10.8g (sat 2.1g, mono 4.7g, poly 2.5g); PROTEIN 34.9g; CARB 25.9g; FIBER 3.1g; CHOL 113mg; IRON 4.8mg; SODIUM 625mg; CALC 95mg
EXCHANGES: 1 Starch, 2 Vegetable, 4 Lean Meat

LEMONY PEPPER CHICKEN

Dark meat chicken has only about 8 grams of fat per 3-ounce serving.

8   (6-ounce) chicken thighs, skinned
1½   teaspoons dried oregano
½   teaspoon salt
¼   teaspoon black pepper
¼   teaspoon paprika
Cooking spray
1½   cups red bell pepper strips
1½   cups green bell pepper strips
1   tablespoon grated lemon rind
¼   cup fresh lemon juice
½   cup fat-free, less-sodium chicken broth
2   tablespoons ketchup

1. Sprinkle chicken with oregano, salt, black pepper, and paprika. Heat a large nonstick skillet coated with cooking spray over medium-high heat. Add chicken; sauté 3 minutes. Turn chicken; top with bell peppers, rind, and juice. Cover, reduce heat, and simmer 30 minutes or until chicken is done. Remove from pan.
2. Combine broth and ketchup. Stir ketchup mixture into pan; bring to a boil. Serve pepper mixture with chicken. Yield: 4 servings (serving size: 2 chicken thighs and ½ cup pepper mixture).

CALORIES 267 (26% from fat); FAT 7.8g (sat 2g, mono 2.4g, poly 2g); PROTEIN 39.4g; CARB 8.7g; FIBER 1.9g; CHOL 161mg; IRON 2.8mg; SODIUM 609mg; CALC 40mg
EXCHANGES: 2 Vegetable, 4 Lean Meat

LEMON-PEPPER ROASTED CHICKEN

Be sure to remove the skin before eating the chicken; the skin is where most of the fat is located.

1   (5- to 6-pound) roasting chicken
1   tablespoon grated lemon rind
1   teaspoon cracked black pepper
½   teaspoon garlic powder
½   teaspoon salt

1. Preheat oven to 400°.
2. Remove and discard giblets and neck from chicken. Rinse with cold water; pat dry. Trim excess fat. Starting at neck cavity, loosen skin from breast and drumsticks by inserting fingers, gently pushing between skin and meat.
3. Combine lemon rind, pepper, garlic powder, and salt. Rub lemon mixture under and over loosened skin. Lift wing tips up and over back; tuck under chicken. Place chicken, breast side up, on a foil-lined broiler pan. Insert meat thermometer into meaty part of thigh, making sure not to touch bone. Bake chicken at 400° for 1 hour and 15 minutes or until thermometer registers 180°. Let stand 10 minutes. Discard skin. Yield: 8 servings (serving size: about 3 ounces).

CALORIES 221 (35% from fat); FAT 8.7g
(sat 2.4g, mono 3.3g, poly 2g); PROTEIN 33g;
CARB 0.4g; FIBER 0.2g; CHOL 99mg;
IRON 1.7mg; SODIUM 245mg; CALC 18 mg
EXCHANGES: 4 Lean Meat

ROAST CHICKEN WITH CUMIN AND HONEY

1   (3-pound) roasting chicken
¼   cup honey
1½ tablespoons grated orange rind
1   tablespoon ground cumin
¼   teaspoon salt
⅛   teaspoon black pepper
1   garlic clove, minced

1. Preheat oven to 400°.
2. Remove and discard giblets from chicken. Rinse chicken with cold water; pat dry. Trim excess fat. Starting at neck cavity, loosen skin from breast and drumsticks by inserting fingers, gently pushing between skin and meat.
3. Combine honey and remaining ingredients. Rub honey mixture under loosened skin and over breast and drumsticks. Lift wing tips up and over back; tuck under chicken. Place chicken, breast side up, on a foil-lined broiler pan. Pierce skin several times with a meat fork. Insert meat thermometer into meaty part of thigh, making sure not to touch bone. Bake at 400° for 30 minutes; cover loosely with foil. Bake 40 minutes or until thermometer registers 180°. Let stand 10 minutes. Discard skin. Yield: 4 servings (serving size: about 3 ounces).

CALORIES 273 (27% from fat); FAT 8.2g
(sat 2.2g, mono 3g, poly 1.9g); PROTEIN 31.2g;
CARB 19g; FIBER 0.2g; CHOL 95mg;
IRON 2.4mg; SODIUM 241mg; CALC 37mg
EXCHANGES: 1 Starch, 4 Lean Meat

TURKEY JAMBALAYA

We've lightened a Cajun classic by reducing the amount of sausage and replacing it with shredded turkey.

1	tablespoon olive oil
1½	cups chopped onion
1	teaspoon bottled minced garlic
1	cup chopped green bell pepper
1	cup chopped red bell pepper
2½	teaspoons paprika
½	teaspoon salt
½	teaspoon dried oregano
½	teaspoon ground red pepper
½	teaspoon black pepper
1	cup uncooked long-grain rice
2	cups fat-free, less-sodium chicken broth
1	(14.5-ounce) can diced tomatoes, undrained
2	cups shredded cooked turkey
6	ounces andouille sausage, chopped
2	tablespoons sliced green onions

1. Heat oil in a large Dutch oven over medium-high heat. Add onion and garlic; sauté 6 minutes or until lightly browned. Stir in bell peppers and next 5 ingredients; sauté 1 minute. Add rice; sauté 1 minute. Stir in broth and tomatoes; bring to a boil. Cover, reduce heat, and simmer 15 minutes.

2. Add shredded turkey and andouille sausage; cover and cook 5 minutes.

Sprinkle with green onions. Yield: 8 servings (serving size: 1 cup).

CALORIES 249 (27% from fat); FAT 7.6g (sat 2.4g, mono 3.4g, poly 1.3g); PROTEIN 17.3g; CARB 27.4g; FIBER 2.7g; CHOL 42mg; IRON 2.7mg; SODIUM 523mg; CALC 37mg
EXCHANGES: 2 Starch, 1 High-Fat Meat

TURKEY-VEGETABLE PARMESAN

1	teaspoon olive oil
1	cup chopped onion (about 1)
1½	cups chopped green bell pepper
2	garlic cloves, minced
1	pound ground turkey breast
1	(28-ounce) can diced tomatoes, drained
1	(8-ounce) can tomato sauce with garlic and onion
½	teaspoon salt
¼	teaspoon black pepper
2	zucchini, sliced
3	cups hot cooked ziti (about 6 ounces uncooked pasta)
3	tablespoons chopped fresh basil
3	tablespoons grated Parmesan cheese

1. Heat oil in a nonstick skillet over medium-high heat. Add onion, green bell pepper, and garlic; sauté 7 minutes. Add turkey; cook until turkey is browned, stirring to crumble.

2. Add diced tomatoes, tomato sauce, salt, and black pepper. Bring to a boil;

cover, reduce heat, and simmer 20 minutes, stirring occasionally.

3. Add zucchini; simmer 3 minutes. Add pasta and basil; return mixture to a boil. Remove from heat. Let stand 5 minutes. Sprinkle with cheese. Yield: 5 servings (serving size: 1½ cups).

CALORIES 347 (27% from fat); FAT 10.3g (sat 3g; mono 3.6g; poly 2.1g);
PROTEIN 24.3g; CARB 39.2g; FIBER 5.1g;
CHOL 75mg; IRON 3.4mg; SODIUM 728mg;
CALC 107mg
EXCHANGES: 1½ Starch, 3 Vegetable, 2 Lean Meat, 1 Fat

Turkey Lo Mein

You can use one pound of skinless, boneless chicken breast, pounded and cut into strips, instead of turkey.

> 6 ounces uncooked linguine
> Cooking spray
> 2½ teaspoons dark sesame oil
> 1 pound turkey cutlets, cut into strips
> 2 cups snow peas, trimmed
> 1 cup red bell pepper strips
> 1 cup broccoli florets
> ½ cup shredded carrot
> 2 tablespoons chopped green onions
> 1 teaspoon minced peeled fresh ginger
> ⅛ teaspoon crushed red pepper
> 2 garlic cloves, crushed
> 3 tablespoons low-sodium soy sauce

1. Cook pasta according to package directions, omitting salt and fat. Drain.

2. Coat a large nonstick skillet with cooking spray; add 1 teaspoon oil. Place over high heat. Add turkey, and stir-fry 5 minutes or until done. Add snow peas and next 7 ingredients; stir-fry 4 minutes. Add pasta and soy sauce; cook 2 minutes. Remove from heat; add remaining 1½ teaspoons oil, and toss well to coat. Yield: 4 servings (serving size: 2 cups).

CALORIES 404 (23% from fat); FAT 10g (sat 2.3g; mono 4.4g; poly 3.6g);
PROTEIN 33.1g; CARB 43.8g; FIBER 5.6g;
CHOL 60mg; IRON 4.5mg; SODIUM 520mg;
CALC 72mg
EXCHANGES: 2 Starch, 2 Vegetable, 3 Very Lean Meat, 1 Fat

Turkey Talk

Look for packaged turkey cutlets in the poultry section of the grocery store. If you can't find cutlets, you can use turkey breast tenderloins and pound them to ¼-inch thickness.

Keep fresh uncooked turkey in its original packaging for up to 3 days in the refrigerator. Or you can freeze it for up to 3 months.

GRILLED TURKEY TENDERLOINS WITH MANGO-PAPAYA SALSA

Turkey is not just for Thanksgiving. This grilled version with salsa is great for summertime entertaining.

SALSA:

¾ cup diced peeled mango
¾ cup diced peeled papaya
½ cup diced red onion
½ cup diced plum tomato
3 tablespoons chopped fresh cilantro
2 tablespoons fresh lime juice
2 teaspoons olive oil
1½ teaspoons grated lime rind
⅛ teaspoon salt
⅛ teaspoon ground red pepper

TURKEY:

¼ cup fresh lime juice
1 tablespoon olive oil
½ teaspoon salt
¼ teaspoon ground cumin
¼ teaspoon ground red pepper
2 (½-pound) turkey tenderloins
Cooking spray

1. To prepare salsa, combine first 10 ingredients in a medium bowl; toss gently. Cover and chill.
2. To prepare turkey, combine lime juice and next 5 ingredients in a large heavy-duty zip-top plastic bag; seal bag, and marinate in refrigerator 30 minutes.
3. Prepare grill.

4. Remove turkey from bag, reserving marinade. Place marinade in a saucepan. Bring to a boil; remove from heat. Coat grill rack with cooking spray; place turkey on rack over medium-hot coals (350° to 400°). Grill, covered, 10 minutes on each side or until turkey is done, turning and basting frequently with reserved marinade. Cut turkey diagonally across grain into thin (¼-inch-thick) slices. Serve turkey with Mango-Papaya Salsa. Yield: 4 servings (serving size: 3 ounces turkey and ½ cup salsa).

CALORIES 223 (35% from fat); FAT 8.7g (sat 1.7g; mono 5.1g; poly 1.7g); PROTEIN 24.4g; CARB 12.3g; FIBER 1.6g; CHOL 55mg; IRON 1.5mg; SODIUM 422mg; CALC 36mg
EXCHANGES: 1 Fruit, 3 Lean Meat

Chapter 42

Salads

If your idea of salad is just a bowl of lettuce,
we'd like to give you a few new ideas.

SPICY MELON SALAD

Tingle your taste buds with this
combination of sweet melon and fiery
jalapeño pepper.

- ⅔ cup water
- ½ cup minced fresh mint
- ¼ cup sugar
- 1 jalapeño pepper, seeded and minced
- 8 cups chopped melon (such as cantaloupe and honeydew)
- ½ teaspoon ground cumin

1. Combine first 4 ingredients in a small saucepan. Bring to a boil; reduce heat, and simmer 5 minutes. Combine melon and cumin in a large bowl; drizzle with mint mixture. Toss well to combine. Yield: 8 servings (serving size: 1 cup).

CALORIES 83 (3% from fat); FAT 0.3g (sat 0.1g, mono 0g, poly 0.1g); PROTEIN 1.2g; CARB 20.9g; FIBER 1.3g; CHOL 0mg; IRON 0.3mg; SODIUM 16mg; CALC 16mg EXCHANGES: ½ Starch, 1 Fruit

STRAWBERRIES-AND-FETA SALAD

Both strawberries and orange juice are
excellent sources of disease-fighting
vitamin C.

- 2 tablespoons orange juice
- 1 tablespoon white wine vinegar
- 2 teaspoons extra-virgin olive oil
- ¾ teaspoon sugar
- 6 cups gourmet salad greens
- 1 cup quartered strawberries
- ¼ cup (1 ounce) crumbled feta cheese

1. Combine first 4 ingredients in a small bowl; stir with a whisk. Combine greens, strawberries, and cheese in a large bowl; add orange juice mixture, tossing to coat. Serve immediately. Yield: 4 servings (serving size: 1½ cups).

CALORIES 70 (53% from fat); FAT 4.1g (sat 1.4g, mono 2g, poly 0.4g); PROTEIN 2.7g; CARB 6.6g; FIBER 2.3g; CHOL 6mg; IRON 1.1mg; SODIUM 87mg; CALC 71mg EXCHANGES: ½ Fruit, 1 Fat

FIELD SALAD WITH ROASTED LEEKS, MUSHROOMS, AND FETA

Roasting vegetables is one of the best ways to bring out their natural rich sweetness.

1 cup thinly sliced leek
1 teaspoon olive oil
Cooking spray
3 cups trimmed arugula
3 cups spinach leaves
1 cup sliced mushrooms
¼ cup (1 ounce) crumbled feta cheese
3 tablespoons light dill-mustard dressing (such as Maple Grove Farms of Vermont)

1. Preheat oven to 450°.

2. Combine sliced leek and oil. Spread leek mixture into a jelly roll pan coated with cooking spray. Bake at 450° for 10 minutes or until browned.

3. Combine leek mixture, arugula, spinach, mushrooms, and cheese in a large bowl. Drizzle with dressing, and toss gently to coat. Yield: 4 servings (serving size: 1¾ cups).

CALORIES 88 (51% from fat); FAT 5g (sat 1.6g, mono 1.7g, poly 1.4g); PROTEIN 2.6g; CARB 8.6g; FIBER 1.4g; CHOL 6mg; IRON 1.4mg; SODIUM 197mg; CALC 103mg EXCHANGES: 2 Vegetable, 1 Fat

SIMPLEST GREEN SALAD

10 cups mixed salad greens
¼ teaspoon kosher salt
5 teaspoons extra-virgin olive oil
2 teaspoons fresh lemon juice
⅛ teaspoon freshly ground black pepper

1. Sprinkle greens with salt; toss. Add remaining ingredients; toss. Yield: 5 servings (serving size: 2 cups).

CALORIES 58 (73% from fat); FAT 4.7g (sat 0.6g, mono 3.3g, poly 0.5g); PROTEIN 1.8g; CARB 2.9g; FIBER 1.9g; CHOL 0mg; IRON 1.3mg; SODIUM 65mg; CALC 41mg EXCHANGES: ½ Vegetable, 1 Fat

CAESAR SALAD

Try a light version of a classic salad.

8 cups torn romaine lettuce
⅓ cup light Caesar dressing
3 tablespoons grated fresh Parmesan cheese
1 cup croutons

1. Combine lettuce and dressing, tossing to coat. Top with Parmesan cheese and croutons. Yield: 6 servings (serving size: about 1½ cups).

CALORIES 70 (37% from fat); FAT 2.9g (sat 1.1g, mono 1.1g, poly 0.6g); PROTEIN 3.3g; CARB 8.6g; FIBER 1.6g; CHOL 3mg; IRON 1.1mg; SODIUM 290mg; CALC 79mg EXCHANGES: ½ Starch, ½ Fat

CLASSIC LAYERED SALAD

Light mayonnaise gives the dressing a rich and creamy texture without all the fat of regular mayonnaise.

½ cup light mayonnaise
2 tablespoons grated Parmesan cheese
2 teaspoons sugar
⅛ teaspoon salt
⅛ teaspoon black pepper
1 large ripe tomato, cut into 8 wedges
4 cups torn iceberg lettuce
2 cups small cauliflower florets
½ cup thinly sliced red onion
1 tablespoon bottled real bacon bits

1. Combine first 5 ingredients; stir well with a whisk. Arrange tomato wedges in bottom of a 2-quart serving bowl. Top with lettuce and cauliflower. Spread mayonnaise mixture over cauliflower. Top with onion and bacon bits.

2. Cover and chill 8 hours or overnight. Toss gently before serving. Yield: 7 servings (serving size: 1 cup).

CALORIES 65 (33% from fat); FAT 2.4g (sat 0.8g, mono 0.7g, poly 0.8g); PROTEIN 2.1g; CARB 9.5g; FIBER 1.3g; CHOL 2mg; IRON 0.4mg; SODIUM 261mg; CALC 36mg EXCHANGES: 2 Vegetable, ½ Fat

FRESH-FROM-THE-GARDEN VEGETABLE SALAD

Your mother will be happy because you're eating your vegetables; you'll be happy because this sweet and tangy vegetable recipe tastes so good.

4 quarts water
¾ pound green beans, trimmed
¾ pound carrots, cut into 3½ x ¼-inch sticks
1 tablespoon sugar
2 tablespoons cider vinegar
2 tablespoons Dijon mustard
1 tablespoon vegetable oil
¾ teaspoon salt
1 cup yellow bell pepper strips
¼ cup finely chopped onion

1. Bring water to a boil in an 8-quart stockpot. Add beans; cook 1 minute. Add carrot; cook 2 minutes or until crisp-tender. Drain; place vegetables in ice water. Let stand 1 minute or until cool; drain.

2. Combine sugar, vinegar, mustard, oil, and salt in a large bowl; stir well with a whisk. Add beans, carrot, bell pepper, and onion; toss gently to coat. Yield: 6 servings (serving size: 1 cup).

CALORIES 84 (31% from fat); FAT 2.9g (sat 0.5g, mono 0.7g, poly 1.2g); PROTEIN 1.8g; CARB 14g; FIBER 3.4g; CHOL 0mg; IRON 1.1mg; SODIUM 466mg; CALC 39mg EXCHANGES: ½ Starch, 1 Vegetable, ½ Fat

CHIPOTLE, TOMATO, AND ROASTED VEGETABLE SALAD

1½ cups chopped onion
1⅓ cups chopped green bell pepper
1⅓ cups chopped yellow bell pepper
      Cooking spray
1⅓ cups chopped seeded tomato
¼   cup minced fresh cilantro
1   (7-ounce) can chipotle chiles in
      adobo sauce
2   tablespoons cider vinegar
2   teaspoons extra-virgin olive oil
½   teaspoon salt

1. Preheat broiler.
2. Place first 3 ingredients on a baking sheet coated with cooking spray. Lightly coat mixture with cooking spray; broil 8 minutes or until vegetables begin to blacken, stirring once. Cool mixture. Add tomato and cilantro.
3. Remove 1 chile from can, and chop to measure 1½ teaspoons. Reserve remaining chiles for another use.
4. Combine chile, vinegar, oil, and salt, and stir with a whisk. Drizzle over onion mixture; toss gently to coat. Yield: 12 servings (serving size: ⅓ cup).

CALORIES 28 (37% from fat); FAT 1.1g
(sat 0.1g, mono 0.6g, poly 0.2g); PROTEIN 0.7g;
CARB 4.5g; FIBER 1.1g; CHOL 0mg;
IRON 0.6mg; SODIUM 106mg; CALC 8mg
EXCHANGE: 1 Vegetable

RIPE TOMATO SALAD

Tomatoes are a powerhouse of disease-fighting, age-defying nutrients: Vitamin C, vitamin A, and lycopene top the list.

2   tablespoons balsamic vinegar
2   tablespoons brown sugar
3   cups mixed salad greens
1   large yellow tomato, sliced
1   large red tomato, sliced
¼   teaspoon salt
1   tablespoon pine nuts

1. Combine vinegar and brown sugar; microwave at MEDIUM (50% power) until mixture comes to a boil (about 1½ to 2 minutes). Let stand until cool and slightly thick (about 5 minutes).
2. Place ¾ cup salad greens on each of 4 plates. Arrange tomato slices evenly on top of salad greens. Sprinkle salt evenly over tomatoes. Drizzle evenly with vinaigrette, and sprinkle with pine nuts. Yield: 4 servings.

CALORIES 58 (23% from fat); FAT 1.5g
(sat 0.2g, mono 0.5g, poly 0.6g); PROTEIN 2.1g;
CARB 10.8g; FIBER 1.9g; CHOL 0mg;
IRON 1.4mg; SODIUM 177mg; CALC 38mg
EXCHANGES: 2 Vegetable

CRUNCHY NOODLE SALAD

Napa cabbage is a filling and fiber-filled alternative to lettuce. And it's rich in folate, a vitamin that helps prevent birth defects.

3 tablespoons rice or cider vinegar
2 tablespoons sugar
1 tablespoon vegetable oil
1 tablespoon honey
1 tablespoon low-sodium soy sauce
1½ teaspoons margarine
2 tablespoons slivered almonds, toasted
1 tablespoon sunflower seed kernels
1 (5-ounce) package Japanese curly noodles (chucka soba), crumbled
4 cups shredded napa (Chinese) cabbage
1 cup shredded carrot
½ cup thinly sliced green onions

1. Combine first 5 ingredients in a small saucepan. Bring to a boil, and cook 1 minute, stirring constantly. Spoon mixture into a bowl; cover and chill.
2. Melt butter in a large nonstick skillet over medium-high heat. Add almonds, sunflower kernels, and noodles; cook 2 minutes or until lightly toasted, tossing occasionally. Spoon mixture into a large bowl; cover and chill.
3. Add vinegar mixture to noodle mixture; let stand 15 minutes.
4. Add cabbage, carrot, and onions, tossing to coat. Yield: 6 servings (serving size: ¾ cup).
Note: This recipe is a reader recipe makeover. The original recipe serves 12 (see page 159), but we modified this version for smaller families.

CALORIES 192 (28% from fat); FAT 5.9g
(sat 0.5g, mono 2.9g, poly 1.7g); PROTEIN 4.6g;
CARB 31.6g; FIBER 3.1g; CHOL 0mg;
IRON 0.9mg; SODIUM 273mg; CALC 42mg
EXCHANGES: 1½ Starch, 1 Vegetable, 1 Fat

BLACK BEAN SALAD

Black beans are naturally low in fat and packed with protein, vitamins, and minerals. Plus, they're full of fiber, so they help you feel full.

1 (15-ounce) can black beans, drained and rinsed
2 chopped green onions
1 plum tomato, chopped
1 tablespoon chopped fresh cilantro
1 tablespoon fresh lime juice
1 tablespoon olive oil

1. Combine all ingredients in a medium bowl, stirring well. Cover and chill. Yield: 4 servings (serving size: ½ cup).

CALORIES 72 (44% from fat); FAT 3.5g
(sat 0.5g, mono 2.5g, poly 0.3g); PROTEIN 2.8g;
CARB 10.1g; FIBER 3.4g; CHOL 0mg;
IRON 1.1mg; SODIUM 191mg; CALC 30mg
EXCHANGES: 2 Vegetable, ½ Fat

White Bean Salad with Asparagus and Artichokes

If you can't find baby artichokes, use fresh artichoke bottoms. Canned artichokes will also work, but they're higher in sodium than the fresh.

10 fresh baby artichokes, peeled and quartered
2 cups (1-inch) diagonally cut asparagus
1/3 cup thinly sliced radishes
3 tablespoons thinly sliced green onions
2 tablespoons thinly sliced fresh basil
2 tablespoons fresh lemon juice
1 tablespoon extra-virgin olive oil
1/4 teaspoon salt
1/8 teaspoon black pepper
1 (19-ounce) can Great Northern beans or other white beans, rinsed and drained

1. Steam artichokes, covered, 10 minutes or until tender. Steam asparagus, covered, 2 minutes.
2. Combine radishes and remaining ingredients in a bowl, and gently stir in artichokes and asparagus. Yield: 4 servings (serving size: 1 cup).

CALORIES 170 (22% from fat); FAT 4.2g
(sat 0.7g, mono 2.5g, poly 0.6g); PROTEIN 10.3g;
CARB 26.7g; FIBER 5g; CHOL 0mg;
IRON 2.7mg; SODIUM 400mg; CALC 89mg
EXCHANGES: 1 Starch, 2 Vegetable, 1 Fat

Tabbouleh

Pack this flavor-filled Middle Eastern salad for your next picnic, or stuff it in pita bread for a light lunch on the go.

4 cups diced tomato
2/3 cup chopped fresh flat-leaf parsley
1/3 cup thinly sliced green onions
1/4 cup uncooked bulgur
1/4 cup chopped fresh mint
2 1/2 teaspoons extra-virgin olive oil
2 tablespoons fresh lemon juice
1/2 teaspoon kosher salt
1/2 teaspoon ground allspice
1/4 teaspoon ground cinnamon
1/4 teaspoon freshly ground black pepper
5 large iceberg lettuce leaves

1. Combine first 5 ingredients in a large bowl. Cover and let stand 30 minutes.
2. Stir in oil and next 5 ingredients; toss well. Serve on lettuce leaves. Yield: 5 servings (serving size: 1 cup salad and 1 lettuce leaf).

CALORIES 83 (31% from fat); FAT 2.9g
(sat 0.4g, mono 1.8g, poly 0.5g); PROTEIN 2.6g;
CARB 14g; FIBER 3.6g; CHOL 0mg;
IRON 1.6mg; SODIUM 255mg; CALC 31mg
EXCHANGES: 1/2 Starch, 1 Vegetable

WARM POTATO SALAD

You'll never want to go back to regular fat-laden potato salad once you try this light and savory version.

    3   Yukon gold or red potatoes, cut
        into 1/4-inch-thick slices (about
        1 pound)
  1/4   cup sliced onion, separated into
        rings
    2   tablespoons quartered pitted
        kalamata olives
    3   tablespoons red wine vinegar
    1   tablespoon olive oil
    2   tablespoons chopped fresh
        parsley
    1   teaspoon chopped fresh or
        1/4 teaspoon dried thyme
  1/2   teaspoon salt
  1/4   teaspoon pepper

1. Cook potatoes in boiling water 5 minutes or until tender, and drain well.
2. Combine potatoes, onion, and olives in a bowl. Combine vinegar and remaining ingredients, stirring well with a whisk. Pour over potato mixture; toss gently. Serve warm. Yield: 6 servings (serving size: 1/2 cup).

CALORIES 85 (30% from fat); FAT 2.8g
(sat 0.4g, mono 2g, poly 0.3g); PROTEIN 1.8g;
CARB 13.7g; FIBER 1.7g; CHOL 0mg;
IRON 1.3mg; SODIUM 242mg; CALC 18mg
EXCHANGE: 1 Starch

CRAB SALAD WITH WHITE BEANS AND GOURMET GREENS

If you're in a rut with the usual grilled chicken or tuna salads, top your greens with sweet crabmeat and tender white beans.

  1/3   cup chopped yellow bell pepper
  1/3   cup chopped red onion
  1/4   cup chopped celery
    2   tablespoons white wine vinegar
    1   tablespoon fresh lemon juice
    1   tablespoon olive oil
  1/4   teaspoon salt
  1/8   teaspoon hot sauce
    2   (6-ounce) cans lump crabmeat,
        drained
    1   (16-ounce) can cannellini beans
        or other white beans, rinsed and
        drained
    6   cups torn gourmet salad greens

1. Combine first 10 ingredients; toss gently. Cover and chill 20 minutes.
2. Serve over greens. Yield: 6 servings (serving size: 2/3 cup salad and 1 cup greens).

CALORIES 149 (25% from fat); FAT 4.1g
(sat 0.6g, mono 2g, poly 1g); PROTEIN 12.8g;
CARB 16.6g; FIBER 4.3g; CHOL 29mg;
IRON 3.3mg; SODIUM 353mg; CALC 117mg
EXCHANGES: 1 Starch, 2 Very Lean Meat

SESAME SHRIMP-AND-COUSCOUS SALAD

The peanuts sprinkled on this salad add a little fat, but it's monounsaturated fat, a good kind of fat that may help ward off heart disease.

3¼ cups water, divided
½ pound medium shrimp, peeled and deveined
1 cup uncooked couscous
¼ cup seasoned rice vinegar
2 teaspoons vegetable oil
1½ teaspoons low-sodium soy sauce
½ teaspoon dark sesame oil
1 garlic clove, crushed
1½ cups thinly sliced romaine lettuce
1 cup chopped red bell pepper
¾ cup frozen green peas, thawed
¼ cup chopped fresh cilantro
2 tablespoons finely chopped unsalted, dry-roasted peanuts

1. Bring 2 cups water to a boil in a medium saucepan. Add shrimp; cook 3 minutes or until done. Drain and rinse with cold water; cut shrimp in half.
2. Bring 1¼ cups water to a boil in pan; gradually stir in couscous. Remove from heat; cover and let stand 5 minutes. Fluff with a fork; cool.
3. Combine vinegar, vegetable oil, soy sauce, sesame oil, and garlic in a large bowl; stir well with a whisk. Add shrimp, couscous, lettuce, bell pepper, peas, and cilantro; toss well. Sprinkle with peanuts.

Yield: 4 servings (serving size: 1½ cups).

CALORIES 276 (21% from fat); FAT 6.5g (sat 1g, mono 2.1g, poly 2.5g); PROTEIN 16.8g; CARB 35.6g; FIBER 4.1g; CHOL 65mg; IRON 3.2mg; SODIUM 164mg; CALC 49mg EXCHANGES: 2 Starch, 1 Vegetable, 1 Very Lean Meat, 1 Fat

GAZPACHO SHRIMP SALAD

Even though shrimp is a little higher in sodium and cholesterol than other types of seafood, it's a terrific protein source with only 1 gram of fat for a 3-ounce portion.

1½ cups (1½-inch) diagonally sliced green beans (about ½ pound)
1 pound large shrimp, cooked and peeled
2 cups cubed seeded cucumber
2 cups chopped tomato
⅓ cup diced green bell pepper
¼ cup diagonally sliced green onions
¼ cup thinly sliced fresh basil
¼ cup tomato juice
3 tablespoons red wine vinegar
4 teaspoons extra-virgin olive oil
¼ teaspoon sugar
¼ teaspoon salt
⅛ teaspoon black pepper
⅛ teaspoon hot sauce
2 garlic cloves, minced
8 cups gourmet salad greens

1. Steam beans, covered, 4 minutes or until crisp-tender. Drain and rinse with cold water; drain well. Combine beans, shrimp, and next 5 ingredients.

2. Combine juice and next 7 ingredients in a small bowl; stir well with a whisk. Pour over shrimp mixture; toss well. Serve over greens. Serve at room temperature or chilled. Yield: 4 servings (serving size: 2 cups salad and 2 cups greens).

CALORIES 200 (28% from fat); FAT 6.2g (sat 1g, mono 3.6g, poly 1.1g); PROTEIN 22.3g; CARB 15.6g; FIBER 5g; CHOL 166mg; IRON 5.3mg; SODIUM 417mg; CALC 122mg EXCHANGES: 3 Vegetable, 2 Lean Meat

SEARED SCALLOPS AND FRESH ORANGE SALAD

Scallops are even lower in fat than shrimp, and their tender sweetness complements the oranges and greens.

SHALLOTS:

2 tablespoons vegetable oil

⅓ cup sliced shallots

SALAD:

3 cups trimmed watercress

3 cups coarsely chopped curly endive

1 cup orange sections

½ cup diced peeled avocado

1½ pounds sea scallops

¼ teaspoon salt

1 teaspoon vegetable oil

DRESSING:

½ cup fresh lemon juice (about 2 lemons)

2 tablespoons brown sugar

1½ tablespoons Thai fish sauce

1 tablespoon minced seeded Thai, hot red, or serrano chiles

2 garlic cloves, crushed

⅓ cup chopped fresh mint

1. To prepare shallots, heat 2 tablespoons oil in a small saucepan over medium-high heat. Add shallots, and sauté 2 minutes or until crispy. Remove shallots from pan with a slotted spoon; drain and cool. Set aside.

2. To prepare salad, arrange watercress and endive on a serving platter. Top with orange sections and avocado. Sprinkle scallops with salt. Heat 1 teaspoon oil in a nonstick skillet over medium-high heat. Add scallops, and cook 4 minutes, turning once. Spoon scallops over greens mixture.

3. To prepare dressing, combine lemon juice and next 4 ingredients in a bowl; stir well with a whisk. Heat dressing in a small saucepan over medium heat 1 minute; pour over salad. Sprinkle with mint and shallots. Yield: 4 servings.

CALORIES 292 (27% from fat); FAT 8.9g (sat 1.5g, mono 3.2g, poly 3.1g); PROTEIN 31.4g; CARB 22.7g; FIBER 3.4g; CHOL 56mg; IRON 1.4mg; SODIUM 933mg; CALC 126mg EXCHANGES: 1 Fruit, 2 Vegetable, 4 Very Lean Meat, 1 Fat

GRILLED SALMON SALAD

Because it contains omega-3 fatty acids, salmon may help prevent heart disease and ease joint pain.

$3/4$ cup chopped seeded peeled cucumber

3 tablespoons plain low-fat yogurt

2 tablespoons lemon juice

$1\frac{1}{2}$ teaspoons chopped fresh parsley

$1\frac{1}{2}$ teaspoons chopped fresh chives

$1\frac{1}{4}$ teaspoons grated lemon rind

$1/4$ teaspoon black pepper

1 garlic clove, sliced

4 (6-ounce) salmon fillets (about 1 inch thick)

1 teaspoon black pepper

$1/2$ teaspoon salt

Cooking spray

4 cups gourmet salad greens

$3/4$ cup basil leaves

$1/2$ cup cubed peeled ripe mango

1. Prepare grill.

2. Place first 8 ingredients in a blender; process until almost smooth.

3. Sprinkle fish with 1 teaspoon pepper and salt. Place fish, skin sides up, on grill rack coated with cooking spray; grill 5 minutes on each side or until fish flakes easily when tested with a fork. Remove skin from fillets; discard skin. Break fish into chunks.

4. Place greens and basil in a large bowl; add $1/4$ cup cucumber dressing,

tossing well. Arrange salad on 4 plates. Divide salmon evenly among salads; top each serving with 2 tablespoons dressing and 2 tablespoons mango. Yield: 4 servings.

CALORIES 317 (41% from fat); FAT 14.6g (sat 2.6g, mono 6.9g, poly 3.3g); PROTEIN 37g; CARB 8.1g; FIBER 2g; CHOL 112mg; IRON 1.9mg; SODIUM 392mg; CALC 75mg EXCHANGES: $1/2$ Fruit, 5 Lean Meat

CHICKEN TACO SALAD

Low-fat tortilla chips have 83 percent less fat than regular tortilla chips.

$3/4$ cup bottled salsa

3 tablespoons white wine vinegar

1 teaspoon sugar

$1/2$ teaspoon ground cumin

$1/4$ teaspoon dried thyme

$1/4$ teaspoon bottled minced garlic

Dash of ground red pepper

$1/2$ pound skinless, boneless chicken breast, cut into 1-inch strips

1 cup halved cherry tomatoes (about 12 tomatoes)

1 cup canned kidney beans, rinsed and drained

$1/4$ cup minced fresh cilantro

1 tablespoon olive oil

Cooking spray

4 cups coarsely chopped iceberg lettuce

1 cup (4 ounces) reduced-fat shredded Cheddar cheese

32 low-fat baked tortilla chips

1. Combine first 7 ingredients in a bowl. Combine ½ cup of salsa mixture and chicken in a zip-top plastic bag; seal and marinate in refrigerator 30 minutes. Add tomatoes, beans, cilantro, and oil to remaining salsa mixture; cover and marinate in refrigerator 30 minutes.

2. Place a medium nonstick skillet coated with cooking spray over medium-high heat until hot. Add chicken mixture; sauté 5 minutes or until chicken is done.

3. Arrange lettuce on 4 plates; top each with ½ cup bean mixture and one-fourth of chicken mixture. Sprinkle each serving with ¼ cup cheese. Serve each salad with 8 tortilla chips. Yield: 4 servings.

CALORIES 391 (25% from fat); FAT 11g (sat 3.9g, mono 2.8g, poly 1g); PROTEIN 30.4g; CARB 43.8g; FIBER 6g; CHOL 51mg; IRON 4mg; SODIUM 767mg; CALC 320mg EXCHANGES: 3 Starch, 3 Lean Meat

RINSE CYCLE

When you rinse canned beans in a strainer under cool running water, you can reduce the sodium content by about 40 percent.

TABBOULEH WITH ARUGULA AND CHICKEN

You get more salt in deli-roasted chicken than in chicken you cook yourself, but the fat is about the same in both when you remove the skin.

1	cup uncooked bulgur or cracked wheat
1	cup boiling water
1½	cups chopped ready-to-eat roasted skinless, boneless chicken breasts (about 2 breasts)
1	cup diced tomato
½	cup chopped arugula
⅓	cup diced red onion
¼	cup finely chopped fresh parsley
2	tablespoons finely chopped fresh mint
2	tablespoons fresh lemon juice
1	tablespoon olive oil
¼	teaspoon salt
⅛	teaspoon black pepper
24	arugula leaves

1. Combine bulgur and water in a large bowl. Cover and let stand 25 minutes. Stir in chicken and next 9 ingredients; cover and chill. Serve on arugula-lined plates. Yield: 4 servings (serving size: 1½ cups).

CALORIES 218 (21% from fat); FAT 5g (sat 0.9g, mono 2.9g, poly 0.8g); PROTEIN 14.9g; CARB 31g; FIBER 7.5g; CHOL 26mg; IRON 1.5mg; SODIUM 379mg; CALC 43mg EXCHANGES: 2 Starch, 1 Lean Meat

GRILLED THAI CHICKEN SALAD WITH MANGO AND GINGER

Not only are they fat-free, but both mango and ginger have been heralded as stomach-soothing remedies.

DRESSING:

¼   cup fresh lemon juice
3   tablespoons Thai fish sauce
2   tablespoons brown sugar
2   tablespoons minced seeded Thai, hot red, or serrano chiles

SALAD:

12   ounces skinless, boneless chicken breast
Cooking spray
2   cups sliced peeled mango (about 2 mangoes)
⅔   cup thinly sliced shallots
¼   cup matchstick-cut peeled fresh ginger
4   cups mixed salad greens
⅔   cup torn mint leaves

1. To prepare dressing, combine first 4 ingredients in a bowl, and stir well with a whisk. Set dressing aside.
2. Prepare grill or broiler.
3. To prepare salad, combine 1 table-spoon dressing and chicken, and toss to coat. Place chicken on grill rack or broiler pan coated with cooking spray; cook 6 minutes on each side or until chicken is done.

4. Cut chicken diagonally across grain into thin slices. Combine chicken, mango, shallots, and ginger. Toss with remaining dressing. Divide salad greens evenly among 3 plates. Top salad greens with chicken salad; sprinkle with mint.
Yield: 3 servings (serving size: 1 cup chicken salad, 1⅓ cups salad greens, and about 3 tablespoons mint).

CALORIES 278 (7% from fat); FAT 2.1g (sat 0.5g, mono 0.5g, poly 0.5g); PROTEIN 30.3g; CARB 37.1g; FIBER 4.1g; CHOL 66mg; IRON 3.1mg; SODIUM 1,390mg; CALC 115mg EXCHANGES: 2 Fruit, 4 Very Lean Meat

TOMATO PANZANELLA WITH PROVOLONE AND HAM

Balsamic vinegar adds a distinctive tangy flavor to this bread salad, and, like other vinegars, it's fat- and calorie-free.

3½   cups diced tomato
1   tablespoon capers
⅛   teaspoon salt
¼   teaspoon freshly ground black pepper
1   garlic clove, minced
2   tablespoons balsamic vinegar
4   cups (1-inch) cubed day-old rosemary bread (about 8 ounces)
½   cup (3 ounces) diced 33%-less-sodium ham
½   cup (2 ounces) diced sharp provolone cheese
½   cup chopped fresh basil

1. Combine first 5 ingredients in a large bowl; cover and marinate in refrigerator 8 hours. Stir in vinegar.

2. Add bread and remaining ingredients just before serving; toss gently. Yield: 4 servings (serving size: 1¾ cups).

Note: Any sturdy peasant-type bread will work in this dish, but we liked rosemary the best. The bread should be slightly stale; if not, arrange bread cubes on a baking sheet and bake at 350° for 10 minutes.

CALORIES 272 (25% from fat); FAT 7.6g (sat 3.4g, mono 2.4g, poly 1g); PROTEIN 13.8g; CARB 38.3g; FIBER 3.5g; CHOL 22mg; IRON 2.5mg; SODIUM 940mg; CALC 168mg EXCHANGES: 2 Starch, 1 Vegetable, 1 Lean Meat, 1 Fat

FIERY THAI BEEF SALAD

The bold flavors of the herbs and spices in this salad add plenty of flavor without adding fat and calories.

DRESSING:

⅓ cup fresh lime juice
¼ cup chopped fresh cilantro
2 tablespoons brown sugar
1 tablespoon water
1 tablespoon Thai fish sauce
5 garlic cloves, minced
2 Thai, hot red, or serrano chiles, seeded and minced

SALAD:

1 (1-pound) flank steak
¼ teaspoon salt
⅛ teaspoon black pepper
Cooking spray
6 cups torn romaine lettuce
1¾ cups quartered cherry tomatoes
1 cup thinly sliced red onion, separated into rings
¼ cup coarsely chopped fresh mint
2 tablespoons sliced peeled fresh lemon grass

1. To prepare dressing, combine first 7 ingredients in a bowl; stir well with a whisk.

2. Prepare grill or broiler.

3. Sprinkle both sides of steak with salt and pepper. Place steak on grill rack or broiler pan coated with cooking spray, and cook 6 minutes on each side or until desired degree of doneness. Let stand 10 minutes. Cut steak diagonally across grain into thin slices; cut each slice into 2-inch pieces.

4. Combine steak, lettuce, and remaining ingredients in a large bowl; add dressing, tossing to coat. Yield: 4 servings (serving size: 2 cups).

CALORIES 265 (38% from fat); FAT 11.3g (sat 4.7g, mono 4.3g, poly 0.6g); PROTEIN 25.5g; CARB 16g; FIBER 3g; CHOL 57mg; IRON 4.1mg; SODIUM 572mg; CALC 65mg EXCHANGES: ½ Starch, 2 Vegetable, 3 Lean Meat

Chapter 43

Side Dishes

Eating more fruits and vegetables helps you
lose weight and stay healthy. With these easy recipes,
you'll be happy doing both.

CRAN-APPLE RELISH

This relish is packed with antioxidants
that fight heart disease and soluble
fiber that lowers cholesterol.

5	cups chopped peeled apple
2	cups fresh cranberries
2	cups water
¾	cup packed dark brown sugar
½	cup white wine vinegar
¼	teaspoon ground cloves
1	(3-inch) cinnamon stick

1. Combine all ingredients in a large
heavy saucepan. Bring to a boil. Reduce
heat; simmer 1 hour, stirring occasionally;
continue to cook until thick (about 30
minutes), stirring frequently.
2. Discard cinnamon. Mash with a
potato masher. Cover and chill. Yield:
18 servings (serving size: ¼ cup).

CALORIES 69 (3% from fat); FAT 0.2g (sat 0g,
mono 0 g, poly 0.1g); PROTEIN 0.1g;
CARB 17.8g; FIBER 1.4g; CHOL 0mg;
IRON 0.3mg; SODIUM 5mg; CALC 12mg
EXCHANGE: 1 Fruit

MUSTARD-DRESSED ASPARAGUS

In one serving of asparagus, you get
about one-third of your recommended
daily amount of folate—a B-vitamin
that can reduce the risk of heart
attack, boost the immune system, and
reduce the risk of birth defects.

4	pounds asparagus
2	tablespoons Dijon mustard
2	tablespoons lemon juice
¼	teaspoon salt
1	tablespoon mustard seeds

1. Snap off tough ends of asparagus.
Bring 4 quarts water to a boil in an
8-quart stockpot. Add half of asparagus;
cook 3 minutes. Remove asparagus
from stockpot. Rinse with cold water;
drain and pat dry. Repeat procedure
with remaining asparagus.
2. Combine Dijon mustard, lemon
juice, and salt in a small bowl. Place a

large nonstick skillet over medium heat until hot. Add mustard seeds; sauté 1 minute. Add asparagus and mustard mixture, and cook 2 minutes or until thoroughly heated. Yield: 8 servings.

CALORIES 51 (19% from fat); FAT 1.1g (sat 0.1g, mono 0.3g, poly 0.3g); PROTEIN 4.5g; CARB 8.3g; FIBER 4.4g; CHOL 0mg; IRON 1.3mg; SODIUM 222mg; CALC 74mg
EXCHANGES: 2 Vegetable

STIR-FRIED BROCCOLI WITH OYSTER SAUCE

Broccoli is nutrient- and fiber-rich, and known for its cancer-fighting properties.

2	pounds broccoli
6	cups water
½	cup fat-free, less-sodium chicken broth
3	tablespoons oyster sauce
1½	tablespoons rice wine or sake
1½	teaspoons cornstarch
1½	teaspoons sugar
1	teaspoon low-sodium soy sauce
1	teaspoon dark sesame oil
1½	tablespoons vegetable oil
¼	cup minced green onions
1½	tablespoons minced peeled fresh ginger
2	tablespoons minced garlic

1. Cut broccoli florets and stems into bite-size pieces to measure 10 cups.
2. Bring water to a boil in a large Dutch oven; add broccoli. Cook broccoli 4 minutes or until crisp-tender; drain.
3. Combine broth and next 6 ingredients; stir well with a whisk. Heat vegetable oil in a large nonstick skillet over medium-high heat. Add onions, ginger, and garlic; sauté 15 seconds. Add broth mixture; bring to a boil. Cook 1 minute or until thick, stirring constantly. Add broccoli; cook 30 seconds, tossing to coat. Yield: 8 servings (serving size: 1 cup).

CALORIES 80 (40% from fat); FAT 3.5g (sat 0.6g, mono 1g, poly 1.7g); PROTEIN 3.8g; CARB 10.3g; FIBER 3.6g; CHOL 0mg IRON 1.1mg; SODIUM 275mg; CALC 62mg
EXCHANGES: 2 Vegetable, 1 Fat

STIR-FRY STRATEGIES

Stir-frying (or sautéing) is a great low-fat cooking method because you use only in a small amount of fat. And because you're cooking the food in a short amount of time, you preserve nutrients.

Keep the following pointers in mind for stir-fry success.
• Cut pieces of food the same size so they'll cook evenly.
• Heat the oil until it's very hot but not burning or smoking.
• Stir constantly, pushing the food quickly back and forth across the skillet or wok.

BRUSSELS SPROUTS AND CARROTS WITH ALMONDS

Topping your vegetables with almonds is a tasty way to get vitamin E, a vitamin that has been shown to reduce cholesterol and the risk of heart disease. Almonds are one of the top sources of this important vitamin.

1   tablespoon butter or margarine
1½ cups julienne-cut carrot
3   cups trimmed Brussels sprouts, quartered (about ¾ pound)
2   tablespoons minced fresh parsley
1   tablespoon sliced almonds, toasted
1   teaspoon brown sugar
¼   teaspoon salt
⅛   teaspoon black pepper

1. Melt butter in a large nonstick skillet over medium-high heat. Add carrot; sauté 4 minutes. Reduce heat to medium. Add Brussels sprouts; sauté 5 minutes or until crisp-tender. Add parsley and remaining ingredients; cook 30 seconds or until sugar melts, stirring constantly. Yield: 4 servings (serving size: ¾ cup).

CALORIES 84 (42% from fat); FAT 3.9g (sat 1.9g, mono 1.4g, poly 0.4g); PROTEIN 3g; CARB 11.3g; FIBER 4.4g; CHOL 8mg; IRON 1.3mg; SODIUM 208mg; CALC 47mg EXCHANGES: 2 Vegetable, 1 Fat

BRAISED RED CABBAGE AND PEARS

Cabbage is in the same vegetable family as broccoli and cauliflower—a family known for its cancer-fighting power.

1   teaspoon olive oil
1½ cups thinly sliced onion, separated into rings
6   cups sliced red cabbage
⅓   cup red wine vinegar
2   tablespoons sugar
2   bay leaves
1   (3-inch) cinnamon stick
1½ cups thinly sliced peeled Anjou pear (about 2 pears)
½   teaspoon salt
¼   teaspoon black pepper

1. Heat oil in a large Dutch oven over medium-high heat. Add onion; sauté 5 minutes. Stir in cabbage, vinegar, sugar, bay leaves, and cinnamon stick; cover, reduce heat, and simmer 15 minutes or until cabbage is tender.
2. Stir in pear, salt, and pepper; cover and cook 5 minutes. Discard bay leaves and cinnamon stick. Yield: 8 servings (serving size: ¾ cup).

CALORIES 59 (13% from fat); FAT 0.9g (sat 0.1g, mono 0.5g, poly 0.2g); PROTEIN 1.1g; CARB 13.2g; FIBER 2.2g; CHOL 0mg; IRON 0.4mg; SODIUM 153mg; CALC 35mg EXCHANGES: ½ Fruit, 1 Vegetable

KALE-CABBAGE SAUTÉ

Kale is one of the top sources of lutein, an antioxidant that may protect against macular degeneration—a leading cause of blindness.

2	teaspoons vegetable oil
½	teaspoon cumin seeds
2	teaspoons minced peeled fresh ginger
2	cups vertically sliced onion
1	tablespoon chopped seeded jalapeño pepper
1	teaspoon sugar
½	teaspoon salt
½	teaspoon ground turmeric
5	cups chopped kale
2	cups presliced green cabbage
2	tablespoons water

1. Heat oil in a large nonstick skillet over medium heat. Add cumin seeds; cook 1 minute. Add ginger; sauté 1 minute. Add onion; cook 5 minutes. Stir in jalapeño and remaining ingredients. Cover and cook 15 minutes or until kale is tender; stir occasionally. Yield: 6 servings (serving size: ½ cup).

CALORIES 67 (28% from fat); FAT 2.1g (sat 0.4g, mono 0.5g, poly 1g); PROTEIN 2.7g; CARB 11.4g; FIBER 2.2g; CHOL 0mg; IRON 1.4mg; SODIUM 226mg; CALC 98mg
EXCHANGES: 2 Vegetable

LEMON-DILL CARROTS

Serve this simple side dish during the holidays when you need a low-fat item to accompany roast or turkey.

1	teaspoon olive oil
3	cups diagonally sliced carrot
¼	cup fat-free, less-sodium chicken broth
1	teaspoon grated lemon rind
1	tablespoon fresh lemon juice
½	teaspoon celery salt
¼	teaspoon black pepper
1	tablespoon minced fresh or 1 teaspoon dried dill

1. Heat oil in a large nonstick skillet over medium-high heat. Add carrot; sauté 2 minutes. Stir in broth and next 4 ingredients. Cover; reduce heat to medium-low, and cook 10 minutes or until tender, stirring occasionally. Remove from heat; stir in dill. Yield: 6 servings (serving size: ½ cup).

CALORIES 33 (25% from fat); FAT 0.9g (sat 0.1g, mono 0.6g, poly 0.1g); PROTEIN 0.7g; CARB 6.1g; FIBER 1.8g; CHOL 0mg; IRON 0.4mg; SODIUM 214mg; CALC 20mg
EXCHANGE: 1 Vegetable

HOLIDAY GREEN BEANS

Don't wait for a special occasion to serve these high-flavor beans. Green beans have folate, which helps prevent birth defects and protects against heart disease.

2½ tablespoons Dijon mustard
¼ teaspoon salt
¼ teaspoon freshly ground black pepper
¼ teaspoon dried tarragon
1½ pounds green beans, trimmed
2 teaspoons butter or margarine
¾ cup thinly sliced shallots
2 tablespoons low-fat sour cream

1. Combine first 4 ingredients; set aside.
2. Steam green beans, covered, 5 minutes or until tender. Keep warm.
3. Melt butter in a Dutch oven over medium heat. Add shallots; sauté 3 minutes. Stir in mustard mixture and green beans; toss well. Cook 2 minutes or until thoroughly heated. Stir in sour cream, and remove from heat. Serve immediately. Yield: 10 servings (serving size: ½ cup).

CALORIES 45 (29% from fat); FAT 1.5g (sat 0.8g, mono 0.5g, poly 0.1g); PROTEIN 1.6g; CARB 7.3g; FIBER 1.5g; CHOL 3mg; IRON 0.9mg; SODIUM 185mg; CALC 33mg
EXCHANGE: 1 Vegetable

ROASTED GREEN BEANS

Roasting is an ideal low-fat cooking method for vegetables because cooking at a high temperature helps bring out their natural sweetness in a short amount of time.

1¼ pounds green or wax beans, trimmed
2 tablespoons slivered almonds
1 tablespoon lemon juice
2 teaspoons olive oil
½ teaspoon salt
¼ teaspoon garlic powder
¼ teaspoon dried basil
¼ teaspoon freshly ground black pepper

1. Preheat oven to 450°.
2. Combine all ingredients in a jelly roll pan, tossing well. Bake at 450° for 10 minutes or until beans are tender and browned, stirring occasionally. Yield: 4 servings (serving size: 1 cup).

CALORIES 83 (43% from fat); FAT 4g (sat 0.5g, mono 2.7g, poly 0.6g); PROTEIN 3.2g; CARB 11.3g; FIBER 3.4g; CHOL 0mg; IRON 1.6mg; SODIUM 302mg; CALC 63mg
EXCHANGES: 2 Vegetable, 1 Fat

GREENS WITH GARLIC AND LEMON

Try using any mixture of other greens, such as beet (minus the stems), chard, dandelion, and mustard. They're all good sources of indoles—antioxidants that can boost cancer-fighting enzymes. See page 64 for more information.

4	quarts water
6	cups torn turnip greens
6	cups torn collard greens
1½	teaspoons olive oil
2	garlic cloves, finely chopped
⅛	teaspoon salt
4	lemon wedges

1. Bring 4 quarts water to a boil in an 8-quart stockpot. Add greens; cover and cook 20 minutes. Drain well.
2. Heat oil in a skillet over medium-high heat. Add garlic, and sauté 30 seconds or until lightly browned. Combine greens, sautéed garlic, and salt in a medium bowl; toss well. Serve with lemon wedges. Yield: 4 servings (serving size: ½ cup).

CALORIES 63 (31% from fat); FAT 2.2g;
(sat 0.3g, mono 1.3g, poly 0.3g); PROTEIN 2.6g;
CARB 10.3g; FIBER 4g; CHOL 0mg;
IRON 1.8mg; SODIUM 140mg; CALC 317mg
EXCHANGES: 2 Vegetable

OKRA STEWED WITH TOMATOES

This recipe uses a simple trick to keep the texture of the okra firm: Coat with vinegar and salt before cooking.

1	pound small okra pods
1½	tablespoons white vinegar
¼	teaspoon salt, divided
2	teaspoons olive oil
1½	cups chopped onion
1	cup chopped tomato
⅛	teaspoon sugar
⅛	teaspoon black pepper
¼	cup chopped fresh parsley

1. Combine okra, vinegar, and ⅛ teaspoon salt in a bowl. Let stand 1 hour, stirring occasionally.
2. Heat oil in a medium nonstick skillet over medium-high heat. Add onion, and sauté 7 minutes or until tender. Stir in ⅛ teaspoon salt, tomato, sugar, and pepper. Reduce heat, and simmer 15 minutes.
3. Add okra mixture; cook 40 minutes or until tender, stirring occasionally. Stir in parsley. Yield: 8 servings (serving size: ¾ cup).

CALORIES 50 (23% from fat); FAT 1.3g
(sat 0.2g, mono 0.9g, poly 0.2g);
PROTEIN 1.8g; CARB 8.5g; FIBER 1.5g;
CHOL 0mg; IRON 0.8mg; SODIUM 82mg;
CALC 56mg
EXCHANGES: 2 Vegetable

Baked Spaghetti Squash with Tomato Sauce and Olives

If you're looking for a switch from pasta, try spaghetti squash. Its long, thin strands resemble spaghetti when you scrape it out.

1	spaghetti squash (about 3¼ pounds)
1½	tablespoons olive oil
1	cup minced fresh onion
1	teaspoon dried oregano
½	teaspoon dried thyme
2	bay leaves

Dash of crushed red pepper

3	garlic cloves, minced and divided
1	cup dry red wine
½	cup water
⅓	cup coarsely chopped pitted kalamata olives
1	tablespoon capers
¼	teaspoon freshly ground black pepper
⅛	teaspoon salt
1	(28-ounce) can crushed tomatoes, undrained
¼	cup (1 ounce) grated fresh Parmesan cheese
¼	cup chopped fresh parsley

1. Preheat oven to 375°.

2. Pierce squash with a fork. Place squash on a baking sheet; bake at 375° for 1½ hours or until tender. Cool. Cut squash in half lengthwise; discard seeds. Scrape inside of squash with a fork to remove spaghetti-like strands to measure 6 cups. Keep warm.

3. While squash is baking, heat oil in a large nonstick skillet over medium heat. Add onion, oregano, thyme, bay leaves, and red pepper; sauté 5 minutes. Add 2 minced garlic cloves, wine, and next 6 ingredients; bring to a boil. Reduce heat, and simmer until thick (about 30 minutes).

4. Discard bay leaves. Serve sauce over squash. Combine 1 minced garlic clove, Parmesan cheese, and parsley. Sprinkle over each serving. Yield: 6 servings (serving size: 1 cup squash, ¾ cup sauce, 1 tablespoon topping).

CALORIES 128 (28% from fat); FAT 3.9g (sat 1.2g, mono 1.9g, poly 0.6g); PROTEIN 4.8g; CARB 20.4g; FIBER 3.5g; CHOL 3mg; IRON 2.2mg; SODIUM 505mg; CALC 159mg
EXCHANGES: 1 Starch, 1 Vegetable, 1 Fat

Winter Storage

Because of their thick skins, winter squash (such as acorn, butternut, hubbard, pumpkins, and spaghetti squash) can be stored longer than summer squash. You don't have to refrigerate winter squash; keep in a paper bag in a cool, dark place (about 50°F) for about a month. Don't store winter squash in a plastic bag for more than 3 days because the plastic traps moisture and causes the squash to rot.

SUMMER SQUASH-AND-CORN SAUTÉ

This makes a terrific side to just about any entrée—particularly roasted chicken or grilled steak.

1   teaspoon olive oil
2   teaspoons cumin seeds
2   cups fresh corn kernels (about 4 ears)
1   cup sliced onion
3   garlic cloves, minced
2   cups (¼-inch-thick) sliced diagonally cut zucchini (about ¾ pound)
2   cups (¼-inch-thick) sliced diagonally cut yellow squash (about ¾ pound)
½   teaspoon salt
1   (4.5-ounce) can chopped green chiles
2   tablespoons chopped fresh cilantro
½   cup (2 ounces) shredded reduced-fat Monterey Jack cheese

1. Heat oil in a large nonstick skillet over medium-high heat; add cumin seeds and cook 30 seconds or until toasted, stirring frequently. Add corn, onion, and garlic; sauté 5 minutes or until lightly browned. Add zucchini, yellow squash, salt, and chiles, and sauté 6 minutes or until tender. Stir in cilantro. Remove from heat; sprinkle with cheese. Cover and let stand 5 minutes or until cheese melts. Yield: 6 servings (serving size: 1 cup).

CALORIES 109 (29% from fat); FAT 3.5g (sat 1.4g, mono 1.5g, poly 0.6g); PROTEIN 6.1g; CARB 16.7g; FIBER 3.4g; CHOL 6mg; IRON 1.3mg; SODIUM 517mg; CALC 108mg
EXCHANGES: 1 Starch, ½ Fat

BRAISED ZUCCHINI AND LEEKS

A little bit of butter is all it takes to add big flavor to this vegetable dish.

1   tablespoon butter
2   cups finely chopped leek (about 2 large)
6   cups finely chopped zucchini (about 5 small)
1   teaspoon salt
2   garlic cloves, minced

1. Melt butter in a large nonstick skillet over medium heat. Add leek; sauté 2 minutes. Add zucchini, salt, and garlic. Cover; reduce heat to medium-low, and cook 20 minutes, stirring occasionally.
2. Uncover and cook over medium-high heat 10 minutes or until most of liquid evaporates. Serve immediately. Yield: 8 servings (serving size: about ⅔ cup).

CALORIES 52 (26% from fat); FAT 1.5g (sat 0.9g, mono 0.4g, poly 0.1g); PROTEIN 1.7g; CARB 8.4g; FIBER 2.9g; CHOL 4mg; IRON 0.9mg; SODIUM 313mg; CALC 40mg
EXCHANGES: 2 Vegetable

CRISPY ZUCCHINI STICKS WITH CREAMY SALSA DIP

Here's a low-fat alternative to the fried mozzarella sticks that are so popular on restaurant appetizer menus.

- ½ cup bottled salsa
- ¼ cup fat-free sour cream
- 2 zucchini (about ¾ pound)
- ⅔ cup Italian-seasoned breadcrumbs
- ½ cup yellow cornmeal
- 2 tablespoons grated fresh Parmesan cheese
- 2 tablespoons minced fresh parsley
- ¼ teaspoon salt
- ⅓ cup all-purpose flour
- 3 large egg whites, lightly beaten
- Cooking spray

1. Preheat oven to 450°.
2. Combine salsa and sour cream; set aside.
3. Cut each zucchini lengthwise into quarters; cut each quarter crosswise into 3 pieces. Combine breadcrumbs and next 4 ingredients in a shallow dish. Dredge 6 zucchini pieces in flour. Dip in egg whites, and dredge in bread-crumb mixture. Repeat procedure with remaining zucchini, flour, egg whites, and breadcrumb mixture. Place zucchini on a large baking sheet coated with cooking spray. Lightly coat zucchini with cooking spray. Bake at 450° for 25 minutes or until lightly browned and crisp, carefully turning after 12 minutes. Serve zucchini immediately with salsa dip. Yield: 6 servings (serving size: 4 zucchini pieces and 2 tablespoons dip).

CALORIES 153 (9% from fat); FAT 1.6g (sat 0.6g, mono 0.4g, poly 0.2g); PROTEIN 7.6g; CARB 27g; FIBER 1.5g; CHOL 2mg; IRON 1.7mg; SODIUM 620mg; CALC 71mg
EXCHANGES: 2 Starch

GRILLED VEGETABLES WITH RANCH DRESSING

Grilling brings out the natural robust flavor in vegetables.

- 2 red bell peppers, seeded
- 2 yellow bell peppers, seeded
- 1 small eggplant, cut in half lengthwise (about 1 pound)
- 16 asparagus spears (about 1 pound)
- 1 medium zucchini or yellow squash, cut in half lengthwise
- 8 plum tomatoes
- 2 tablespoons olive oil
- ½ teaspoon black pepper
- ¼ teaspoon salt
- Cooking spray
- Ranch Dressing

1. Prepare grill.
2. Brush first 6 ingredients with oil; sprinkle evenly with black pepper and salt. Place bell peppers on grill rack coated with cooking spray; grill 5 minutes. Add eggplant; grill 5 minutes.

Add asparagus; grill 5 minutes. Add zucchini; grill 5 minutes. Add tomatoes; grill 5 minutes or until all vegetables are tender, turning as needed. Remove from grill. Cut each pepper into quarters; cut eggplant and zucchini halves each into 4 pieces. Serve with Ranch Dressing.

Yield: 8 servings (serving size: 2 pepper quarters, 1 eggplant piece, 2 asparagus spears, 1 zucchini piece, 1 tomato, and 2 tablespoons dressing).

(Totals include Ranch Dressing) CALORIES 105 (39% from fat); FAT 4.6g (sat 0.8g, mono 2.7g, poly 0.6g); PROTEIN 4.6g; CARB 13.9g; FIBER 3.5g; CHOL 0mg; IRON 1.6mg; SODIUM 181mg; CALC 57mg EXCHANGES: 3 Vegetable, 1 Fat

RANCH DRESSING

- ¾ cup low-fat buttermilk
- ¼ cup fat-free sour cream
- ½ teaspoon dry mustard
- ½ teaspoon dried oregano
- ½ teaspoon dried basil
- ¼ teaspoon salt
- ¼ teaspoon dried dill
- ¼ teaspoon black pepper
- 1 garlic clove, minced

1. Combine all ingredients in a bowl; stir well with a whisk. Cover and chill.

Yield: 1 cup (serving size: 2 tablespoons).

CALORIES 18 (20% from fat); FAT 0.4g (sat 0.3g, mono 0.1g, poly 0g); PROTEIN 1.4g; CARB 1.9g; FIBER 0.1g; CHOL 0mg; IRON 0.1mg; SODIUM 90mg; CALC 33mg EXCHANGE: Free

SPICY STEAK FRIES

When you just can't give up French fries, here's a low-fat version with about 13 grams less fat per serving than a medium-sized order of fast-food fries.

- 1 tablespoon vegetable oil
- 2 large baking potatoes, each cut lengthwise into 12 wedges (about 1½ pounds)
- 2 teaspoons Cajun or blackening seasoning
- ¼ teaspoon salt

1. Preheat oven to 400°.
2. Spread oil in a jelly roll pan. Place potato wedges on pan. Sprinkle with seasoning; toss gently to coat. Bake at 400° for 40 minutes or until tender. Sprinkle with salt. Yield: 4 servings (serving size: 6 wedges).

CALORIES 216 (15% from fat); FAT 3.6g (sat 0.7g, mono 1g, poly 1.7g); PROTEIN 3.7g; CARB 42.9g; FIBER 3.1g; CHOL 0mg; IRON 2.3mg; SODIUM 275mg; CALC 17mg EXCHANGES: 2½ Starch, ½ Fat

ROSEMARY-GARLIC MASHED POTATOES

Yukon golds whip up creamier than russets, but you can use either variety.

2 whole garlic heads
2 pounds cubed peeled Yukon gold potato
1 cup chopped onion
2 tablespoons plain fat-free yogurt
1 teaspoon dried rosemary, chopped
½ teaspoon salt
¼ teaspoon black pepper

1. Preheat oven to 350°.
2. Remove papery skin from garlic heads (do not peel or separate cloves). Wrap each head in foil. Bake at 350° for 1 hour; cool 10 minutes. Separate cloves; squeeze to extract pulp. Discard skins.
3. Place potato and onion in a saucepan; cover with water, and bring to a boil. Cover, reduce heat, and simmer 15 minutes. Drain, reserving ¼ cup liquid. Combine garlic, potato mixture, ¼ cup liquid, and remaining ingredients; mash. Yield: 8 servings (serving size: ½ cup).

CALORIES 93 (2% from fat); FAT 0.2g (sat 0.1g, mono 0g, poly 0.1g); PROTEIN 2.8g; CARB 21g; FIBER 2.1g; CHOL 0mg; IRON 0.9mg; SODIUM 230mg; CALC 30mg
EXCHANGE: 1 Starch

SPICY GARLIC-ROASTED POTATOES

Roasting potatoes gives them a wonderfully rich and hearty flavor, and you only need a small amount of oil.

4 teaspoons vegetable oil
5 garlic cloves, minced
2 teaspoons ground cumin
¼ teaspoon ground red pepper
1½ pounds red potatoes, cut into 1½-inch pieces
½ teaspoon salt
Cooking spray

1. Preheat oven to 400°.
2. Heat oil in a large skillet over medium-high heat. Add garlic; sauté until golden (about 30 seconds). Add cumin and red pepper. Add potatoes and salt; toss well. Place potato mixture in a roasting pan coated with cooking spray. Bake at 400° for 25 minutes or until tender. Yield: 4 servings (serving size: 1 cup).

CALORIES 176 (26% from fat); FAT 5.1g (sat 0.6g, mono 1.2g, poly 1.8g); PROTEIN 4.2g; CARB 30g; FIBER 3.3g; CHOL 0mg; IRON 3mg; SODIUM 307mg; CALC 39mg
EXCHANGES: 2 Starch, 1 Fat

Spicy Grilled Sweet Potatoes

High in vitamins A and C, these savory grilled sweet potatoes are a nutrient-packed addition to a casual patio meal.

- ¾ teaspoon ground cumin
- ½ teaspoon garlic powder
- ¼ teaspoon salt
- ⅛ teaspoon ground red pepper
- 1 tablespoon olive oil
- 1 pound peeled sweet potatoes, cut into ¼-inch-thick slices
- Cooking spray
- 2 tablespoons chopped fresh cilantro

1. Combine first 4 ingredients in a small bowl.

2. Combine oil and sweet potatoes in a medium bowl; toss to coat. Heat a large grill pan coated with cooking spray over medium heat. Add potatoes, and cook 10 minutes, turning occasionally.

3. Place potatoes in a large bowl; sprinkle with cumin mixture and cilantro. Toss gently. Yield: 4 servings (serving size: ½ cup).

CALORIES 157 (25% from fat); FAT 4.3g (sat 0.6g, mono 2.7g, poly 0.7g); PROTEIN 2g; CARB 28.1g; FIBER 3.5g; CHOL 0mg; IRON 1.1mg; SODIUM 163mg; CALC 31mg EXCHANGES: 2 Starch, 1 Fat

Lemon Couscous

Take a break from rice and serve couscous. It's fat-free and takes only 5 minutes to prepare. Look for boxes of couscous in the rice and grain section of the supermarket.

- 1¼ cups water
- ¾ cup uncooked couscous
- ¼ cup sliced green onions
- 2 tablespoons chopped fresh parsley
- 2 tablespoons orange juice
- 1 teaspoon grated lemon rind
- 1 tablespoon fresh lemon juice
- ¼ teaspoon salt
- ⅛ teaspoon black pepper

1. Bring water to a boil in a medium saucepan; gradually stir in couscous. Remove from heat; cover and let stand 5 minutes. Fluff with a fork. Stir in onions and remaining ingredients. Yield: 4 servings (serving size: ½ cup).

CALORIES 102 (3% from fat); FAT 0.3g (sat 0g, mono 0g, poly 0g); PROTEIN 3.7g; CARB 21.8g; FIBER 1.3g; CHOL 0mg; IRON 0.8mg; SODIUM 151mg; CALC 9mg EXCHANGE: 1 Starch

Spiced Fruity Oatmeal

High in soluble fiber, oatmeal has been labeled a heart-healthy food due to its cholesterol-lowering benefits. And if you're not taken by the idea of plain ol' oatmeal for breakfast, try this version with brown sugar, cinnamon, and fruit.

1 1/2	cups apple juice
1/2	cup water
1/8	teaspoon salt
1 1/3	cups regular oats
1/4	cup sweetened dried cranberries (such as Craisins) or raisins
1/4	cup 1% low-fat milk
1	tablespoon brown sugar
3/4	teaspoon ground cinnamon
1/8	teaspoon ground nutmeg
2	tablespoons chopped walnuts

1. Combine first 3 ingredients in a medium saucepan; bring to a boil. Stir in oats and cranberries; reduce heat, and simmer 4 minutes, stirring occasionally. Stir in milk, sugar, cinnamon, and nutmeg; cook 1 minute. Spoon into bowls; sprinkle with walnuts. Yield: 4 servings (serving size: 3/4 cup oatmeal and 1 1/2 teaspoons walnuts).

Microwave variation:
Combine first 5 ingredients in a 2-quart glass measure or bowl, and microwave at HIGH 4 minutes or until slightly thick, stirring after 2 minutes. Stir in milk, sugar, cinnamon, and nutmeg; let stand, covered, 1 minute. Spoon into bowls; sprinkle with walnuts.

CALORIES 212 (18% from fat); FAT 4.2g (sat 0.6g, mono 1.1g, poly 2.1g); PROTEIN 5.8g; CARB 38.9g; FIBER 3.7g; CHOL 1mg; IRON 1.8mg; SODIUM 86mg; CALC 49mg EXCHANGES: 2 Starch, 1/2 Fruit, 1 Fat

Vermicelli with Garlic and Herbs

Instead of a high-fat cream sauce, the flavor in this low-fat pasta dish comes primarily from herbs.

1	(8-ounce) package vermicelli
2	tablespoons chopped fresh parsley
2	tablespoons olive oil
2	tablespoons lemon juice
2	teaspoons bottled minced garlic
1	teaspoon dried basil
1	teaspoon salt
1	teaspoon freshly ground black pepper

1. Cook pasta according to package directions, omitting salt and fat. Drain.
2. Combine parsley and next 5 ingredients. Toss parsley mixture with pasta. Sprinkle with freshly ground black pepper. Yield: 4 servings (serving size: 1/2 cup).

CALORIES 144 (24% from fat); FAT 3.9g (sat 0.5g, mono 2.6g, poly 0.5g); PROTEIN 3.9g; CARB 23.3g; FIBER 1.6g; CHOL 0mg; IRON 1.3mg; SODIUM 295mg; CALC 14mg EXCHANGES: 1 1/2 Starch, 1/2 Fat

MINNESOTA WILD RICE PILAF

1¼   cups water
2   (16-ounce) cans fat-free, less-
      sodium chicken broth
1½   cups uncooked wild rice
1   tablespoon butter or margarine
3   cups sliced mushrooms
1   cup chopped onion
½   cup finely chopped fresh parsley
⅓   cup chopped pecans, toasted
¾   teaspoon poultry seasoning
½   teaspoon salt
¼   teaspoon black pepper
Cooking spray

1. Bring water and broth to a boil in a saucepan. Add wild rice; cover, reduce heat, and simmer 1 hour or until tender. Drain.

2. Preheat oven to 325°.

3. Melt butter in a nonstick skillet over medium-high heat. Add mushrooms and onion; sauté 6 minutes. Remove from heat; stir in parsley and next 4 ingredients. Combine rice and mushroom mixture in a 2-quart casserole coated with cooking spray. Cover and bake at 325° for 25 minutes. Yield: 8 servings (serving size: 1 cup).

CALORIES 177 (27% from fat); FAT 5.4g
(sat 1.2g, mono 2.6g, poly 1.1g);
PROTEIN 6.9g; CARB 27.2g; FIBER 2.8g;
CHOL 4mg; IRON 1.4mg; SODIUM 347mg;
CALC 21mg
EXCHANGES: 1½ Starch, 1 Vegetable, 1 Fat

PEANUT RICE

When you add peanuts to a recipe, you add heart-healthy fat as well as a tasty crunch.

2¼   cups water
1   cup uncooked white basmati rice
½   teaspoon salt
¼   teaspoon ground turmeric
½   cup dry-roasted peanuts
½   cup frozen petite green peas,
      thawed

1. Bring water to a boil in a medium saucepan. Add rice, salt, and turmeric; cover, reduce heat, and simmer 20 minutes or until liquid is absorbed. Remove from heat; stir in peanuts and peas. Yield: 4 servings (serving size: 1 cup).

CALORIES 288 (29% from fat); FAT 9.3g
(sat 1.3g, mono 4.5g, poly 2.9g); PROTEIN 9g;
CARB 42.9g; FIBER 3g; CHOL 0mg;
IRON 2.7mg; SODIUM 465mg; CALC 33mg
Exchanges: 3 Starch, 1 Fat

ON THE WILD SIDE
Wild rice is not really rice—it's a long-grain marsh grass with a nutty flavor that has almost five times more fiber than long-grain white rice.

Chapter 44

Soups and Sandwiches

Whether you prefer them simmered, stuffed, or stacked, soups and sandwiches make simple meals that can take the stress out of your weight-loss journey.

STRAWBERRY SOUP

Strawberries in soup? Absolutely—they make for a unique, refreshing first course or low-fat dessert.

3⅓ cups quartered strawberries
½   cup orange juice
½   cup Riesling or other slightly sweet white wine
2½ tablespoons sugar
1⅓ cups plain fat-free yogurt
2   teaspoons chopped fresh mint

1. Place first 4 ingredients in a blender; process until smooth. Pour strawberry puree into a bowl, and add yogurt, stirring with a whisk. Cover and chill.
2. Spoon soup into 5 bowls, and sprinkle with mint. Yield: 5 servings (serving size: 1 cup).

CALORIES 116 (4% from fat); FAT 0.5g (sat 0.1g, mono 0.1g, poly 0.2g); PROTEIN 4.3g; CARB 21.2g; FIBER 2.4g; CHOL 1mg; IRON 0.7mg; SODIUM 48mg; CALC 139mg
EXCHANGES: ½ Starch, 1 Fruit

CURRIED SQUASH SOUP

Low-fat buttermilk adds a rich creaminess to this savory soup.

2   teaspoons curry powder
1¼   pounds yellow squash, cubed
½   cup chopped onion
1   (14½-ounce) can vegetable broth
1¾   cups low-fat buttermilk
1   tablespoon chopped fresh mint
½   teaspoon salt

1. Cook curry powder in a saucepan over medium heat 1 minute. Add squash, onion, and broth. Bring to a boil; cover, reduce heat, and simmer 25 minutes or until tender.
2. Place mixture in a blender; process until smooth. Pour into a bowl; cover and chill. Stir in buttermilk, mint, and salt. Yield: 5 servings (serving size: 1 cup).

CALORIES 82 (24% from fat); FAT 2.2g (sat 1g, mono 0.6g, poly 0.4g); PROTEIN 4.8g; CARB 12.3g; FIBER 2.5g; CHOL 0mg; IRON 0.8mg; SODIUM 681mg; CALC 136mg
EXCHANGES: 1 Vegetable, ½ Skim Milk

Golden Corn Chowder with Roasted Chiles

Yukon gold potatoes have a naturally rich, buttery flavor, but no more fat than any other kind of potato.

6   jalapeño peppers
3   cups cubed peeled Yukon gold or red potato (about 1 pound)
2   tablespoons butter or margarine
1   cup chopped onion
2/3 cup diced orange or yellow bell pepper
3   tablespoons chopped celery
3   cups fresh corn kernels (about 4 ears)
3   cups 1% low-fat milk
2   cups chopped seeded yellow tomato (about 1 pound)
3/4 teaspoon salt
1/4 teaspoon white pepper
6   tablespoons shredded reduced-fat Monterey Jack cheese
2   tablespoons chopped fresh cilantro

1. Preheat broiler.
2. Place jalapeño peppers on a foil-lined baking sheet; broil 10 minutes or until blackened, turning occasionally. Place in a zip-top plastic bag; seal. Let stand 15 minutes.
3. Peel peppers; cut in half lengthwise, discarding seeds and membranes. Finely chop jalapeño peppers; set aside.
4. Place potato in a medium saucepan, and cover with water; bring to a boil. Reduce heat, and simmer 15 minutes or until tender. Drain; partially mash potato with a potato masher.
5. Melt butter in a Dutch oven over medium heat. Add onion, bell pepper, and celery; cook 10 minutes, stirring frequently. Add jalapeño peppers, potato, corn, milk, tomato, salt, and white pepper; cook until thick (about 30 minutes), stirring occasionally. Ladle soup into each of 6 bowls, and sprinkle with cheese and cilantro. Yield: 6 servings (serving size: 1 1/3 cups soup, 1 tablespoon cheese, and 1 teaspoon cilantro).

CALORIES 265 (26% from fat); FAT 7.8g (sat 4.2g, mono 2.3g, poly 0.8g); PROTEIN 11.4g; CARB 41.5g; FIBER 5.4g; CHOL 20mg; IRON 1.8mg; SODIUM 466mg; CALC 230mg
EXCHANGES: 2 Starch, 1/2 Skim Milk, 1 Fat

Heat Warning

The heat in peppers ranges from hot to very hot, and most of the heat is in the seeds and veins (or membranes). It's a good idea to wear gloves when you're handling fresh jalapeños so you don't burn your hands. When you want to reduce the fire in a recipe, discard the pepper seeds and membranes.

LENTIL-VEGETABLE SOUP

This is one of those soups that tastes even better the next day, so take a break from sandwiches and pack a thermos of soup for your lunch at work.

1½	tablespoons olive oil
1⅓	cups finely diced onion
⅓	cup finely diced celery
⅓	cup finely diced carrot
2	bay leaves
2	tablespoons tomato paste
1	teaspoon salt
2	garlic cloves, minced
6	cups water
1	cup dried French dark green or other lentils
6	cups chopped spinach
⅓	cup chopped fresh parsley
2	teaspoons red wine vinegar
2	teaspoons Dijon mustard
¼	teaspoon black pepper
¾	cup (3 ounces) shaved fresh Parmesan cheese

1. Heat olive oil in a large Dutch oven or stockpot over medium-high heat. Add diced onion, celery, carrot, and bay leaves; sauté 10 minutes. Add tomato paste, salt, and minced garlic; sauté 1 minute. Add 6 cups water and lentils; bring mixture to a boil. Partially cover, reduce heat, and simmer 25 minutes.

2. Stir in chopped spinach, parsley, vinegar, mustard, and pepper; cook 15 minutes. Discard bay leaves. Ladle soup into bowls; top with cheese. Yield: 6 servings (serving size: 1 cup soup and 2 tablespoons cheese).

CALORIES 234 (30% from fat); FAT 7.8g
(sat 2.9g, mono 3.7g, poly 0.7g);
PROTEIN 16.6g; CARB 26.6g; FIBER 7.3g;
CHOL 10mg; IRON 5.1mg; SODIUM 729mg;
CALC 260mg
EXCHANGES: 2 Starch, 1 Very Lean Meat, 1 Fat

TOMATO-BASIL SOUP

Serve this quick version of the classic soup with cheese toast for a refreshingly light supper. Toasted French bread spread with light Boursin cheese is a tasty stand-in for the standard high-fat grilled cheese sandwich.

2	teaspoons olive oil
3	garlic cloves, minced
3	cups fat-free, less-sodium chicken broth
¾	teaspoon salt
3	(14.5-ounce) cans no-salt-added diced tomatoes, undrained
2	cups fresh basil leaves, thinly sliced
	Basil leaves (optional)

1. Heat oil in a large saucepan over medium heat. Add garlic; sauté 30 seconds. Stir in broth, salt, and tomatoes; bring to a boil. Reduce heat; simmer 20 minutes. Stir in basil.

2. Place half of soup in a blender;

process until smooth. Pour pureed soup into a bowl, and repeat procedure with remaining soup. Garnish with basil leaves, if desired. Yield: 4 servings (serving size: 1 1/2 cups).

CALORIES 103 (24% from fat); FAT 2.8g (sat 0.4g, mono 1.7g, poly 0.4g); PROTEIN 5.8g; CARB 15.9g; FIBER 4g; CHOL 0mg; IRON 2.4mg; SODIUM 809mg; CALC 129mg EXCHANGES: 1 Starch, 1/2 Fat

NORTH WOODS BEAN SOUP

What better way to increase iron in your diet than with a hearty soup full of dried beans, sausage, and spinach?

Cooking spray
1   cup baby carrots, halved
1   cup chopped onion
2   garlic cloves, minced
7   ounces turkey kielbasa, halved lengthwise and cut into 1/2-inch pieces
4   cups fat-free, less-sodium chicken broth
1/2 teaspoon dried Italian seasoning
1/2 teaspoon black pepper
2   (15.8-ounce) cans Great Northern beans, drained and rinsed
1   (6-ounce) bag fresh baby spinach leaves

1. Heat a large saucepan coated with cooking spray over medium-high heat. Add carrots, onion, garlic, and kielbasa;

sauté 3 minutes, stirring occasionally. Reduce heat to medium; cook 5 minutes. Add broth, Italian seasoning, pepper, and beans. Bring to a boil, reduce heat, and simmer 5 minutes.

2. Place 2 cups of soup in a food processor or blender, and process until smooth. Return pureed mixture to pan. Simmer 5 minutes. Remove soup from heat. Add spinach, stirring until spinach wilts. Yield: 5 servings (serving size: about 1 1/2 cups).

CALORIES 227 (15% from fat); FAT 3.9g (sat 1.2g, mono 1.3g, poly 1.2g); PROTEIN 18.1g; CARB 30.8g; FIBER 6.7g; CHOL 26mg; IRON 3.5mg; SODIUM 750mg; CALC 112mg EXCHANGES: 2 Starch, 2 Very Lean Meat

IRON NEEDS

For women ages 25-50, the recommended intake of iron is 18 milligrams per day. Women over 50 and men over 24 need 8 milligrams a day.

Iron is an essential part of the blood cells that help carry oxygen from your lungs to every part of your body. A deficiency of iron can lead to anemia, fatigue, and susceptibility to infections.

The best and most well-absorbed sources of iron are from animal products such as beef liver, lean ground beef, dark meat chicken, and lean pork. Fortified breakfast cereals are the best non-animal source of iron.

QUICK SHRIMP-AND-CORN SOUP

By using reduced-fat versions of cream cheese, milk, and cream soup, we were able to get a velvety consistency and rich taste without a lot of fat.

Cooking spray
1 cup chopped onion
1 cup chopped green bell pepper
1 garlic clove, minced
¾ cup (6 ounces) ⅓-less-fat cream cheese, softened
2 cups fat-free milk
1 (15-ounce) can cream-style corn
1 (10.75-ounce) can condensed reduced-fat, reduced-sodium cream of mushroom soup, undiluted
1 (10-ounce) can diced tomatoes and green chiles, undrained
1¼ pounds medium shrimp, peeled and deveined
4 teaspoons sliced green onions

1. Heat a Dutch oven or large saucepan coated with cooking spray over medium-high heat. Add onion, bell pepper, and garlic, and sauté 5 minutes. Stir in cream cheese; reduce heat, and cook until cheese melts. Add milk, corn, soup, and tomatoes; cook 10 minutes, stirring occasionally.
2. Bring milk mixture to a boil. Add shrimp; cook 5 minutes or until shrimp

are done. Remove from heat. Sprinkle each serving with green onions. Yield: 8 servings (serving size: 1 cup soup and ½ teaspoon green onions).

CALORIES 228 (29% from fat); FAT 7.4g (sat 3.8g, mono 1.9g, poly 1.1g); PROTEIN 18.8g; CARB 20.8g; FIBER 1.5g; CHOL 118mg; IRON 2.4mg; SODIUM 663mg; CALC 176mg EXCHANGES: 1 Starch, 1 Vegetable, 2 Very Lean Meat, 1 Fat

EASY FISH STEW

To keep your heart healthy, experts recommend eating fish twice a week.

1 tablespoon olive oil
1 cup chopped onion
¼ cup minced celery
1 teaspoon chili powder
2 cups water
1½ cups frozen whole-kernel corn, thawed
1 tablespoon Worcestershire sauce
¾ teaspoon salt
1 (14.5-ounce) can no-salt-added diced tomatoes, undrained
1 pound cod or other lean white fish fillets, cut into bite-size pieces
¼ cup minced fresh parsley

1. Heat olive oil in a Dutch oven over medium-high heat. Add chopped onion, celery, and chili powder; sauté 3 minutes or until tender.
2. Stir in water and next 4 ingredients; cook 10 minutes. Add fish; cook 3

minutes or until fish flakes easily when tested with a fork. Stir in parsley. Yield: 6 servings (serving size: 1 cup).

CALORIES 143 (20% from fat); FAT 3.1g
(sat 0.5g, mono 1.8g, poly 0.5g);
PROTEIN 15.7g; CARB 14.6g; FIBER 1.8g;
CHOL 33mg; IRON 1mg; SODIUM 380mg;
CALC 51mg
EXCHANGES: 1 Starch, 2 Very Lean Meat

RED CHICKEN CHILI

If you're not a red meat eater, here's a chili for you. It's full of beans, chicken, and lots of chili powder. (The chili powder makes the chicken red.)

2 teaspoons olive oil
3 cups chopped onion
¼ cup chili powder
1½ teaspoons dried oregano
1½ teaspoons ground cumin
¾ teaspoon salt
2 garlic cloves, minced
3 cups fat-free, less-sodium chicken broth
1 (16-ounce) can kidney beans, drained
1 (15-ounce) can black beans, drained
1 (14.5-ounce) can whole tomatoes, undrained and chopped
3 cups diced cooked chicken
½ cup (2 ounces) shredded reduced-fat extra-sharp Cheddar cheese
½ cup low-fat sour cream

1. Heat oil in a large Dutch oven over medium-high heat. Add onion; sauté 5 minutes. Add chili powder and next 4 ingredients; sauté 30 seconds. Add chicken broth, beans, and tomatoes; bring to a boil. Reduce heat to medium-low; simmer 30 minutes.

2. Stir in chicken; simmer 15 minutes. Serve with cheese and sour cream. Yield: 8 servings (serving size: 1 cup chili, 1 tablespoon cheese, and 1 tablespoon sour cream).

CALORIES 280 (30% from fat); FAT 9.2g
(sat 3.3g, mono 3.3g, poly 1.6g); PROTEIN 24.5g;
CARB 26.6g; FIBER 5.4g; CHOL 54mg;
IRON 3.6mg; SODIUM 743mg; CALC 150mg
EXCHANGES: 1 Starch, 2 Vegetable, 3 Lean Meat

BETTER BEANS

Beans are high in fiber and protein, low in fat, and good sources of B-vitamins and iron. Because they have so many nutrients, specifically soluble and insoluble fiber, beans can help reduce the risk of diabetes, heart disease, and some types of cancer.

If convenient canned beans have been off-limits for you because of their sodium content, take heart. Most types of beans are now available in low-sodium canned versions. You can substitute the low-sodium beans for regular in any recipe that calls for canned beans.

QUICK CHILI CON CARNE

1   pound ground round
1   cup coarsely chopped onion
1   chopped red bell pepper
2   teaspoons ground red pepper
1½   cups spicy-hot vegetable juice
1   cup frozen whole-kernel corn
1   cup beef broth
1   (15-ounce) can black beans,
     rinsed and drained
6   tablespoons reduced-fat shredded
     sharp Cheddar cheese
6   tablespoons fat-free sour cream
6   tablespoons minced fresh
     cilantro

1. Cook beef in a large nonstick skillet over medium-high heat until browned, stirring to crumble. Add onion, bell peppers, and ground red pepper; sauté 10 minutes or until tender.
2. Add juice, corn, broth, and beans; bring to a boil. Reduce heat, and simmer 10 minutes.
3. Spoon into bowls, and top each with shredded cheese, sour cream, and cilantro. Yield: 6 servings (serving size: 1 cup chili, 1 tablespoon cheese, 1 tablespoon sour cream, and 1 tablespoon cilantro).

CALORIES 269 (23% from fat); FAT 6.9g
(sat 2.6g, mono 2.5g, poly 0.7g);
PROTEIN 26.9g; CARB 25.2g; FIBER 4.4g;
CHOL 51mg; IRON 3.7mg; SODIUM 600mg;
CALC 120mg
EXCHANGES: 1 Starch, 2 Vegetable, 3 Lean Meat

SONORA GRILLED CHEESE

¼   cup low-fat mayonnaise
¼   teaspoon ground cumin
⅛   teaspoon black pepper
8   (1-ounce) slices hearty white
     bread
8   (¼-inch-thick) slices tomato
½   cup (2 ounces) shredded
     Monterey Jack cheese with
     jalapeño peppers
⅛   teaspoon salt
½   cup fat-free black bean dip
Cooking spray

1. Combine first 3 ingredients. Spread mixture evenly over 4 bread slices. Top each with 2 tomato slices and 2 tablespoons cheese; sprinkle with salt. Spread each remaining bread slice with 2 tablespoons black bean dip; place, dip sides down, on top of sandwiches.
2. Heat a large nonstick skillet coated with cooking spray over medium heat. Coat each side of sandwiches with cooking spray. Place sandwiches in pan; cook 2 minutes on each side or until golden brown. Yield: 4 servings (serving size: 1 sandwich).

CALORIES 270 (26% from fat); FAT 7.8g
(sat 2.6g, mono 2.6g, poly 1.5g);
PROTEIN 10.5g; CARB 35.6g; FIBER 2.7g;
CHOL 17mg; IRON 2.4mg; SODIUM 697mg;
CALC 190mg
EXCHANGES: 2 Starch, 1 Vegetable, 1½ Fat

ITALIAN PORTOBELLO SANDWICHES

Instead of high-fat cold cuts, try filling your sandwich with meaty portobello mushrooms and tender sautéed onion.

1 teaspoon olive oil

2 cups sliced portobello mushroom caps

2 (¼-inch-thick) slices red onion, separated into rings

¼ cup fat-free mayonnaise

2 tablespoons chopped fresh basil

¼ teaspoon freshly ground black pepper

4 (1½-ounce) slices sourdough bread

⅔ cup bottled roasted red bell peppers

2 (1-ounce) slices provolone cheese

1. Heat oil in a large nonstick skillet over medium heat. Add mushrooms and onion; cover and cook 7 minutes or until onion is tender, stirring occasionally. Remove from heat; cool.

2. Combine mayonnaise, basil, and black pepper. Spread 1 tablespoon mayonnaise mixture on each bread slice; layer each of 2 slices with ⅓ cup bell peppers, ½ cup mushroom mixture, and 1 slice cheese. Top with remaining bread slices. Yield: 2 servings (serving size: 1 sandwich).

CALORIES 412 (27% from fat); FAT 12.3g (sat 5.3g, mono 3.8g, poly 0.8g); PROTEIN 18.3g; CARB 60.1g; FIBER 2.6g; CHOL 20mg; IRON 5.9mg; SODIUM 1,117mg; CALC 320mg
EXCHANGES: 4 Starch, 1 Medium-Fat Meat, 1 Fat

PORTOBELLO POINTERS

Portobello mushrooms (the big brown ones) have a hearty, meaty flavor and texture.

Freshly harvested portobellos are light tan and slightly rough-textured with uneven edges and visible gills. As they mature, the caps become flatter, and the surface gets darker and more wrinkled. These more mature mushrooms actually have a richer flavor than the younger ones.

Most grocery stores sell the mushrooms either loose (with stems attached), or packaged as slices or caps only. The size varies, but size is not an indicator of flavor or texture.

CURRIED EGG SALAD SANDWICHES

We used only two egg yolks (all of the egg's fat content is in the yolk) and still got a creamy texture and rich flavor.

- 6 hard-cooked large eggs
- 1 tablespoon finely chopped red onion
- 1 tablespoon sweet pickle relish
- 3 tablespoons low-fat mayonnaise
- 1/4 teaspoon salt
- 1/4 teaspoon ground curry
- 1/8 teaspoon freshly ground black pepper
- 4 green leaf lettuce leaves
- 4 English muffins, split and toasted

1. Cut eggs in half lengthwise, removing yolks. Reserve 4 egg yolks for another use. Chop whites and remaining 2 yolks. Combine egg, onion, and relish in a small bowl.
2. Combine mayonnaise, salt, curry, and pepper; add to egg mixture.
3. Place 1 lettuce leaf on bottom half of each English muffin. Spoon one-fourth egg salad over each leaf, and top with remaining muffin halves. Yield: 4 servings (serving size: 1 sandwich).

CALORIES 215 (19% from fat); FAT 4.4g (sat 1g), mono 1.2g, poly 0.9g); PROTEIN 11.2g; CARB 31.7g; FIBER 1.8g; CHOL 106mg; IRON 2mg; SODIUM 634mg; CALC 122mg
EXCHANGES: 2 Starch, 1 Lean Meat

SPINACH CALZONE

Most women don't get enough iron or calcium. This hot sandwich, packed with spinach and five different cheeses, provides plenty of both.

- 3/4 cup 1% low-fat cottage cheese
- 1/2 cup low-fat sour cream
- 1/4 cup (2 ounces) 1/3-less-fat cream cheese, softened
- 3 tablespoons grated fresh Parmesan cheese
- 1 (10-ounce) package frozen chopped spinach, thawed, drained, and squeezed dry
- 1 (7-ounce) bottle roasted red bell peppers, drained and chopped
- 1 teaspoon garlic powder
- 1/4 teaspoon black pepper
- 1 (10-ounce) can refrigerated pizza crust

Cooking spray
- 1/4 cup (1 ounce) shredded part-skim mozzarella cheese
- 1/4 cup (1 ounce) shredded reduced-fat sharp Cheddar cheese
- 1 1/2 cups bottled fat-free Italian herb pasta sauce

1. Preheat oven to 425°.
2. Combine first 4 ingredients; beat with a mixer at medium speed 2 minutes or until blended. Stir in spinach, bell peppers, garlic powder, and black pepper.

3. Unroll pizza crust onto a baking sheet coated with cooking spray; pat into a 14 x 10-inch rectangle. Spread spinach mixture over half of crust, leaving a 1-inch border. Sprinkle mozzarella and Cheddar over spinach mixture. Fold dough over filling; press edges together to seal.

4. Bake at 425° for 15 minutes or until browned. Cool on a wire rack 5 minutes. Heat pasta sauce in a small saucepan over medium heat. Cut calzone into 6 squares, and top with sauce. Yield: 6 servings (serving size: 1 square and ¼ cup sauce).

CALORIES 289 (30% from fat); FAT 9.6g (sat 5g, mono 2.9g, poly 1.2g); PROTEIN 15.7g; CARB 35.4g; FIBER 2.8g; CHOL 24mg; IRON 3mg; SODIUM 778mg; CALC 227mg EXCHANGES: 2 Starch, 1 Vegetable, 1 High-Fat Meat

IRON AID

Even though spinach is a good source of iron, the iron in plant sources is not absorbed as well as that in animal sources.

To help your body better absorb the iron in spinach, include a vitamin C food (such as red bell pepper) at the same meal. The Spinach Calzone above is a great way to do just that.

TUNA MELTS

Eating an omega-3 fatty fish such as tuna at least twice a week might help ward off a heart attack.

1	(12-ounce) can solid white tuna in water, drained
⅓	cup chopped celery
3	tablespoons light mayonnaise
2	tablespoons Dijon mustard
2	teaspoons lime juice
½	teaspoon coarsely ground black pepper
4	English muffins, split and toasted
8	(¼-inch-thick) slices tomato
½	cup (2 ounces) shredded reduced-fat Swiss cheese

1. Preheat broiler.

2. Combine first 6 ingredients. Spread 3 tablespoons tuna mixture onto each muffin half. Top each with 1 tomato slice and 1 tablespoon cheese. Broil 5 minutes or until cheese melts. Yield: 4 servings (serving size: 2 muffin halves).

Note: Women who are pregnant, or planning to become pregnant, should not eat more than one serving of tuna per month because of mercury levels in several types of fish, including tuna.

CALORIES 368 (23% from fat); FAT 9.3g (sat 2.7g, mono 2.8g, poly 2.9g); PROTEIN 29.7g; CARB 39.8g; FIBER 0.9g; CHOL 42mg; IRON 2.8mg; SODIUM 954mg; CALC 282mg Exchanges: 2½ Starch, 3 Lean Meat

SHRIMP PO'BOYS WITH RÉMOULADE SLAW

This recipe features one of our "tried and true" methods for oven-frying fish.

2	tablespoons chopped green onions
1	tablespoon chopped fresh parsley
1½	tablespoons sweet pickle relish
1	tablespoon Creole mustard
2	tablespoons light mayonnaise
2	tablespoons white wine vinegar
¼	teaspoon salt
2½	cups packaged cabbage-and-carrot coleslaw
1¼	pounds jumbo shrimp
3	garlic cloves, minced
3	tablespoons yellow cornmeal
2	teaspoons all-purpose flour
½	teaspoon salt
¼	teaspoon ground red pepper
2	tablespoons peanut oil
3	(3-ounce) submarine rolls

1. Preheat oven to 450°.
2. Combine first 7 ingredients. Pour over slaw; toss gently to coat. Set aside.
3. Peel and devein shrimp. Combine shrimp and garlic in a large zip-top plastic bag; shake to coat. Combine cornmeal and next 3 ingredients. Add to shrimp; shake until well coated.
4. Coat a jelly roll pan evenly with oil; place in oven for 3 minutes or until very hot. Arrange shrimp on pan in a single layer. Bake at 450° for 3 minutes; turn and bake 1 minute or until golden. Remove shrimp from pan.
5. Spoon slaw mixture over bottom halves of rolls; top each with 4 shrimp. Cover with top halves of rolls. Yield: 6 servings (serving size: ½ sandwich).

CALORIES 253 (29% from fat); FAT 8.3g (sat 1.8g, mono 3.3g, poly 2.1g); PROTEIN 18.3g; CARB 27.2g; FIBER 2.3g; CHOL 129mg; IRON 4mg; SODIUM 724mg; CALC 77mg
EXCHANGES: 2 Starch, 2 Very Lean Meat, 1 Fat

ROAST BEEF SANDWICHES WITH HORSERADISH CREAM

Instead of grabbing fast food during your lunch hour, pack a healthier lunch with a satisfying roast beef sandwich.

8	(1-ounce) slices rye bread
1½	tablespoons reduced-fat sour cream
1½	tablespoons fat-free mayonnaise
2	teaspoons prepared horseradish
½	pound thinly sliced deli roast beef
2	ounces reduced-fat Swiss cheese, thinly sliced
4	green lettuce leaves
8	small tomato slices

1. Preheat oven to 450°.
2. Arrange bread on a jelly roll pan. Bake at 450° for 5 minutes or until golden.
3. Stir together sour cream, mayonnaise, and horseradish; spread evenly on toasted bread. Top with roast beef,

cheese, lettuce, and tomato. Top with remaining bread slices. Cut in half diagonally. Yield: 4 servings (serving size: 1 sandwich).

CALORIES 273 (23% from fat); FAT 6.9g
(sat 3.4g, mono 1.7g, poly 0.7g);
PROTEIN 19.6g; CARB 32.5g; FIBER 3.9g;
CHOL 34mg; IRON 2.7mg; SODIUM 876mg;
CALC 184mg
EXCHANGES: 2 Starch, 2 Lean Meat

RUM-PEPPER STEAK SANDWICHES

Instead of rum, you can use an equal amount of pineapple juice.

MARINADE:

- ½   cup dark rum
- 2   tablespoons brown sugar
- 1   tablespoon coarsely ground black pepper
- ¼   teaspoon salt
- 5   garlic cloves, crushed, or 2½ teaspoons bottled minced garlic
- 1   (1½-pound) flank steak

FLAVORED MAYONNAISE:

- ½   cup fat-free or light mayonnaise
- 2   teaspoons prepared horseradish

REMAINING INGREDIENTS:

- 8   (½-inch-thick) slices red onion (about 2 onions)
- Cooking spray
- 16   (1-ounce) slices sourdough bread
- 2   cups thinly sliced romaine lettuce
- 16   (¼-inch-thick) slices tomato

1. To prepare marinade, combine first 5 ingredients in a large zip-top plastic bag. Trim fat from steak; add steak to bag. Seal and marinate in refrigerator at least 2 hours, turning bag occasionally. Remove steak from bag, reserving marinade. Pour marinade into a microwave-safe dish. Microwave at HIGH 1 minute.
2. To prepare flavored mayonnaise, combine mayonnaise and horseradish.
3. Prepare grill.
4. Place steak and red onion slices on grill rack coated with cooking spray, and grill onions 4 minutes on each side, basting with reserved marinade. Remove onions from grill. Turn steak, and grill 8 minutes or until steak is desired degree of doneness. Remove steak from grill. Place bread slices on grill rack, and grill 2 minutes on each side or until toasted.
5. Cut steak diagonally across grain into thin slices. Spread 1 tablespoon flavored mayonnaise on one side of each toasted bread slice. Divide steak, onion slices, lettuce, and tomato evenly among bread slices. Top with remaining bread. Yield: 8 servings (serving size: 1 sandwich).

CALORIES 345 (29% from fat); FAT 11g
(sat 4.4g, mono 4.6g, poly 0.7g);
PROTEIN 22.6g; CARB 39.2g; FIBER 2.6g;
CHOL 45mg; IRON 3.8mg; SODIUM 640mg;
CALC 84mg
EXCHANGES: 2½ Starch, 2 Lean Meat, 1 Fat

STUFFED BLUE CHEESE BURGERS

Ground round has about 15 percent fat compared to about 27 percent for ground beef.

    1   pound ground round
   1/4 cup (1 ounce) crumbled blue
        cheese
    1   teaspoon olive oil
    1   large sweet onion, thinly sliced
        and separated into rings
    2   cups sliced mushrooms
   1/8 teaspoon salt
   1/8 teaspoon pepper
        Cooking spray
    4   (2.4-ounce) Kaiser rolls
    4   teaspoons creamy mustard blend

1. Divide beef into 4 equal portions. Roll each portion into a ball; make a pocket in the side of each ball, and insert 1 tablespoon blue cheese. Roll back into a ball, and flatten into a 3 1/2-inch patty. Cover and chill.
2. Prepare grill.
3. Heat oil in a large nonstick skillet over medium-high heat. Add onion, and sauté 12 to 14 minutes or until golden. Add mushrooms; sauté until tender and liquid is absorbed. Add salt and pepper. Set aside, and keep warm.
4. Place patties on grill rack coated with cooking spray; grill, covered, 6 minutes on each side or until done.

5. Place one patty on bottom half of each roll; top each with 1/4 cup onion mixture. Spread 1 teaspoon mustard on cut side of remaining roll halves. Cover burgers with roll tops. Yield: 4 servings (serving size: 1 sandwich).

CALORIES 378 (32% from fat); FAT 13.4g (sat 4.1g, mono 4.4g, poly 0.7g); PROTEIN 33.2g; CARB 29.5g; FIBER 2g; CHOL 70mg; IRON 4.4mg; SODIUM 600mg; CALC 77mg
EXCHANGES: 2 Starch, 3 Medium-Fat Meat

BARBECUE PORK-AND-COLESLAW HOAGIES

Starting with lean pork tenderloin is the way to get low-fat pork barbecue.

    1   (1-pound) pork tenderloin
   1/2 cup spicy barbecue sauce, divided
        Cooking spray
  2 1/2 cups packaged coleslaw
  2 1/2 tablespoons low-fat sour cream
  1 1/2 tablespoons light mayonnaise
  1 1/2 teaspoons sugar
  2 1/2 teaspoons prepared horseradish
    4   (2 1/2-ounce) hoagie rolls

1. Prepare broiler.
2. Cut pork in half lengthwise; brush with 3 tablespoons barbecue sauce. Place on a broiler pan coated with cooking spray; broil 15 minutes or until a meat thermometer registers 155° (slightly pink), turning occasionally. Cut into 1/4-inch-thick slices.

3. Combine coleslaw and next 4 ingredients. Combine pork and 3 tablespoons sauce. Brush cut sides of bread with 2 tablespoons sauce. Divide pork evenly among bottom halves of rolls. Top each roll half with about ½ cup coleslaw; cover with roll tops. Yield: 4 servings (serving size: 1 sandwich).

CALORIES 398 (23% from fat); FAT 10.2g (sat 3.6g, mono 4g, poly 1.7g); PROTEIN 34g; CARB 45g; FIBER 3.4g; CHOL 88mg; IRON 4.6mg; SODIUM 717mg; CALC 106mg Exchanges: 3 Starch, 3 Lean Meat

SPICY RANCH CHICKEN WRAPS

Take a break from the sandwich routine and make a wrap filled with spicy chicken, peppers, and tomatoes.

2	teaspoons chili powder
2	teaspoons vegetable oil
1½	teaspoons ground cumin
½	teaspoon salt
1¼	pounds skinless, boneless chicken breasts, cut into ½-inch strips
½	cup low-fat buttermilk
¼	cup light mayonnaise
2	tablespoons minced fresh parsley
2	tablespoons fresh lime juice
2	jalapeño peppers, seeded and diced
2	garlic cloves, crushed
4	(8-inch) fat-free flour tortillas
3	cups chopped romaine lettuce
1⅓	cups chopped seeded tomato

1. Combine first 4 ingredients in a heavy-duty zip-top plastic bag. Add chicken; seal and shake to coat. Remove chicken from bag.

2. Combine buttermilk and next 5 ingredients in a small bowl, and stir well with a whisk.

3. Place a large nonstick skillet over medium-high heat until hot. Add chicken, and sauté 2 minutes or until chicken is done. Add buttermilk mixture; cover and cook 1 minute. Remove from heat.

4. Warm tortillas according to package directions. Spoon about ¾ cup chicken mixture onto each tortilla, and top each serving with ¾ cup chopped lettuce and ⅓ cup chopped tomato. Roll up wrap. Yield: 4 servings (serving size: 1 wrap).

CALORIES 362 (20% from fat); FAT 7.9g (sat 1.8g, mono 2.2g, poly 3.2g); PROTEIN 38.7g; CARB 32.9g; FIBER 2.9g; CHOL 87mg; IRON 3.4mg; SODIUM 724mg; CALC 84mg EXCHANGES: 2 Starch, 4 Very Lean Meat, 1 Fat

TORTILLA TIP
We've found that the best way to warm flour tortillas without drying them out is to place them between two damp paper towels and heat in the microwave on HIGH for about 7 to 10 seconds per tortilla.

OPEN-FACED MEDITERRANEAN GRILLED CHICKEN SANDWICHES

Marinate the chicken 8 hours or overnight for maximum flavor.

  4 (4-ounce) skinless, boneless chicken breast halves
 ½ cup plus 1 tablespoon sun-dried tomato dressing, divided
    Olive oil-flavored cooking spray
  4 slices reduced-fat provolone cheese
  4 (1½-ounce) slices French bread
 1½ cups shredded romaine lettuce
  2 plum tomatoes, thinly sliced
  2 teaspoons chopped fresh basil
 ¼ teaspoon freshly ground black pepper

1. Place each chicken breast half between 2 sheets of heavy-duty plastic wrap; flatten to ½-inch thickness, using a meat mallet or rolling pin. Combine chicken breast halves and ½ cup dressing in a heavy-duty zip-top plastic bag; seal bag securely, and marinate in refrigerator at least 8 hours.
2. Prepare grill.
3. Remove chicken from marinade, discarding marinade. Place chicken on grill rack coated with cooking spray; grill, covered, 4 minutes on each side or until done. Top with cheese, and grill 1 minute or until cheese melts. Coat bread with cooking spray; grill, covered, 1 minute on each side or until toasted.
4. Toss lettuce with 1 tablespoon dressing. Top bread slices evenly with lettuce and tomato. Place a chicken breast over each. Sprinkle with basil and pepper. Yield: 4 servings (serving size: 1 open-faced sandwich).

CALORIES 305 (26% from fat); FAT 8.8g (sat 2.2g, mono 0.9g, poly 0.7g); PROTEIN 35.6g; CARB 19.7g; FIBER 1.7g; CHOL 71mg; IRON 2.2mg; SODIUM 602mg; CALC 199mg
EXCHANGES: 1 Starch, 1 Vegetable, 4 Very Lean Meat, 1 Fat

TURKEY COBB SANDWICHES

We reduced the fat significantly in this sandwich version of a Cobb salad by using reduced-fat Cheddar, fat-free mayonnaise, and reduced-fat bacon.

 ½ cup (2 ounces) reduced-fat shredded Cheddar cheese
 ⅓ cup fat-free mayonnaise
 ¼ cup (1 ounce) crumbled blue cheese
 ¼ teaspoon black pepper
  1 green onion, thinly sliced
  4 green leaf lettuce leaves
  8 (0.6-ounce) slices light white bread, lightly toasted
 12 large watercress sprigs, trimmed
 ¼ pound thinly sliced deli turkey
  4 slices 40%-less-fat bacon, cooked and halved
  8 thin slices tomato

1. Combine first 5 ingredients in a small bowl, stirring well.

2. Place lettuce leaves on 4 bread slices; top evenly with watercress. Layer turkey, bacon, and tomato evenly on watercress. Spread mayonnaise mixture evenly on remaining bread slices; top sandwiches with bread.

3. Slice sandwiches in half diagonally, using a wooden pick to hold each half together. Yield: 4 servings (serving size: 1 sandwich).

CALORIES 231 (30% from fat); FAT 8.2g (sat 3.7g, mono 0.6g, poly 0.4g); PROTEIN 17.5g; CARB 25.4g; FIBER 5.6g; CHOL 28mg; IRON 2.1mg; SODIUM 987mg; CALC 223mg
EXCHANGES: 2 Starch, 1 Lean Meat, 1 Medium-Fat Meat, ½ Fat

HOLD THE MAYO

People tend to have strong preferences when it comes to mayonnaise, especially the reduced-fat versions. In our test kitchens, we've found that the fat-free brands are fine for spreading on sandwiches, but for stirring into dips or sauces, the reduced-fat or light versions add a bit more creaminess.

Of course, if you're a real mayonnaise connoisseur, you may prefer just using smaller amounts of the real thing.

ASIAN-STYLE TURKEY BURGERS

Ground turkey includes light and dark meat. You can trim the fat even more by using ground turkey breast.

1	pound ground turkey
⅓	cup finely chopped onion
3	tablespoons chopped fresh parsley
2	tablespoons Worcestershire sauce
2	tablespoons minced green bell pepper
1	tablespoon low-sodium soy sauce
1	tablespoon cold water
2	teaspoons grated peeled fresh ginger
½	teaspoon salt
¼	teaspoon pepper
2	garlic cloves, minced
	Cooking spray
4	(1½-ounce) hamburger buns

1. Combine first 11 ingredients. Divide turkey mixture into 4 portions, shaping each into a ¾-inch-thick patty.

2. Place a nonstick skillet coated with cooking spray over medium-high heat until hot. Add patties; cook 5 minutes on each side. Serve on buns. Yield: 4 servings (serving size: 1 burger).

CALORIES 329 (35% from fat); FAT 12.7g (sat 3.6g, mono 4.7g, poly 2.9g); PROTEIN 25g; CARB 25.2g; FIBER 1.3g; CHOL 58mg; IRON 2.9mg; SODIUM 751mg; CALC 48mg
EXCHANGES: 1½ Starch, 3 Medium-Fat Meat

Chapter 45

Menus for
a New You

Eating healthy is easy when you use
Cooking Light recipes. Here's a whole week of no-denial,
no-stress meals guaranteed to satisfy.

Putting together healthy meals is easy with these handy menu plans. We've set up a week's worth of menus for breakfast, lunch, dinner, and a snack. The recipes in bold are from the recipe section of this book, with page numbers provided for easy reference. The other items—fresh fruits, vegetables, breads, and grains—are simple ways to round out the meals.

Our suggested menu plan is not meant to be an exact prescription, but an example. For each day, we've given you two different calorie levels: 1,600 and 2,000. The daily calorie percentage is about 55 percent calories from carbohydrate, 20 percent from protein, and 25 percent or less from fat.

Everyone's preferences and needs differ, so don't hesitate to tailor the menus to meet your needs. If you're a woman, try the 1,600-calorie plan. If you need to cut back from that, choose smaller portions, or trim a few of the snacks from the menu. We don't advise eating less than 1,500 calories, especially if you are moderately active. If you're an "average" active man, you might need to add about 700 calories to the 2,000-calorie plan. Do this by doubling up on nutrient-rich foods. For example, have two muffins at breakfast, or drink a double dose of a smoothie. Add 2 to 3 extra ounces of low-fat meat to your sandwich, and have one or two pieces of fresh fruit for a mid-morning snack.

For further fine tuning, pay attention to your special needs regarding allergies, heart disease, diabetes, and lactation. If one rule applies to everyone, it's this: Eat a balanced, varied, and moderate diet.

Meal Planning 101

Planning menus is a matter of creating meals that are pleasing to the senses in both flavor and appearance. Ask the following questions when planning meals.

1. Is there variety in the type and shape of the foods? A meal with all round foods, for example, is not visually appealing.
2. Are the textures of the foods interesting and varied?
3. Are the colors varied and contrasting, but not clashing?
4. Are the flavors compatible?
5. Do the temperatures of the foods vary within the meal? A good example of temperature variation is a soup and sandwich meal.
6. Is there more than one type of food preparation method for the meal? For example, it's hectic in the kitchen if everything on the menu has to be cooked in a skillet. Plus, it's boring if all the foods on the plate have been cooked the same way.
7. Are the foods appropriate for the individuals who will be eating with regard to special dietary needs, allergies, or religious preferences?

Day 1

	1600 calories	2000 calories
Breakfast	**Banana-Bran Soy Muffins, page 180,** 2 muffins Fat-free fruit yogurt, 8 ounces Orange juice, ½ cup	**Banana-Bran Soy Muffins, page 180,** 2 muffins Fat-free fruit yogurt, 8 ounces Orange juice, ½ cup
Lunch	**Grilled Salmon Salad, page 270,** 1 serving Crisp breadsticks, 4 Red grapes, ½ cup	**Grilled Salmon Salad, page 270,** 1 serving Crisp breadsticks, 8 Red grapes, ½ cup **Espresso Meringue Cookies, page 197,** 3 cookies
Dinner	**Grilled Tuna Steaks with Garlic and Oregano, page 212,** 1 serving **Rosemary-Garlic Mashed Potatoes, page 284,** 1 serving Steamed green beans, ½ cup Whole wheat roll, 1	**Grilled Tuna Steaks with Garlic and Oregano, page 212,** 1 serving **Rosemary-Garlic Mashed Potatoes, page 284,** 1 serving Steamed green beans, 1 cup Whole wheat rolls, 2 Light butter, 1 tablespoon
Snack	**Curried Popcorn, page 167,** 1 serving **Passion Potion, page 175,** 1 serving	**Curried Popcorn, page 167,** 2 servings **Passion Potion, page 175,** 1 serving
	Total calories: 1574	Total calories: 2017

	DAY 2		**DAY 3**	
	1600 calories	2000 calories	1600 calories	2000 calories
Breakfast	Wheat bran cereal, 1 cup Banana, 1 Fat-free milk, 1 cup Orange juice, ½ cup	Wheat bran cereal, 1 cup Bagel, toasted, 1 Light butter, 1 tablespoon Banana, 1 Fat-free milk, 1 cup Orange juice, ½ cup	**Buckwheat-Honey Pancakes, page 181,** 2 pancakes Reduced-calorie syrup, 1 tablespoon Turkey sausage, 2 ounces Blueberries, ½ cup Fat-free milk, 1 cup	**Buckwheat-Honey Pancakes, page 181,** 3 pancakes Reduced-calorie syrup, 2 tablespoons Turkey sausage, 2 ounces Blueberries, ½ cup Fat-free milk, 1 cup
Lunch	**Tuna Melts, page 297,** 1 serving Reduced-fat potato chips, 1 ounce Baby carrots, ½ cup	**Tuna Melts, page 297,** 1 serving Reduced-fat potato chips, 1 ounce Baby carrots, ½ cup	**Tabbouleh with Arugula and Chicken, page 271,** 1 serving Whole wheat pita bread, 1 round Orange sections, 1 cup	**Tabbouleh with Arugula and Chicken, page 271,** 1 serving Whole wheat pita bread, 1 round Orange sections, 1 cup **Spicy Oatmeal Crisps, page 198,** 2 cookies
Dinner	**Chicken-and-Sweet Pepper Fajitas, page 250,** 1 serving **Black Bean Salad, page 265,** 1 serving **Pineapple-Mint Ice, page 396,** 1 serving	**Chicken-and-Sweet Pepper Fajitas, page 250,** 1 serving **Black Bean Salad, page 265,** 2 servings **Pineapple-Mint Ice, page 396,** 1 serving	**Mediterranean Lasagna, page 227,** 1 serving **Simplest Green Salad, page 262,** 1 serving French bread, 1 slice **Cappuccino Granita, page 190,** 1 serving	**Mediterranean Lasagna, page 227,** 1 serving **Simplest Green Salad, page 262,** 2 servings French bread, 2 slices **Cappuccino Granita, page 190,** 1 serving
Snack	**Asian Party Mix, page 168,** 2 servings	**Asian Party Mix, page 168,** 2 servings	**Strawberry-Banana Soy Smoothie, page 174,** 1 serving	**Strawberry-Banana Soy Smoothie, page 174,** 1 serving
	Total calories: 1626	Total calories: 1943	Total calories: 1603	Total calories: 1987

	DAY 4		**DAY 5**	
	1600 calories	2000 calories	1600 calories	2000 calories
Breakfast	Banana-Oat Quick Bread, page 184, 1 slice Light butter, 1 tablespoon Fresh fruit cup, 1 cup Fat-free milk, 1 cup	Banana-Oat Quick Bread, page 184, 2 slices Light butter, 2 tablespoons Fresh fruit cup, 1 cup Fat-free milk, 1 cup	Blueberry-Bran Muffins, page 181, 2 muffins Banana-Mango Smoothie, page 174, 1 serving	Blueberry-Bran Muffins, page 181, 2 muffins Banana-Mango Smoothie, page 174, 1 serving
Lunch	Turkey Cobb Sandwiches, page 302, 1 serving Pretzel sticks, 2 ounces Grapes, ½ cup Fat-free milk, 1 cup	Turkey Cobb Sandwiches, page 302, 1 serving Pretzel sticks, 2 ounces Ultradecadent Double-Chip Brownies, page 199, 1 brownie Grapes, ½ cup Fat-free milk, 1 cup	Lentil-Vegetable Soup, page 290, 1 serving Greek Bread, page 177, 1 slice Pear, 1	Lentil-Vegetable Soup, page 290, 1 serving Greek Bread, page 177, 2 slices Pear, 1 Fat-free milk, 1 cup
Dinner	Meatballs and Peppers, page 236, 1 serving Mixed green salad with low-fat vinaigrette, 1½ cups Whole wheat roll, 1 Light butter, 1 teaspoon Chocolate low-fat ice cream, ½ cup	Meatballs and Peppers, page 236, 1 serving Mixed green salad with low-fat vinaigrette, 1½ cups Whole wheat rolls, 2 Light butter, 1 tablespoon Chocolate low-fat ice cream, ½ cup	Balsamic Chicken, page 251, 1 serving Roasted asparagus, 1 cup Spicy Melon Salad, page 261, 1 serving	Balsamic Chicken, page 251, 1 serving Roasted asparagus, 1 cup Spicy Melon Salad, page 261, 1 serving Whole wheat roll, 1 Light butter, 1 tablespoon
Snack	String cheese, 1 stick Apple, 1, cut into wedges	String cheese, 1 stick Apple, 1, cut into wedges	Spicy Oatmeal Crisps, page 198, 2 cookies Fat-free milk, 1 cup	Spicy Oatmeal Crisps, page 198, 3 cookies Fat-free milk, 1 cup
	Total calories: 1577	Total calories: 2085	Total calories: 1563	Total calories: 1972

	DAY 6		DAY 7	
	1600 calories	2000 calories	1600 calories	2000 calories
Breakfast	Whole wheat toast, 1 slice Fruit spread, 1 tablespoon Scrambled egg, 1 Bacon, 1 slice Orange juice, ½ cup Fat-free milk, 1 cup	Whole wheat toast, 2 slices Fruit spread, 2 tablespoons Scrambled egg, 1 Bacon, 2 slices Orange juice, ½ cup Fat-free milk, 1 cup	**Feta Omelet with Breadcrumbs, page 219,** 1 serving English muffin, 1 muffin Grapefruit sections, ½ cup Fat-free milk, 1 cup	**Feta Omelet with Breadcrumbs, page 219,** 1 serving English muffin, 2 muffins Fruit spread, 2 tablespoons Grapefruit sections, ½ cup Fat-free milk, 1 cup
Lunch	**Roast Beef Sandwiches with Horseradish Cream, page 298,** 1 serving Bagel chips, 1 ounce Nectarine, 1	**Roast Beef Sandwiches with Horseradish Cream, page 298,** 1 serving Bagel chips, 2 ounces Nectarine, 1	**Spicy Ranch Chicken Wraps, page 301,** 1 serving Baked tortilla chips, 1 ounce Watermelon cubes, 1 cup	**Spicy Ranch Chicken Wraps, page 301,** 1 serving Baked tortilla chips, 2 ounces Watermelon cubes, 1 cup
Dinner	**Indian-Spiced Roast Salmon, page 211,** 1 serving **Lemon Couscous, page 285,** 1 serving Steamed broccoli, 1 cup Raspberry sorbet, ½ cup	**Indian-Spiced Roast Salmon, page 211,** 1 serving **Lemon Couscous, page 285,** 1 serving Steamed broccoli, 1 cup Raspberry sorbet, ½ cup	**Pork, Kale, and Bok Choy Stir-Fry, page 243,** 1 serving Steamed snow peas, 1 cup Fresh pineapple chunks, ½ cup	**Pork, Kale, and Bok Choy Stir-Fry, page 243,** 1 serving Steamed snow peas, 1 cup Fresh pineapple chunks, ½ cup
Snack	**Puffed-up Chocolate-Chip Cookies, page 198,** 2 cookies Fat-free milk, 1 cup	**Puffed-up Chocolate-Chip Cookies, page 198,** 3 cookies Fat-free milk, 1 cup	Graham crackers, 3 squares Fat-free milk, ½ cup	Graham crackers, 6 squares Peanut butter, 2 tablespoons Fat-free milk, 1 cup
	Total calories: 1597	Total calories: 1996	Total calories: 1635	Total calories: 1999

Chapter 46

Food and Weight-Loss Journal

When it comes to weight loss, the power's in the pen.

Weight loss experts say that one of the best weight-loss tools is a food journal. To keep a basic food journal, write down everything that you eat and drink during the day, including amounts. To really get a good picture of your eating habits, you can also record where you were when you were eating (in front of the television, at your desk, in your car) and your mood when you were eating (stressed, nervous, happy).

A food journal can give you information about what you are eating, plus it can reveal important information about why you might be eating, and also give you some clues about what behavior changes you can make. For example, you may believe that you always eat 5 servings of fruits and vegetables a day, but when you write it down, you see that you actually get those 5 servings about twice a week. You can also see where your food weaknesses are. Review your journal and see if you tend to hit the vending machine for a chocolate candy bar every Monday afternoon after stressful staff meetings. Or maybe you get the munchies on Friday night when you're home by yourself watching old movies or when you're out celebrating with friends.

Whatever your situation, a food journal can be a powerful motivator for change. It can help you see the areas where you can improve, and, for some people, keeping a journal actually helps keep them from overeating. There's something about knowing that you will have to record every bite you take that keeps you from eating one more handful of M&M's.

Set up your journal in whatever way works for you: a pocket- or purse-sized notebook, a spiral notebook, or your laptop computer. Use the example on the next page to see what information you need to include to get a glimpse of your eating style.

Food	Amount	Time	Location	Mood
orange juice blueberry muffins	1 cup 2	7 a.m.	kitchen	rushed
peanuts	1 bag	10 a.m.	work-desk	busy
tuna sandwich pretzels Diet Coke	1 bag 1 can	1 p.m.	work-desk	busy
apple	1	5 p.m.	den-watching TV	tired
vegetable-beef soup crackers fruit salad milk	1 bowl (2 cups) 8 ½ cup 1 cup	7 p.m.	kitchen table	relaxed
low-fat ice cream	1 cup	9 p.m.		

Fit Kids

Help your children have a happy, healthy life by
showing them how to eat well and stay active.

Chapter 47

Teach Your Children Well

How to keep your children fit and healthy for life

Super parents that we are—busy fighting the forces of society that are ready to pounce on our innocent children at any moment, forces such as sex, drugs, rock and roll, or more likely, MTV, Power Station II, and Cheetos—there is no doubt that our fast-paced, ever-vigilant lifestyle presents a challenge to our attempts at good nutrition. And overnutrition has recently emerged as a problem of affluence, convenience, and hectic living. Not every child is overweight, but without a concerted effort to maintain a balanced diet and a balanced environment, many children are at risk for developing weight problems. Just take a look at the numbers.

The Centers for Disease Control and Prevention (CDC) has categorized children at risk of being overweight as those greater than the 85th percentile Body Mass Index (BMI). Children who are greater than the 95th percentile BMI are considered overweight. BMI is based on a relative measurement of an adult or child's height to weight; however, the children's BMI chart is different than the one used for adults. Children tend to have less fat than adults do, with that percentage dipping fairly low by age 6 and then increasing into adulthood. Girls carry slightly more fat than boys do, so BMI charts for children reflect these subtle differences.

> Without a concerted effort to maintain a balanced diet and a balanced environment, many children are at risk for developing weight problems.

Based on the CDC's definition of overweight, about 8 percent of children 4 to 5 years of age are overweight, as are 13 percent of children aged 6 to 11 years, and 14 percent of adolescents. That equates to roughly one in five children being overweight—more than double the number two decades ago, and for adolescents, a triple effect.

LIKE PARENT, LIKE CHILD

The initial concern about overweight children seems to be the fact that most of them end up in a vicious cycle of dieting, weight gain, and low self-esteem that reaches far into adulthood. Genetics has something to do with a child's weight as an adult, but our genetic pool hasn't changed enough in the past 20 years to support such rapid increases in obesity. Since 40 percent of children with one overweight parent end up overweight as adults, and 80 percent of children with two overweight parents also end up overweight, it's likely that parents pass on not only their genetic body types, but also habits and lifestyles.

DIABETES ON THE RISE

The incidence of type 2 diabetes, which most people assume is an adult disease, is rising at an alarming rate in children in this country. About 85 percent of all new cases of children with type 2 diabetes are children with weight problems. What normally wouldn't show up until adulthood—or the time when most people gain extra pounds—is now appearing earlier than expected. Although this phenomenon occurs across the board, gender and race complicate the issue. Young girls are more likely to develop type 2 diabetes than young boys, and Native Americans, African-Americans, Hispanics, and Asian-Americans/Pacific Islanders are also more likely to develop the disease than Caucasian children.

OTHER HEALTH PROBLEMS

While type 2 diabetes may be one of the greatest health concerns among health care providers who work with overweight children, so too is the increased risk of heart disease and high blood pressure. The spectrum of potential health problems includes an increased risk for gall bladder disease, sleep apnea, asthma, and discomfort in the legs and joints that limits the ability of the child to move and play.

However, the most immediate consideration for the parents and the child is the social isolation that overweight children face. We've all been kids and we all know how overweight children get teased. It's not unusual at all for these kids to develop a lifelong dysfunctional relationship with food—evidenced through anorexia, binge eating, failed diets, or just a disregard for good nutrition. The emotional toll exhibits itself not only in how children view food, but how they view themselves. And that, after all, is really the most important reason why all children, regardless of size, should be taught the principles of a balanced diet.

A Guide to Kids' Daily Nutritional Needs

Anyone who's ever tried to feed kids knows that at times, they seem like Martians. After all, given a choice, what earthly creature could eat a cheese sandwich every day for lunch for two straight years? Who knew that the right way to eat a banana was to peel one side, leaving the other side to cradle the fruit, which of course must be sliced diagonally?

As much as it may seem like our children are from another planet, their actual basic nutritional needs aren't that different from ours. The main difference is that kids require smaller portion sizes, and, often, more frequent snacks. But aside from that, their dietary intake should reflect ours. And therein lies the rub—how can we expect our children to eat right if we don't? Children are tiny mirrors of adults, and they learn to eat as we eat, enjoy what we enjoy, and develop similar attitudes towards food. For that reason, any child with special dietary needs—a sensitivity to gluten, diabetes, or extra weight—should not be isolated from the rest of the family by a special diet. The best method for instituting change in a child's diet is to change the diet of the entire family. In other words, it's a group effort. While this concept of the family eating a healthful diet is easy to understand, making the actual change is where the work really starts.

> Children learn to eat as we eat, enjoy what we enjoy, and develop similar attitudes toward food.

Reality Check

It's important to understand how to set realistic weight goals for children. Overweight children should not be placed on a diet. First, these kids should be encouraged to eat a healthful diet and increase their physical activity in an attempt to maintain their weight while they grow taller. Over time, this approach allows a child's body mass index (BMI) to fall more in line with that of his peers, or, in more simple terms, it lets children "grow into their weight." Second, if a child is really overweight, a reduction in calories may be necessary, but only a reduction of calories back to a child's normal level—not to levels promoted for adult low-calorie diets. It boils down to a common sense approach to food selection and portions, such as the difference between a super-sized McDonald's meal (about 1800 calories) or a regular-sized McDonald's meal (roughly 600 calories).

In general, it is not recommended that overweight kids lose weight unless the child is extremely overweight, in which case the weight loss should be minimal—five to ten percent of the original weight—and it should be supervised by a physician and registered dietitian. A combination of setting realistic weight-loss goals or controlling weight gain, establishing a healthy diet, and increasing physical activity is really the best, long-term solution in maintaining a healthy weight for both children and adults.

For many overweight children, the goal of achieving an ideal body weight or becoming as thin as their thinnest friends is elusive. To some extent, these children may always be a little larger, so it's critical to provide a supportive and accepting environment at home. Make sure your child feels loved no matter what weight he or she is. Emphasize talents, not weight. And if it hasn't been said enough already, make sure your child doesn't feel alone with the weight problem. Approach the solution as a family's initiative to eat better rather than as a prohibitive diet for a singled-out child. Include other caregivers such as grandparents, daycare providers, and family friends in the lifestyle change. Research has shown that children rebel when placed on diets, but seem to be able to control their calorie intake much better when parents provide healthy food choices and then let the kids decide how much they want to eat.

HEALTHY KIDS

What constitutes a healthy diet for kids? Pretty much the same as what adults should be eating, only not quite as much for younger children. The Food Guide Pyramid and its number of servings and portion sizes are the same for children aged 7 to 10 and adults. Once puberty starts—usually around 11 years of age for both girls and boys— food intake for boys seems to rocket off the charts, while adolescent girls need only slightly more food than normal. Younger children (aged 2 to 6) tend to eat less, but usually by around age 7 or 8, most kids can eat portions close to the size of those on the adult menu. The children's version of the Food Guide Pyramid recommends six servings of grains, three servings of vegetables, two servings of fruits, two servings of meat, two servings of milk, and like adults, modest use of fats and sweets. Generally, a 2- to 3-year old eats about two-thirds the portion size of a 4- to 6-year old. See the chart on pages 316 and 317 for examples of serving sizes from each food category.

> What constitutes a healthy diet for kids? Pretty much the same as what adults should be eating, only not as much for younger children.

Recommended Daily Servings and Portion Size Guidelines for Children 2-6 Years Old*

Recommended Daily Servings	2-3 years	4-6 years
Grain Group—6 servings		
Bread	¼-½ slice	1 slice
Cooked rice or pasta	¼-⅓ cup	½ cup
Cooked cereal	¼-⅓ cup	½ cup
Ready-to-eat cereal	¼-⅓ cup	½ cup or 1 ounce
Graham cracker squares	1-2	2-3
Whole grain crackers	3-4	5-6
Buns, bagels, muffins	¼-½	½
4-inch pancake	½-⅔ pancake	1 pancake
Popcorn	2 cups	3 cups
Taco shells	May cause choking	2 shells
7-inch corn tortilla	½-⅔ tortilla	1 tortilla
Fruit/Vegetable Groups		
Vitamin C Sources—1 serving or more		
Whole fruit	½ small	½-1 small
Cooked, canned, chopped raw	⅓ cup	½ cup
Juice	¼-⅓ cup	½-¾ cup
Large kiwi fruit	½-⅓ kiwi	1 whole kiwi
Medium orange	½-⅓ orange	1 whole orange
Grapefruit	½ grapefruit	½ grapefruit
Tomato or spaghetti sauce	¼-⅓ cup	½ cup
Cherry tomatoes	May cause choking	5 tomatoes
Vitamin A Sources—1 serving or more		
Whole fruit	½ small	½-1 small
Cooked, canned, chopped raw	⅓ cup	½ cup
Juice	¼-⅓ cup	½-¾ cup
Broccoli spears	1 spear	2 spears
3-inch-long carrot sticks	May cause choking	7-8 sticks
Squash	⅓ cup	½ cup
Cantaloupe	1-2 slices	¼ medium melon

RECOMMENDED DAILY SERVINGS AND PORTION SIZE GUIDELINES FOR CHILDREN 2-6 YEARS OLD*

Recommended Daily Servings	2-3 years	4-6 years
Other Fruits and Vegetables—3 servings or more		
Whole fruit	½ small	½-1 small
Cooked, canned, chopped raw	⅓ cup	½ cup
Dried	¼ cup	¼ cup
Medium-sized baked potato	½ potato	1 potato
Banana	½ banana	1 banana
Applesauce	¼-⅓ cup	½ cup
Small pear	½ pear	1 pear
Milk Group—2 servings		
Milk	1 cup	1 cup
Yogurt	½ cup	1 cup
Cheese	1-1½ ounces	2 ounces
Soy milk, calcium fortified	1 cup	1 cup
Pudding	½ cup	1 cup
Meat Group—2 servings to total 3.5 ounces/day		**5 ounces/day**
Lean meat, chicken, fish	1-2 ounces or 3-6 tablespoons	2-3 ounces
Dry bean and peas	1-2 ounces or 3-6 tablespoons	2-3 ounces
Egg	1 egg	1 egg
Peanut butter	2 tablespoons= 1 ounce	2 tablespoons= 1 ounce
Salmon or tuna, canned	¼ cup=1 ounce	¼ cup=1 ounce
Soy burger patty	1 patty=1 ounce	1 patty=1 ounce
Tofu	½ cup=1 ounce	½ cup=1 ounce
Fat Group—3-4 servings		
Margarine, butter, oil	1 teaspoon	1 teaspoon

*Adapted from the USDA Food Guide Pyramid for Young Children 2 to 6 Years Old

While the American Heart Association and the American Academy of Pediatrics support a 30 percent restriction of fat in a child's diet—similar to adults—it is not okay to restrict fat for children under the age of 2 years. Infants and toddlers need dietary fat for brain development, energy, and to protect their internal organs. Parents should be cautious not to get carried away with low-fat diets for their children because these diets may cause more harm than good. A more balanced approach would be to slowly move a child to the recommended percentage of fat intake as the child reaches adolescence. If parents follow the concepts of the children's Food Guide Pyramid, the percentage of fat intake really shouldn't be an issue, and it will self-correct based on making wise choices from the other food groups.

FUN WITH FOOD

Eating healthfully shouldn't be a chore, and whether your child is at his or her ideal weight or not, there are basic tips that can be shared by all families to make nutritious dining fun.

- Eat together as a family as often as possible. Savor the experience by talking, laughing, and enjoying the time together. The family that dines together is fine together.
- Turn off the TV during mealtimes, and limit overall television watching and other sedentary activities like video games and computer time. The American Academy of Pediatrics recommends that children watch no more than one to two hours of television a day. Limit TV watching by offering enjoyable alternatives—a trip to the park or a romp with a pet.
- Avoid turning food into weapons of punishment, or for that matter, into rewards. Instead, reward kids by spending quality time with them. Play a game of cards with them or take them to the skating rink.
- Teach children where foods come from by growing a garden or even just a pot of herbs. Encourage them to help you prepare healthful foods. This is an easy and fun way to get kids excited about nutrition.
- Set an example by avoiding foods high in fat, sugar, and calories, and focus on eating at least five servings of fruits and vegetables a day. A sure-fire way to do this is to stock the kitchen with nutritious snacks such as apple wedges, bananas, orange sections, and raw veggies rather than tempting, high-calorie, fatty foods.
- Swap out water for soft drinks, fruit juice drinks, and sports drinks. Children of any age only need $\frac{1}{2}$ cup to $\frac{3}{4}$ cup of 100 percent fruit juice a day. Beyond that, juice can be a huge source of extra calories.

- Learn, measure, and use correct portion sizes. Though this is a challenge at first, it will eventually become second nature to the point where you could do it in your sleep. As if by osmosis, your child will pick up on these portion sizes and consider them normal.
- Don't force children to eat when they are not hungry. Contrary to what our parents told us, the clean plate club is not a good idea. Kids have their own internal regulators, which, when left untainted by adults, work well to regulate calorie intake. As long as your child is active and growing, calories don't need to be forced. Remember, adults determine what foods are available, and children choose how much of them they want to eat.
- Limit eating out or ordering in. Research studies show that the more people eat away from home, the higher the likelihood that they will become overweight. This is true for kids as well. A good rule of thumb to follow here is to limit dining out to one time per week. Sound tough? It is at first, but over time, this too will soon seem customary.
- Learn to spot healthy choices or better choices on the menu when you are eating out. Many fast-food restaurants offer salads, chili, baked potatoes, or broiled chicken or fish. But hold the salad dressing, mayonnaise, or tartar sauce. Have a game plan in place before setting foot into a restaurant, and stick to it!
- Practice a life of activity. Divvy up household chores to kids as well as adults. Plan a big adventure like a camping or hiking trip. Understand that your child can be active even if he or she isn't athletic and be flexible to your child's need to participate in team sports versus individual sports like dancing, swimming, or martial arts. Spend weekends touring your local city by foot. Recruit your neighbors to help create a safe environment for the kids to play outside, and plan pastimes like tag or touch football for the whole family. Most of all, be sensitive to your overweight child's needs and avoid embarrassing scenarios where he or she is likely to fail.
- Be consistent. Again, easier said than done, but sending children mixed messages only adds to the confusion.

At all costs, help your child avoid commercial weight-loss centers, fad diets, or dietary supplements. In general, these have not been determined to be safe weight-loss methods for kids. Stick with the basics—the Food Guide Pyramid, increased physical activity, and family support—for a successful, lifetime approach to food, nutrition, and weight control.

—Tamara Schryver

Chapter 48

Family Food Feuds

Use these tactics to wrangle a cease-fire with
your kids in the war over junk foods.

Getting children to trade in their cookielike cereals or any other food smothered in frosting or cheese for something plucked from a tree or spaded up from a field is a torturous experience for many parents who regularly battle through mealtime skirmishes.

The end game is predictable: Either flustered adults surrender to the hard sells of the snack-food establishment, or they try to force the food pyramid onto their kids as if their home were a police state. Obviously, neither "solution" engenders a healthy, balanced attitude toward food and nutrition.

While the family food feuds have left many parents tired and confused, they also have left many children at higher risk for serious health problems when they reach adulthood. Only 20 percent of kids get the recommended five daily servings of fruits and vegetables that have been shown to help reduce the risk of heart disease and cancer in adults. Because kids are exercising less, too, it's not surprising that the percentage of overweight children has doubled since the 1980s.

"Some kids never learn what nutritious foods can do for them," says Lilian Cheung, a lecturer in the department of nutrition at the Harvard School of Public Health in Boston. "They don't learn it at school, and they don't learn it at home. Some kids I've talked with don't even know where foods come from—they think food just pops out of the refrigerator."

Meanwhile, research has consistently shown that kids who learn early to eat nutritiously hang on to those habits as adults. Eating the right foods at the right time might even affect a child's report card. In a study conducted by Massachusetts General Hospital in Boston, children who regularly ate breakfast earned better grades in math than those who didn't have a morning meal. It didn't have to be anything fancy: Cereal, milk, bread or muffins, and fruit or fruit juice worked just fine.

WINNING STRATEGIES

How, then, can adults give their kids a healthy respect for food? We asked several experts—whose unenviable job is to help children appreciate a wide array of foods—for their winning strategies. Here are their suggestions.

Don't dictate. Turning healthy eating into a domestic crusade draws battle lines between you and the kids. Preaching sermons about the evils of fat, delivering supper-table threats—"Eat your broccoli or you can't watch TV"—and forcing kids to eat dishes they don't like will just breed antagonism toward healthy foods.

But don't be a pushover, either. If your child balks at what you've put on the table, it's perfectly acceptable to say, "Sorry, but this is what we're having for dinner." When the child eventually gets hungry, he'll understand that there are consequences to his actions.

Be creative. If your child doesn't like apples fresh from the crisper, maybe the turnoff isn't the taste, but the shape or skin. Cut them up, peel them, and see what happens. If you know she's a fan of Thousand Island dressing, drizzle it over the broccoli that she's not crazy about. According to William Dietz, M.D., Ph.D., of the Centers for Disease Control and Prevention in Atlanta, your obligation is clear-cut: "Make the right foods available, and make them attractive."

> Research has consistently shown that kids who learn early to eat nutritiously hang on to those habits as adults.

Create a food adventure. Few children are familiar with the history of foods or their cultural origins, information that might help them become more adventurous in their eating habits. So take the international approach: Buy foods from different cultures and countries, and take your child to the market to help. Pinch-hit kiwis and mangoes for oranges and bananas, or quinoa and bulgur for rice and pasta. Let your children come up with menus and help prepare the foods. Kids who help prepare a meal will usually try it.

Try a Sunday-night special. Convene for dinner on Sunday night, or any night, at the dining-room table. Add ambiance with candles and fancy plates. When you slow down and ritualize a meal, it confers importance on the act of eating and the foods themselves.

Adjust your strategies to their age. Be flexible enough to slot nutrition into your child's way of life rather than coerce him to conform to your own ironclad wishes. "Young children are great imitators, so parents should strive to be especially good nutritional role models during the younger years," Cheung says. That means avoiding overindulgence and the no-fat-no-fun approach. In fact, let your child occasionally choose his favorite high-fat foods—remember, all foods are appropriate; they're just not appropriate at all times.

Teenagers, on the other hand, are tuned in to one wavelength—their peers'—so mimicking you is the last thing they'll do. Instead, adapt your tactics to their on-the-run lifestyle by buying nutritious foods that make a great movable feast, such as snack or energy bars, microwavable soups, and low-fat mozzarella sticks. (See "Fast Food Fake-Out," page 323, for recipes for teens and others easily tempted by junk food.)

If they don't like it, be cool. Persuading children to try a variety of foods doesn't mean they'll like all of them. Once your kids have had several opportunities to taste a certain food—and they finally try it but give it a thumbs-down—move on. "The human taste buds are more receptive to sweeter tastes, especially in children," Cheung says, "so don't be surprised if bitter vegetables like broccoli or cabbage turn them off, and sweet veggies like carrots and corn don't." But parents shouldn't do a soul-check if their kids aren't big fans of, say, Brussels sprouts or lentils. Perhaps they'll like another green vegetable or legume.

Remember that tastes do change as a child matures. A child who would never touch a vegetable that wasn't potatoes or corn may suddenly start eating broccoli because he read that the lead singer in his favorite band was crazy for the florets. In the generational food fights, you take a victory any way you can get it.

—*Wayne Kalyn*

Chapter 49

Fast Food
Fake-Out

These lower-fat, less-salty variations of your kids'
favorite junk foods are so good, you'll have to put
a drive-through lane in your kitchen.

A s most parents painfully discover, it's one thing to talk to kids about nutrition and quite another to get them to actually eat healthfully. (See "Family
Food Feuds," page 320.) Even when you're armed with the right strategies and a
creative approach, it's not easy selling a plate of steamed cauliflower to a child who
is dead set on dining at the golden arches. The reality is that kids (and a lot of
adults, too) love ooey, gooey, cheesy, sugary, salty foods.

So why not give them what they want—sort of. We've created kid-friendly
recipes for nachos, pizza, and cookies that will rival, and even beat, the lure of fatty
snacks and fast food. The knockoffs are so similar in taste and appearance to the
regular versions that kids won't be able to tell the difference.

But there is one: The appearance may be the same, but the ingredients are
lighter and healthier. Our streamlined version of pizza, made with reduced-fat pepperoni and part-skim mozzarella cheese, weighs in with a mere 7.1 grams of fat and
230 calories. A slice of pepperoni pizza from a neighborhood pizzeria can carry
more than twice the fat (16 grams or more if the chef is liberal with the pepperoni)
and nearly 300 calories. The same goes for the rest of our fast-food clones.

Your kids probably won't even care that the nachos, besides being loaded with
meat and cheese, also have a few servings of vegetables: roasted red peppers and
tomatoes for powerful carotenoids that may help ward off cancer and heart disease,
and lean refried beans with the kind of soluble fiber that keeps cholesterol down
and blood sugar on an even keel. All that matters to the younger set is that the
appearance is familiar and the flavor is awesome. But you'll know the difference.

Corn Dogs

¼ cup toasted wheat germ, divided
2 tablespoons seasoned breadcrumbs
1 (11.5-ounce) can refrigerated corn bread twists
1 tablespoon all-purpose flour
8 teaspoons prepared mustard
1 (14-ounce) package fat-free turkey-and-beef hot dogs
2 large egg whites

1. Preheat oven to 375°.
2. Combine 2 tablespoons wheat germ and breadcrumbs in a shallow dish. Set aside.
3. Unroll dough. Working with 2 dough portions at a time, pinch perforations to seal. Roll dough into a 6 x 3-inch rectangle on a surface sprinkled with 2 tablespoons wheat germ and flour. Spread 1 teaspoon mustard over rectangle. Place 1 hot dog on rectangle. Wrap dough around hot dog; pinch ends to seal. Repeat procedure with remaining dough, mustard, and hot dogs.
4. Dip each corn dog in egg whites; dredge in breadcrumb mixture. Place corn dogs on a baking sheet. Bake at 375° for 25 minutes or until golden brown. Yield: 8 servings (serving size: 1 corn dog).

CALORIES 211 (28% from fat); FAT 6.6g
(sat 1.6g, mono 2.6g, poly 2.3g);
PROTEIN 11.3g; CARB 25.3g; FIBER 0.6g;
CHOL 15mg; IRON 1.9mg; SODIUM 949mg;
CALC 8mg
EXCHANGES: 1½ Starch, 1 Medium-Fat Meat

Oven "Fried" Chicken Fingers with Honey-Mustard Dipping Sauce

SAUCE:
¼ cup honey
¼ cup spicy brown mustard

CHICKEN:
1½ pounds chicken breast tenders (about 16 pieces)
½ cup low-fat buttermilk
½ cup coarsely crushed cornflakes
¼ cup seasoned breadcrumbs
1 tablespoon instant minced onion
1 teaspoon paprika
¼ teaspoon dried thyme
¼ teaspoon black pepper
1 tablespoon vegetable oil

1. To prepare sauce, combine honey and mustard in a small bowl; cover and chill.
2. Preheat oven to 400°.
3. To prepare chicken, combine chicken and buttermilk in a shallow dish; cover and chill 15 minutes. Drain chicken, discarding liquid.
4. Combine cornflakes and next 5 ingredients in a large zip-top plastic bag; add 4 chicken pieces to bag. Seal and shake to coat. Repeat procedure with remaining chicken. Spread oil evenly in a jelly roll pan, and arrange chicken in a single layer in pan. Bake at 400° for 4 minutes

on each side or until done. Serve with sauce. Yield: 8 servings (serving size: 2 chicken tenders and 1 tablespoon sauce).

CALORIES 185 (18% from fat); FAT 3.7g
(sat 0.8g, mono 1.2g, poly 1.2g);
PROTEIN 21.6g; CARB 16g; FIBER 0.3g;
CHOL 49mg; IRON 1.3mg; SODIUM 306mg;
CALC 46mg
EXCHANGES: 1 Starch, 3 Very Lean Meat

LOADED NACHOS

    8   ounces ground round
   ½   cup chopped bottled roasted red
        bell peppers
    1   teaspoon chili powder
   ½   teaspoon dried oregano
   ¼   teaspoon salt
    1   (14.5-ounce) can no-salt-added
        diced tomatoes, undrained
    1   garlic clove, crushed
Cooking spray
    1   (16-ounce) can fat-free refried
        beans with mild chiles
   ¼   cup minced fresh cilantro,
        divided
   ¼   cup chopped green onions,
        divided
   27 baked tortilla chips (about 3
        ounces)
    1   cup (4 ounces) shredded
        Monterey Jack cheese
    3   tablespoons low-fat sour cream
   27 pickled jalapeño pepper slices
        (optional)

1. Preheat oven to 375°.

2. Cook meat in a large nonstick skillet over medium-high heat until browned, stirring to crumble. Stir in bell peppers and next 5 ingredients; cook 8 minutes or until thick, stirring occasionally. Remove from pan.

3. Place pan coated with cooking spray over medium heat until hot. Add beans, 2 tablespoons cilantro, and 2 tablespoons green onions; cook 2 minutes or until thoroughly heated. Place chips on a large ovenproof serving platter; spread warm bean mixture evenly over chips. Spoon meat mixture over bean mixture; top with cheese. Bake at 375° for 9 minutes or until cheese melts. Remove from oven; top with sour cream, 2 tablespoons cilantro, and 2 tablespoons green onions. Top with jalapeño pepper slices, if desired. Serve immediately. Yield: 9 servings (serving size: 3 loaded chips).

CALORIES 183 (30% from fat); FAT 6.2g
(sat 3.2g, mono 2g, poly 0.4g); PROTEIN 37.3g;
CARB 19.2g; FIBER 2.9g; CHOL 26mg;
IRON 2.3mg; SODIUM 449mg; CALC 152mg
EXCHANGES: 1 Starch, 1 Vegetable, 2 Lean
Meat

PEPPERONI PIZZA

SAUCE:

Cooking spray
2 garlic cloves, minced
1 teaspoon dried oregano
¼ teaspoon salt
⅛ teaspoon crushed red pepper
1 (8-ounce) can no-salt-added tomato sauce
1 tablespoon minced fresh parsley

CRUST:

1 (10-ounce) can refrigerated pizza crust dough
2 teaspoons cornmeal

REMAINING INGREDIENTS:

16 slices turkey pepperoni (such as Hormel)
1½ cups (6 ounces) preshredded part-skim mozzarella cheese
2 tablespoons grated Parmesan cheese

1. To prepare sauce, place a small saucepan coated with cooking spray over medium heat until hot. Add garlic, and sauté 1 minute. Add oregano, ¼ teaspoon salt, red pepper, and tomato sauce; reduce heat, and simmer 20 minutes, stirring occasionally. Stir in parsley, and keep warm.

2. Preheat oven to 450°.

3. Roll dough into a 12-inch circle on a 12-inch pizza pan or baking sheet coated with cooking spray and sprinkled with cornmeal.

4. Spread sauce over pizza crust, leaving a ½-inch border; top with pepperoni. Sprinkle with cheeses. Bake at 450° for 10 minutes or until crust is puffy and lightly browned. Remove pizza to cutting board; cut into 6 slices. Yield: 6 servings (serving size: 1 slice).

CALORIES 230 (28% from fat); FAT 7.1g (sat 3.4g, mono 1.6g, poly 0.3g); PROTEIN 12.8g; CARB 27.1g; FIBER 1.2g; CHOL 21mg; IRON 1.8mg; SODIUM 641mg; CALC 219mg
EXCHANGES: 2 Starch, 1 High-Fat Meat

Chapter 50

Finding Time for Family Fitness

Couch-potato kids can become fit and healthy—if Mom and Dad get into the act.

When Helene and David Gugerty saw the Bayville 5K looming on their calendar last May, the decision was a no-brainer. The whole crew would enter the race: David would run, and Helene would push a stroller carrying 4-year-old Emma and 2-year-old Paige. This family-wide fitness approach is daily Gugerty practice—a pledge that these outdoor-minded attorneys made to each other when they started their family. "We were so active before we had the kids," Helene says. "Now, we're active with the kids." Their daily walks, weekend bike rides, and joyrides in the jogging stroller will set the stage, these parents hope, for lifelong habits in their children.

When a family culture includes regular, fun-oriented exercise, a child is more likely to develop good fitness habits.

The Gugerty family has the right approach to a national problem: overweight, out-of-shape children. Twenty years ago, 10 percent of American children were considered overweight. The figure has doubled to 20 percent. "Some people would call that an epidemic," says Leonard H. Epstein, Ph.D., professor of psychology, social and preventive medicine, and nutrition at State University of New York-Buffalo. Not only are overweight children between the ages of 10 and 13 six times as likely to become overweight adults, but childhood obesity has also been linked to the adult onset of stroke and cancer, regardless of adult weight.

A big part of the problem is that American children just don't exercise enough. Figures from the third National Health and Nutrition Examination Survey show that 20 percent of American children participate in fewer than three sessions of vigorous activity per week, and the American Council on Exercise reports that 62 percent of American teenagers don't exercise regularly. While parents may carp at their children to get off the couch and get some real exercise, this may not be enough. "There's a lot of evidence that the best predictor of child activity levels is parent activity levels," Epstein says. When a family culture includes regular, fun-oriented exercise, a child is more likely to join in and develop good fitness habits.

Lucky for today's families, the world is catching on to the idea. Whereas kids have always had their Little League and soccer teams, there is more opportunity now than ever for families to exercise together. Fitness facilities of all sorts now offer activities for children, from wee sports at health clubs and kids' classes at yoga studios to multigenerational sessions at martial-arts studios. That makes it easier for parents to include kids in their fitness regimens.

Some health clubs are even putting their bricks and mortar into luring active-minded families. For instance, the Newtown Athletic & Aquatic Club in Newtown, Pennsylvania, built a 33,000-square-foot addition exclusively for kids. One of its most popular offerings is a program for girls aged 11 to 14 that includes speakers on fitness and nutrition and access to "cool" classes such as cardio-kickboxing—just like mom and dad sign up for.

Efforts by fitness centers, family organizations, and even schools to tug on family ties and roust today's kids from their couches and computers promise to spread in the future. But there's plenty you can do at home now to get kids into the swing of things. In fact, you've got to set the example and exercise, says Shannon Entin, a fitness instructor and publisher of Fitness Link, an online fitness-information service.

Helene and David Gugerty can hardly imagine what life might be like when their two girls are teenagers. But it promises to be active. During the Bayville 5K, they had to make sure Emma was securely strapped into the double jogging stroller with her little sister because the budding athlete wanted to walk the whole race on her own—a little dangerous with so many runners going by. "Can you believe it?" her mother asked. "She wants me to find a shorter fun run she can do with other children."

—*Tracey Minkin*

Fit Kids: A Game Plan

Help your kids develop into solid-citizen athletes with these tips.

Ages 2 to 5

- **Prescription:** Encourage basic skills that lay the foundation for athletics such as jumping, hopping, skipping, and running; also promote ball skills, including catching, rolling, bouncing, kicking, tossing, and batting.
- **Strategies:** Set up "toddlercize" sessions once a week, employing these basic movements in activities that allow kids and parents to play together.

Ages 6 to 8

- **Prescription:** Redouble efforts to get kids outside, away from TV and computers, to enjoy more complex skills such as biking, roller skating, ice skating, and swimming.
- **Strategies:** Kids at this age are already influenced by peer dynamics, so find ways to make exercise "cool." Include friends in the deal; offer an afternoon at the rink or a bike outing on a Saturday.

Ages 9 to 12

- **Prescription:** Encourage preteens to enjoy the rigors of team sports; if they're intimidated by the team experience, look around for individual activities that have a real fitness component such as hiking, biking, even strength training under close supervision. Kids this age aren't yet physically ready for serious training, but they need some aerobic conditioning.
- **Strategies:** Be supportive, even if your child picks a sport that isn't your personal favorite. Expand your network of family fitness activities—scout out a health club with kid-friendly programming. Or plan an active family vacation; several soft-adventure travel outfitters, including Backroads and Butterfield & Robinson, tailor their biking, hiking, and watersports trips to families.

Ages 13 and over

- **Prescription:** Take advantage of the competitive juices that kick in at this age to guide your teenager into sports. Also encourage kids in competitive athletics to explore other realms they're now old enough to try: rock climbing, kayaking, and mountain biking.
- **Strategies:** A nod to their "grownup" status may be just the motivator to get a teenager to lift weights or enter a race. At home, look for excuses to get moving together outside, even to walk the dog. You may actually get a chance to talk with your teenager. When you're out in the fresh air, you loosen up. You communicate better.

Chapter 51

Family Feat: Eating Healthy, Staying Fit

From cycling mountain peaks to kayaking raging rivers, the Keoghans are up for any challenge, including their greatest feat: keeping themselves, and 4-year-old Elle, fit and eating smart.

Preparations for Phil and Louise Keoghan's Saturday-morning bike ride with their 4-year-old daughter, Elle, actually begin the night before. That's when Mom and Dad sketch out a map of their route through gritty, brush-country mountains near their home, where the Santa Monica Mountains National Recreation Area keeps L.A.'s urban sprawl at bay. Not that Phil and Louise need help navigating the 27-mile trail; the map is to guide Elle, a sometimes-reluctant passenger, to treats hidden by "fairies" along the way.

Some might call this bribery, but you can't deny its creativity. The promise of a treat or a toy boosts Elle's enthusiasm for what she calls a "big adventure" and makes less noticeable any bumping and jarring as she rides through the hills on the back of Phil's bike. And with Elle's attention occupied, her parents can relish the fresh air, the exertion, and the views of the distant ocean and scrub-covered valleys.

This ingenuity promises to help the Keoghans succeed where many parents struggle: in encouraging healthy habits in their children and managing to stay active and fit despite the demands of parenthood and professional life. Both Phil and Louise pour lots of energy into their careers—he as an executive producer and host of The Travel Channel's *Adventure Crazy*, she as an independent television documentary producer.

"Having a child has not stopped us from doing the things we love; it has only changed the way that we do them," Phil says. When Elle was an infant, her parents passed her back and forth as they were working out. Phil lifted her above his head in impromptu shoulder presses, to Elle's delight; Louise did lunges with baby on board in a backpack-like child carrier. Now, Elle can handle more ambitious adventures, such as the Saturday bike rides.

THE PITTER-PUTTER OF LITTLE FEET

The Keoghans see these family activities as an investment in Elle's future. "When you see exercise while growing up, it becomes a part of your life," Phil says. Both he and Louise were encouraged to be active as children, to "get out there and just experience stuff," he says. Elle is already showing signs that she has inherited her parents' love for fitness. She mimics her mom as Louise does sit-ups on the living-room floor, and she putts alongside her dad when he uses the room as a makeshift green. Elle even has her own club—not a pint-sized plastic knock-off, but a bona fide metal putter that Phil had a pro shop cut down to size.

STIMULATE THE MIND; THE APPETITE WILL FOLLOW

No doubt the playful attitude Elle's parents have for exercise makes it infectious, but healthy foods can be a harder sell. "I am very conscious of what goes in Elle's precious body," Louise says. She and Phil stock their home with fresh vegetables, fruit, seafood, poultry, and whole grains—most of them organic. Elle couldn't care less, though: "Most of our food feuds are not so much about Elle choosing the wrong food, but her skipping meals altogether," Louise says.

But while she may not always be interested in eating, Elle, like most preschoolers, is hungry for knowledge. So Louise turns shopping for groceries into fact-finding missions, hoping that Elle's curiosity will influence her appetite. "When we shop, we talk about how healthy the food is and where it comes from," Louise says. This approach seems to be working: Elle has developed a taste for whole grain bread, several kinds of fruit, eggs from free-range chickens, even soy milk.

Sweets are reserved for special occasions. "This instills in her mind that treats aren't just for the taking whenever she wants them," Louise says.

OUT OF THE COMFORT ZONE

In his role as travel-show host, Phil has climbed an active volcano in Italy, swum in underwater Mexican caves, and slept in a Finnish ice castle. He and Louise have renewed their wedding vows submerged in scuba gear off the coast of the Bahamas, and biked around the Caribbean island of Antigua. If there's any doubt that Elle has the spirit of adventure in her DNA, take note: At age 4, she's already a United Airlines Premier Member, a designation for those who have flown more than 25,000 miles.

But if you ask the Keoghans to define adventure, you might not get the answer you'd expect. Adventure isn't restricted to feats of physical endurance or fortitude; it's about personal challenge. "The best adventures are of the mind as much as the body," Phil says. "Any time you leave your safety net, let go of the hand rails, and leave the comforts that you know behind, you're on an adventure," he says.

Louise and Phil agree that their biggest adventure is one they share with many people: being parents, and everything that entails—such as carrying your child up a mountain on the back of a bike. But there are treats at the top. And many other rewards besides.   —*Kerri Westenberg*

KEOGHANS' COUNSEL

Louise Keoghan and her husband, Phil, have found "every weird way imaginable" to stay fit and eat healthy despite the pressures of parenthood and careers—and to foster a healthy heritage for their daughter, Elle. Here are some of their secrets.

- To get Elle to eat more fruit, Louise gives her a bowl of cut-up produce to snack on while watching a video: "She wolfs her way through three or four varieties of fruit during one program."
- Invest in solid home-exercise equipment. Examples include a treadmill or resistance-training equipment. "When Elle came along, getting to the gym became even harder, so we adapted things," Phil says.
- Buy (or borrow) safe, sturdy child-carrying equipment such as backpack-style carriers and jogging strollers. "I always keep a lookout for equipment that will enable Elle to join us on hikes and bike rides," Phil says.
- The world is your gym. Playground equipment, hotel stairs, furniture, even phone books are workout tools for the Keoghans.

Part

8

Good Moves

If you want to do something over a lifetime,
it's important to find joy or a sense of
accomplishment within the activity itself.

Chapter 52

Strong, Lean, and Healthy

Being fit is about more than just losing weight.

Y ou're ready to put all of your motivation and confidence to work and get moving. While there's no doubt that exercise is good for the body, mind, and soul, you may feel overwhelmed trying to figure out what to do, how often, and how. Relax. Your body was made to move. It has all of the right parts, and will respond quite well when you learn a little bit about the three different types of exercise: (1) cardiovascular or aerobic, (2) muscle strength and endurance, and (3) flexibility.

Each type is vital to overall fitness, and while some individuals tend to focus on one or two areas, a training program that incorporates them all is the best way to achieve peak performance and satisfying results. And it's really rather easy to enjoy all fitness has to offer in a quick, efficient manner. On page 351, see the complete, easy-to-use *Cooking Light* fitness plan to help you become stronger, leaner, and healthier in just 12 weeks.

Cardiovascular Exercise

Cardiovascular fitness is how well your heart and lungs work together to deliver blood and oxygen to your muscles. In the muscles, your body uses oxygen to continually make the energy you need; this type of exercise is called cardiovascular or aerobic exercise. (You'll hear both terms, or even "cardio.") With training, the heart strengthens, can pump more blood with each beat, and your body becomes an awesome power producer. While working hard, you're producing power and you're burning calories. In addition to power production and calorie burning, the benefits of aerobic exercise are numerous. (See the sidebar on the next page.)

You can choose walking, running, cycling, swimming, step aerobics, jumping rope, stair-climbing, or any other exercise that increases your heart rate. There is no *best* aerobic exercise. Each one is effective for increasing aerobic fitness and the only thing that makes one better than another is that you do it. They all burn fat and calories. The rule is that the longer and harder you work, the more you burn. What's important is that you work at a level of intensity and for the duration that fits your fitness level and goals. (See "Get Moving" on page 337 for a list of cardiovascular/aerobic exercise activities.)

BENEFITS OF AEROBIC EXERCISE

- increased health and well-being
- improved appearance
- improved posture
- reduced blood pressure
- reduced cholesterol levels
- reduced blood sugar levels
- better relaxation
- better sleep
- reduced fatigue

Determining Intensity The most common way to measure the intensity of cardiovascular exercise is with a pulse or heart rate check. Two different heart rates are important—the resting pulse and the working pulse. Certain medications, especially those for high blood pressure, can affect your heart rate, so you might discuss an appropriate heart rate range with your doctor.

Resting Heart Rate It's best to take your resting heart rate first thing in the morning, before you get out of bed. However, if you take it another time, make sure you are calm, seated, and not exerting yourself. To find your pulse, place two fingers (not your thumb) on the side of your neck and count the number of beats you feel, starting with zero. Count for a full 60 seconds. Resting heart rates vary according to age and fitness level, with a normal range from 40 to 100. You should see a decrease in the number as you become fitter, indicating that your cardiovascular system is becoming stronger and more efficient.

Working Heart Rate The working heart rate should be taken during your workout, and helps you to determine if you are exercising too hard or not hard enough. To determine what your working heart rate should be, use the following formula.

220 – age = maximum heart rate x desired percentage of intensity

Here's an example. A 40-year-old wants to work at 70% of her maximum heart rate: 220 minus 40 = 180 (her maximum heart rate) x 70% = 126. This number is a target for her to maintain during her workout. Okay, so you're thinking, "How do I know what percentage to shoot for?"

That depends on your fitness level and goals. The following chart gives heart rate ranges for age and personal goals, whether those goals are for increased health, fitness, or athletic performance. To measure your working heart rate during exercise, start with zero and count the number of beats for 10 seconds and then multiply that number by 6.

WORKING HEART RATE RANGES

AGE	HEALTH		FITNESS	PERFORMANCE
	Active Living	Moderate Activity	Conditioning	High Intensity
	<50% max	50-70% max	70-85% max	>85% max
20	<100	100-140	140-170	>170
25	<98	98-137	137-166	>166
30	<95	95-133	133-162	>162
35	<93	93-130	130-157	>157
40	<90	90-126	126-153	>153
45	<88	88-123	123-149	>149
50	<85	85-119	119-145	>145
55	<83	83-116	116-140	>140
60	<80	80-112	112-136	>136
65	<78	78-109	109-132	>132
70	<75	75-105	105-128	>128

Personal Fitness Levels/Goals

Active Living—the least amount of intensity from which you will experience health benefits

Moderate Activity—greater promotion of general health and additional prevention of disease

Conditioning—all the health benefits associated with increased aerobic fitness and sports performance

High intensity—for those desiring a high level of athletic performance

max = maximum heart rate

If you don't want to worry about numbers, the simplest way to determine how hard you're working is the talk test. You should speed up if talking is too easy, slow down if talking is difficult and you are gasping for air, and you know you're just right if you can talk in short bursts and are breathing comfortably.

GET MOVING

For many people, the term "aerobics" is synonymous with "aerobics class." But aerobics is any activity that increases your heart rate. When it comes to exercise, the terms "cardiovascular" and "aerobic" are interchangeable, and there are plenty of activities that you can choose to increase your heart rate and burn calories. See the list below for a few examples.

- Group exercise classes such as Step, Spinning, Jazzercise*
- Cross-country skiing
- Cycling
- Elliptical trainers
- In-line skating
- Rowing
- Running
- Stair climbing
- Swimming
- Walking (15 minutes/mile)

*Most group classes include some strength and stretching exercise in addition to the cardio/aerobic portion.

DON'T SHIRK THAT WARMUP

As busy as most of us are, we barely have time to exercise at all, let alone waste five minutes on a warmup. But warming up isn't a waste, it's a must. Here's why.

- An easy walk or jog before the main part of your workout raises your body temperature gradually, making muscles more fluid so they contract more efficiently during exercise, and tendons and ligaments more flexible, reducing your chances of injury.
- By increasing blood flow, warming up prepares your heart for the higher physical demands of exercise. It also helps deliver fuel to your muscles.
- A warmup causes the body's cooling system—its sweat glands—to switch on. The more you sweat, the less likely you are to overheat during strenuous exercise.
- The slow transition from rest to workout helps protect muscles from excessive soreness.

Muscle Strength/Endurance

The number of people who weight train as part of their regular exercise routine has grown tremendously in the past decade. That's because they've discovered how great it is for their bodies and how great it makes them feel. Weight training (also called resistance training or strength training) keeps muscles functioning as they should. Over the years, some individuals lose up to 50 percent of the muscle mass they had as young adults. Weight training dramatically reduces that loss. It improves your posture and balance, your ability to carry out daily activities, and—what's very appealing to many—it helps you burn more calories all day long. The more muscles you have, the more calories it takes to keep them nourished.

Strength vs Endurance It's important to understand strength and endurance in order to decide what type of weight training best suits your goals. Muscle strength is simply how much total weight you can move, while muscle endurance is the number of times you can move the weight, or how many repetitions. Is one more important than the other? That depends. An Olympic power-lifter is not concerned with lifting that enormous amount of weight more than once. One lift gets the medal. He/she will train with very heavy weight and low repetitions. Body builders want to be strong, but they also must do a high volume of training to accomplish the muscle growth they seek, so they train for a combination of strength and endurance. People who want to experience the general health and fitness benefits of weight training should engage in a program that balances strength and endurance.

> Weight training improves posture, balance, ability to carry out daily activities, and helps you burn more calories all day long.

Here's a good rule of thumb:
- fewer than 8 repetitions with heavy weights: maximal strength and power training
- 8 to 12 repetitions with moderate weights: balance of strength and endurance training
- 12 or more repetitions with light to moderate weights: endurance training

Choices and Options You can do weight training in the weight room, with a selection of equipment, such as Nautilus or Cybex, and free weights (dumbbells and plates). Or you can train with tubes, rubber balls, and instructor-led classes using all types of equipment. Which one is for you?

WEIGHT-TRAINING BASICS

Before you get started on a weight-training program, here are a few basic terms you need to know.

Repetition or "rep": doing a single exercise one time. If you are lifting weights for general fitness, you should do 4-second reps, 2 seconds to lift the weight and 2 seconds to lower it.

Set: doing a specific exercise a number of times consecutively without stopping. For example, if you perform 8 triceps curls, then put the weights down, you've done one set of curls.

Routine: everything you do in one weight-lifting session. Your routine includes the type of equipment you use, the number of exercises, sets, and reps you do, and the order in which you do the exercises.

Circuit: the logical arrangement of the weight-training machines so that you can move from machine to machine working muscles in the correct order.

Sequence: the order in which you do the exercises. When choosing the sequence of your workout, think about your body being divided into three different zones: lower, middle (or core), and upper. It doesn't matter which zone you work first, but it's best to work the large muscles before the small ones. For example, if you are working your upper body, work the chest and back muscles first, then the shoulders, biceps and triceps, then the wrists.

Fitness trainers: trained professionals, sometimes certified through professional organizations, who help you plan your workout routine and guide your progress. Some of the reputable certifying organizations are the American College of Sports Medicine, the National Strength and Conditioning Association, and the American Council on Exercise.

That depends on your experience with weights, your current strength and balance, and your goals. A new exerciser will be most successful at first in a class where an instructor can teach correct form and alignment, or on equipment, such as Nautilus or others like it, that guides you to correct positioning. After experimenting with different types of strength training, you will probably decide that certain activities suit you best.

The muscle strength exercises for lower body, core, and upper body on the next several pages are examples of good exercises to work specific muscles. For other exercises that you can do, consult with an instructor at your local health club, attend group classes at a health club or community center, read fitness articles in *Cooking Light* and other reputable health magazines, or use exercise videotapes.

MAJOR MUSCLES

It's important to balance your workout by strengthening all of your major muscle groups. So let's review the major muscle groups. Have you ever been in an aerobic exercise class when the instructor urged the class to "work those quads!"—and you had no clue what she was talking about? Take a look at the diagram below that identifies the muscle groups in your body. You don't need to know the scientific names of the muscles in order to tone them, but it sure will help you figure out what's going on in aerobics class. Then turn to the muscle strength exercises beginning on the next page for specific moves to tone muscles in the lower, middle, and upper body.

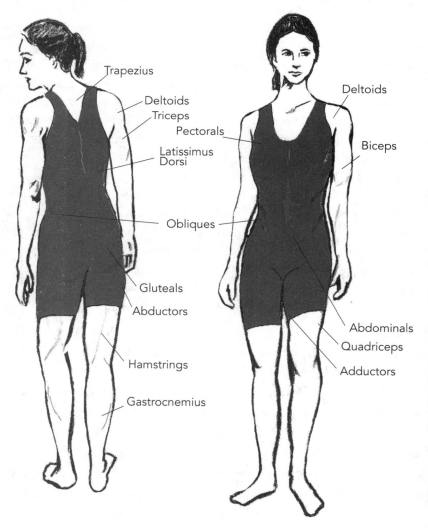

Trapezius
Deltoids
Triceps
Pectorals
Latissimus Dorsi
Deltoids
Biceps
Obliques
Gluteals
Abductors
Abdominals
Quadriceps
Adductors
Hamstrings
Gastrocnemius

LOWER BODY STRENGTH EXERCISES

The main muscles of the lower body are the quads, abductors and adductors (outer and inner thighs), hamstrings, and buttocks. Note that several of the moves will work more than one muscle group at a time. These are not the only exercises that tone these muscles, but they're good basic exercises for any fitness program.

Quads

▶ **Left Lunge with Lateral Raise:** Stand with left leg back, weights at sides. Bend knees, and raise arms to the side until they reach shoulder height, leading with elbows. Slowly lower arms back to sides as you return to start position. Repeat on opposite leg. Perform 8 repetitions on each leg.

Right Lunge with Biceps Curl: Stand with right leg back, holding weights at sides, palms turned forward. Bend knees, keeping torso straight and curling weights toward your shoulders. Lower arms as you rise to start position. Repeat on opposite leg. Perform 8 repetitions on each leg. (See photo on page 373.)

◀ **Squats with Overhead Press:** Stand with legs shoulder-width apart, weights level with shoulders. Bend knees as if you're going to sit back on a chair, keeping your back straight. (If you lower your eyes, you should be able to see your toes past your knees.) Straighten your legs and move up onto toes, bringing the weights above your head, palms turned in. Hold for 2 seconds. Slowly lower to start position. Perform 6 to 8 repetitions.

When you do squats with hand weights, as pictured, you can work the lower body and upper body at the same time. If you're a beginner, start with 2- or 3-pound weights, then increase as you get stronger.

Abductors

▶ **Side Kick:** Stand upright, shoulders back, holding onto a chair or wall with your left hand for balance, if necessary. Turn left toe out slightly. Lean to the left side with your torso, and lift right leg up, knee bent. Your leg should be almost parallel to the floor. Slowly straighten the right leg by pushing out with the heel of the foot, as if you're driving your heel into something next to you. Bend your right knee back, and straighten torso as you lower foot to start position. Perform 8 to 12 repetitions. Repeat on opposite leg.

◀ **Seated Leg Lifts** (for fronts of thighs):
A. Sit in front of platform, leaning back slightly with elbows resting on platform. Bend right leg into butterfly position, with side of leg resting on floor and bottom of foot against knee of left leg; left leg should be extended on floor. Lift left leg, with foot flexed.
B. Lower leg, and lift again, turning foot out to side toward floor. Keep foot flexed and inner thigh facing upward. Bring leg back to start position. Perform 8 to 12 repetitions. Repeat with opposite leg. Hint: Try to keep back as straight as possible, allowing as little weight as possible to rest on platform.

Hamstrings

▶ **Standing Hamstring Curl:** Holding onto a chair or wall for balance, bring your heel up toward your buttocks. Squeeze a 3-pound weighted ball or dumbbell behind the calf and hamstring (in the bend of the knee). Flexing the foot, pull your heel toward your buttocks to contract your hamstring. Perform 12 to 16 repetitions on each leg.

Buttocks

◀ **Donkey Kick:** Kneel on platform top, with knees and forearms resting on surface. Extend left leg up and off back of platform, keeping right knee on platform (place a towel under knee for comfort, if needed). Lift and lower extended leg slowly, allowing 4 counts in each direction. Perform 8 to 12 repetitions. Repeat on opposite side.

Hints: Tighten buttocks before you lift; don't allow foot to rest on floor between reps; keep knee of lifting leg soft; raise platform to highest level to achieve greatest range of motion.

▶ **Rear Raises:** With your right hand on a chair back or wall for balance, hold a 5-pound weight at the small of your back with your left hand. Draw your left leg behind and to the left of your right foot, left knee turned out (right knee should be soft). Bend forward from the hip 60 degrees or until your bottom tightens. Lift your left leg, knee turned out, leading with the little toe. Hold for 2 seconds; slowly release. Perform 8 to 12 repetitions. Repeat on opposite leg.

CORE/MIDDLE BODY STRENGTH EXERCISES
Abdominals

◁ **Five-Count Crunch:**

A. Lie on your back with your knees bent, feet flat on the floor and hip-width apart, abdominals pulled inward. Place your hands behind your head, fingertips touching but not laced together, thumbs behind your ears. Point your elbows outward, and tuck your chin in slightly. **B.** Curl your head, neck, and chest up and forward off the floor; pause. Extend your arms straight out toward your knees; pause. Lift a bit further; pause. Place your hands back behind your head; pause again, then lower to starting position. Perform 8 to 12 repetitions.

▷ **Abdominal Twister** (for upper and lower abdominals and obliques): Lie on your back with knees bent and lifted toward chest. Hold one 5- to 8-pound dumbbell with one hand on each end, palms facing each  other. Extend arms toward ceiling over chest. Slowly straighten left leg (knees should remain soft), and drop it toward the ground as you twist your upper torso to the left side, lowering the dumbbell toward the ground. Lift right side of your bottom off the ground and hold for 2 seconds. Return to start, and repeat. Perform 8 to 12 repetitions.

Bent-Leg V-Sit (also works hips, lower back, backs of shoulders, and torso):

A. Sit on ground, leaning back slightly and supporting body with hands. Your fingers should be spread, thumbs forward; elbows should be soft, abdominals tight. Bend knees, and pull toward the chest, contracting stomach muscles.

B. Point toes, and slowly lower one leg toward the ground, keeping knee bent. Tap toe, if possible, then bring knee back to chest. Repeat with opposite leg. Perform 4 to 6 repetitions.

UPPER BODY STRENGTH EXERCISES

The following moves help you tone your triceps, biceps, shoulders, and chest.

Biceps

▶ **Standing Curls:** Stand upright with one weight in each hand, arms at sides. Bend both arms at the elbow, slowly bringing weights toward the shoulders. Keep arms and elbows close to body; lower slowly. Perform 8 to 12 repetitions.

Triceps

▶ **Dips:** Sit on the edge of a chair. With elbows relaxed, firmly grip the edge and slide your bottom off the chair. Legs should be together, knees bent, toes pointing up. Slowly lower bottom, keeping back close to chair seat; then push up until arms are straight. Straighten the legs slightly to intensify the exercise. Perform 8 to 12 repetitions.

Shoulders

◄ **Arm Arc:**

A. Start with a 3- to 5-pound dumbbell in each hand. Bend forward from your hips with knees bent, shoulders back, and arms at your sides with palms facing inward. Slowly lift the weights up and straight out to sides, letting elbows lead, as you begin to stand erect.

B. Continue to straighten the spine until you're upright, bringing your arms up in an arc until they meet above your forehead, palms out, forming a complete circle. Lower arms to your sides, and repeat. Perform 8 to 12 repetitions.

Chest

▶ **Push-Ups:** This exercise works most of your upper-body muscles. Start out on your hands and knees, with your hands shoulder-width apart and flat on the floor at chest level and middle fingers pointing straight ahead. Inhale as you slowly lower your upper body away from the floor directly below you. Keep your elbows close to your waist and your eyes

on the floor directly below you. Exhale, and push your body away from the floor with your eyes focusing on the same spot so that your neck is aligned with your spine. Inhale as you slowly return to start position. Perform 12 repetitions.

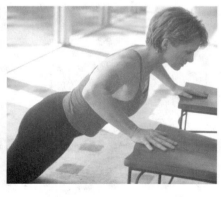

◄ **Alternate Push-Ups:** Position chairs about a torso-distance away. Chairs should be placed at an angle so that their front legs are shoulder-width apart and back legs are several inches farther apart. On your knees, lean forward and place palms on chair seats. Lower chest to chairs until elbows are at a 90-degree angle; press body upward until elbows are extended; lower until elbows are at a 90-degree angle again. Perform 8 to 12 repetitions.

Flexibility

Flexibility is the amount of movement around a joint, and is often referred to as Range of Motion (ROM). Insufficient ROM can limit our ability to perform activities of daily living (zip a dress, reach into a cabinet, tie our own shoes), and can throw us out of alignment and cause muscle imbalance and poor posture. Inflexible joints are more likely to be injured, especially when exercising.

Flexibility tends to decrease with age. The fluid around joints gets thicker, sometimes because of disease, but most often because of disuse. Women tend to be more flexible than men, but neither age nor gender is reason to suffer from tight joints. Flexibility can always be improved.

You should stretch every time you work out, especially the muscle groups that you've worked.

While flexibility tends to be the most ignored of the fitness components, its popularity has grown as yoga and stretching classes are more attended than ever. Avid exercisers find that good flexibility can increase their performance and their enjoyment.

Stretch It Out How often and how should you stretch? You should stretch every time you work out, especially the muscle groups you've worked. Stretch even more often if you can. For most of us, over-stretching is not a concern. Stretch all muscle groups, and target areas known to be inflexible. Most low back pain is a result of inflexibility and poor muscle strength. A good abdominal and low back training program and stretching of tight areas can alleviate low back pain. While there are different methods of stretching, the best and safest is static stretching. In a static stretch, you take the stretch to its limit (without pain) and hold it for 10-30 seconds. It's best to stretch muscles and joints when warm, so the cool down portion of a workout is the most effective time to stretch. Stretching while warming up should be very light and part of movement to warm up the muscles.

Our 12-Week Fitness Plan (page 351) includes stretching sessions at least three times a week. Use the stretching routine starting on the next page to improve posture, prevent muscle soreness, and increase range of motion. Or vary your stretching routine with any of the yoga exercises beginning on page 378.   —*Carol Kutik*

◀ Calf Stretch

A. Stand with both feet on the bottom step of a staircase or lower platform, hands on a nearby banister or wall for support. Rest your left foot on the back of your right heel, and lower the right heel toward the floor until you feel a stretch in your right calf. Then bend your right knee slightly to move the stretch into the back of your ankle. Hold for 18 seconds, release, and switch legs.

B. With both feet on level ground, lift your right leg slightly to the front. Flex the toe back toward the shin until you feel a stretch in the calf. Slightly bend your knee to deepen the stretch. Hold for 18 seconds, release, and switch legs. Repeat Step A.

▶ Hamstring Stretch

Lie on your back with one knee bent and one leg extended. Wrap a small towel around the ankle of the extended foot. Grasping the ends of the towel, bend your elbows and, keeping your leg straight and knee slightly bent, gently pull the extended leg toward your chest until you feel a comfortable stretch. Avoid locking

your knee. Keep the leg in that position as you release the ends of the towel. Hold for 15 to 18 seconds. Relax. Repeat a total of 3 times with each leg.

Lower-Back/Torso Stretch

A. Lie on your back, knees bent and pulled toward chest. Stretch right arm out to the side, perpendicular to your body. Use the left hand to pull your knees to the left side until you feel a stretch in your lower back. Keep your back and shoulders pressed into the ground. Hold for 18 seconds, release, and switch sides.

B. From the starting position, stretch both arms out to the sides so that your body forms a cross (not shown). Rotate knees to the left without using your hands, keeping your back and shoulders pressed into the ground. Hold for 18 seconds, release, and switch sides. Repeat Step A.

Quadriceps Stretch

Lie on your side with both legs extended. Sit up on your elbow as shown at left. Grasp the foot (not the toes) that's on top, and pull it toward your bottom while tilting your hips forward. Keep knees together. Hold the stretch for 15 to 18 seconds. Release. Repeat a total of 3 times with each leg.

Standing Hamstring/Shoulder Stretch

A. Stand facing a chair about 2 feet away, with your left foot on the chair seat. Fold right elbow behind the back. Lean slightly forward from the hip with a flat back until you feel a tug-of-war between your tailbone and the tops of your shoulders. Next, release your left hand, and reach forward, palm toward the ceiling. Hold for 18 seconds, release, and switch legs.

B. Stand upright in starting position with left foot on chair seat. Tighten the front of your left thigh, forcing the hamstring to lengthen. This is a very small movement; your left heel may lift slightly off the chair. Hold for 18 seconds, release and switch legs. Repeat Step A.

Chapter 53

12 Weeks to a Leaner You

Use this easy-to-follow plan to get started on a fitness program today.

If you want to lose weight, you've got to start moving—and now is the time. Begin this fitness plan today and stick with it for 12 weeks. You'll be on the road to weight loss and feel stronger and more energized than you do right now. It doesn't take much of your time to get started—a maximum of 20 minutes three times a week. As you improve your fitness level and become stronger (as you will), you'll want to increase your time and your intensity.

How to Use the Plan Find the week that corresponds to your current fitness level—active living, moderate activity, or conditioning—and start there. If you have not been exercising regularly, you'll probably want to start with Weeks 1-2. (Refer to the chart on page 336 for more information about fitness levels.) The plan has three components based on the three types of exercises that you learned about in Chapter 52: (1) cardiovascular/aerobic, (2) muscle strength and endurance, and (3) flexibility. Each week you will do a combination of these types of exercises; the plan gives you the number of minutes to spend on each type. It's up to you to decide what exercise combinations you do each day. Just make sure that by the end of the week you've done each kind of exercise for the suggested amount of time and the recommended number of sessions. Turn back to Chapter 52 to review all of the choices you have for cardiovascular/aerobic activities and for specific muscle strength exercises and stretching moves. There are other exercises that you can do; we've just given you some examples to get you started.

After about six weeks, you'll probably begin to feel more adventuresome and will want to try some of the options that you'll read about later in this section. —*Carol Kutik*

12-Week Fitness Plan

Let's get started! For best results, keep the following tips in mind when you start using this plan.

- Make the plan work for your schedule. On our sample schedule, the exercise sessions are spread out over 5 to 7 days, but you can do the same number of sessions all in 3 or 4 days and take a day or two off. Do what works for you.
- When you're doing strength exercises, never work the same muscles on consecutive days. Your muscles need at least 48 hours to rest and grow. You can do strength exercises on consecutive days if you work different muscles.
- Vary your cardio activities so you don't get bored.
- Always warm up. See "Don't Shirk That Warmup" on page 337.

WEEKS 1-2: ACTIVE LIVING TO MODERATE ACTIVITY

Exercise	Mon	Tues	Wed	Thurs	Fri	Sat	Sun
Cardiovascular/ aerobic activity such as walking*	10-20 minutes		10-20 minutes		10-20 minutes		
Muscle strength/ endurance		10 minutes		10 minutes			
Flexibility/ stretching		10 minutes		10 minutes	10 minutes		

* See page 337 for a list of suggested cardiovascular/aerobic activities.

WEEKS 3-4: MODERATE ACTIVITY

Exercise	Mon	Tues	Wed	Thurs	Fri	Sat	Sun
Cardiovascular/ aerobic activity such as walking	15-20 minutes		15-20 minutes		15-20 minutes		
Muscle strength/ endurance		15-20 minutes		15-20 minutes			
Flexibility/ stretching		10 minutes		10 minutes	10 minutes		

WEEKS 5-6: MODERATE ACTIVITY

Exercise	Mon	Tues	Wed	Thurs	Fri	Sat	Sun
Cardiovascular/ aerobic activity such as walking	20-25 minutes		20-25 minutes			20-25 minutes	
Muscle strength/ endurance		15-20 minutes		15-20 minutes	15-20 minutes		
Flexibility/ stretching		15 minutes		15 minutes	15 minutes		

WEEKS 7-8: CONDITIONING

Exercise	Mon	Tues	Wed	Thurs	Fri	Sat	Sun
Cardiovascular/ aerobic activity such as walking	20-30 minutes		20-30 minutes			20-30 minutes	
Muscle strength/ endurance		20-30 minutes		20-30 minutes	20-30 minutes		
Flexibility/ stretching		15 minutes		15 minutes	15 minutes		

WEEK 9: CONDITIONING

Exercise	Mon	Tues	Wed	Thurs	Fri	Sat	Sun
Cardiovascular/ aerobic activity such as walking	25-35 minutes		25-35 minutes			25-35 minutes	
Muscle strength/ endurance		30-40 minutes		30-40 minutes	30-40 minutes		
Flexibility/ stretching		15 minutes		15 minutes	15 minutes		15 minutes

WEEK 10: CONDITIONING

Exercise	Mon	Tues	Wed	Thurs	Fri	Sat	Sun
Cardiovascular/ aerobic activity such as walking	30-35 minutes		30-35 minutes			30-35 minutes	
Muscle strength/ endurance		30-40 minutes		30-40 minutes	30-40 minutes		
Flexibility/ stretching		15 minutes		15 minutes	15 minutes		15 minutes

WEEK 11: CONDITIONING

Exercise	Mon	Tues	Wed	Thurs	Fri	Sat	Sun
Cardiovascular/ aerobic activity such as walking	35+ minutes		35+ minutes		35+ minutes	35+ minutes	
Muscle strength/ endurance		40 minutes		40 minutes	40 minutes		
Flexibility/ stretching		20 minutes		20 minutes	20 minutes		20 minutes

WEEK 12: CONDITIONING

Exercise	Mon	Tues	Wed	Thurs	Fri	Sat	Sun
Cardiovascular/ aerobic activity such as walking	40+ minutes		40+ minutes		40+ minutes	40+ minutes	
Muscle strength/ endurance		40+ minutes		40+ minutes	40+ minutes		
Flexibility/ stretching		20 minutes		20 minutes	20 minutes		20 minutes

Chapter 54

Exercise Worksheet

Keeping track of your physical activity
will help you see in black and white how successful
you've been at keeping up with your fitness plan.

G et your daily planner out and schedule those workouts! While it's tempting to go all out at first, too much too soon may set you up for injury and burnout. Set short-term, realistic goals, things like, "I'm going to work out 3 days this week," rather than "I want to lose 5 pounds this week." The top reasons for dropping out of a new exercise program are unrealistic goals and injury. Remember, regular exercise and eating well are not a quick fix. They are part of a healthy, gratifying lifestyle.

Keeping a log of your workouts will help you progress wisely and see how successful you've been in keeping your goals. We all have days when nothing goes as planned, so don't beat yourself up if your plans have to change. Mental flexibility is as important as physical flexibility when it comes to exercise. If you have to skip a day or change an activity, it's okay. Long-term well-being will not suffer from small obstacles.

Mental flexibility is as important as physical flexibility when it comes to exercise.

This worksheet is designed to go along with the 12-Week Fitness Plan that begins on page 351. Make copies so that you'll have a page for each week. Here's how to use the worksheet.

- Record the number of the week (or the date) at the top of the page.
- Record your activities: for example, "aerobic—20 minutes on the treadmill."
- For strength exercises, make a check mark for the muscles worked. You can also record the weight used and the number of repetitions.
- In the notes section, include highlights, barriers, and positive thoughts like, "I really enjoyed my stretching today."

EXERCISE WORKSHEET   WEEK:

Exercise		Mon	Tues	Wed	Thurs	Fri	Sat	Sun
Cardiovascular/ aerobic activity such as walking								
Muscle strength/endurance								
Lower Body	Quads							
	Hamstrings							
	Abductors/ Adductors							
	Buttocks							
Middle	Abdominals							
Upper Body	Biceps							
	Triceps							
	Shoulders							
	Chest							
Flexibility/ stretching								

Notes:

Chapter 55

Lifestyle Exercise

Lifestyle exercise can be as good as a gym visit.
But how do you know how much is enough?

Did you know that "lifestyle exercise"—the everyday workouts you get from carrying groceries, walking up stairs, mowing the lawn, and the like—can do you as much good as a trip to the gym? If it is indeed a viable alternative to time-consuming workout routines, how does it actually work? What exactly do you need to do? And how much of it?

In assessing the ways people can do a minimum of 30 minutes of meaningful cardiovascular activity a day, the Cooper Institute for Aerobics Research conducted a study on lifestyle exercise and concluded that almost anything would work—if people did the activity regularly. "Regardless of what activity the people in the study did, we saw changes," says Bess Marcus, Ph.D., a professor at Brown University School of Medicine and a coauthor of the study. "What they did was up to them. Some chose to work two minutes at a time; some did all of their activity at once. We tried to encourage people to shape their behavior to what would work for them and to get away from all-or-nothing thinking. If you have 15 minutes, use them. Turn any time you have into an opportunity to be more active."

The strategy paid off. Although those who went to the gym initially showed higher fitness levels than the lifestylers, they evened out by the end of the two-year study period, and the lifestylers were actually better at maintaining their fitness over the long term.

MEASURE YOUR STEPS

The Cooper Institute researchers quickly realized that motivation had a lot to do with setting goals and monitoring progress. A wristwatch could help keep track of exercise time, and journals could record behavior changes, but for immediate and ongoing activity feedback, nothing said movement like digits on a pedometer. The little device could also emphasize one of the best ways of stockpiling those exercise minutes: brisk walking (at 3 to 4 mph). (See Keeping Pace, page 359.) The Institute calculated that 7,000 steps a day (minimum) and up to 10,000 (optimum) would easily meet the goal of 30 minutes of moderately intense physical activity most days of the week. (One important note: The Institute of Medicine's Food and Nutrition Board now recommends 60 minutes of exercise daily.)

ESTIMATING DAILY ACTIVITY

We couldn't decide if lifestyle exercising was easy or difficult. Were we already fit by those standards, or far from it? So some of the *Cooking Light* staff volunteered to go about their normal business, duly pedometered, and report the results. And, prior to the experiment, the participants were asked to estimate how active they were.

We discovered we basically didn't have a clue what paces—literally—our bodies went through, badly underestimating our movements. Several expected their totals to be about 3,000 steps, but the averages in fact ranged from 3,500 to 8,000. Just a little extra effort and planning, and bingo, most of us could be lifestyle-healthy without a single step into the gym or on the track.

On the other hand, hitting the optimum 10,000 mark (about 4.7 miles) proved a challenge. One volunteer recorded between 4,800 and 5,700 steps with no extra effort, but to reach 10,000, he had to spend 2½ hours gardening—pushing a wheelbarrow from one end of the yard to another and trudging back and forth to the compost pile and garage. One of the editors confessed that in a moment of desperation, she considered folding laundry at one end of her house and putting it away at the other, one piece at a time. "You have to be as inefficient as possible," she joked. This editor is a runner, and at the end of the experiment, she said that she'd rather get her total on the running trail than around the house.

> The key is to think about exercise not as a separate item on your schedule, but as part of your daily routine. Take a hard look at your day with this new mind-set and ask, "Where are there opportunities to be less sedentary?"

But others who took the test strongly preferred the lifestyle option. "Wearing the pedometer, even though it's a bit geeky, helps me focus on walking more," one editor said. "It will take a while to work up to 10,000 steps, but I intend to do it."

Former *Cooking Light* editor Doug Crichton, who logged nearly 8,000 steps on days when he went on his usual evening walk with his wife, Ginger, agreed: "It was great to have a goal to shoot for. It kept me motivated more than I thought it would." By adding a 15-minute walk at lunchtime, he figured he could reach 10,000 steps—on weekdays, that is. Then one Saturday, the father of four logged 13,078 steps. "I had no idea I was walking that much," he says. "I never felt strained, pushed, or uncomfortable. If it's that easy to hit 13,000 on a Saturday, surely I can work a little harder to reach 10,000 steps on weekdays."

The key is to think about exercise not as a separate item on your schedule, but as part of your daily routine. Take a hard look at your day with this new mind-set and ask, "Where are there opportunities to be less sedentary?" Try keeping an activity log that breaks your entire waking day into 15-minute blocks and searching each block for chances to add to your exercise tally. Get off the subway one stop early and walk the rest of the way, or on your lunch hour, instead of standing around the cafeteria, go for a 10-minute walk. When done in increments of 10 minutes or more for a total of at least 30 minutes a day, these kinds of activities provide solid health benefits.

In addition, the health benefits gained

GETTING FIT THE NO-SWEAT WAY

Fifteen ways to make your days more active.

1. Take the stairs, up and down, whenever possible.
2. Go for a five-minute "non smoking" walk around the block when coworkers take a cigarette break.
3. Walk every supermarket aisle, whether or not you need to.
4. Get up from your desk and take a three-minute walk every hour.
5. Park at the end of the mall that's farthest away from your shopping destination.
6. Walk the perimeter of the field while your kids play soccer.
7. Have "walking meetings" at work.
8. Deliver things to coworkers in person instead of using inter-office mail or e-mail.
9. Use a cordless phone and walk while you talk.
10. Exercise—walk, play a sport, visit a park—on a date.
11. Play music and dance around the house.
12. Cut your own grass and consider using a push mower.
13. Hang your laundry outside.
14. Vacuum your house more often.
15. Spend an evening out dancing instead of at the movies.

by a sedentary person who begins exercising are much greater than those gained by moving from lifestyle activity to more vigorous exercise. "Simply going from below-average to average fitness dramatically reduces the risk of disease," says Arthur Leon, M.D., a cardiologist and physiologist and a professor at the University of Minnesota. "It's well worth it."

You don't have to be an athlete or a fanatic, or have any special equipment, or even need a special space or time of day to get enough exercise to stay healthy.

You just have to get moving. —*Karen Baar*

KEEPING PACE

Pedometers have been around for years, but only fairly recently have they become popular with the average person. Not only did they used to be dorky, but clunky, too; a decade ago, the typical unit was heavy, ugly, and fat as a deck of cards.

Time has been kind. The brand we used, FreeStyle, is matchbox-size and feather-light. The new breed is also smarter than the old: Basic models tell you how many steps you're taking, but sophisticated versions also keep track of your weight, calories burned, and time spent in motion.

Razzle-dazzle or plain, pedometers work on a fairly simple principle: Worn on the waistband over the hip, each unit houses a weight attached to a spring that moves up and down as you walk. A counter keeps track of how many times the weight moves and records each movement as a step.

Why use one? Literally, to keep you moving. "A pedometer is a helpful piece of motivation," says Bess Marcus, Ph.D., Brown University. "You just hook it on and do your thing."

Pedometers range in cost from about $12 to $50 and can be found in most sporting-goods stores.

Chapter 56

Find the Fun
in Fitness

It's all about attitude.

Michela Larsen has stuck with her exercise plan (two strength-training sessions, a yoga class, and three to five walks a week) for almost two years now. She's tenacious, despite a hectic life that includes raising two sons and running two busy Boston-area restaurants with her partners. But Larsen's fitness streak only hints at her perseverance—she has tinkered for nine years to find the right routine.

Being consistent is no easy feat, but the key, say many experts, has as much—or more—to do with your mind as your body. And the name of the game is willpower. "Whether you're an NBA player or a casual runner, it's all about attitude," says Greg Shelley, Ph.D., a sports psychologist and professor at Ithaca College in Ithaca, New York. The can-do spirit that propels you out of bed and to the gym or your walking route, day in and day out, isn't something that you either have or you don't, like blue eyes or flat feet. It can be built, just like your sculpted biceps.

"People think of willpower as a trait, but it's really a willingness to engage in a problem-solving process," explains Andrea Dunn, Ph.D., of the Cooper Institute for Aerobics Research in Dallas. Larsen's case proves the point. After sporadic attempts and a restaurant opening that brought her fitness regimen to a complete halt, she kept experimenting—both in and out of the gym, with a trainer, with friends, with different disciplines and intensities—until things clicked.

FEELIN' GOOD

Along the way, Larsen developed another psychological ingredient critical to maintaining a fitness streak: a sense of self-worth. Sports psychologists report that people with high self-esteem, whether they're U.S. soccer champs or dedicated walkers, stick with fitness not to look good for a high-school reunion, but because exercising makes them feel good. And that good feeling in turn flows into other important aspects of their lives, such as work and family.

VISUALIZE THE BIG PICTURE

Successful exercisers also perceive the big picture. "Great athletes focus on clear visions. Every day, they take a little step closer to their goals," says psychologist Terry Orlick, Ph.D. "The same is true for someone who wants a balanced life that includes being active."

If you don't see yourself as a loyal exerciser now, don't give up; your vision may come later, suggests new Cooper Institute research. It seems true with smoking, for example, that you should see yourself changed—as a nonsmoker—first. But research shows that with exercise, the more you do something, the more it becomes part of your self-concept. That may be because exercise takes constant planning. Once smokers have quit for a year, many say they stop thinking about having a cigarette—it just becomes a nonissue. But staying active is always an issue, and you have to keep it in the forefront of your mind. Even the experts admit it's a challenge. "We're all creatures of habit," Shelley says. To change those habits and find the exerciser within, start with these tips on attitude adjustment.

> Research shows that with exercise, the more you do something, the more it becomes a part of your self-concept.

Make a mental commitment. It doesn't take a lot for the hustle of everyday life to distract you from your good intentions. So before you slide out of bed each day, think about two or three things that you'll do that day to relate to your exercise goals. "It could be meeting a friend for a walk or recalling a good feeling from completing an exercise session," Orlick says. "It doesn't have to be perfectly clear, just a flash or a feeling to direct what you do that day."

Control the controllables. Just as a basketball player at the free-throw line learns to block out a chanting crowd, you must also develop the power to overcome obstacles. Shelley calls this "controlling the controllables." For instance, you can't stop snow and ice, but you can join a gym in the winter months. That's helped Texas native Rose Ann Miller run five to seven miles every other day through eleven New England winters.

Stay focused on your own progress. You just did two pull-ups. Are you elated because you only did one last week, or discouraged because the woman next to you just cranked out five? Staying focused on your own progress reinforces positive feelings that are keys to your success.

Choose activities because you like them. "We have a conventional one-size-fits-all idea of exercise, and that's a mistake," Dunn says. Choose activities, places, and situations because you like them, not because you think you should. Larsen, for instance, found that she could feed a spiritual craving by exercising outdoors. "If I couldn't feel the wind or smell the flowers, it would be harder for me to exercise," she says.

Tell your spouse about your amazing hike. Or bring him along. Both exercising together and talking about it will enhance your enjoyment and reinforce your commitment, Dunn says.

Write it down. Take five minutes each evening to record the best moments of your day—the things that made you feel best—in a notebook. It's a small but powerful gesture, as a study of 600 students at the University of Ottawa found. "Within eight weeks, they were dwelling less on the negative, and more than 90% reported a significant change in their perspective for the better," Orlick says. "You'll find yourself writing down things you saw or how you felt during or after exercising, and that motivates you to continue."

"If you want to do something over a lifetime, you have to find joy or a sense of accomplishment within the activity itself," Orlick explains. "All high-level performers have a passion for what they're doing, though parts of it may not be joyful." Pinpoint those feel-good moments—zooming down a big hill, paddling in perfect rhythm, easing into your favorite yoga position. Soak them up. Recall them later.

Truly, it all comes down to that feel-good vibe. Miller wouldn't trade the well-oiled, clear-headed sensation that stays with her after a run for the world. And Larsen? "At age 50, I feel great," she says. "Trying new things keeps me interested in the process, and that helps me grow." If that's not reason to keep a good thing going, what is?

—Tracy Teare

Chapter 57

Make Exercise Your Passion

Get into the exercise groove in five easy steps.

What separates die-hard exercisers from the rest of us? Why is it that some people can't wait to go to the gym, while others want only to grab a bowl of ice cream, put their feet up, and catch yet another Seinfeld rerun?

"There is a certain type of individual who thrives on exercise," says Susan Bartlett, Ph.D., a clinical psychologist and assistant professor of medicine at Johns Hopkins Medical Institutions in Baltimore. "But it's not common, encompassing only about 10 percent of the population. These are the people who really love to exercise. They tend to be structured, focused, goal-oriented, and good at follow-through."

So what can the rest of us unstructured, unfocused people do to feel, if not passionate about exercise, at least more enthusiastic? We put this question to the experts—and to the hundreds of fitness fans among our readers at CookingLight.com. Here are their fail-safe ways to light your exercise fire.

Mix it up. If there's one generalization we can make about our respondents, it's that they vary their routines to stave off boredom. "I love exercise so much because I change it constantly," reader Renee told us. "Being inspired by the experience and success of a new routine, getting educated, and being involved in the cutting edge of fitness makes me passionate! Trying the new class, signing up for the latest challenge at the gym—you name it, I want to taste it."

"Variety is important for most of us to help us avoid boredom and injury," Bartlett adds. "For people who don't get that exercise 'high,' having options can make a huge difference."

Find a buddy. Working out with a friend can make time pass more quickly. Plus, many of our dedicated exercisers actually view their workouts as social time, which makes them more eager to exercise. According to one fitness buff, "Exercise is fun—and not a chore—for me since I have two walking buddies, one for the weekend and one at work. It's great to have two wonderful confidantes."

Another respondent, Stephanie, enjoys catching up with her buddies at the gym: "It's so nice to walk into the club and be able to say hi to all my friends. For me, working out is almost like my social hour. If you go to the club enough, people will start to look familiar, and all of the regulars will soon become your good friends."

Do what you love. A big bonus of trying all that's available inside and outside the gym is the likelihood that you'll eventually hit on a workout that you just can't get enough of. It may seem obvious, but it's virtually impossible to stick with an activity that you dislike. Margie, one Web-site respondent, advises, "Do whichever sport or exercise you love; don't force yourself to run if you dread it."

Carl Foster, Ph.D., a professor of exercise and sport science at the University of Wisconsin-La Crosse, agrees. "Try different forms of exercise until you find something you like well enough that you would do it even if it weren't for your health," he says. Keep in mind that exercise doesn't have to be in a gym or require shorts and a T-shirt. Ballroom dancing, martial arts, swimming, even playing Frisbee with your kids are all workouts if done energetically.

Set realistic goals. Do you start an exercise program imagining a marathon, but never get past your first sprint? "It's fun and necessary to have goals for achievement, but the key is to have very realistic ones," notes Web-site respondent Sherri. "I started running two years ago, after my son was born. Each year I had a goal: first a 5K run, then last year a 10K, this year, half-marathons."

Shelley, another respondent, adds, "Remember that learning to exercise regularly is a process."

Examine your goals regularly, too. For example, if you want to exercise a given number of times during the week, figure out what's standing in your way if you're coming up short, Foster says. Were your fitness goals realistic? Did you make excuses for failing to live up to them? What are those excuses telling you? Regularly reviewing your goals and keeping records of your progress helps keep you on track.

Think time and place. You've no doubt heard the expression "timing is everything." To make workouts more enjoyable, it's important to pick a time that works for you. "I run in the morning because it fits into my schedule and because I want to put it first literally and figuratively," respondent Sarah says. "I lay out my running clothes the night before, then just get up and get right into them."

Where you choose to work out is also important. If going to the gym intimidates you, buy or rent workout videos that you can use at home. Can't stand wearing a bathing suit in front of other people? Don't force yourself into a public pool; instead, look for a workout that doesn't require you to wear revealing clothes (for example, self-defense disciplines such as karate, judo, or tae kwon do).

"Understand what works best for you and don't try to fit into someone else's mold," Bartlett says. "We all need to redefine what exercise is. Remember—you don't have to be in Lycra for your exercise to count." —*Linda Rao*

Chapter 58

The Easiest Exercise

Walking is one of the cheapest, easiest ways to
get in shape. Why not make it social, too?

What fitness activity could be easier than walking? It doesn't require extensive training or complicated equipment. You don't need a health club to
do it in. And, with the exception of a decent pair of shoes, it doesn't cost a thing.
Team up with other people, and the list of reasons to walk for exercise grows.
Joining a walking club can transform a solitary pursuit into a social occasion,
providing an opportunity not only to get some exercise but also to fulfill—and
exceed—your own expectations.

First Steps

When you commit to joining a walking club, your fellow members are counting on
you to show up, just as you're expecting them to be there for you. That mutual
accountability is an essential component of consistent participation, says Gwen
Hyatt, a spokesperson for the American Council on Exercise. "Just keeping a
commitment to a walking club is a success for some people," she says. "Maybe they
can't commit to exercise on their own."

That was Susie Bump's problem. A college student the last time she worked
out regularly, Bump had gained weight over the years and lost her resolve to start
exercising again. It wasn't until she relocated to Castro Valley, California, four
years ago that she decided to give walking a try.

Her new clubmates invited her to join them for walks along area nature trails.
"It wasn't easy," Bump says, recalling those first outings. "I was short of breath,
especially on the slight grades. But I liked the vegetation and wildlife." Gradually,
those occasional walks got easier—and she began to notice positive results. "I felt
stronger and more energetic, and I slept better," she says.

Amy Silberman, of Baltimore, also enjoys the support of her fellow walkers.

Two and a half years ago, she joined a walking and running club, hoping to make new friends, get more exercise, and lose weight. Members bond during their outings and over healthy meals, occasionally alternating with volunteer work; their efforts include cooking and delivering meals to homebound people and doing yard work at an inner-city school.

Achieving her fitness goals was more of a challenge, but Silberman credits her fellow club members with keeping her on track through her early walks and, later, training runs. "Being able to accomplish the goal every week and having people cheer me on kept me going," she says. "I never could have done it by myself."

SHARING THE WALKER'S HIGH

Camaraderie is an excellent motivator, according to John Foreyt, Ph.D., professor of medicine at Baylor College of Medicine in Houston. "Social support is one of the key predictors for long-term success in any fitness program."

Indeed, walking clubs can bolster your self-confidence by providing a forum for social connection. They provide a gathering place to share information and discuss things, such as family or financial problems. Lynda O'Connor eagerly anticipates weekly walks with friends through her Lake Forest, Illinois, neighborhood. The seven-member group walks for one hour and 15 minutes every Monday morning. "It really feels good to fulfill a commitment, do something healthy, and spend some time with friends," she says. "We just walk, talk, and listen. It's like a support group."

Sometimes, the club may even be a forum for some friendly rivalry, with one walker inspiring another. "Walkers use competition to make each other better," Seabourne says. Rachel Cohen, a recreational runner who walked and ran with Silberman, says her friend often pushed her along during the more grueling training they did for a marathon. "I'd be dying, and she'd say, 'Let's just go to the fire hydrant,' and we'd keep going," Cohen remembers.

A STEPPING STONE

The biggest benefit of walking clubs may be that they inspire participants to reach for greater fitness goals. Encouraged by her previous accomplishments, Bump joined San Jose Fit, a local running club. When she ran her first marathon, the members of her walking club showed up to support her. "Just knowing you're not in there by yourself is enough to keep you going," she says. "It helps knowing that somebody is waiting for you at the finish line."

Bump went on to run a marathon at Walt Disney World in Florida and another in Big Sur, California, three months later. She also joined the Leukemia and Lymphoma Society's Team in Training program and completed two 100-mile cycling events last fall. "I never expected to run marathons and complete major bike rides," she says. "The walking club showed me I could do anything I set my mind to."

—*Winifred Yu*

LOOK FOR A CLUB

You can find walking clubs through the local YMCA, health clubs, or your job. Or surf the Web for resources like the American Volkssport Association (800-830-9255 or www.ava.org), which helps organize noncompetitive community clubs. If you like to walk indoors, find out whether a mall near you is part of the WalkSport program (800-757-9255 or www.walksport.com). Prefer to do it outside? Team up with fellow hikers through the American Hiking Society (www.americanhiking.org or 301-565-6704).

...OR START YOUR OWN

1. Recruit. Post a flier in your local library, call your friends, or round up coworkers.
2. Arrange a meeting time—and stick to it. Determine whether you'll meet daily, weekly, or monthly; select a time and a place that's convenient for everyone.
3. Set goals. Every walker should have personal goals such as losing weight, improving endurance, or increasing speed. The group should also strive toward a common goal, such as preparing for a local race or walkathon.
4. Keep things interesting. Instead of walking the same route every week, try heading to a nearby park or looping through a different neighborhood. Vary the distance, or look for a route with hills if you're used to walking on flat surfaces.
5. Take responsibility for your club. That means acknowledging and encouraging regular members, contacting those who miss a walk, going out of your way to make new people feel welcome, and spreading the word about the club. It also means missing as few events as possible.

Chapter 59

Take the Plunge:
Try a New Sport

Four things that can help any new-sport novice
get over the fear of trying.

As adults, we often feel self-conscious about trying a new activity, especially a new sport. We feel that we're too old, too awkward, too late. But there are four important reasons why it's always worth trying a new sport, even if there's a chance of exposing yourself to expensive public humiliation.

1. No one cares how you look.

There are few arenas in life where people will praise you for being initially inept, but sports is one of them. That was one of the most pleasant discoveries Nada Milakovic, a Chicago speechwriter, made when she signed up for swimming lessons at a local pool at the age of 28. "I had gotten by for years doing a sort of panicked dog paddle," Milakovic explains. "The first time I was able to swim across the pool face down, without flailing my arms, my class actually applauded."

Like other neophytes, Milakovic was intimidated by what she perceived as the condescension of the more masterly lap swimmers in the fast lanes. "But as I got more confident, I realized that people who are enjoying their sport aren't paying any attention at all to how silly you look," she says.

2. It might be just what you need.

Kerry Burak, a human services administrator from the Minneapolis-St. Paul area, never got much pleasure out of the sports she participated in as a kid. "I was on the swim team and played softball just because that's what you did at that age," she says. She was skeptical when a coworker persuaded her to try rock climbing last year, but when she cinched into her harness for the first time, she was hooked.

"Rock climbing was just what I was looking for—a sport that was challenging for both my body and my mind," Burak says. "At first my goal was simply to try it. Now I want to get really good at it."

3. SPORTS CHANGE—AND SO CAN YOU.

A bad experience with a sport years ago doesn't mean you're doomed for failure if you give it another go. For one thing, sports are evolving all the time—inline skates have far better brakes than they did just a few years back; shorter, wider skis have added more speed to cross-country skiing; and golf courses now actively court women players. For another, you're evolving, too. If you found yourself falling asleep in a yoga class when you were nineteen, today you might find the rhythmic breathing and slow, contemplative pace calming and energizing.

4. EVERYONE ELSE IS LEARNING, TOO—EVEN THE PROS.

The challenges of a new sport may make you wonder if it's worth the time and effort. But bear in mind that the people who get the most out of their pursuits are those who learn from their mistakes and keep going. The pros may be great—but like you, they're still students of the game.   —*Laura Billings*

A BASIC DESIRE: FUN EXERCISE

Many people have a fundamental desire to get moving, but don't follow up on the urge. Psychologists at Ohio State University (OSU) surveyed 2,500 people to find out what they really want to do in life. Among the 15 basic desires—believe it or not—was exercise. So why do we often find it a struggle just to get to the gym?

Psychologist and OSU researcher Steven Reiss, Ph.D., believes that people want to exercise for the fun of it—not for their health or even their looks. So it follows that most people aren't going to work up a sweat doing something they don't enjoy.

If your motivation wanes, first re-evaluate the fun factor of your fitness activity of choice; explore other options until you find something that keeps your interest. If that doesn't work, try looking at exercise as a step toward a goal that does offer you some enjoyment—for instance, if you stay in shape, you'll be better able to keep up with your kids in a game of touch football. "Become clear on why you want to exercise," Reiss says, "and focus on that goal. It will make exercise much easier."

Chapter 60

No Excuses Exercises for Couch Potatoes

Should you watch TV tonight or exercise?
This real-life workout plan lets you do both.

Let's face it, over the course of a typical week, chances are someone on your favorite TV show will persuade you to skip the gym or that evening walk and sit down on the couch. But here's a way to enjoy your favorite show without sacrificing fitness: Exercise while you watch TV.

OK, there's nothing new there. Thousands do it regularly. The problem is that most home exercisers don't have a plan. If you accept that sometimes you're going to spend an evening in front of the tube, why not complete a workout routine that fits the format of most hour-long TV shows?

In fact, this moderate-intensity circuit program, which alternates cardio and strength segments, works perfectly with any show that has commercial breaks. You'll perform strength moves during the commercials (so that you can focus on counting and form) and cardiovascular routines while the show's on. And while the following workout doesn't equal a full-blown step class, you will burn about 325 calories if you maintain a moderate intensity level for the entire hour.

Remember, though, that this shouldn't be your only exercise regimen. For one thing, you probably won't work as intensely as you really should during a TV workout, because at least part of you will be more concerned with what's happening on the program than with breaking a sweat. Also, your workout repertoire should include lots of different activities. But if you're going to watch TV anyway, you might as well be an active spectator.

So get into your sweats and sneaks, turn on your favorite show, and get ready to work while you watch.

TV Workout

You'll need two 8- to 12-pound dumbbells, a chair or sofa, and a mat if you're not on carpet. You'll also need to clear a little space in front of the TV so you can move 3 to 5 feet in each direction.

STRENGTH EXERCISES
In a slow, controlled fashion, perform two strength moves per commercial break. Do 8 to 12 repetitions of each move on each side, but feel free to continue any of the exercises for approximately 2 minutes, resting when necessary, if you want to work during the entire commercial break. Perform exercises in the order shown for best results. Complete each strength segment before moving on to a cardio routine, even if the commercials have ended.

Push-Ups: Begin in "down" phase, with your knees or toes on floor, arms shoulder-width apart. Push up, then slowly lower.

Squats: Stand with feet shoulder-width apart, toes forward. Hold weights on shoulders. Slowly, lower down and back, as if sitting in a chair. Pause before slowly rising, tightening the buttocks as you lift.

Lunges with Biceps Curls: Stand with right leg back, left knee bent and behind the toes. Hold weights at sides, palms turned forward. Lower your right knee as you curl weights toward shoulder. Repeat on opposite side.

Bent-Over Rows: Bend at waist, placing right hand on arm of sofa or chair. Step back into lunge position with left leg. Hold weight in left hand, arm extended toward floor. Pull the weight up to the hip, leading with the elbow. Repeat on opposite side.

Rear Leg Extensions: Place hands on back of chair. Bend the left knee slightly. Slowly raise your right leg back and slightly out to the side. Pause, then lower. Perform 4 lifts with the right leg, then 4 with the left. Repeat for 2 minutes.

Shoulder Arcs: Hold weights at sides with palms turned out. Tap weights together behind your back. Bring the weights forward to chest or forehead level, rotating palms toward your face. Tap weights together, then return to back, rotating palms. Repeat for 2 minutes.

Side Leg Lifts: Lie on left side with bottom leg slightly bent, right leg extended. Support upper body on elbow, making sure not to sink into the shoulder. Hold weight on your right thigh. Taking 4 counts, lift leg as high as possible without rolling back onto your hip. Pause, then slowly lower. Repeat for 1 minute, then repeat on opposite side.

◄ **Triceps Dips with Inner-Thigh Lifts:** Sit on sofa or sturdy chair with hands on edge of seat, feet on floor. Lift buttocks off seat, supporting weight with arms. Extend right leg, turning foot to the right. Slowly bend elbows and lower, keeping back close to chair. Lower the right leg as you dip. As you push back up, lift right leg. Repeat for 1 minute, then repeat on opposite side.

Abdominals: Lie on floor with feet on chair seat or sofa. Place your fingertips on sides of head, elbows out. While holding abs in, lift your shoulders off floor without pulling on neck. Once up, follow this sequence: Move left elbow toward left hip, return to center, move right elbow toward right hip, return to center, lower. Repeat, starting with a lift and leading with your right elbow to the right hip. Continue alternating for 1½ to 2 minutes.

CARDIO EXERCISES

The cardio segments use simple, repetitive moves so you can enjoy your show. You can perform one routine for the full segment, or you can alternate routines.

▶ **Lateral Shuffles:** Keeping feet wide apart, shuffle sideways to the right then back to the left, following this pattern: shuffle, shuffle, shuffle, hold with a clap. To increase intensity, add a hamstring curl on the hold, kicking the inside leg toward the buttocks. To increase intensity further, jump on the hold.

Jacks: Do a four-count jack by stepping to the right with the right foot and raising arms to sides (to shoulder level). Step back in and repeat with left leg. To increase intensity, perform a traditional jumping jack at half tempo:

Jump out, hold, jump in, hold (raise arms to shoulder level on outward jumps). To increase intensity further, do full-tempo jacks, raising arms above and slightly in front of your head.

Diagonal Boxing Lunges: Step to your right with the right foot, bend left knee, and punch across the chest (to the left) with the right arm. Step back together, then repeat on the opposite side. To increase intensity, add a slight jump when pushing off with the lunged leg. To increase intensity further, lift the knee of the bent leg before lunging to the side.

Jump-Rope Jogs: Setting your own pace, jog in place, lifting the knees as you turn an imaginary jump rope. To increase the intensity, jump faster or with your feet together as you turn the "rope." To increase intensity further, hop on one foot for two counts, and then repeat on opposite side.

Other Cardio Options: Stepping, marching, running in place, performing routines from aerobics classes or videos, or using a treadmill or any other piece of cardio equipment.   —*Gin Miller*

Chapter 61

Try the Latest
Exercise Trends

Here are some of the latest fashions in the exercise world,
and why they'll help you lose weight.

We've come a long way from being lined up in gym class performing jumping
jacks and sit-ups to classes with soothing music and stretching, playing
with oversized balls, and even water workouts. Before you dismiss these activities
as mere diversions from a serious workout, read on.

Yoga Moves
Build Core Power

Yoga—once the domain of swamis, seekers, and far-out philosophers—has become a
mainstream fitness activity in the past few years. And why not? It increases circulation
and lung capacity, builds strength and endurance, and improves flexibility and balance
while at the same time calming the mind and boosting energy. Because it strengthens
core muscles—including the transverse abdominal muscles and the spinal muscles—
yoga, when done properly and regularly, can help you develop a stronger lower back,
flatter torso, and straighter posture. And that can make you look years younger. Since
core strength and flexibility protect against injuries, yoga also helps prevent the kinds of
aches, pains, pulls, and strains you often encounter while going about everyday tasks.

Yoga encourages steady breathing (see "Focus on Your Breath" on page 388)
and controlled motion, so a yoga workout can serve as a great way to take the edge
off a hard day. But don't be fooled by the "easy-does-it" format; yoga is not all gentle stretches and quiet meditation. Today's yoga classes cater to Western students,
offering lots of intense movement followed by guided relaxation.

Most classes include a series of postures (called asanas) that require you to breathe smoothly as you stretch, lift, and support your body weight all at once. The movements are tough. You might, for example, balance on one foot while holding the other one aloft, or lift your legs and arms off the ground using only the strength of your back muscles.

The routines beginning on page 378 (Swan, Stingray, Python, Giraffe, and Gazelle) draw on many of the principles and movements used in both yoga and Pilates—an exercise system that combines yogalike moves with strength work. (See "Pilates" on page 388.) These workouts offer many of the same benefits as yoga and Pilates, but the moves are modified so that you can perform them effectively and safely without individualized instruction. Even if you're an advanced yogini, the workout will still benefit and challenge you simply because these exercises are different from those your muscles are used to performing. The routine's not easy, but it is energizing and—when combined with smooth, deep breathing—very relaxing. Do it on a regular basis, and you'll thank yourself right down to the core.

YOGA WORKOUT PLAN

Wear loose, comfortable clothing and no shoes or socks. Before beginning the workout, warm up long enough so that your blood is pumping and you feel slightly warm. Then take several slow, deep breaths to center yourself and help you feel relaxed.

Move gently through the exercises without jerking, bouncing, or relying on momentum. At the end of the routine, you can expect to feel restored both physically and mentally; you'll be energized, calm, and relaxed. Expect to feel some slight soreness and stiffness after you perform the exercises the first few times. (You should never feel joint pain, however.)

As a side note, if weight loss is your goal, don't expect these moves to produce rapid decreases at the scale. They will, however, help reshape and tone your muscles, resulting in lost inches.

Swan

The Swan routine works fronts of thighs, abs, and upper and lower back.
Allow 2 seconds for each move; perform them slowly and with a full range of motion.
Do 5 to 10 repetitions of this exercise.

1. Sit leaning slightly back with knees bent and pressed together, feet flat on floor, chest lifted. Support body weight on your hands, placed slightly behind you with palms flat and fingers splayed.

2. Straighten left leg and lift, toes pointed forward, while reaching above your head.

3. Return to start position.

4. Repeat leg lift and arm movement.

5. Return to start position.

6. Straighten and lift right leg, and raise arms above your head.

7. Return to start position.

8. Repeat leg lift and arm movement.

SIMPLIFY: Sit with back against wall and a small pillow between base of spine and wall.

INTENSIFY: Sit upright without supporting weight on hands. Do not allow hands to touch floor between reps.

TIPS: Keep your chest and chin lifted, abs tight, and shoulders back. Maintain a natural arch in spine. Do not allow back or shoulders to round forward. If your back tires, simplify as described above.

Stingray

The Stingray routine works backs of legs, lower back, and shoulders.
Allow 2 seconds for each move; perform them slowly and with a full range
of motion. Do 5 to 10 repetitions of this exercise on each side.

1. Stand with left foot slightly to the rear, toes resting on floor.

2. Take a deep breath, and extend arms above your head.

3. Bend forward at hips, keeping arms extended.

4. Sweep arms back as you lift your left leg behind you.

5. Slowly lower leg while returning arms to the front.

6. Repeat arm movement and leg lift.

7. Slowly lower leg, and return arms to the front.

8. Return to standing position with arms overhead. Slowly release arms to sides.

SIMPLIFY: Start with both feet firmly planted on floor, and eliminate leg lifts.
TIPS: When bending from hips, lift chest and squeeze shoulder blades together.
Look down in bent position, and keep knees soft (slightly bent).

Python

The Python routine works hips, inner and outer thighs, shoulders, and obliques. Allow 2 seconds for each move; perform them slowly and with a full range of motion. Do 5 to 10 repetitions of this exercise on each side.

1. Lie on right side with bottom knee bent and top leg extended. Straighten your right arm to support upper body on right hand, palm flat, fingers splayed.

2. Lift hips while extending left arm above head.

3. Raise bottom knee to top knee.

4. Lower.

5. Raise top leg.

6. Lower.

7. Lift bottom knee to top knee again.

8. Lower.

SIMPLIFY: Support upper body on forearm instead of hand, squeezing bottom knee to top knee.

INTENSIFY: Extend legs in a V position with top leg slightly behind front leg. Raise bottom leg to top leg rather than raising bent knee to top knee.

TIPS: Abs should be contracted during entire exercise. Keep supporting arm straight and head and neck in line with rest of body. Your hips should be stacked and shouldn't roll forward or backward.

Giraffe

The Giraffe routine works buttocks, backs of thighs, chest, and calves. Allow 2 seconds for each move; perform them slowly and with a full range of motion. Do 5 to 10 repetitions of this exercise on each side.

1. Lie face down with hands on floor, level with lower chest, palms flat and elbows bent.

2. Push up onto hands and knees.

3. Lift hips toward ceiling as you move onto feet and into an inverted V (arms extended, palms flat on floor, and legs as straight as possible with heels toward floor).

4. Lift right leg straight up.

5. Lower.

6. Repeat lift.

7. Lower.

8. Return to start position.

SIMPLIFY: Bend knee on leg lifts, and lift leg directly to the rear, foot flexed.
INTENSIFY: Push up to forearms rather than hands.
TIPS: Keep abs tight and back straight. Keep head and neck relaxed. Spread your fingers to help distribute weight.

Gazelle

The Gazelle routine works all trunk muscles. Allow 2 seconds for each move; perform them slowly and with a full range of motion. Do 5 to 10 repetitions of this exercise on each side.

1. Lie on back with knees toward chest. Hold a rolled towel at the nape of the neck to support your head.

2. Lift shoulders off floor.

3. Lower left leg, keeping knee slightly bent and small of back pressed to floor.

4. Lift left leg halfway.

5. Lower.

6. Lift left leg halfway.

7. Lift left leg so that it's even with right.

8. Return to start position.

SIMPLIFY: Keep knees bent at a 90° angle throughout exercise.

INTENSIFY: Extend arms overhead, allowing upper arms to support head.

TIPS: Keep small of back pressed into floor and abs contracted during entire exercise. Keep head and neck in line with rest of body, and do not initiate upper-body movement with head. As you lower one leg, move the other leg toward chest.

Breathing properly is important during any type of physical activity, but it's key in yoga—just as time is the focus for a competitive runner or adding more pounds is the goal for a weight lifter. In this workout, concentrate on breathing rhythmically and smoothly, without gasping or holding your breath. Inhale at the beginning of each movement and exhale on exertion. Your breathing rhythm should follow this pattern:

1. Fill your lower lungs, expanding your belly.

2. Bring the air into the middle chest, expanding through the ribs.

3. Continue to inhale into the upper chest so the collarbone lifts slightly. As you exhale, reverse the pattern: Release air from the chest, then from your belly. This type of breathing—called complete breath—increases oxygen flow and aids in relaxation. It also helps focus the mind and increase mental clarity. Plus, proper deep, steady breathing is a great calming device, especially when paired with exercise.

Pilates

Pilates (pronounced "pill-AH-teez") is an exercise system that incorporates aspects of yoga, martial arts, physical therapy, and strength training. It was developed in the 1920s by physical trainer Joseph Pilates as a way of developing strong, flexible muscles without adding bulk. Originally called Contrology, the Pilates method was adopted by dancers such as Martha Graham and George Balanchine, and remains popular today not only with dancers but also with models and actors.

The method relies on simple mat work and sophisticated machines called Reformers. The exercises focus on proper alignment and full range of motion instead of high repetitions or heavy resistance. The focus of Pilates is to strengthen the entire abdominal muscle system—the rectus abdominis, obliques, and transversus abdominis (the deep abdominal muscle that you contract when you take in a breath), as well as the back muscles. By focusing on the entire torso rather than just one muscle at a time, you elongate and tighten the whole pelvic girdle—producing a longer, leaner core.

Visit The Pilates Studio online at www.pilates-studio.com to learn more about Pilates. If you'd like to try a Pilates workout at home, we recommend the Stott Pilates Primary Matwork for Beginners video ($14.95), a great workout for beginners. Call Stott Pilates at 800-910-0001, or go to www.stottpilates.com.

Water Workout

As the temperature soars, you may see your workout willpower plummet. And no wonder: Summer heat and humidity can make you feel so sluggish that you're tempted to forgo high-intensity exercise in favor of lower-intensity activities such as lounging poolside. But a water workout will help keep you cool and challenge you physically at the same time. You just have to be willing to get a little wet. Rather than swimming laps (which is great exercise in itself), a water aerobics routine combines a series of simple movements performed upright in waist- to chest-deep water.

WATER WORKS?

If you've never tried water exercise, you may be skeptical: How can splashing around in a pool measure up to a landlocked workout? Water has been used for years for exercise of the nonswimming kind, mostly to rehabilitate regular folks and athletes from injury—even hamstrung racehorses start their journey back to the track in the water. Wet workouts aren't just for people (and horses) on the mend, though. Lots of healthy people, even serious athletes, have begun cross-training in water. Why? You're constantly working against water's resistance, which challenges both your muscles and cardiovascular system. Water is so dense—approximately 12 times denser than air—that it's more difficult to work out in the pool than on dry land. The faster you try to move, the greater the resistance.

Because water keeps your body cooler, you are able to work harder and longer without realizing it. Water helps dissipate body heat, so you don't feel drained as quickly as you would during a high-speed interval workout or a circuit-training session. And no matter how strenuous the workout, there's little risk of injury, thanks to water's most famous property: buoyancy. That means you're able to run, jump, and stomp your feet—all of those high-impact movements that, on dry land, could leave you sore or worse—without jarring your joints.

To find out about water fitness classes in your area, call the YMCA or a local community center. For more information, you can call the Aquatic Exercise Association (AEA) at 1-888-AEAWAVE.　　　　　　　　　　　　　　　—*Gin Miller*

Chapter 62

10 Best Exercise Buys

Want to start exercising, but not sure where
to start? Here are ten affordable must-haves for
starting your fitness program.

Jumping into an exercise program can be a bit overwhelming, especially if you haven't picked up a weight in ages. But it's not as difficult as it might seem. You can be on your way to being a fitness diva by investing in a few necessities. The best part is, whether you can invest in one or all ten of these fitness fundamentals, you'll get a head start on achieving that healthier lifestyle.

1 FITNESS SHOES

Because walking is the starting point for most beginning exercisers, a good pair of walking or running shoes—experts say either style is fine for fitness walking—is probably the most important thing for you to have in your fitness closet. Shoes can run anywhere from $30 to $150. If you're completely clueless about what shoes are best for you, go to a store that specializes in walking and running shoes and get an expert opinion. A good tip: Walking shoes are typically more rigid than running shoes, so if you want a little more flexibility, opt for a running shoe. Be sure to give them a thorough test walk before you buy.

2 AN APPOINTMENT WITH A PERSONAL TRAINER

Personal trainers are experts in fitness. They are affordable (around $25 to $50 per session), and they can help set up an individualized program to meet your needs. Be sure your prospective trainer is certified by a credible fitness organization like the American Council on Exercise (ACE). For information on qualified trainers near you, visit the ACE Web site at www.acefitness.org.

3 FREE WEIGHTS

You're probably thinking of those tough-looking ironclad weights that you find in the gym. But weights designed for home use are very gentle, on your hands and on the furniture. These weights are typically covered with rubber so they're easier to grip and more comfortable to use. You'll probably want to start out with a set of 2- or 5-pound weights. You can find free weights at most any variety or sporting goods store for around $10.

4 EXERCISE VIDEOS

If you don't have time, or simply don't like, to go to the gym, but you want the benefit of an expert instructor, videos are a great option. There are plenty of exercise styles available on video—from salsa dancing to boxing. The Complete Guide to Exercise Videos is a top-notch catalog published by Collage Video Specialties. Visit their Web site at www.collagevideo.com.

5 EXERCISE BANDS

These bands are basically rubber tubing with handles. They come in varying resistances and are used by exercise classes and fitness experts across the country. They cost about $15 each, and can be used for doing everything from biceps curls to leg lifts.

6 A GOOD BOOK

If you'd rather not spend the money on a personal trainer, you can always invest in a book by a professional. Be sure to look for a book that is authored or reviewed by a certified personal trainer or an exercise physiologist. And be sure it's right for your level of fitness. Fitness for Dummies ($19.99, IDG Books) is a good bet for beginner exercisers.

7 STABILITY BALL

These big, plastic balls have been on the exercise scene for a while, but fitness experts have only recently discovered how useful they are. Perfect for developing balance, these balls were also found by the American Council on Exercise to be extremely effective in building abdominal muscles. Plus they're fun to bounce around on. They come in two sizes, 55 cm (for people under 5'8") and 65 cm (for people over 5'8") and cost around $30. Be sure to buy a stability ball that comes with a video or a wall chart that explains how to use the ball.

8 ANKLE WEIGHTS

Ankle weights are great for adding some resistance when you work your lower body—like doing leg lifts. They are made for strength training only—don't use ankle weights while you do cardiovascular exercises like walking or aerobics, or you'll be asking for knee problems. The vast majority of ankle weights range from 1 to 5 pounds and cost around $20 to $25.

9 EXERCISE MAT

These are great for stretching, doing yoga moves, or simply doing some strength-training moves that require you to lie down or get on your knees. You get some extra padding and a clean place to exercise so you can avoid carpet burn or bruises from your hardwood floors. They are inexpensive (around $20) and roll up or fold to store inconspicuously in a corner or in the closet.

10 TREADMILL

If you're willing to shell out a bit more money for your home gym, you would be wise to invest in a treadmill. A review by Consumer Reports found that treadmills are used more than any other home exercise equipment, and they're very effective. You can find worthwhile treadmills that cost as little as $500 or as much as $3,000. Don't think more money means better quality, though. Consumer Reports ranked a $500 model as a good buy. There are many questions to ask when investing in a treadmill, so before you buy, think about where you're going to put it and how much room you've got. And when you start shopping, be sure to give the treadmill a test walk before you buy.

—*Michele Mann*

Part

9

Secrets of Success

How to Beat the Top 10 Weight-Loss Challenges

We polled our readers for the top 10 challenges to losing weight. Here's what they said, and our secrets to overcoming these obstacles.

Chapter 63

A Sweet Tooth

"I have all kinds of good intentions about losing weight, but my downfall is desserts. I just can't resist sweets!"

Secret: Guilt-Free Desserts

Nature's Sweet Treats

Sometimes the sweetest treat is also the simplest. Fruit is nature's way of encouraging us to enjoy sweet, juicy flavors, pleasing textures, and vibrant colors.

Fruit-based desserts are usually low in calories because the flavor comes from fruit instead of large amounts of fat and sugar. Plus, you get fiber, vitamins, and minerals to boot. There is quite a bit of promising research showing that the antioxidants found in fruits can help reduce the risk of heart disease and certain cancers.

So dig in. These desserts are so good for you, it's almost a crime to pass up dessert!

CITRUSY MELON AND STRAWBERRY CUP

1   tablespoon sugar
1   tablespoon lemon juice
3   tablespoons frozen orange juice
    concentrate, thawed
1½ cups cantaloupe cubes
1½ cups honeydew melon cubes
1   cup halved fresh strawberries

1. Combine first 3 ingredients in a large bowl; stir well. Add remaining ingredients; stir gently. Yield: 4 servings (serving size: 1 cup).

CALORIES 86 (4% from fat); FAT 0.4g (sat 0.1g, mono 0g, poly 0.2g); PROTEIN 1.3g; CARB 21.2g; FIBER 1.8g; CHOL 0mg; IRON 0.4mg; SODIUM 11mg; CALCIUM 20mg EXCHANGES: 1½ Fruit

MIXED BERRY DESSERT

    3 tablespoons orange juice
    ½ teaspoon grated fresh orange
        rind
    1 tablespoon sugar
    1 cup blueberries
    1 cup blackberries or raspberries
    ½ cup frozen reduced-calorie
        whipped topping, thawed

1. Combine first 3 ingredients in a medium bowl, stirring until sugar dissolves. Add blueberries and blackberries, tossing gently.

2. Spoon mixture into individual dessert dishes. Top each serving with 2 tablespoons whipped topping. Yield: 4 servings (serving size: ½ cup).

CALORIES 77 (15% from fat); FAT 1.3g (sat 1g, mono 0g, poly 0.1g); PROTEIN 0.6g; CARB 16.1g; FIBER 2.4g; CHOL 0mg; IRON 0.3g; SODIUM 2mg; CALC 15g EXCHANGE: 1 Fruit

TUTTI-FRUTTI SMOOTHIE

    1 cup sliced ripe banana
        (about 1 large)
    1 cup orange juice
    ¾ cup sliced peeled peaches
    ¾ cup sliced strawberries
    1 tablespoon honey

1. Combine all ingredients in a blender; cover and process until smooth. Serve immediately. Yield: 3 servings (serving size: 1 cup).

SMOOTHIE SAVVY

Most smoothie shop drinks are fruit-based, which may make you think they're always low in calories. But extras like protein powder can boost the calories in a single serving to 500 or more. Smoothies can be good additions to your diet if you follow these guidelines.

- Sip sparingly. Make that blueberry blast or mango madness a once-a-week treat. Drinking smoothies in place of meals on occasion is fine, but remember, they're mostly carbohydrates. They don't offer all the nutrients you need, like fiber and protein.
- Be a detective. Ask specifically what's in the drink. If one of the ingredients is a premade mix, find out what's in that, too. Many are loaded with sugar.
- Nix the herbs and supplements. Some places offer smoothies made with everything from ginseng to echinacea. Skip them, because you can't be sure how much of the herb you're getting, and some herbs are toxic at extremely high doses.

CALORIES 134 (3% from fat); FAT 0.5g (sat 0.1g, mono 0.1g, poly 0.1g); PROTEIN 1.6g; CARB 33.8g; FIBER 3.3g; CHOL 0mg; IRON 0.5mg; SODIUM 2mg; CALC 18mg EXCHANGES: 2 Fruit

Minted Watermelon Granita

If you're seeding and cubing 6 cups of watermelon, you'll end up with at least ⅓ cup of juice. If you use pre-packaged cubes, just use water in the recipe.

- ⅓ cup sugar
- ⅓ cup watermelon juice or water
- 6 cups seeded watermelon cubes
- ¼ cup lime juice
- ½ teaspoon peppermint extract
- 2 teaspoons chopped fresh mint

1. Combine sugar and watermelon juice in a small saucepan; bring to a boil. Cook, stirring constantly, until sugar dissolves.
2. Place watermelon cubes, lime juice, and peppermint in a blender; process until smooth, stopping once to scrape down sides. Add sugar mixture; cover and process until blended. Pour mixture into a 13 x 9-inch pan; cover and freeze at least 8 hours or until firm.
3. Remove mixture from freezer, and scrape entire mixture with tines of a fork until fluffy. Toss mint into granita; serve immediately. Yield: 6 servings (serving size: 1 cup).

CALORIES 98 (6% from fat); FAT 0.7g (sat 0.1g, mono 0.2g, poly 0.2g); PROTEIN 1g; CARB 23.4g; FIBER 0.8g; CHOL 0mg; IRON 0.3mg; SODIUM 3mg; CALC 14mg EXCHANGES: ½ Starch, 1 Fruit

Pineapple-Mint Ice

Use any 20-ounce can of fruit in this easy, two-ingredient dessert.

- 1 (20-ounce) can pineapple chunks in juice, chilled and undrained
- 2 tablespoons coarsely chopped fresh mint
- Fresh mint sprigs (optional)

1. Set aside 3 pineapple chunks for garnish. Place remaining pineapple and juice into an 8-inch square pan. Cover and freeze 1½ to 2 hours or until almost frozen.
2. Process frozen pineapple and chopped mint in a food processor until smooth, but not melted. Serve immediately; garnish with reserved pineapple chunks and mint sprigs, if desired.
Yield: 3 servings (serving size: ¾ cup).

CALORIES 117 (0% from fat); FAT 0g (sat 0g, mono 0g, poly 0g); PROTEIN 0g; CARB 28.9g; FIBER 1.4g; CHOL 0mg; IRON 0.6mg; SODIUM 2mg; CALC 20mg EXCHANGES: 2 Fruit

STRAWBERRY-MERLOT ICE

For a nonalcoholic version, use 2 cups of red grape juice instead of the red wine.

- 2 cups Merlot or other dry red wine
- 1 cup white grape juice concentrate
- 1 (16-ounce) package frozen whole strawberries

1. Combine all ingredients in a blender; process until smooth, stopping once to scrape down sides. Pour mixture into a 13 x 9-inch pan; cover and freeze at least 8 hours or until firm.

2. Remove mixture from freezer, and scrape entire mixture with the tines of a fork until fluffy. Serve immediately, or spoon into a freezer-safe container; cover and freeze up to 1 month. Yield: 12 servings (serving size: ½ cup).

CALORIES 98 (2% from fat); FAT 0.3g (sat 0g, mono 0g, poly 0g); PROTEIN 0.1g; CARB 18.2g; FIBER 0.5g; CHOL 0mg; IRON 0.2mg; SODIUM 10mg; CALC 9mg EXCHANGE: 1 Fruit

GINGERED GRAPEFRUIT SORBET

Use a package of melon, strawberries, or peaches alone if you prefer a single fruit dessert.

- 1 (1-pound) package frozen melon, peach, and strawberry mixture
- 2 cups red grapefruit juice
- ½ cup honey
- 1 tablespoon lemon juice
- 1 tablespoon grated fresh ginger

1. Combine all ingredients in a large bowl; stir well. Pour one-third of mixture into a blender; process until smooth, stopping once to scrape down sides. Pour mixture into a 13 x 9-inch pan. Repeat procedure in 2 batches with remaining mixture. Cover and freeze at least 8 hours or until firm.

2. Remove mixture from freezer, and let stand 10 minutes. Serve immediately, or spoon into an airtight freezer-safe container; cover and freeze up to 1 month. Yield: 6 servings (serving size: 1 cup).

CALORIES 158 (1% from fat); FAT 0.1g (sat 0g, mono 0g, poly 0.1g); PROTEIN 0.7g; CARB 45.1g; FIBER 1.1g; CHOL 0mg; IRON 0.9mg; SODIUM 18mg; CALC 3mg EXCHANGES: 1 Starch, 2 Fruit

PEACH SUNDAES WITH BLUEBERRY SAUCE

The sauce can be served over waffles, angel food cake, or pancakes.

Blueberry Sauce
1 cup cubed peeled fresh peaches
1⅓ cups low-fat vanilla ice cream

1. Prepare Blueberry Sauce.
2. Place ¼ cup peaches in each of 4 dessert dishes; top each with ⅓ cup ice cream and ¼ cup Blueberry Sauce. Serve immediately. Yield: 4 servings.

BLUEBERRY SAUCE

3 tablespoons sugar
1½ teaspoons cornstarch
½ cup water
1 cup fresh blueberries

1. Combine sugar and cornstarch in a small saucepan; gradually stir in water. Bring mixture to a boil over medium-high heat, stirring constantly. Add blueberries, and cook 4 minutes or until mixture boils in center, stirring often. Reduce heat to medium, and cook 2 minutes, stirring often; cool slightly. Yield: 1 cup.

CALORIES 145 (9% from fat); FAT 1.5g (sat 1g, mono 0g, poly 0.1g); PROTEIN 2.5g; CARB 32.0g; FIBER 2.5g; CHOL 7mg; IRON 0.1mg; SODIUM 6mg; CALC 71mg
EXCHANGES: 1½ Starch, 1½ Fruit

THE ROOT OF YOUR SWEET TOOTH

Do you find yourself raiding the refrigerator after dinner in search of something sweet? Could be it's in your genes.

"The liking for sweet foods seems to be universal among humans," says Marcia Pelchat, Ph.D., a biological psychologist at the Monell Chemical Senses Center in Philadelphia. We seem to be genetically programmed to prefer sweet foods from birth: Babies instinctively go for sweet over salty foods.

The theory behind this is that we've evolved to enjoy sweet foods; they tend to be safe to eat, while bitter foods, which can contain toxins, may signal danger.

But there's a difference between liking sweet foods and craving them. Researchers question whether a hankering for chocolate cake reflects a craving for sugar or a craving for fat, since cake, candies, cookies, and ice cream are high-fat foods. If you really wanted sugar, they say, then you'd probably reach for a piece of hard candy or a fruit drink.

8 Great Desserts

The *Cooking Light* food editors reviewed the dessert recipe files and picked some of their favorites that were low in fat and calories, but had an especially high "indulgence factor." We think these will satisfy your sweet tooth.

1 EASY LEMON SQUARES

If you've always been a fan of old-fashioned lemon bars, you'll love this lightened version that is remarkably similar to the traditional bar.

CRUST:

¼	cup granulated sugar
3	tablespoons butter or margarine, softened
1	cup all-purpose flour

TOPPING:

3	large eggs
¾	cup granulated sugar
2	teaspoons grated lemon rind
⅓	cup fresh lemon juice
3	tablespoons all-purpose flour
½	teaspoon baking powder
⅛	teaspoon salt
2	teaspoons powdered sugar

1. Preheat oven to 350°.

2. To prepare crust, beat ¼ cup granulated sugar and butter with a mixer at medium speed until creamy. Lightly spoon 1 cup flour into a dry measuring cup; level with a knife. Gradually add 1 cup flour to sugar mixture, beating at low speed until mixture resembles fine crumbs. Gently press mixture into bottom of an 8-inch square baking pan. Bake at 350° for 15 minutes; cool on a wire rack.

3. To prepare topping, beat eggs at medium speed until foamy. Add ¾ cup granulated sugar and next 5 ingredients, and beat until well blended. Pour mixture over partially baked crust. Bake at 350° for 20 to 25 minutes or until set. Cool on wire rack. Sift powdered sugar evenly over top. Yield: 16 servings (serving size: 1 square).

CALORIES 118 (24% from fat); FAT 3.2g (sat 1.7g, mono 1g, poly 0.3g); PROTEIN 2.2g; CARB 20.5g; FIBER 0.3g; CHOL 47mg; IRON 0.6mg; SODIUM 68mg; CALC 16mg EXCHANGES: 1 Starch, 1 Fat

2 WHITE RUSSIAN TIRAMISU

We reduced the fat and calories, but not the creaminess, in this traditional Italian dessert by replacing some of the high-fat mascarpone cheese with fat-free cream cheese.

1½	cups brewed coffee
¼	cup Kahlúa (coffee-flavored liqueur), divided
½	cup (3½ ounces) mascarpone cheese
1	(8-ounce) block fat-free cream cheese, softened
⅓	cup packed brown sugar
¼	cup granulated sugar
24	ladyfingers (2 [3-ounce] packages)
2	teaspoons unsweetened cocoa, divided

1. Combine brewed coffee and 2 tablespoons Kahlúa in a shallow dish; cool.
2. Combine cheeses in a large bowl. Beat with a mixer at high speed until smooth. Add 2 tablespoons Kahlúa and sugars; beat until well blended.
3. Split ladyfingers in half lengthwise.
4. Quickly dip 24 ladyfinger halves, flat sides down, into coffee mixture. Place halves, dipped sides down, in the bottom of an 8-inch square baking dish (halves will be slightly overlapping). Spread half of cheese mixture over ladyfingers; sprinkle with 1 teaspoon cocoa. Repeat procedure with remaining ladyfinger halves, coffee mixture, cheese mixture, and 1 teaspoon cocoa.
5. Place 1 toothpick in each corner of dish and 1 in center of tiramisu (to prevent plastic wrap from sticking to cheese mixture); cover with plastic wrap. Chill 2 hours. Yield: 12 servings.

CALORIES 134 (30% from fat); FAT 4.5g (sat 2.2g, mono 1.5g, poly 0.4g); PROTEIN 3.3g; CARB 21.7g; FIBER 0g; CHOL 31mg; IRON 0.3mg; SODIUM 139mg; CALC 77mg EXCHANGES: 1 Starch, 1 Fat

3 CHOCOLATE-TOFFEE PUFFS

This cookie took first place in a chocolate recipe contest among *Cooking Light* readers.

4	large egg whites
⅓	cup granulated sugar
1	cup sifted powdered sugar
½	cup unsweetened cocoa
2	(1.4-ounce) chocolate-covered toffee bars (such as Heath), crushed

Cooking spray

1. Preheat oven to 350°.
2. Beat egg whites in a large bowl with a mixer at high speed until soft peaks form. Gradually add granulated sugar, beating until stiff peaks form.
3. Combine powdered sugar, cocoa, and candy bars in a small bowl; mix well.

Fold half of cocoa mixture into egg mixture (egg whites will deflate quickly). Fold in remaining cocoa mixture until smooth. Drop mixture by rounded tablespoonfuls onto a baking sheet coated with cooking spray. Bake at 350° for 15 minutes (puffs will be soft in center). Yield: 2 dozen cookies (serving size: 1 cookie).

CALORIES 52 (24% from fat); FAT 1.4g (sat 0.9g, mono 0.5g, poly 0.1g); PROTEIN 1.1g; CARB 9.9g; FIBER 0.7g; CHOL 1.7mg; IRON 0.3mg; SODIUM 19mg; CALC 7mg EXCHANGE: ½ Starch

4 CHOCOLATE MOUSSE

Sinfully creamy and rich, this chocolate mousse is good for you because it contains tofu.

¾ cup semisweet chocolate chips
1 (12.3-ounce) package reduced-fat extra-firm silken tofu
¼ teaspoon salt
3 large egg whites
½ cup sugar
¼ cup water
Frozen fat-free whipped topping, thawed (optional)
Grated chocolate (optional)

1. Place chocolate chips in a small glass bowl; microwave at HIGH 1½ minutes or until almost melted, stirring after 1 minute. Place chocolate and tofu in a food processor or blender; process 2 minutes or until smooth.

2. Place salt and egg whites in a medium bowl; beat with a mixer at high speed until stiff peaks form. Combine sugar and water in a small saucepan; bring to a boil. Cook, without stirring, until candy thermometer registers 238°. Pour hot sugar syrup in a thin stream over egg whites, beating at high speed. Gently stir one-fourth of meringue into tofu mixture; gently fold in remaining meringue. Spoon ½ cup mousse into each of 8 (6-ounce) custard cups. Cover and chill at least 4 hours. Garnish with whipped topping and grated chocolate, if desired. Yield: 8 servings.

CALORIES 147 (34% from fat); FAT 5.6g (sat 3.3g, mono 1.8g, poly 0.5g); PROTEIN 5.2g; CARB 22.5g; FIBER 0.2g; CHOL 0mg; IRON 0.9mg; SODIUM 134mg; CALC 26mg EXCHANGES: 1½ Starch, 1 Fat

5 EASY CHOCOLATE-CARAMEL BROWNIES

Use a cake mix that contains pudding; the recipe won't work otherwise. Cut brownies after they've cooled. To make ahead, cool completely, wrap tightly in heavy-duty plastic wrap, and freeze.

2 tablespoons fat-free milk
27 small soft caramel candies (about 8 ounces)
½ cup fat-free sweetened condensed milk (not evaporated fat-free milk)
1 (18.25-ounce) package devil's food cake mix with pudding
7 tablespoons reduced-calorie margarine, melted
1 large egg white, lightly beaten
Cooking spray
1 teaspoon all-purpose flour
½ cup reduced-fat chocolate baking chips

1. Preheat oven to 350°.
2. Combine fat-free milk and candies in a bowl. Microwave at HIGH 1½ to 2 minutes or until caramels melt and mixture is smooth, stirring with a whisk after every minute. Set aside.
3. Combine sweetened condensed milk, cake mix, margarine, and egg white in a bowl; stir well (batter will be very stiff). Coat bottom only of a 13 x 9-inch baking pan with cooking spray; dust lightly with flour. Press two-thirds of batter into prepared pan using floured hands; pat evenly (layer will be thin).
4. Bake at 350° for 10 minutes. Remove from oven; sprinkle with chocolate chips. Drizzle caramel mixture over chips; carefully drop remaining batter by spoonfuls over caramel mixture. Bake at 350° for 30 minutes. Cool completely in pan on a wire rack. Yield: 3 dozen (serving size: 1 brownie).

CALORIES 122 (30% from fat); FAT 4g (sat 1.6g, mono 1.3g, poly 0.6g); PROTEIN 1.6g; CARB 20.4g; FIBER 0.4g; CHOL 1mg; IRON 0.5mg; SODIUM 224mg; CALC 34mg EXCHANGES: 1 Starch, 1 Fat

6 DOUBLE-CHOCOLATE CHEWS

Double chocolate. Less than 2 grams of fat per cookie. What else need be said?

1¾ cups all-purpose flour
⅔ cup sifted powdered sugar
⅓ cup unsweetened cocoa
2¼ teaspoons baking powder
⅛ teaspoon salt
1 cup semisweet chocolate minichips, divided
3 tablespoons vegetable oil
1 cup packed brown sugar
2½ tablespoons light-colored corn syrup
1 tablespoon water
2½ teaspoons vanilla extract
3 large egg whites
Cooking spray

1. Preheat oven to 350°.

2. Combine first 5 ingredients in a bowl; stir well, and set aside.

3. Combine ¾ cup chocolate minichips and oil in a small saucepan; cook over low heat until chocolate melts, stirring constantly. Pour melted chocolate mixture into a large bowl, and cool 5 minutes. Add brown sugar, corn syrup, water, vanilla extract, and egg whites to chocolate mixture; stir well. Stir in flour mixture and remaining chocolate minichips.

4. Drop dough by level tablespoons 2 inches apart onto baking sheets coated with cooking spray. Bake at 350° for 8 minutes. Cool 2 minutes or until firm. Remove cookies from pans; cool on wire racks. Yield: 4 dozen (serving size: 1 cookie).

CALORIES 64 (23% from fat); FAT 1.6g (sat 0.6g, mono 0.5g, poly 0.5g); PROTEIN 0.9g; CARB 11.8g; FIBER 0.1g; CHOL 0mg; IRON 0.5mg; SODIUM 13mg; CALC 19mg EXCHANGE: 1 Starch

10 SWEET WAYS TO SATISFY YOUR SWEET TOOTH

In addition to the heavenly recipes in this section, here are a few secret weapons—all around 100 calories or less.

1. If you're a coffee drinker, indulge in a cup of flavored coffee after your meal. Chocolate-almond and hazelnut are two examples.

2. Finish off your meal with a piece of sweet, juicy fruit—not only will the fruit tingle your taste buds, it's good for you, too!

3. Dump a can of peaches, pineapple, or pears (packed in juice) into a shallow dish and freeze. When you're ready for dessert, plop the frozen fruit in your blender, and you've got a quick fruit sorbet.

4. Blend fresh berries in the food processor for a quick fruit sauce. Spoon it over fat-free vanilla ice cream or frozen yogurt.

5. Put a single layer of seedless grapes on a baking sheet and freeze for about 20 minutes. It's almost like eating candy!

6. Top a piece of angel food cake with fresh strawberries and a spoonful of reduced-calorie whipped topping.

7. Make mini ice cream sandwiches with about 2 tablespoons softened fat-free ice cream sandwiched between 2 ginger snaps.

8. Top fat-free lemon yogurt with a few fresh berries, and serve in a fancy dessert glass.

9. Add a splash of fruit-flavored liqueur to mixed fresh fruit, and serve in a stemmed glass.

10. Crumble a low-fat sandwich cream cookie over a scoop of fat-free frozen yogurt or ice cream.

7 BUTTERMILK-APPLE COFFEE CAKE

The low-fat buttermilk helps give the cake a rich, homestyle flavor.

CAKE:

1½ cups thinly sliced peeled Granny Smith apple
3 tablespoons brown sugar
1 tablespoon lemon juice
½ teaspoon ground cinnamon
1 cup all-purpose flour
½ teaspoon baking soda
⅛ teaspoon salt
⅓ cup granulated sugar
2 tablespoons butter, softened
1 large egg
1 teaspoon vanilla extract
½ teaspoon almond extract
½ cup low-fat buttermilk
   Cooking spray
2 tablespoons sliced almonds

GLAZE:

¼ cup sifted powdered sugar
1 teaspoon low-fat buttermilk
¼ teaspoon vanilla extract

1. Preheat oven to 350°.

2. To prepare cake, combine first 4 ingredients in a small saucepan over medium-high heat. Cook 5 minutes or until syrupy, stirring frequently; cool.

3. Lightly spoon flour into a dry measuring cup; level with a knife. Combine flour, baking soda, and salt in a small bowl, stirring well with a whisk. Combine granulated sugar and butter in a large bowl; beat with a mixer at medium speed until well blended; add egg and extracts, beating well. Add flour mixture to sugar mixture alternately with buttermilk, beginning and ending with flour mixture; beat well after each addition.

4. Spoon batter into an 8-inch round cake pan coated with cooking spray. Arrange apple mixture over cake; top with almonds. Bake at 350° for 25 minutes or until cake begins to pull away from sides of pan. Cool in pan on a wire rack for 10 minutes. Quickly invert cake onto wire rack. Then invert onto a serving plate.

5. To prepare glaze, combine powdered sugar, 1 teaspoon buttermilk, and ¼ teaspoon vanilla in a small bowl; stir with a whisk. Drizzle glaze over cake. Serve warm or at room temperature. Yield: 8 servings (serving size: 1 wedge).

CALORIES 185 (24% from fat); FAT 5g (sat 2.3g, mono 1.7g, poly 0.6g); PROTEIN 3.4g; CARB 31.8g; FIBER 1g; CHOL 35mg; IRON 1mg; SODIUM 162mg; CALC 36mg EXCHANGES: 1 Starch, 1 Fruit, 1 Fat

8 PECAN TASSIES IN CREAM CHEESE PASTRY

One way to serve these miniature tarts during the holidays is on a dessert bar, with an assortment of winter fruits and hot drinks.

PASTRY:

1   cup all-purpose flour
1   tablespoon granulated sugar
Dash of salt
¼   cup (2 ounces) ⅓-less-fat cream cheese, softened
2   tablespoons butter or margarine, softened
2   tablespoons fat-free milk
Cooking spray

FILLING:

⅓   cup finely chopped pecans
½   cup packed brown sugar
⅓   cup light-colored corn syrup
1   teaspoon vanilla extract
⅛   teaspoon salt
1   large egg
1   large egg white

1. Preheat oven to 350°.
2. To prepare pastry, lightly spoon flour into a dry measuring cup; level with a knife. Combine flour, 1 tablespoon sugar, and dash of salt in a small bowl. Combine cream cheese, butter, and milk in a large bowl; beat with a mixer at medium speed until well blended. Add flour mixture; beat at low speed just until blended (mixture will be crumbly). Press flour mixture into a ball.

3. Turn dough out onto a lightly floured surface, and knead lightly 3 to 4 times. Divide dough into 24 portions. Place 1 dough portion into each of 24 miniature muffin cups coated with cooking spray. Press dough into bottom and up sides of cups, using lightly floured fingers.

4. To prepare filling, divide pecans evenly among muffin cups. Combine brown sugar and remaining ingredients; spoon about 2 teaspoons filling over pecans in each muffin cup.

5. Bake at 350° for 20 minutes or until pastry is lightly browned and filling is puffy. Cool in cups 10 minutes on a wire rack. Run a knife around outside edge of each tassie; remove from pan. Cool completely on a wire rack. Yield: 2 dozen tassies (serving size: 1 tassie).

CALORIES 77 (35% from fat); FAT 3g (sat 1.1g, mono 1.2g, poly 0.4g); PROTEIN 1.4g; CARB 11.3g; FIBER 0.2g; CHOL 14mg; IRON 0.4mg; SODIUM 50mg; CALC 9mg EXCHANGE: 1 Starch

Chapter 64

Challenge 2

Heaping Helpings

"I just love to eat! I guess I don't have any
self-control when it comes to food."

Secret: Super-Size Smarts

First, fast-food restaurants gave us "super-size" fries. Then 2-ounce muffins turned into 400-calorie monstrosities. Now supermarkets sell 600-calorie baking potatoes, leading us to presume that spuds should be the size of Volkswagens. Who even knows what a reasonable serving size is supposed to look like anymore?

Use the guide on the next page to help estimate portion sizes. These portions correspond to the serving sizes recommended by the Food Pyramid and the leading health and nutrition agencies. (See page 164 for more information on the Food Pyramid and portion sizes.)

WEIGH TO GO

Most of us are accustomed to using cups and spoons when we measure, but if pinpoint accuracy is your goal, a kitchen scale is your means. You'll get a much more precise measurement, and weighing on a scale is easier than packing dry ingredients in a cup or scraping margarine and shortening off a spoon.

The preferred method of measurement in many foreign countries, weighing ingredients is gaining popularity in the United States. People are starting to cook more at home, and many of them are trying recipes, like baked goods or exotic dishes, that rely on consistent measurements for the best results.

In addition to helping you cook better, scales can encourage healthier eating. Even if you don't want to weigh all your food, putting a few items to the test may open your eyes to just how much you're eating. Bagels and muffins can vary in size from a modest serving to those monstrous things. It would definitely be good to measure such items in terms of weight because there's a big difference in calories and fat from one size to another. Or use the chart below to help you judge portion sizes.

HELP YOURSELF TO HEALTHY PORTIONS

When you're away from home and don't have scales and measuring cups on hand, use these visual examples to make quick estimates of healthy serving sizes.

Food	Modern Equivalent
3 ounces meat, poultry, or fish 3 ounces grilled fish	diskette
1 ounce cheese	lipstick tube
2 tablespoons peanut butter	golf ball
1 tablespoon oil or salad dressing	individual eye-shadow compact
½ cup chopped fresh vegetables	3 regular ice cubes
1 medium apple or orange	baseball
1 medium potato	computer mouse or 1 small soap bar
1 cup potatoes, rice, or pasta	tennis ball
1 standard bagel	6-ounce can tuna
1 serving pretzels or other snack food	a coffee mug full
1 scoop ice cream	round iMac mouse

Chapter 65

No Time to Exercise

"I get up at 5 a.m., get the kids off to daycare, work, pick up kids, make dinner, clean up the kitchen, put the kids to bed, and by the time I'm done at 8 p.m., I'm exhausted. And I'm just not willing to get up at 4:40 a.m. to exercise."

Secret: Fitness in Minutes a Day

Strength at Lightning Speed

This warp-speed workout is perfect for anyone on a tight schedule. The concept is simple: Do one set of an exercise as quickly as you can without sacrificing form, rest only as long as it takes to get in position for the next move, and hustle.

The 11-exercise circuit we've created here takes only about 20 minutes. It's a total-body strength workout in less time than it takes most people to walk a mile. And there's a bonus: Reducing the amount of rest between exercises keeps your heart pumping, so your cardiovascular system benefits, too.

If you prefer weight-training machines at the gym, we've included the heavy-equipment equivalent in italics following each of our low-tech exercises. But with a set of dumbbells and a weight bench, you can do the whole routine in your own home.

1 Abdominal Crunch Lie on your back with your knees bent and feet flat on the floor, hip-width apart. Place your fingertips lightly behind your ears—don't clasp your fingers behind your head—and keep your elbows out to the sides. Tilt your chin slightly toward your chest. Gently pulling your abdominals inward, exhale and curl up so that your head, neck, and shoulder blades lift off the floor. Pause, inhale, and then slowly lower back down. Do 16 repetitions. *Alternate: ab-crunch machine*

2 ▶ **S q u a t** (for the buttocks and legs) Stand with feet hip-width apart, weight back on your heels and hands on your hips. With abdominals tight, lower your rear as far as you can without leaning more than a few inches forward. Don't let your knees extend beyond your toes. Once you feel your upper body fold forward over your thighs, straighten legs, and stand up. Don't lock your knees at the top of the movement. Do 16 repetitions. *Alternate: leg-press machine*

3 ◀ **P u s h - U p s** (for the chest, shoulders, and arms) Lying stomach-down on an exercise mat, bend your knees, keeping your palms on the floor next to your shoulders and your ankles crossed behind you. Straighten your arms, and lift your body so that you're balanced on palms and knees. Keep your back straight, your chin tucked, and your abs tight. Pause. Then lower your entire body at once until your upper arms are parallel to the floor; don't rest your body on the floor. Do 8 repetitions. *Alternate: chest- or bench-press machine*

4 **Alternate Lunges** (for buttocks and thighs) Stand with your feet hip-width apart and hands on hips. Keep your back straight and shoulders square as you step your right foot forward, leading with your heel, about a stride's length. As your foot touches the floor, bend both knees until your right thigh is parallel to the floor and your left thigh is perpendicular to it. Press off the ball of your right foot; step back to the standing position. Switch legs. Do 8 repetitions on each side. *Alternate: leg-extension machine*

5 ▶ **Dumbbell Row** (for upper back, shoulders, and arms) Stand to the left of a weight bench, holding a dumbbell in your left hand with your palm facing in. With your abdominals tight and knees slightly bent, lean forward from your hips so that your back is roughly parallel with the floor; keep your neck in line with your spine. Allow your right hand

to rest on the bench for support and your left arm to hang down. Pull your left arm up until your upper arm is parallel to the floor and your hand brushes against your waist. Lower the weight slowly. Do 8 repetitions, and switch arms. *Alternate: machine row*

6 ▶**Kneeling Leg Curl** (for hamstrings and buttocks) Get down on your hands and knees with elbows bent and forearms on the floor, fingers laced together. Pull your stomach in to keep your back from sagging, and tilt your chin toward your chest. Keeping your knee bent and foot flexed, lift your

right leg so your knee is level with your hip. Slowly straighten your right leg without locking your knee. Then bend the knee, and lower your leg until your calf is parallel to the floor. Do 8 repetitions; switch legs. *Alternate: leg-curl machine*

7 ◀**Shoulder Press** (for shoulders and arms) Sit on a chair or bench, feet firmly on the floor about hip-width apart, and with a dumbbell in each hand. Bend your elbows, and raise the dumbbells so that they are level with your ears, palms facing in. With your stomach tight, press the dumbbells toward the ceiling, straightening your arms without locking elbows. Slowly lower the weights until they are once again level with your ears. Do 8 repetitions. *Alternate: shoulder-press machine*

8 **Back Raise** (for lower back) Lie on your stomach with your forehead on the floor, arms straight out in front of you with your palms down. With your stomach tight, lift your right arm and left leg about 1 inch off the floor, stretching out as much as you can. Pause for two slow counts, lower arm and leg, and switch sides. Alternate sides until you've completed a total of 16 repetitions. *Alternate: back raise on a hyperextension bench*

9 **Biceps Curl** Stand with your feet hip-width apart, arms at your sides. Hold a dumbbell in each hand, palms facing in. Keep your stomach tight, back straight, and knees relaxed as you curl your right arm up to your shoulder, twisting your palm so it's facing your shoulder at the top of the movement.

Slowly lower the dumbbell; switch sides. Alternate sides until you've completed a total of 16 repetitions. *Alternate: arm-curl machine*

10 ►**Calf Raises** Stand on the edge of a stairstep or step-aerobics platform that's about 1 foot off the ground. The balls of your feet should be firmly planted on the step, your heels hanging over the edge. Hold onto a wall or sturdy object for balance. Slowly raise onto your toes, pause, and return to starting position. Do 8 repetitions. *Alternate: standing calf machine*

11 ◄**Bench Dips** (for triceps) Sit on the edge of a bench with legs together straight in front of you, toes pointing up. With elbows relaxed, firmly grip the edge of the bench. Slide your backside off the front of the bench, supporting your weight with your arms, keeping your stomach tight. Bend your elbows and lower your body, keeping your upper body

perpendicular to the floor, until your upper arms are parallel to the floor; then push yourself back up. Complete 8 repetitions. *Alternate: triceps press*

—Liz Neporent

At-Work Workout (pages 412-413)

For the time-pressed and work-stressed, here's a quick, full-body exercise routine that you can do at the office in about 30 minutes. Sneak away during the first half of your lunch hour to a quiet stairwell where the doors are kept unlocked. You don't even need workout clothes, though you will want to wear athletic shoes and perhaps change into a T-shirt. If your stairwell is too hot or stuffy, find some outdoor stairs, or substitute power walking in place of stair climbing for the cardio segments.

AT-WORK WORKOUT

Warm up by walking up and down stairs for 5 minutes. Then do the stretches. Next, alternate 5 minutes of cardio work with the strength moves. Do 10 to 12 repetitions (reps) of each strength exercise. Cool down with 5 minutes of walking and stretching.

Hamstring/calf: Place one heel on second or third step. Bend knee of supporting leg, pressing hips back until you feel a stretch in the back of the forward leg, and hold. Lean forward, bending the front knee and straightening the rear leg until you feel stretch in calf. Slide rear foot back to intensify stretch. Hold, then repeat with opposite leg.

Back: Standing at top of stairs, grasp stair post with both hands. (Use a wide grip, with one hand over the other.) Squat and lean back with arms extended.

▶ **Chest:** From back stretch position, release one hand, and turn away from the opposite hand to stretch chest and shoulders. Hold, then repeat on opposite side.

◀ **Quads:** Stand with feet close together. Grasp right foot with right hand, and pull heel toward buttocks. Roll hips under to intensify stretch in front of thigh. (Place other hand on wall or grasp banister for support, if needed.) Hold stretch, then repeat on left side.

▶ Each cardio segment comprises 5 minutes of stair climbing. Begin by running up one flight of stairs and walking back down. Then run up two flights of stairs and walk down. Continue adding one flight at a time and walking back to the bottom between each set. When you're able to run up all the flights in your stairwell, continue this run/walk pattern for 5 minutes. *To decrease intensity, walk up the stairs, or walk up every other flight. To increase intensity, run up two steps at a time.*

▶ **Bent-Knee Push-Ups:** Stand at bottom of stairs, about 3 feet from bottom step. Bend forward, placing hands on second step and keeping feet on floor with knees bent (but not resting on ground). Slowly lower chest toward step, then slowly push back up. Engage core torso muscles to target abs as well as chest. *To decrease intensity, allow knees to rest on a mat on the floor. To increase intensity, place hands on first step.*

◀ **Triceps Swing-Backs:** Sit on bottom step (use towel if steps are dirty), with legs extended to front; keep knees slightly bent to protect back. Grip step with hands slightly wider than hips, fingertips forward. Lift up and to front of step, straightening arms. Slowly lower hips toward ground, keeping elbows bent to back and hips close to front of step. Press with your arms, raising back up until arms are extended. Then swing hips back through arms until legs are straight and hips brush over top of step. Bring hips back to front of step, with arms straight and knees bent. Slowly lower in front of step to begin second rep. *To decrease intensity, place feet closer to bottom of step, with knees more bent. To intensify, hold one leg up as you lower and move hips back through arms; alternate legs.*

▶ **Rows:** Standing at top of stairs, grasp stair post hand over hand, or wrap a towel around post and grasp ends of towel with both hands. With feet hip-width apart and positioned 2 feet from stair post, sit back into squat position. Flex elbows, and pull chest toward post, working biceps and back. Slowly release.

▼ **Bent-Over Leg Extensions:** Standing at top of stairs, grasp top of stair post with both hands; feet should be about 2 feet away from bottom of post. Lean forward from hips. Lift one leg to the back and slightly to the side diagonally. Curl heel to buttocks. Straighten leg, and slowly lower. Perform 10 to 12 reps on one side before switching to opposite side, or alternate legs between each lift.

Chapter 66

Challenge 4

Constant Cravings, Hidden Binges

"Once I start snacking, I just can't stop, especially when I'm home at night."

Secret: Appetite-Taming Tricks

THE SKINNY ON SNACKING

Many nutrition experts—including the ones at *Cooking Light*—often recommend munching between meals to maintain your energy and prevent you from devouring too much at lunch or dinner. A new study questions that advice, though, even suggesting that the only thing snacking thwarts is your ability to manage the size of your middle.

Here's the scoop: French researchers gave lunch to a group of young men and then monitored when they requested dinner and how many calories they consumed. On three subsequent days, they were served the identical lunch plus a 250-calorie snack of toast, jam, and cheese. The researchers suspected the men would want to delay or at least eat less during dinner. But the snack didn't curb their appetite for supper at all. On each occasion, they asked for dinner at the same time and ate just as much of it as they did on the day they went snackless.

The researchers suspect that the men may have nibbled primarily because they thought they had to, rather than because they were hungry. While the study's sample was limited to men, which makes it difficult to draw general conclusions, it does raise an interesting point: Lots of people—57 percent of women and 47 percent of men, according to a recent national survey—snack when their tummies aren't rumbling.

So where does that leave them? "Overweight," says Leslie Bonci, R.D., a Pittsburgh-based spokesperson for The American Dietetic Association. "An extra 250 calories a day can pack on a pound every two weeks."

But this doesn't mean that you should give up between-meal noshing altogether in the name of waist control. Snacking is still an effective way of giving you much-needed bursts of energy throughout the day, helping you meet your daily quotas for important nutrients, and keeping your appetite from getting the best of you at mealtime—if, that is, you snack smart.

"Nutrition experts are not wrong about the healthfulness of snacking, but perhaps we haven't been clear that you should have a snack only when your stomach wants it," states Connie Roberts, R.D., a nutritionist at Brigham & Women's Hospital in Boston. "Even people in the French study may not have accepted the snack if they thought they had a choice."

If you're one of those folks who visit the vending machine, pantry, or convenience store for reasons other than hunger, work on identifying why. Are you bored? Join a book group or call a friend. Tense? Take a lavender bath. Mad? Go out to the driving range and see how far you can hit the ball. "Distract yourself in healthy ways until they become a habit," suggests Mike Bowers, Psy.D., former chief clinical psychologist at the University of Colorado's Weight Management Center in Denver.

Once you learn to snack only when your stomach calls, chances are you will eat less at subsequent meals, Roberts adds. Why? She explains that it takes the food you eat about 20 minutes to start making a dent in your hunger. If you begin a meal ravenous, you may eat so quickly that you've polished off a second helping before you feel even the slightest bit full. In this case, a modest premeal snack could keep you from stuffing yourself. Which brings us to this question: When your stomach sounds like a symphony, what should you snack on?

SNACK STRATEGIES

Use the following advice to make healthy snack selections.

Check out the calories. Opt for 50- or 100-calorie snacks if your next meal is within an hour or two, 150 to 200 if it's going to be longer than that. It'll be just enough to keep you satisfied. (For suggestions, see "16 Superior Snacks" on the next page.)

16 SUPERIOR SNACKS

Snack time's a prime time to work nutritious foods into your diet. If you're hungry for something—but not sure what—figure out how many calories to consume (50 to 100 if your next meal is within two hours; 150 to 200 if it's more than that). Then reach for one of these no-fuss, stay-full snacks that deliver energy and much-needed nutrients. You can even find a few of them in your office vending machine.

50 calories

- 1 mini milk chocolate candy bar
- 1½ cups low-fat microwave popcorn with ¾ tablespoon grated Parmesan cheese
- ⅓ cup low-fat cottage cheese
- 1 tomato, sliced, with a small piece (about ½ ounce) of part-skim mozzarella cheese
- ¾ cup cantaloupe, cubed, and 1 slice deli turkey

100 calories

- 1 fat-free pudding cup
- 15 baby carrots and 2 tablespoons low-fat ranch dressing
- ½ cup whole-fruit sorbet
- ½ cup fat-free frozen yogurt
- 1 (1-ounce) box raisins
- 1 ounce pretzels

150 calories

- 1 cup fat-free milk and 2 ginger snaps
- 1 Nutri-Grain cereal bar
- 1 hard-cooked egg on a slice of whole wheat toast
- 1 baked apple topped with 1 teaspoon cinnamon and 1 tablespoon caramel sauce
- 1 ounce soy nuts
- 1 ounce Terra Chips (flavors such as Spiced Taro, Jalapeño Sweet Potato, and Yukon Gold)

200 calories

- 1 cup plain low-fat yogurt with ½ cup raspberries and 1 teaspoon chopped walnuts
- 25 red grapes, 3 tablespoons feta cheese, and 6 Ry-Krisp crackers
- 1 (1¼-ounce) bag peanuts
- 1 (1⅓-ounce) package peanut butter-on-wheat crackers

Think outside the bag. Sure, it's easy to grab a bag of chips (Americans ate 11 million pounds of them on Super Bowl Sunday alone). But look beyond the usual choices—pretzels, popcorn, and chips—and focus on fruits, vegetables, and dairy products.

Focus on fiber and protein. A snack containing at least a little protein will keep you fuller longer. Snacks that are high in fiber are also more filling than low-fiber snacks. Fruits, vegetables, and whole grains are fiber-rich; low-fat dairy products, legumes, nuts, and lean meat are packed with protein. Whenever you can, combine the two—spread a little peanut butter on your banana, or top your whole wheat crackers with tuna salad or hummus.

Don't forsake your favorites. Sweet snacks are unlikely to contain enough protein or fiber to fill you up until mealtime. But you needn't—and shouldn't—banish them completely. "You just can't say, 'I'll never eat another Oreo again.' It's a surefire way to devour the whole bag," Bowers says. You may be able to pair your snack-of-choice with a protein- or fiber-rich food—Oreos and fat-free milk, for instance. If it's not that easy, build small portions of your favorite snack foods—no matter how vitamin-vacant they are—into your regular meals when you're hungry. "Plan to have two Oreos with your lunch on Wednesdays or for dessert on Friday," Bowers suggests.

Avoid a snack-food rut. Have different kinds of snacks every day so you get a variety of nutrients.

—*Karen Cicero*

SURVIVING THE SNACK BAR

Making it through a Saturday night at the movies without hitting the snack bar is a supreme test of anyone's will. Is there any hope? Can a health-conscious cinephile find any joy in noshing at the multiplex?

Act I: A Savory Solution. Movie popcorn is no low-fat treat. Although many theaters now pop up fresh batches using heart-friendly canola oil, a small bag of just the plain stuff—even without the fake-butter flavoring used by some vendors—still contains 360 calories and 22 grams of fat. Want salt with your flicks? Try a baked pretzel instead.

Act II: Sweet Success. Stay away from Godzilla-size confections. One super-size Snickers, for example, weighs in at 510 calories and 24 grams of fat. If you can't find your favorite candy in a smaller package, it's OK to go gargantuan—just split it with your movie mate.

Act III: Think Small. Some theaters offer a kid-size popcorn bag (usually about two-thirds the size of a small), and other theaters even offer a kind of kid's meal—a trio of scaled-down popcorn, candy, and drink. Consider buying the small-fry size to keep your intake low.

Act IV: Surprise Ending. Many theaters offer coffee or even cappuccino. Order yours with fat-free milk, and sip slowly through the show. You may lose your appetite for the snack-bar stuff altogether.

10 LOW-CALORIE CHOCOLATE TREATS

Satisfy your sweet tooth with any one of these guilt-free chocolate snacks. They're all under 120 calories.

1. 1 sugar-free chocolate soft drink: 0 calories
2. 1 chocolate-flavored rice cake with 1 tablespoon reduced-calorie whipped topping: 86 calories
3. 2 tablespoons chocolate-covered raisins: 95 calories
4. 4 bite-size chocolate-coated caramel and creamy nougat bars: 97 calories
5. 1 chocolate fudge pop: 100 calories
6. 1 individual chocolate fat-free pudding cup: 100 calories
7. 4 milk chocolate kisses: 104 calories
8. 2 cream-filled chocolate sandwich cookies: 107 calories
9. 1 packet hot chocolate mix (prepared with water): 112 calories
10. 1 cup chocolate chip cookie-flavored dry cereal: 120 calories

TOP 10 BINGE BUSTERS

1. **Curb your cravings.** If it's a fudge brownie or other rich sweet that tempts you, indulge just a little. Buy one small treat, or split it with a friend. You'll skimp on calories and satisfy your cravings. If chocolate is your weakness, see the list on the previous page of "low-calorie" chocolate snacks.

2. **Plan to indulge.** That's right. It's okay to enjoy high-fat, high-calorie foods now and then. Cutting certain foods completely from your diet only makes you want them more. So enjoy a treat occasionally.

3. **Know your limits.** It's important to realize what triggers your overeating. If you know you can't stop with just a few potato chips, don't buy a super-size bag. Buy an individual serving bag.

4. **Shop smart.** If the food's not in your pantry, you can't reach for it when a crisis strikes. Before you head to the grocery store, decide what you are and aren't going to buy.

5. **Drink up.** Too often, people mistake thirst for hunger. Aim for a minimum of 8 (8-ounce) glasses of water daily. Sugar-free, non-caffeinated beverages count toward that goal.

6. **Make a move.** If you are physically active, you're less likely to overindulge a craving. Who wants to spoil a fantastic workout by blowing it on a huge slice of cheesecake?

7. **Eat everything.** There's really no such thing as an unhealthy food— just unhealthy portions. Eat a variety of foods, and think moderation, not deprivation.

8. **Open wide.** Tempted to keep eating after a meal? Brush your teeth or gargle with mouthwash as soon as you finish eating. That's a mental cue that you've finished eating, and you'll wash away your taste for food.

9. **Get soupy.** Choose a yummy broth-based soup for your first course at dinner, and you'll fill up fast with very few calories and be less tempted to overeat during the rest of the meal.

10. **Eat breakfast.** A morning meal will help you avoid a raid on the vending machine at 10 a.m., as well as help you burn calories more efficiently during the day.

Chapter 67

Eating Out

"I do just fine with my eating plan when
I'm cooking my own meals and eating at home,
but when I go out, I blow it."

Secret: Savvy Selections

Good Tips

According to a Japanese proverb, your life is extended 75 days for every new food you taste. If that's true, it's becoming easier than ever to lengthen your life span, given the recent explosion of restaurants offering authentic dishes from around the world. Since many restaurants don't inform you whether their dishes are low-fat or low-sodium (yet), *Cooking Light* looked at some popular choices to determine which are the healthiest. But as with all dining—and cooking—some general tips apply:

- Order sauces on the side, especially creamy ones or those high in sodium.
- Remember that grilled or baked entrées tend to be the healthiest.
- Don't be nervous about communicating your needs to a waiter.
- Ask questions about food preparation and be clear about changes you want.
- Be respectful and open to cultural differences if you are eating in an ethnic restaurant.

As French author and gastronome Jean-Anthelme Brillat-Savarin once mused, "The discovery of a new dish does more for human happiness than the discovery of a new star." So head out to that unknown restaurant with confidence—your road to happiness can easily be delicious and healthy. Here are some strategies to help you on your journey.

CARIBBEAN

These are the flavors of Africa and Spain, with a bit of the tropics thrown in. Common ingredients include hot peppers, spicy meat rubs, seafood, tropical fruits (especially coconut and mango), and root vegetables.

Best bets:

Jerk chicken: Seasoned with hot peppers, onions, and spices, then smoked; often served with mango and/or other tropical fruits.

Stew peas and rice: Seasoned pork or beef and kidney beans served over rice; spinners (flour dumplings) are often added.

Escoveitch fish: Lightly pan-fried, then cooked in a marinade of onions, bell peppers, carrots, and vinegar; often served with rice, plantains, and tropical fruit chutney.

Thumbs down:

Rice and beans (or rice and peas): Not a plain mix of healthy basic ingredients, this dish often features coconut milk, which is high in saturated fat.

Tips for the savvy Caribbean diner:

- Most callaloo (one-pot) dishes contain salt pork and coconut milk, so ask before ordering.
- Beware of Scotch bonnet peppers—they're some of the hottest known to man.

JAPANESE

A simple cuisine without lots of seasonings—with the exceptions of soy sauce and wasabi, a spicy horseradish paste served on the side. (The two are mixed together to create a dipping sauce.) Appearance and presentation are extremely important in Japanese cooking. Key ingredients include fish, rice and noodles, soy and soybeans, seaweed, and vegetables (often pickled).

Best bets:

Chicken sukiyaki: One-pot dish of chicken, tofu, bamboo shoots, and vegetables simmered in broth at your table. Try this without the egg-based dipping sauce that's often provided.

Shabu-shabu: Sliced beef and vegetables with noodles, cooked and served at the table. This dish comes with dipping sauces that are high in sodium, so use them sparingly.

Nigiri sushi: Pieces of fresh fish served on vinegared rice, secured with a seaweed wrap (called nori), and served with soy sauce, wasabi, and pickled ginger.

If you're a beginner, ask which types of fish are cooked—not all sushi is raw.

Thumbs down:

Tempura: While assorted vegetables are usually a healthy choice, these have been battered and fried, significantly raising their fat and calorie counts.

Tips for the savvy Japanese diner:

- Go easy on soy and teriyaki sauces as well as miso dressing, since they contain a lot of sodium. Get them on the side when possible, ask for a smaller amount, or ask if low-sodium sauces are available.
- **Sushi eaters:** Don't overdo it on higher-fat fishes such as yellowtail, salmon, and eel.

MEDITERRANEAN, MIDDLE/NEAR EASTERN

Think olives and olive oil—and lots of stuffed dishes. Common ingredients include cheese (feta is extremely popular), bread (especially pita), grains and legumes (lots of chickpeas), eggplant, okra, garlic, lemon, lamb, beef, and yogurt.

Best bets:

Souvlaki: Greek dish of marinated, grilled meat served in a pita with lettuce, tomatoes, onions, and a yogurt-cucumber (tzatziki) sauce.

Gyro: Strips of lean, seared, spicy beef served in a pita with lettuce, tomatoes, and onions. Ask for sauce on the side.

Lah me june (Armenian pizza): Dough topped with ground meat, parsley, tomatoes, onions, and spices.

Couscous: Steamed wheat grain, usually served with fish, beef, chicken, lamb, or vegetables in a spicy red sauce.

Thumbs down:

Falafel: A vegetable patty made with fava beans and chickpeas has to be healthy, right? Unfortunately, it's fried and full of fat.

Tips for the savvy Mediterranean or Middle/Near Eastern diner:

- Recipes that use phyllo dough, such as baklava (pastry filled with nuts and honey) and spanakopita (spinach pie) generally contain lots of butter and oil.
- Tahini, a ground sesame-seed paste used in hummus and other dishes, is virtually all fat. Ask for this on the side, if possible, and use it in small amounts.
- Avoid béchamel (a rich white sauce), which tops such popular dishes as moussaka (eggplant-and-ground-lamb casserole).
- Watch for the Greek word lathera, especially with soups and stews—it indicates a dish has been cooked in lots of olive oil.

KOREAN

Characterized by tabletop cooking and lots of condiments, this cuisine promises a variety of simple but robust flavors. Common ingredients include rice, noodles, mung beans, meat (especially beef), seafood, garlic, soy/miso, and kimchi (a spicy vegetable pickle considered the national dish of Korea).

Best bets:

Pindaettok (Korean pizza): Thick pancake made from ground mung beans and topped with marinated meat and vegetables.

Chongol: Strips of beef, sliced vegetables, and tofu cooked in simmering broth at your table. This is a great one to order because you can control what's added.

Bibimbop: A one-dish meal of rice, beef, and vegetables served with red-pepper sauce and kimchi on the side. An egg usually tops the dish.

Chopchae: Sautéed cellophane noodles often served with vegetables and beef (if desired). Your healthiest bet is to ask for vegetables only.

Bulgogi: Although barbecue may not sound light, this dish—thin slices of marinated beef barbecued at your table and wrapped in lettuce with rice and spicy accompaniments—isn't bad if you forgo the dipping sauces, which can add a lot of sodium.

Tip for the savvy Korean diner:

• Control your sodium intake by going easy on the dipping sauces.

THAI

Thai food is hot, spicy, sweet, sour, and aromatic, with hints of both Indian and Asian cuisines. Some common ingredients include chile peppers, rice and noodles, nam pla (fish sauce), sugar, lime and other fruits, fish, chicken, and fresh vegetables.

Best bets:

Thai chicken: Chicken sautéed with onions, mushrooms, pineapple, scallions, and chiles, served in a pineapple. Request that the chef prepare the dish without nuts.

Poy sian: Seafood sautéed with straw mushrooms, napa cabbage, bamboo shoots, onions, and string beans.

Gai yang: Grilled marinated chicken served on fresh cabbage with a sweet (fat-free) chile sauce and steamed rice. No fat is added to cooked meat. Ask for the sauce on the side.

Thumbs down:

Pad thai: The noodles in this dish are stir-fried with lots of oil to keep them from sticking to the pan. Ground peanuts and egg add to the fat count.

Tips for the savvy Thai diner:

- Skip nam prik (a spicy peanut sauce) and sao nam (which contains coconut); both are very high in fat. Healthier sauce choices include those made with basil, chiles, and lime juice.
- Go easy on the nam pla and soy sauce, which are both high in sodium.
- Ask if the chef is cooking with lard or coconut oil; if so, you should request vegetable oil, which contains less saturated fat, instead.
- Don't be afraid to ask for more vegetables and less protein in a dish.
- When you order, remember that the spiciness of a dish can be adjusted to your tastes.

VIETNAMESE

A balance of understated flavors emphasizing lightness and freshness. Common ingredients include rice, seafood, pork, vegetables, chicken, beef, lemongrass, and herbs. Dipping sauces—nuoc nam (a ubiquitous fish sauce), chile sauce, lime juice—and toppings—bean sprouts, basil, mint, garlic, coriander—are provided at the table.

Best bets:

Pho: Hearty, filling soup with beef or chicken, rice noodles, and herbs. You add the garnishes. The sodium in this dish may be high, so go easy on the soy sauce and nuoc nam.

Bun: Grilled pork, beef, or shrimp marinated in a sweet/hot/sour/salty mixture and served over rice noodles and often topped with nuts. You add your own sauces and seasonings.

Grilled lemongrass chicken: This dish is served with rice papers, lettuce, and fresh herbs that you make into a roll and dip in the sauces of your choice.

Beef fondue: Not the usual oil-based fondue, this dish features meat in a vinegary broth with aromatics and no added fat.

Tips for the savvy Vietnamese diner:

- Ask if meat or fish can be cooked or sautéed in broth instead of oil.
- Nuoc nam is high in sodium, so use it sparingly.
- Clay-pot dishes tend to be heavy on fat and sodium. Ask if the meat or fish in them is fried. If it is, you may want to try something else.

Salad Bar Savvy

At first glance, eating from the salad bar seems like a wise choice for weight control. It can be if you make good choices, but there are plenty of high-fat, high-sugar items that can sabatoge your good intentions. To make the best selections, walk around the salad bar and survey the items before you start piling things on your plate.

- Select low-fat items such as lettuce, broccoli, spinach, carrots, cauliflower, bell peppers, tomatoes, onions, fresh fruit, and low-fat salad dressings.
- Avoid high-fat items such as chow mein noodles, pepperoni, coleslaw, pasta salad, potato salad, pea salad, marinated vegetable salads, and regular salad dressings. And go easy on the cheese and the croutons.
- If there are no low-fat salad dressings, use a regular dressing and dilute it with lemon juice or vinegar. Or dress your salad with oil and vinegar, using less oil and more vinegar.
- Select fresh fruit—the canned variety usually is the kind packed in heavy syrup and is higher in calories than the fresh.
- Select broth-based soups instead of cream soups.
- Eat slowly and fill up so that you don't have time to return to the salad bar for seconds.

Pizza

- Order thin-crust pizzas.
- If you want meat on your pizza, select only one meat topping, and choose a low-fat meat such as chicken or lean ham.
- Go for the low-fat, high-fiber veggie toppings: mushrooms, bell peppers, onions, and tomatoes. Some pizza restaurants have additional vegetable choices such as spinach and broccoli, or even fruit pizzas.
- The meat-free pizzas are often a good choice, but don't ask for extra cheese because that adds a lot more fat.
- Fill up on a salad, so then you'll be less tempted to eat extra slices of pizza.

CHINESE

- Leave off deep-fried items such as tempura, fried won tons and dumplings, egg rolls, crispy noodles, and fried chicken wings.
- Request steamed rice instead of fried.
- Remember that chow mein dishes and egg foo yong dishes are much higher in fat than the vegetable and meat, chicken, or shrimp stir-fries.
- Order individual stir-fry items instead of combination plates, which come with high-fat egg rolls and fried rice.
- If you need to limit sodium, ask if reduced-sodium soy sauce is available.
- Ask about the house specials: Some restaurants offer lobster, scallops, shrimp, and other low-fat seafood stir-fries.
- Pay attention to portion sizes when you are spooning rice onto your plate.
- Eat with chop sticks. It will take you longer to eat, and when you eat slowly, you fill up faster and eat less.

TEX-MEX

- Choose black beans instead of refried beans, which are usually fried in lard.
- Order items with soft flour tortillas instead of crispy fried corn tortillas.
- Ask the waiter not to bring the basket of chips, or, if you can, place it at the opposite end of the table from where you are sitting to help avoid mindless munching.
- Order an appetizer and a tossed green salad, or order individual items and side dishes instead of the large-portioned, high-fat combination dishes.
- Request low-fat sour cream if it's available. Or ask for the sour cream on the side, and use less of the regular.
- Use salsa to add flavor instead of high-fat sour cream or guacamole.
- If you're ordering an alcoholic beverage, order a beer instead of a margarita, which is high in sugar (and salt).   —*Su Reid, Anne Cain*

Chapter 68

No Time to Cook

"It's hard to prepare healthful, low-fat meals
when you work full time and have a family to feed.
There's just no time!"

Secret: Cook-Quick Tricks

Fast-Break Breakfasts

Those of us concerned about our health, waistlines, mental acuity, and physical energy might as well admit it: Mom was right—breakfast is one meal you don't want to miss.

Eating breakfast may actually trigger healthy habits such as keeping a regular meal schedule and avoiding excessive snacking. Plus, it may be instrumental in weight control. Researchers at the Mayo Clinic found that breakfast eaters started their days with significantly higher metabolic rates than breakfast skippers, equivalent to burning an average of 150 additional calories every 24 hours. (Don't scoff: That's about three Oreo cookies.)

> The Mayo Clinic found that breakfast eaters start their day with significantly higher metabolic rates than breakfast skippers.

Eating breakfast doesn't just stoke your calorie-burning furnace, it also fires up your brain. One of many studies on children who ate breakfast found they performed significantly better on standardized tests than kids who didn't eat breakfast. Though such research hasn't been done on adults, many nutritionists suspect breakfast may exert similar effects among mature audiences. If nothing else, eating breakfast prevents that gnawing feeling in your stomach in the middle of the morning.

The morning meal is a great opportunity to stockpile certain nutrients most people don't get enough of—fiber and calcium in particular. The best breakfasts are high in complex carbohydrates such as whole grains and cereals, with some protein to help you sustain your energy. Devising a menu that fits these guidelines is relatively easy on days

QUICK BREAKFAST SOLUTIONS

Within reason, almost any quick breakfast item can be the centerpiece of a healthful morning meal. How? By adding other no-prep foods and by balancing breakfast indulgences with better choices throughout the day. We've analyzed the following fast breakfast staples, particularly focusing on fiber and calcium, which are deficient in most people's diets. Plus, we offer specific suggestions for turning each into a more nutritious meal.

Deli-style bagel, plain (3 ounces) Add "boosters" to increase fiber and calcium intake. Fiber boosters such as 1 cup of raspberries (60 calories, 8.4g fiber) or strawberries (45 calories, 3.4g fiber) will add fiber without many calories. Fat-free milk is the perfect low-calorie calcium-booster; ½ cup contains about 40 calories and 150mg calcium.

Bakery-style blueberry muffin (4 ounces) Consider a low-fat muffin instead, to cut down on both total and saturated fat. If you must indulge, get extra fiber, protein, and calcium later in the day.

Yogurt (8 ounces) Quick and portable, yogurt is a high-protein, high-calcium breakfast choice. Choose low-fat or fat-free yogurt, and, to reduce calories further, select yogurt flavored with a low-calorie sweetener. To increase fiber, stir in low-fat granola or fresh fruit.

McDonald's Egg McMuffin (1) Not bad for fast food. A fat-free milk chaser will increase calcium while keeping calories in line, but you'll have to rely on other meals for fiber.

Kellogg's Corn Flakes (1 cup) Surprisingly low in fiber, as are other standbys such as Rice Krispies. Mix with ¾ cup Kellogg's Bran Flakes (140 calories, 5g fiber) to increase fiber.

when you actually have time to cook. But what about when you're in a rush? How can you make sure those gobble-and-go meals give you what you need nutritionally, without much extra effort?

To aid in your quest for a quick-and-healthy breakfast, we compiled the following chart of favorite "fast-breakers." These suggestions should make it easier for you to start all your days healthfully, as well as tastefully. —*Jim Thornton, Su Reid*

Cheerios (1 cup) Boost fiber with berries and ¼ cup Grape-Nuts (105 calories, 2.5g fiber). Wash it down with calcium-fortified orange juice.

Post Spoon-Size Shredded Wheat (1 cup) Try Post Shredded Wheat 'N Bran, which packs 6.3 grams of fiber per cup. Boost fiber further with berries, and add calcium with ½ cup calcium-fortified orange juice or ½ cup low-fat yogurt.

Quaker 100% Natural Granola (½ cup) Check out the serving size: ½ cup isn't much. Choose a low-fat granola, and add extra fat-free milk and some berries to help you reach optimum nutrient levels.

Quaker Instant Oatmeal, Apples & Cinnamon (2 packets) Prepare with ½ cup water and ½ cup fat-free milk to help you meet your calcium goals. Add extra apple to increase your fiber—one medium apple has 81 calories and 3.7g fiber.

Nutri-Grain Bar, Strawberry (1) Add milk, yogurt, or 1 ounce low-fat Cheddar cheese for additional calcium and protein, and an apple, pear, or banana for fiber.

White toast (2 slices, with 2 teaspoons butter) Use less butter or margarine to reduce saturated fat and/or trans fat. Or top your toast with peanut butter for added protein and heart-healthy monounsaturated fat. For an extra 2.6 grams of fiber, consider using wheat bread.

Eggo Blueberry Waffles (2) Great source of calcium. Complete your meal with a cup of raspberries or an apple and some strawberries for fiber.

5 Superfast Suppers

Calling for pizza delivery is really not necessary when you can get a meal on the table in less than 30 minutes. Not only will it save you time and money, we guarantee you'll feel more satisfied.

Menu 1

- Salmon on Greens with Lime-Ginger Dressing

- Pumpernickel bread

Game Plan

1. Squeeze limes for juice.
2. Peel and slice mangoes; grate ginger.
3. Prepare lime-ginger mixture.
4. Broil salmon.
5. Arrange salmon and mango on greens.

1 SALMON ON GREENS WITH LIME-GINGER DRESSING

Prep: 10 minutes • Cook: 12 minutes

²⁄₃ cup fresh lime juice (about 5 limes)
½ cup honey
½ teaspoon grated peeled fresh ginger
4 (6-ounce) skinned salmon fillets (about 1 inch thick)
Cooking spray
¼ teaspoon salt
8 cups gourmet salad greens
1 cup sliced peeled mango

1. Preheat broiler.

2. Combine first 3 ingredients in a small bowl, reserving ¾ cup juice mixture for dressing. Place salmon fillets on a broiler pan coated with cooking spray. Baste fillets with remaining juice mixture. Broil 4 minutes on each side or until desired degree of doneness, basting once after turning. Sprinkle fillets with salt.

3. Divide salad greens evenly among 4 plates; arrange salmon and mango on top of greens. Drizzle with reserved dressing. Yield: 4 servings (serving size: 2 cups greens, 1 fillet, ¼ cup mango, and 3 tablespoons dressing).

CALORIES 462 (28% from fat); FAT 14.5g (sat 2.5g, mono 6.8g, poly 3.2g); PROTEIN 37.2g; CARB 48.3g; FIBER 2.5g; CHOL 111mg; IRON 2.2mg; SODIUM 243mg; CALC 60mg EXCHANGES: 3 Starch, 4 Lean Meat

- Spicy Thai Coconut Shrimp
- Broiled pineapple spears

Game Plan

1. Peel and devein shrimp.
2. Slice asparagus and onions.
3. Cook rice.
4. Prepare and sauté shrimp mixture.
5. Broil pineapple.

2 SPICY THAI COCONUT SHRIMP

Prep: 20 minutes • Cook: 10 minutes

2	cups uncooked rice
1½	tablespoons water
1½	teaspoons red curry paste or chile paste with garlic
1½	pounds medium shrimp, peeled and deveined
	Cooking spray
2½	cups (1-inch) sliced asparagus (about ¾ pound)
1½	cups sliced green onions
½	teaspoon salt
1	(14-ounce) can light coconut milk

1. Cook rice according to package directions, omitting salt and fat.

2. Combine water and curry paste in a medium bowl; add shrimp, tossing to coat. Place a large nonstick skillet coated with cooking spray over medium-high heat until hot. Add shrimp mixture, and sauté 4 minutes. Add asparagus and green onions; cover and cook 3 minutes or until asparagus is crisp-tender. Stir in salt and coconut milk. Cook 3 minutes or until thoroughly heated, stirring occasionally. Serve over rice. Yield: 4 servings (serving size: 1¼ cups shrimp sauce and 1 cup rice).

CALORIES 457 (16% from fat); FAT 8.1g (sat 4g, mono 1g, poly 1.4g); PROTEIN 32.9g; CARB 57.8g; FIBER 3.9g; CHOL 194mg; IRON 6.9mg; SODIUM 646mg; CALC 135mg EXCHANGES: 3 Starch, 2 Vegetable, 3 Lean Meat

To save even more time, have the seafood market peel and devein the shrimp.

Menu 3

- Bell Pepper-Feta Pasta Toss
- Mixed greens with red onion and cucumber
- Pita wedges

Game Plan

1. Cook pasta.
2. Quarter tomatoes and cut peppers.
3. Prepare salad.
4. Combine pasta, vegetables, and cheese.

3 BELL PEPPER-FETA PASTA TOSS

Prep: 6 minutes • Cook: 15 minutes

6 ounces uncooked linguine
1 large yellow or red bell pepper, seeded and cut into strips
1¼ cups quartered cherry tomatoes
¾ cup finely chopped fresh parsley
¼ teaspoon salt
1 (4-ounce) package crumbled feta cheese with basil
1 (2¼-ounce) can or ¼ cup sliced ripe olives, drained

1. Cook pasta according to package directions, omitting salt and fat.
2. Place bell pepper in a colander; drain pasta over bell pepper.
3. Combine pasta, bell pepper strips, tomatoes, and remaining ingredients in a large bowl; toss gently. Serve immediately.

Yield: 4 servings (serving size: 1¼ cups).

CALORIES 275 (28% from fat); FAT 8.7g (sat 4.7g, mono 2.6g, poly 0.9g); PROTEIN 10.8g; CARB 39.4g; FIBER 3.3g; CHOL 25mg; IRON 3.8mg; SODIUM 602mg; CALC 181mg EXCHANGES: 2 Starch, 1 Vegetable, 1 High-Fat Meat

Draining the pasta over the bell pepper cooks the pepper slightly before you toss the pepper with the pasta.

Menu 4

- Spinach Calzones with Blue Cheese
- Bell pepper strips

Game Plan

1. Slice onion and mushrooms.
2. Top dough with garlic, vegetables, and cheese.
3. Bake calzones.
4. Slice pepper strips.

4 SPINACH CALZONES WITH BLUE CHEESE

Prep: 18 minutes • Cook: 12 minutes

1 (10-ounce) can refrigerated pizza crust
Cooking spray
4 garlic cloves, minced
4 cups spinach leaves
8 (⅛-inch-thick) slices onion
1⅓ cups sliced mushrooms
¾ cup (3 ounces) crumbled blue cheese

1. Preheat oven to 425°.

2. Unroll dough onto a baking sheet coated with cooking spray; cut into 4 quarters. Pat each quarter into a 6 x 5-inch rectangle. Sprinkle garlic evenly over rectangles. Top each rectangle with 1 cup spinach, 2 onion slices, ⅓ cup mushrooms, and 3 tablespoons cheese. Bring 2 opposite corners to center, pinching points to seal. Bring remaining 2 corners to center, pinching all points together to seal. Bake at 425° for 12 minutes or until golden. Yield: 4 servings (serving size: 1 calzone).

CALORIES 297 (28% from fat); FAT 9.1g (sat 4g, mono 3.2g, poly 1g); PROTEIN 13.4g; CARB 40.7g; FIBER 5.1g; CHOL 16mg; IRON 3.8mg; SODIUM 818mg; CALC 180mg EXCHANGES: 2 Starch, 2 Vegetable, ½ High-Fat Meat, 1 Fat

Menu 5

• Orzo with Chicken and Asiago
• Spinach-grapefruit salad
• Breadsticks

Game Plan

1. Cook chicken and pasta.
2. Prepare salad.
3. Combine pasta mixture with peas, herbs, and seasonings.

5 ORZO WITH CHICKEN AND ASIAGO

Prep: 5 minutes • Cook: 25 minutes

1 cup water
1 (16-ounce) can fat-free, less-sodium chicken broth
12 ounces skinless, boneless chicken breast, cut into bite-size pieces
1¼ cups uncooked orzo (rice-shaped pasta)
1 cup frozen green peas, thawed
½ cup (2 ounces) grated Asiago cheese, divided
¼ teaspoon salt
¼ teaspoon dried rosemary, basil, or oregano
⅛ teaspoon black pepper

1. Combine water and broth in a Dutch oven; bring to a boil. Add chicken and pasta; bring to a boil. Reduce heat; simmer 12 minutes, stirring occasionally.

2. Remove from heat; stir in peas, ¼ cup cheese, salt, herbs, and pepper. Top each serving with 1 tablespoon cheese. Yield: 4 servings (serving size: 1¼ cups).

CALORIES 384 (14% from fat); FAT 5.9g (sat 2.9g, mono 1.5g, poly 0.7g); PROTEIN 34.3g; CARB 45.7g; FIBER 2.9g; CHOL 64mg; IRON 3.3mg; SODIUM 656mg; CALC 179mg EXCHANGES: 3 Starch, 3 Lean Meat

Timesaving Appliances

"All you need is a little help from your friends." The friends, in this case,
are a few of your kitchen appliances. With these helpful appliances,
you can save yourself from spending hours in the kitchen, and still end up with
a great meal. Here are some of our best recipes for the pressure cooker,
microwave oven, slow cooker, and yes, even the freezer.

Pressure Cooker

Pressure cookers cut stovetop time significantly while producing some quite succulent meals. And today's retooled versions can withstand human error without blowing their tops, thanks to special new safety devices.

Once you've got the pot closed and cooking, you're free to do other things. In about an hour, our New Mexican Pork Chili or Beef Bourguignonne will be ready for the table. Taste the results. Even the most harried cooks will look forward to the nights they can cook under pressure.

Pressure Cooker Recipes ▶

HIGH-PRESSURE QUESTIONS

How do pressure cookers work so fast? The liquid in the recipe boils and turns to steam. The cooker locks in the steam, and the pressure builds, which allows the temperature inside to superheat very rapidly.

Why brown meats first? Browning produces a caramelized flavor in the meat. The caramelized exterior then dissolves in the liquid in which it's cooked, adding to the overall flavor.

Do they explode? Some of the older models popped their tops if too much steam built up. But the new versions have special safety devices that allow the steam to escape, even with the lid in place.

Which foods work best? Most meats, especially tougher cuts, take very well to pressure cooking and become much more tender. Same with grains and with longer-cooking vegetables such as potatoes. Don't use your pressure cooker for anything that cooks really fast anyway, such as fish, or with fresh vegetables such as tomatoes, asparagus, corn, or summer squash. They'll cook too long and turn mushy.

New Mexican Pork Chili

1 (2-pound) boned pork loin
 roast, cut into 1-inch cubes
2 teaspoons vegetable oil
2 tablespoons chili powder
1 tablespoon ground cumin
½ teaspoon salt
2 cups coarsely chopped onion
6 garlic cloves, chopped
1½ cups water
1 cup coarsely chopped seeded
 Anaheim chiles (about 3 chiles)
¾ cup dried pinto beans
1 tablespoon chopped drained
 canned chipotle chile in adobo
 sauce
1 (14.5-ounce) can no-salt-added
 stewed tomatoes, undrained
1 (10½-ounce) can beef broth
½ cup chopped fresh cilantro
½ cup fat-free sour cream
½ cup chopped tomato

1. Trim fat from pork.
2. Heat oil in a 6-quart pressure cooker over medium heat. Add pork; sprinkle with chili powder, cumin, and salt. Sauté 5 minutes. Add onion and garlic; sauté 2 minutes. Stir in water, Anaheim chiles, beans, chipotle chile, stewed tomatoes, and broth. Close lid securely; bring to high pressure over high heat (about 3 minutes). Adjust heat to medium or level needed to maintain high pressure, and cook 40 minutes. Place pressure

cooker under cold running water. Remove lid; skim fat from surface. Stir in cilantro. Ladle soup into each of 8 bowls; top each serving with sour cream and chopped tomato. Yield: 8 servings (serving size: 1 cup chili, 1 tablespoon sour cream, and 1 tablespoon chopped tomato).

CALORIES 308 (30% from fat); FAT 10g (sat 3.1g, mono 4.2g, poly 1.7g); PROTEIN 30.4g; CARB 24g; FIBER 4.1g; CHOL 64mg; IRON 3.7mg; SODIUM 471mg; CALC 80mg EXCHANGES: 1 Starch, 2 Vegetable, 3 Lean Meat

Beef Bourguignonne

1½ pounds boned chuck roast,
 cut into 1-inch cubes
¼ cup all-purpose flour
½ teaspoon salt
½ teaspoon black pepper
2 bacon slices, diced
½ cup dry red wine
1 (10½-ounce) can beef broth
3 cups baby carrots
3 cups sliced shiitake mushrooms
2 teaspoons dried thyme
6 shallots, halved (about ½ pound)
4 garlic cloves, thinly sliced
7 cups cooked medium egg noodles

1. Combine first 4 ingredients in a zip-top plastic bag. Seal and shake to coat.
2. Cook half of bacon in a 6-quart pressure cooker over medium heat 30 seconds. Add half of beef; cook 5 minutes

or until browned. Remove beef mixture from cooker. Repeat with remaining bacon and beef. Return beef to cooker. Stir in wine and broth, scraping pan to loosen browned bits. Add carrots, mushrooms, thyme, shallots, and garlic. Close lid securely; bring to high pressure over high heat (about 6 minutes). Adjust heat to medium or level needed to maintain high pressure; cook 20 minutes. Remove from heat; place pressure cooker under cold running water. Remove lid. Serve stew over noodles. Yield: 7 servings (serving size: 1 cup stew and 1 cup noodles).

CALORIES 376 (30% from fat); FAT 12.5g (sat 4.5g, mono 5.4g, poly 1.3g); PROTEIN 24.7g; CARB 40.9g; FIBER 3.3g; CHOL 44mg; IRON 5mg; SODIUM 525mg; CALC 53mg EXCHANGES: 2 Starch, 2 Vegetable, 2 Medium-Fat Meat

COOKING WITH WINE

When you cook with wine (or any other type of alcohol), most of the alcohol evaporates and leaves only the rich flavor of the wine. If you don't want to use wine in the Beef Bourguignonne recipe, use ½ cup additional beef broth. Or you can use cooking wine. If you use cooking wine, omit the salt from the recipe because cooking wines usually contain added salt.

Microwave Oven

Use your microwave for more than just reheating—let it help you get the meal on the table in minutes. Try any one of the following speedy spud suppers to see what happens when microwave meets potato. We call it supper.

Potatoes are famous for requiring minimal fuss—and they demand even less if you use your microwave. Most recent models can cook four average-size potatoes (about 1½ pounds) in around 16 minutes. That gives you time to concentrate your creative energy on the final touches.

Microwave Recipes ▼

CHEESY CHICKEN-AND-BROCCOLI POTATOES

4	baking potatoes (about 1½ pounds)
¾	pound skinless, boneless chicken breast, cut into bite-size pieces
1	tablespoon all-purpose flour
1¼	teaspoons paprika, divided
½	teaspoon salt
¼	teaspoon freshly ground black pepper
1	tablespoon butter or margarine
2	cups small broccoli florets
⅔	cup fat-free, less-sodium chicken broth
1	cup (4 ounces) diced light processed cheese (such as Velveeta Light)

1. Pierce potatoes with a fork; arrange in a circle on paper towels in microwave oven. Microwave at HIGH 16 minutes or until done, rearranging potatoes after 8 minutes. Let stand 5 minutes.

2. Combine chicken, flour, 1 teaspoon paprika, salt, and pepper in a large zip-top plastic bag; seal and shake to coat.

3. Melt butter in a large nonstick skillet over medium-high heat. Add chicken mixture and broccoli; sauté 5 minutes. Add broth; bring to a boil, and cook 3 minutes or until chicken is done. Add cheese, stirring just until melted.

4. Split potatoes with a fork, and fluff pulp. Spoon chicken mixture evenly over potatoes; sprinkle with ¼ teaspoon paprika. Yield: 4 servings.

CALORIES 390 (17% from fat); FAT 7.4g (sat 4.2g, mono 1.9g, poly 0.7g); PROTEIN 31.6g; CARB 50.3g; FIBER 4.7g; CHOL 67mg; IRON 3.6mg; SODIUM 904mg; CALC 201mg
EXCHANGES: 3 Starch, 1 Vegetable, 3 Very Lean Meat

WATT'S UP?

Times in these recipes are based on our Test Kitchens' use of several microwave ovens ranging from 650 to 1,000 watts. All cooked the potatoes in 16 minutes and probably would not vary much from your own microwave, but be sure to consult the guide to your own machine for specific instructions. As with all microwave cooking, it's best to monitor for doneness.

PIZZA-TOPPED POTATOES

    4   baking potatoes (about
        1½ pounds)
    2   teaspoons olive oil
    1   cup chopped onion
    1   cup diced green bell pepper
    1   teaspoon bottled minced garlic
    ⅔   cup bottled pizza sauce
    ½   cup turkey pepperoni slices,
        cut in half (about 2 ounces)
    ¼   teaspoon crushed red pepper
    1   cup chopped tomato
    ¼   cup water
    1   cup (4 ounces) preshredded
        part-skim mozzarella cheese

1. Pierce potatoes with a fork; arrange in a circle on paper towels in microwave oven. Microwave at HIGH 16 minutes or until done, rearranging potatoes after 8 minutes. Let stand 5 minutes.

2. Heat oil in a nonstick skillet over medium-high heat. Add onion, bell pepper, and garlic; stir-fry 5 minutes. Add pizza sauce, pepperoni, and red pepper; reduce heat, and simmer 3 minutes. Stir in tomato and water; simmer 3 minutes.

3. Split potatoes with a fork; fluff pulp. Spoon pepperoni mixture over potatoes. Top with cheese. Yield: 4 servings.

CALORIES 374 (24% from fat); FAT 9.9g (sat 4.1g, mono 3.8g, poly 1.3g); PROTEIN 17.1g; CARB 55.4g; FIBER 5.3g; CHOL 37mg; IRON 4.1mg; SODIUM 556mg; CALC 227mg
EXCHANGES: 3 Starch, 2 Vegetable, 1 High-Fat Meat

HAM-AND-SWISS POTATOES

4 baking potatoes (about
   1½ pounds)
1 cup diced 33%-less-sodium ham
   (about 6 ounces)
1 cup (4 ounces) shredded Swiss
   cheese, divided
½ cup thinly sliced green onions,
   divided
½ cup fat-free sour cream
¼ teaspoon freshly ground black
   pepper

1. Pierce potatoes with a fork; arrange
in a circle on paper towels in microwave
oven. Microwave at HIGH 16 minutes
or until done, rearranging potatoes after
8 minutes. Let stand 5 minutes.
2. Preheat broiler.
3. Cut each potato in half lengthwise;
scoop out pulp, leaving a ¼-inch-thick
shell. Combine potato pulp, ham, ½
cup cheese, ⅓ cup green onions, sour
cream, and pepper.
4. Spoon potato mixture into shells.
Combine ½ cup cheese and remaining
green onions, and sprinkle over potatoes.
Place potatoes on a baking sheet; broil 4
minutes or until golden. Yield: 4 servings.

CALORIES 376 (26% from fat); FAT 11g (sat 6.2g,
mono 3.5g, poly 0.7g); PROTEIN 20.1g;
CARB 47.9g; FIBER 3.4g; CHOL 51mg;
IRON 2.9mg; SODIUM 540mg; CALC 359mg
EXCHANGES: 3 Starch, 1 Vegetable,
1 Medium-Fat Meat, 1 Fat

Slow Cooker

Nothing about a slow cooker will slow
you down. This timesaver turns a few
minutes of morning preparation into a
flavor-packed dinner.

On a harried weeknight, there's nothing better than a dinner that takes eight
hours to cook—if you're using a slow
cooker. This device definitely warps time
in your favor. Here's how the magic
works: In the morning, put the ingredients of your choice into the pot, plug it
in, and go do whatever you want. All day
long, your dish will simmer on low heat.
When you return to your kitchen in the
evening, the slow-cooker fairies will be
finished, and your dinner will be fully
cooked. Just pull out the plates, and
you're ready to eat.

Though most popular for cooking
chilis and stews, slow cookers also can
be used for dishes that are usually
prepared in a pan or skillet, such as
chicken Provençale. The slow cooker
is really the way to go. It intensifies
flavor with persistent, gentle heat, giving those few minutes of before-work
prep time a payoff in taste that would
seem to have required hours in the
kitchen. Actually, hours were spent in
the kitchen—but not by you.

Slow Cooker Recipes ▶

THAI-STYLE PORK STEW

Peanut butter melds with classic Asian flavors to lend this one-dish meal a Thai flair. Lime makes a perfect accent.

STEW:

2   pounds boned pork loin, cut into 4 pieces
2   cups (1 x ¼-inch) julienne-cut red bell pepper
¼   cup teriyaki sauce
2   tablespoons rice or white wine vinegar
1   teaspoon crushed red pepper
2   garlic cloves, minced
¼   cup creamy peanut butter

REMAINING INGREDIENTS:

6   cups hot cooked basmati rice
½   cup chopped green onions
2   tablespoons chopped dry-roasted peanuts
8   lime wedges

1. To prepare stew, trim fat from pork. Place pork and next 5 ingredients in an electric slow cooker. Cover with lid, and cook on low-heat setting for 8 hours. Remove pork from slow cooker, and coarsely chop. Add peanut butter to liquid in slow cooker; stir well. Stir in pork.

2. Combine stew and rice in a large bowl. Top each serving with onions and peanuts; serve with lime wedges. Yield: 8 servings (serving size: 1 cup stew, 1 tablespoon green onions, about ½ teaspoon peanuts, and 1 lime wedge).

CALORIES 412 (30% from fat); FAT 13.6g (sat 3.6g, mono 6.2g, poly 2.5g); PROTEIN 28.9g; CARB 42.3g; FIBER 2.1g; CHOL 64mg; IRON 2.9mg; SODIUM 425mg; CALC 37mg EXCHANGES: 2½ Starch, 1 Vegetable, 3 Lean Meat, 1 Fat

PROVENÇALE CHICKEN SUPPER

Use bone-in chicken breasts for this country-French dish.

4   (6-ounce) skinless chicken breast halves
2   teaspoons dried basil
⅛   teaspoon salt
⅛   teaspoon black pepper
1   cup diced yellow bell pepper
1   (16-ounce) can cannellini beans or other white beans, rinsed and drained
1   (14½-ounce) can pasta-style tomatoes, undrained

1. Place chicken in an electric slow cooker; sprinkle with basil, salt, and black pepper. Add bell pepper, beans, and tomatoes. Cover with lid; cook on low-heat setting for 8 hours. Yield: 4 servings (serving size: 1 chicken breast half and 1 cup bean mixture).

CALORIES 296 (10% from fat); FAT 3.4g (sat 0.6g, mono 0.8g, poly 1.3g); PROTEIN 34g; CARB 32.5g; FIBER 5.1g; CHOL 66mg; IRON 4mg; SODIUM 785mg; CALC 81mg EXCHANGES: 2 Starch, 4 Very Lean Meat

CHICKEN AND CARROTS WITH WINE SAUCE

2 cups diagonally sliced carrot (about 8 ounces)

8 chicken thighs (about 2 pounds), skinned

12 garlic cloves, peeled

½ cup dry white wine

1 teaspoon dried thyme

½ teaspoon salt

¼ teaspoon black pepper

1. Combine carrot, chicken, and garlic in an electric slow cooker, and add wine. Sprinkle with thyme, salt, and black pepper. Cover with lid; cook on low-heat setting for 8 hours.

2. Remove carrot, chicken, and garlic with a slotted spoon, reserving cooking liquid. Place ⅓ cup carrot, 3 garlic cloves, and 2 chicken thighs in each of 4 shallow bowls. Spoon 2 tablespoons reserved cooking liquid over each serving. Yield: 4 servings.

CALORIES 243 (25% from fat); FAT 6.8g (sat 1.7g, mono 2.1g, poly 1.7g); PROTEIN 34.6g; CARB 9.4g; FIBER 2g; CHOL 141mg; IRON 2.8mg; SODIUM 463mg; CALC 58mg EXCHANGES: 2 Vegetable, 4 Lean Meat

Freezer

Short on time and tired of store-bought frozen meals? Can't remember the last time you enjoyed a sit-down dinner? How about this for a solution? Cook several meals from scratch on the weekend and then freeze the results for the hurried pace of the week. It's the ultimate make-ahead strategy—all the convenience of quick-and-easy meals but with the flavor of your own healthy home cooking.

For added convenience, freeze your food in handy disposable baking dishes. You can thaw the dish in the microwave, bake, and toss. No mess, no cleanup. (Look for these dishes on the grocery shelves with zip-top plastic bags and aluminum foil.)

From lasagna to chili, you'll move your entrées from freezer to oven to table with minimal effort. In fact, once you try this strategy, you'll find it difficult to look at weeknight planning any other way.

Freezer Recipes ▶

TOMATO-BASIL LASAGNA WITH PROSCIUTTO

Freezing instructions: After assembling the lasagna, cover and freeze up to 1 month. Thaw in refrigerator; bake as directed.

> 5   garlic cloves
> 1   (16-ounce) carton 1% low-fat cottage cheese
> 1/2 cup (4 ounces) block-style fat-free cream cheese
> 1/4 cup (1 ounce) grated fresh Romano cheese, divided
> 2 1/2 teaspoons dried basil
> 1/2 teaspoon crushed red pepper
> 1   large egg
> 1   (26-ounce) bottle fat-free tomato-basil pasta sauce
>   Cooking spray
> 12 cooked lasagna noodles
> 1   cup (4 ounces) chopped prosciutto or ham
> 1   cup (4 ounces) shredded part-skim mozzarella cheese

1. Preheat oven to 375°.

2. Drop garlic through food chute with food processor on, and process until minced. Add cottage cheese; process 2 minutes or until smooth. Add cream cheese, 2 tablespoons Romano, basil, pepper, and egg; process until well blended.

3. Spread 1/2 cup pasta sauce in bottom of a 13 x 9-inch baking dish coated with cooking spray. Arrange 3 noodles over pasta sauce; top with 1 cup cheese mixture, 1/3 cup prosciutto, and 3/4 cup pasta sauce. Repeat layers two times, ending with noodles. Spread remaining pasta sauce over noodles. Sprinkle with 2 tablespoons Romano and mozzarella.

4. Cover and bake at 375° for 45 minutes or until sauce is bubbly. Uncover and bake an additional 15 minutes. Let lasagna stand 5 minutes. Yield: 9 servings.

CALORIES 272 (19% from fat); FAT 5.6g (sat 2.8g, mono 1.8g, poly 0.6g); PROTEIN 20.8g; CARB 33g; FIBER 2.1g; CHOL 47mg; IRON 2.3mg; SODIUM 775mg; CALC 213mg EXCHANGES: 2 Starch, 2 Lean Meat

PASTA SAUCES

Bottled pasta sauces vary in flavors, fat and sodium content, and sometimes significantly in sugar content.

If you can't find the exact sauce called for in a recipe, look for one with a similar flavor and in the same size bottle. Read the label to check for fat, sodium, and sugar content.

Chunky Chipotle-Chicken Chili

Freezing instructions: After adding the chicken and bacon to the corn mixture, spoon into a freezer-safe container. Cool mixture completely in refrigerator; cover and freeze up to 3 months. Thaw in the refrigerator. Place in a large skillet; cook over medium-low heat until thoroughly heated, stirring occasionally.

3   bacon slices
1   pound skinless, boneless chicken breast, cut into 1-inch pieces
½   cup chopped red onion
1   teaspoon ground coriander
5   garlic cloves, minced
1   drained canned chipotle chile in adobo sauce, seeded and minced
1   cup frozen whole-kernel corn, thawed
1   (16-ounce) bottle salsa
1   (15-ounce) can pinto beans, rinsed and drained
1   (7-ounce) bottle roasted red bell peppers, drained and sliced

1. Cook bacon in a large nonstick skillet over medium heat until crisp. Remove bacon from pan; crumble. Add chicken to drippings in pan; sauté 4 minutes. Remove from pan; keep warm.
2. Add onion, coriander, garlic, and chile to pan; sauté 3 minutes. Add corn, salsa, beans, and bell peppers; cover and cook 5 minutes. Return chicken and bacon to pan; cook 5 minutes or until thoroughly heated. Yield: 6 servings (serving size: 1 cup).

CALORIES 293 (30% from fat); FAT 9.8g (sat 3.4g, mono 4.1g, poly 1.5g); PROTEIN 24.7g; CARB 26g; FIBER 4.2g; CHOL 53mg; IRON 2.9mg; SODIUM 686mg; CALC 69mg EXCHANGES: 2 Starch, 2 Very Lean Meat, 1 Fat

Moroccan Chicken with Green Olives

Freezing instructions: After adding chicken to broth mixture, simmer 5 minutes. Place in a freezer-safe container; cool in refrigerator. Freeze up to 2 months. Thaw overnight in refrigerator. Heat a large skillet over medium heat; add chicken mixture, and cook 10 minutes or until heated.

1   teaspoon ground coriander
½   teaspoon dried mint flakes
½   teaspoon ground cinnamon
¼   teaspoon salt
¼   teaspoon black pepper
4   (4-ounce) skinless, boneless chicken breast halves
2   teaspoons olive oil, divided
2   cups sliced onion
1   cup fat-free, less-sodium chicken broth
1   (6-ounce) can thawed orange juice concentrate, undiluted
10   green olives, sliced

1. Combine coriander, mint flakes, cinnamon, salt, and pepper in a small bowl; rub chicken with spice mixture.

2. Heat 1 teaspoon olive oil in a large nonstick skillet over medium-high heat; add chicken. Cook 2 minutes on each side, and set aside.

3. Heat 1 teaspoon olive oil in pan. Add sliced onion, and cook 8 minutes or until onions are golden.

4. Stir in chicken broth, orange juice concentrate, and green olives; bring mixture to a boil. Return chicken to pan; reduce heat, and simmer mixture 15 minutes or until chicken is done.

Yield: 4 servings (serving size: 1 chicken breast half and ½ cup sauce).

CALORIES 253 (17% from fat); FAT 4.7g (sat 0.9g, mono 2.7g, poly 0.6g); PROTEIN 28.9g; CARB 23.1g; FIBER 2g; CHOL 66mg; IRON 1.8mg; SODIUM 456mg; CALC 57mg EXCHANGES: 1 Fruit, 1 Vegetable, 4 Very Lean Meat

TIPS FOR A COLD WORLD

- Don't overcook foods that are intended for the freezer, and be particularly careful to slightly undercook pasta, rice, and vegetables.
- Cool all foods completely by setting meals in the refrigerator for at least an hour before freezing.
- Allow adequate time for your frozen foods to thaw before reheating. About 24 to 48 hours in the refrigerator will completely thaw most freezer items.
- Store foods in any kind of airtight container, such as heavy-duty plastic containers or heavy-duty zip-top plastic bags. For dishes that go from freezer to oven, cover containers with heavy-duty aluminum foil.
- Make certain all freezer containers are sealed completely and that you've removed excess air before sealing.
- Don't forget to label (we use a permanent ink marker) with reheating instructions before freezing. This will streamline your preparation. Include the name of the meal, date frozen, number of servings, temperature and length of time it bakes, and any other necessary information. You can add any personal notes, such as marking extra stars for your favorites.

Chapter 69

Challenge 7

Can't Do It Alone

"When I'm trying to eat better or start a new exercise program, I can always do better if I have a little support from either my husband or my friends."

Secret: Enlisting Family and Friends

TEAM MATES

Couples who share a sport or fitness regimen understand what their spouse's goals are and share a source of joy, which can do wonderful things. It all comes down to a familiar word: communication. In an era of conflicting schedules for many couples, exercising together—running, walking, hiking, or even getting on adjoining treadmills at the gym—will help you both discover whole new meanings of quality time.

One other important benefit: Studies show that married couples who voluntarily begin supervised exercise programs together are far more likely to stay the course than are married men and women who sign up without their spouses. About 50 percent of those who drop out cite family responsibilities and lack of spousal support as their primary excuses.

To help you maximize the benefits of exercising together and minimize the pitfall potential, we asked several experts—including four couples with countless athletic titles, triumphs, and trophies (including a few Olympic gold medals)—to share their strategies for fitness partnerships. Here's their advice.

You're a team. Pace can be a barrier for any couple involved in an activity that moves you from one place to another—walking, cycling, running, and skating, for instance. Even Olympic distance-runners Gwyn and Mark Coogan find it a challenge, because during a serious training run, he's considerably faster than she is. But remember, you're vying for the gold with each other. The Coogans learned to share slower runs and save the hard workouts for when they're with friends or alone. "We also go to the track together and warm up, or drive to a route together and plan to end at the same time," Gwyn says.

Know when to coach. This should be a vehicle for companionship, not an opportunity to tell your companion what to do. "Tailor your activity to the most inexperienced partner's conditioning level," says David Yukelson, Ph.D., a sports psychologist at Pennsylvania State University and a consultant to the USA Track and Field Association. Your partner will ask for help if he or she needs it.

Talk, but listen, too. Three-time national pairs figure-skating champions Jenni Meno and Todd Sand say the fact that they're both good listeners is one of the reasons for their success— both in and out of the rink. "I don't know whether being married helps us with our skating," Meno

> Exercising together will help you both discover whole new meanings of quality time.

says. "But one of the reasons we started skating together is that we felt we could really communicate with each other. And that has really helped our marriage."

Let yourself be moved. See your spouse's early-morning workouts as an inspiration to get out of bed and, say, onto a bike. Odds are, your health will benefit—as will your relationship. An example: In 1982, Mark Allen was a California lifeguard when he watched on TV as Julie Moss crawled her way to second place in the first women's Ironman triathlon. "I didn't know much about the sport then, but Julie's finish was so dramatic, I was intrigued," says Allen, who went on to win the event an unprecedented six times and to marry Moss, a seven-time finisher herself.

Encourage. Don't let your enthusiasm for exercise overwhelm a less-than-enthusiastic partner. Remind yourself that you're courting, not counting laps. "Begin by sharing long walks together after dinner," Yukelson says. "Or set aside an hour every Sunday afternoon for a bike ride around your neighborhood." Keep it light, playful, and a little romantic.

It's the relationship that matters. This is an excellent motto for your tandem workouts and not as no-brainer as it sounds. While getting your body into shape is important, it shouldn't take priority over the health of your marriage. It doesn't for pros like Olympic gold medalists and swimmers Mark Henderson and

Summer Sanders. "As an athlete, you train all your life to get a gold medal," says Henderson. "And I did. But just a week later, when I proposed to Summer at the closing ceremonies of the '96 Olympics, my gold medal felt like a penny. When she said yes, it was much more exciting to me than winning the gold."　　—*Megan Othersen Gorman*

THE BEST OF FRIENDS

The Alabama morning sun hovers on the horizon as Peggy Heal pushes open the garage door of her suburban Birmingham home. Her blond hair is pulled into a ponytail, and she's clad in a crisp, white T-shirt, well-worn running shoes, and shorts as blue as her eyes. Her friend John "Jak" Karn should be arriving any minute. Every Friday, the two, joined by Peggy's dogs—Baxter, a Rottweiler, and Jaibo, a Labrador-German shepherd mix—take an early five-mile run. Emphasis on "early"; when Jak pulls into her driveway at 6 a.m., it's a late start. Most other days, the 39-year-old business manager for an architectural firm is pounding the pavement by 5:30 or driving to the gym for a Muscle Works class.

Running with others is not just for the motivation, but for the camaraderie.

But she's happy to wait for her friend. "I've always enjoyed running with other people," says Peggy, who has pursued the sport since 1985 and has been hitting these hilly, tree-lined streets with Jak for the past three years. "It's not just for the motivation, but for the camaraderie." It's on the trail that Peggy, Jak, and their other runner friends share their life stories, confessions, hopes, and dreams. "Run with someone," Peggy says, "and before you know it, you'll be the best of friends."

Keeping those friends, as well as making new ones through common passions for healthy living—from morning exercise to evening dinner parties—animates Peggy's active life. "Every day, I think how fortunate I am to have my health, such good friends, and a life I really love," she says. The truth is that her good fortune is no accident. She makes it anew every day.

TURN WORKOUTS INTO SOCIAL HOUR

Peggy's initiation into fitness came at age 19, when both her paternal grandparents died of heart failure within eight weeks of each other. The then-college freshman picked up a jump rope shortly thereafter, and she hasn't stopped working out since.

Now she's not only an avid runner but also a captain of the women's tennis team at her sports club and a regular at Muscle Works classes. But she doesn't see fitness as an end in itself. No matter what her choice or challenge, it always involves interaction with others. "Other people push me to be a little bit better," she says. "And besides, working out with friends is fun."

Fun is also functional. When you enjoy what you're doing, Peggy says, you're far more likely to keep at it. That theory has spurred her most recent mission: to put some new kicks into a longstanding-but-staid Saturday-morning run sponsored by the Birmingham Track Club. "Traditionally, there hasn't been a lot of socializing," Peggy says. "People would get their workout in and then go their separate ways." To break that pattern, Peggy introduced a bagel-and-coffee social at the end of the route. Now runners have a reason to hang around, get to know each other better, and enjoy themselves more.

EAT THE BEST TO BE YOUR BEST

When Peggy started pushing herself to run faster (an admitted attempt to defy her 40th birthday), she began to better appreciate how food affects her. "If I'd eat a peach and microwave popcorn for dinner one night and run hard the next morning, I'd be dying midway through the run because I didn't eat to sustain myself," she says.

FRIENDLY ADVICE

As an active professional, Peggy fits friends, fitness, and good food into her life. Here's how.

Meet people through athletics. You're bound to gain friends and improve your fitness. "If you enjoy the same sport, right away you'll have something in common," Peggy says. "My best friends are from running and tennis."

Get a dog. They're not only good friends, they'll keep you in shape. "People have no idea how much exercise they'd get with two dogs," says Peggy, who runs, hikes, and plays fetch with hers regularly.

Eat with friends. You'll find that you have so much to talk about, you won't notice that you're skipping dessert.

Make the important things routine. Peggy has standing dates for running, tennis, and dinner parties with friends. As for exercise: "It's like brushing my teeth. I do it every day."

Peggy usually starts her day with a bran muffin, eats yogurt midmorning, has tofu chili and a salad or soup with a bagel for lunch, munches on fruit in the afternoon, and sits down to a well-rounded meal at night. She hasn't stopped eating what she loves; she's just altered her list of favorites. Tofu now vies with cheesecake somewhere at the top, though she indulges in the former more frequently and reserves the latter for special occasions.

RUN ON OVER TO MY HOUSE

Peggy hosts a "Souper Bowl" party every Super Bowl Sunday for 18 running friends and is also the originator of the group's annual meat loaf cookoff. But her affection for food and entertaining found structural expression three years ago when she decided to redesign her kitchen. "I like to have people over, and that's where they always end up," she explains. She resurfaced the walls, put in a Jenn-Air stove with a grill, and built a curved granite-top island that serves as work station and eating bar.

When her guests come over for dinner, they can gather in a kitchen that encourages both helping out with food preparation and mingling. But never on Friday.

"I come home on Friday nights and usually grill myself some salmon or make another good meal. I like to have at least one night alone when I can just relax and read the paper," Peggy says. The next morning, her alarm will ring before sunrise, and she'll hit the road for a long run with the Saturday morning crew. Then they'll hang around afterward for coffee, bagels, and conversation.

Chapter 70

8
Challenge

Cooking for Just Two

"There's just the two of us, so it's easier
to get takeout or go out to eat instead of
cooking something healthy."

Secret: Tactics for Two

Mealtime should be a relaxed time to enjoy delicious and healthful food—whether it's the two of you, or you're dining alone. Try a few of these ideas for making the most out of mealtime when two's company.

Cook together. Let your child or partner help with the cooking tasks. You cook the main dish one night while your cooking partner prepares the sides. Then swap assignments the next night.

Have a picnic in January—in front of the fireplace or on a favorite quilt.

Eat out. Out of the kitchen, that is. Try eating breakfast on the deck, dinner on the coffee table, or lunch in the rocking chairs on the front porch.

Bring out your dining best. Don't wait for a special holiday—get out the silver and china and serve an elegant meal, just because!

Color the table. Use placemats, tablecloths, napkins, or even a single fresh flower to paint your table, and your mood, a little brighter.

Let the music play. Turn on some of your favorite tunes to add to the pleasant dining atmosphere. Studies show that people tend to eat slower and eat less when there is calm, soothing music playing in the background.

> People tend to eat slower and eat less when there is calm, soothing music in the background.

Supper and the Single Parent

For any family, getting a nutritious meal on the table night after night can be daunting. It's often even harder for the single parent, who juggles work, shopping, cooking, and serving without another adult as a helpmate. But it can be done. Here's your chance to make dinnertime what it should be: a chance to nourish, both physically and mentally, the most important person in your life.

Try to resist being lured by fast-food outlets and grocery stores offering prepackaged takeout. Those temptations are usually second-rate, both nutritionally and gastronomically, and they'll break you financially. A home-cooked meal is the practical and healthy solution, and you just can't go wrong with kids, if you focus on comfort: Meat Sauce Macaroni, Crispy Sesame Shrimp, and Chile-Cheese Rice Burritos, for example. These familiar foods are simple to prepare, and the ingredients are staples in any working kitchen.

Most children are not gastronomes, so don't feel guilty over the simplicity of these meals. With a minimum of effort, you can prepare a wholesome dinner your child will savor, and you'll be able to sit down and do what's really important: Listen carefully as he or she relates the events of the day.

MEAT SAUCE MACARONI

Make a meal with this quick and easy pasta dish by starting with a crisp green salad.

½ pound ground round
½ cup pizza sauce
⅛ teaspoon salt
⅛ teaspoon black pepper
1 cup hot cooked elbow macaroni (about 2 ounces uncooked)
2 tablespoons (about ½ ounce) shredded reduced-fat sharp Cheddar cheese

1. Cook meat in a small nonstick skillet over medium-high heat until browned, stirring to crumble. Drain. Wipe drippings from pan with a paper towel; return meat to pan. Add sauce, salt, and pepper; cook 2 minutes. Add pasta; cook 2 minutes or until thoroughly heated. Sprinkle each serving with 1 tablespoon cheese. Yield: 2 servings (serving size: 1¼ cups).

CALORIES 310 (28% from fat); FAT 9.6g (sat 3.4g, mono 3.9g, poly 0.7g); PROTEIN 30.5g; CARB 24.5g; FIBER 1.5g; CHOL 74mg; IRON 4.1mg; SODIUM 445mg; CALC 90mg
EXCHANGES: 1½ Starch, 3 Very Lean Meat, 1 Vegetable

CRISPY SESAME SHRIMP

If you think sesame shrimp is complicated and best left to Chinese restaurants, this recipe will change your mind. You might serve this with steamed sugar snap peas.

¾ cup herb-seasoned stuffing mix (such as Pepperidge Farm), crushed
1 teaspoon sesame seeds
¼ teaspoon paprika
⅛ teaspoon salt
⅛ teaspoon garlic powder
⅛ teaspoon black pepper
1 large egg white, lightly beaten
10 large shrimp, peeled and deveined (about ¾ pound)
Cooking spray

1. Preheat oven to 425°.
2. Combine first 6 ingredients in a small bowl. Place egg white in a small shallow bowl. Dip shrimp in egg white, and dredge in stuffing mixture. Place shrimp on a large baking sheet coated with cooking spray. Lightly coat shrimp with cooking spray. Bake at 425° for 15 minutes or until golden. Yield: 2 servings (serving size: 5 shrimp).

CALORIES 242 (15% from fat); FAT 4.1g (sat 0.6g, mono 0.7g, poly 1.9g); PROTEIN 30.5g; CARB 18.6g; FIBER 1.7g; CHOL 194mg; IRON 4.3mg; SODIUM 656mg; CALC 104mg
EXCHANGES: 1 Starch, 4 Very Lean Meat

CHILE-CHEESE RICE BURRITOS

Cooking spray
½ cup shredded zucchini
½ cup thinly sliced green onions
1 cup hot cooked rice
¼ cup (1 ounce) shredded Monterey Jack cheese
1 tablespoon chopped green chiles
¼ teaspoon salt
⅛ teaspoon black pepper
¼ cup fat-free sour cream
2 (8-inch) flour tortillas
½ cup shredded iceberg lettuce
½ cup diced tomato
2 tablespoons bottled salsa

1. Place a nonstick skillet coated with cooking spray over medium-high heat until hot. Add zucchini and onions; sauté 3 minutes or until tender. Stir in rice and next 4 ingredients; cook 1 minute, stirring constantly. Remove from heat; stir in sour cream.
2. Warm tortillas according to package directions. Spoon half of rice mixture down center of each tortilla. Top each with half of lettuce and tomato; roll up. Serve with salsa. Yield: 2 servings (serving size: 1 burrito).

CALORIES 358 (20% from fat); FAT 8.1g (sat 3.3g, mono 2.6g, poly 1.7g); PROTEIN 13g; CARB 57.4g; FIBER 3.6g; CHOL 11mg; IRON 3.4mg; SODIUM 726mg; CALC 244mg
EXCHANGES: 3 Starch, 2 Vegetable, 1 High-Fat Meat

Elegant Dinner Duet

Imagine the scene: You and that special someone at a table set for two, a fire crackling in the background, Johnny Mathis crooning smooth tunes, and candlelight sparkling on your wine-glasses. Now imagine a divine meal, punctuated by laughter and prolonged by soulful storytelling.

Are you envisioning your favorite restaurant? Reconsider calling in that reservation, and make one instead at your own dining table. This way, the two of you can enjoy an intimate evening away from the bustle of the daily routine. We can help with a sim-ple, elegant dinner menu for just the two of you. It's special enough for fine dining but requires only ordinary preparation.

After all, what better way to rekindle a romance or simply express affection for a friend than by sharing a home-cooked meal?

Menu
- Artichokes with Roasted Red Pepper Dip
- Bitter Greens with Tarragon Vinaigrette
- Roasted Lobster Tails with Ginger Dipping Sauce
- Snow Peas and Cherry Tomatoes

Serves 2

ARTICHOKES WITH ROASTED RED PEPPER DIP

You'll have some dip left over for impromptu entertaining—try it with raw vegetables, pita chips, or plain crackers. It also makes a delicious sandwich spread.

2	red bell peppers
2	artichokes (1 pound)
12	cups water
3	lemon slices
1	bay leaf
2	teaspoons olive oil
2	teaspoons Dijon mustard
1	teaspoon red wine vinegar
1/4	teaspoon dried fines herbes
1/8	teaspoon black pepper
1	tablespoon finely crumbled feta cheese
1/2	teaspoon capers

1. Preheat broiler.

2. Cut bell peppers in half lengthwise, discarding seeds and membranes. Place pepper halves, skin sides up, on a foil-lined baking sheet; flatten with hand. Broil 10 minutes or until blackened. Place in a zip-top plastic bag; seal. Let stand 20 minutes. Peel and set aside.

3. Cut off artichoke stems, and remove bottom leaves. Trim about 1 inch from tops of artichokes. Bring water, lemon slices, and bay leaf to a boil in a large Dutch oven. Add artichokes; cover, reduce heat, and simmer 25 minutes or until a leaf near the center of each artichoke pulls out easily. Drain well; discard lemon and bay leaf. Set aside.

4. Combine bell peppers, oil, mustard, and vinegar in a blender; process until smooth. Combine bell pepper mixture, fines herbes, and black pepper. Spoon ⅔ cup into a serving bowl; sprinkle with feta and capers. Serve with artichokes. Cover and chill remaining dip. Yield: 2 servings: (serving size: 1 artichoke and ⅓ cup dip).

CALORIES 105 (30% from fat); FAT 3.5g (sat 0.9g, mono 1.9g, poly 0.4g); PROTEIN 4.2g; CARB 17.3g; FIBER 7.1g; CHOL 3mg; IRON 2.6mg; SODIUM 234mg; CALC 80mg
EXCHANGES: 1 Starch, ½ Fat

SNOW PEAS AND CHERRY TOMATOES

1½	cups snow peas, trimmed
3	tablespoons water
½	teaspoon butter or margarine
¼	teaspoon sugar
12	cherry tomatoes, halved
½	teaspoon dark sesame oil
⅛	teaspoon salt
⅛	teaspoon black pepper

1. Combine first 4 ingredients in a large nonstick skillet. Cook over medium-high heat 2 minutes or until liquid almost evaporates. Add tomatoes, and

cook 2 minutes or until tomatoes are thoroughly heated. Remove from heat; stir in remaining ingredients. Yield: 2 servings (serving size: 1 cup).

CALORIES 88 (28% from fat); FAT 2.7g (sat 0.9g, mono 0.8g, poly 0.8g); PROTEIN 3.8g; CARB 13.6g; FIBER 4g; CHOL 3mg; IRON 2.8mg; SODIUM 170mg; CALC 53mg
EXCHANGES: 2 Vegetable, ½ Fat

BITTER GREENS WITH TARRAGON VINAIGRETTE

2	tablespoons white wine vinegar
2	tablespoons plain fat-free yogurt
1	tablespoon chopped fresh or
	1 teaspoon dried tarragon
2	teaspoons Dijon mustard
2	teaspoons honey
1	teaspoon olive oil
⅛	teaspoon salt
⅛	teaspoon black pepper
5	cups mixed bitter greens
1	tablespoon pine nuts, toasted

1. Combine first 8 ingredients in a small bowl; stir well with a whisk. Place greens and pine nuts in a large bowl, and drizzle with vinaigrette. Yield: 2 servings (serving size: 2 cups).

CALORIES 74 (36% from fat); FAT 3g (sat 0.4g, mono 1g, poly 1.1g); PROTEIN 4g; CARB 9.2g; FIBER 2.2g; CHOL 0mg; IRON 0.8mg; SODIUM 337mg; CALC 136mg
EXCHANGES: 2 Vegetable, ½ Fat

ROASTED LOBSTER TAILS WITH GINGER DIPPING SAUCE

- ¾ teaspoon dry mustard
- ½ teaspoon water
- 3 tablespoons low-sodium soy sauce
- 1 tablespoon plum sauce
- 1 tablespoon dry sherry
- ¾ teaspoon minced peeled fresh ginger
- 2 (8-ounce) frozen lobster tails, thawed

Cooking spray

- 1 teaspoon vegetable oil
- ¼ teaspoon dark sesame oil
- ¼ teaspoon black pepper

Sliced green onions (optional)

1. Preheat oven to 425°.

2. Combine mustard and water in a small bowl; stir well with a whisk. Stir in soy sauce, plum sauce, sherry, and ginger; set aside.

3. Make a lengthwise cut through the top of each lobster shell using kitchen shears, cutting to, but not through, lobster meat; press shell open. Place lobster tails, cut sides up, in a shallow roasting pan coated with cooking spray. Combine oils and pepper, and spoon over lobster meat.

4. Bake at 425° for 13 minutes or until lobster meat turns opaque. Serve lobster with sauce, and garnish with onions, if desired. Yield: 2 servings (serving size: 1 lobster tail and 2 tablespoons sauce).

CALORIES 194 (23% from fat); FAT 5g (sat 0.8g, mono 1.4g, poly 2.1g); PROTEIN 27.6g; CARB 8.3g; FIBER 0.2g; CHOL 92mg; IRON 1.2mg; SODIUM 1,263mg; CALC 86mg EXCHANGES: ½ Starch, 4 Very Lean Meat

Desserts à Deux

Downsizing recipes intended for four or six can be fairly easy—sometimes all you have to do is halve the ingredients and everything works out fine. Or you can freeze the extras for another meal.

Desserts are not always so simple. A favorite soufflé originally intended for several couples is going to start looking a lot less compelling the third or fourth night down the road. And that same halving or quartering of a recipe you used to cut back on the entrée might be a chemistry experiment waiting to fail in a dessert, where the measurements are extra-precise. Did we mention the equipment? It's not all that easy to find a cake pan or tart shell that's made for just two people.

The best bet is to plan for two from the start, and that's what we've done here with three recipes perfect for you and anyone else you think is worth it.

Dessert Recipes for Two ▶

Chocolate Chip Meringues with Strawberries

1 large egg white
⅛ teaspoon cream of tartar
Dash of salt
¼ cup powdered sugar
1 tablespoon semisweet chocolate chips
¼ teaspoon vanilla extract
½ cup sliced strawberries
½ teaspoon granulated sugar

1. Preheat oven to 250°.

2. Cover a baking sheet with parchment paper. Draw 2 (3-inch) circles on paper. Turn paper over, and secure with masking tape. Beat egg white, cream of tartar, and salt with a mixer at high speed until foamy. Add ¼ cup powdered sugar, 1 tablespoon at a time, beating until stiff peaks form. Fold in chips and vanilla.

3. Divide egg white mixture evenly between the 2 circles. Shape into nests using the back of a spoon. Bake at 250° for 1 to 1½ hours or until dry. Turn oven off, and cool meringues in closed oven for at least 3 hours. Carefully remove meringues from paper. Combine strawberries and granulated sugar. Spoon strawberry mixture evenly over meringues. Yield: 2 servings.

CALORIES 113 (17% from fat); FAT 2.1g
(sat 1.1g, mono 0.6g, poly 0.1g); PROTEIN 2.2g;
CARB 22.4g; FIBER 1g; CHOL 0mg, IRON
0.3mg, SODIUM 98mg, CALC 9 mg
EXCHANGE: 1½ Starch

Banana Bread Pudding with Caramel Sauce

⅓ cup 1% low-fat milk
1 tablespoon dark brown sugar
⅛ teaspoon ground cinnamon
1 large egg
2 cups (½-inch) cubed French bread (about 2 [1-ounce] slices)
Cooking spray
½ cup mashed ripe banana (about 1 banana)
1 tablespoon granulated sugar
2 tablespoons fat-free caramel topping

1. Combine first 4 ingredients in a small bowl, and stir with a whisk. Place ½ cup bread cubes into each of 2 (8-ounce) ramekins coated with cooking spray. Spoon 2 tablespoons milk mixture over each serving, and top each with ¼ cup banana. Sprinkle each serving with 1½ teaspoons granulated sugar. Repeat procedure with remaining bread and milk mixture. Chill 30 minutes.

2. Preheat oven to 350°.

3. Bake at 350° for 50 minutes or until done. Spoon 1 tablespoon caramel sauce over each serving. Yield: 2 servings.

CALORIES 297 (14% from fat); FAT 4.5g
(sat 1.4g, mono 1.6g, poly 0.9g); PROTEIN 8g;
CARB 57.2g; FIBER 2.3g; CHOL 108mg;
IRON 1.4mg; SODIUM 265mg; CALC 92mg
EXCHANGES: 3 Starch, 1 Fat

CHOCOLATE SOUFFLÉS FOR TWO

Cooking spray

2	teaspoons granulated sugar
½	cup water
¼	cup powdered sugar
2	tablespoons unsweetened cocoa
2	tablespoons 1% low-fat milk
1½	teaspoons all-purpose flour
1	large egg yolk
⅛	teaspoon vanilla extract
1	large egg white
⅛	teaspoon cream of tartar
1	tablespoon granulated sugar
2	teaspoons powdered sugar

1. Preheat oven to 350°.

2. Coat 2 (8-ounce) ramekins with cooking spray; sprinkle with 2 teaspoons granulated sugar. Place ramekins on a baking sheet; set aside.

3. Combine water and next 5 ingredients in top of a double boiler. Cook over simmering water until thick (about 10 minutes), stirring constantly with a whisk. Remove from heat; add vanilla.

4. Beat egg white and cream of tartar with a mixer at high speed until soft peaks form. Gradually add 1 tablespoon granulated sugar, beating until stiff peaks form. Fold one-fourth of egg white mixture into chocolate mixture; fold in remaining egg white mixture. Spoon evenly into prepared ramekins. Bake at 350° for 20 minutes or until puffy and set. Sprinkle each soufflé with 1 teaspoon powdered sugar. Serve immediately. Yield: 2 servings.

Note: If you're having two other people over for dinner, see Individual Chocolate Soufflés on page 200. It's the same recipe, but for 4 servings instead of two.

CALORIES 188 (19% from fat); FAT 3.9g (sat 1.4g, mono 1.4g, poly 0.6g); PROTEIN 5.4g; CARB 33g; FIBER 0g; CHOL 110mg; IRON 1.4mg; SODIUM 41mg; CALC 40mg
EXCHANGES: 2 Starch, 1 Fat

Chapter 71

Holiday Weight Gain

Challenge

"Help! I've lost 20 pounds so far, but with the holidays coming soon, I'm afraid I'll blow it and gain all my weight back."

Secret: Merry Moderation

HONEST INDULGENCE

Marisa Ronan is nervous. It's the same anxiety this busy bank vice president feels every year at holiday time. But it's not about family tensions or even all the extra shopping and gift wrapping. It's about food.

Every year, from Thanksgiving to New Year's, she worries that she will fall irretrievably out of shape by succumbing to the temptation of the season's dishes. "Every day at work, people are getting gifts from clients, and they're always food gifts," she says. "So every single day for six weeks, the office is filled with chocolates, flavored popcorn, nuts, Christmas cookies. You almost find that you start eating before you even realize what you're doing, and then you feel really bad afterwards."

> Research suggests that contrary to popular belief, people do not gain 5 to 10 pounds over the holidays.

Marisa is far from alone. "I get lots of calls about holiday eating," says Daniel Kirschenbaum, Ph.D., a professor of psychiatry at Northwestern University and director of Chicago's Center for Behavioral Medicine. "People struggle with it," he continues, explaining that the holidays are among the top three "environmental challenges" that can lead to overindulgence (the other two are traveling and going to a restaurant).

But the anxiety many people feel about food throughout December is generally unnecessary. Research suggests that contrary to popular belief, people do not gain 5 to 10 pounds over the holidays. They gain, on average, only one, according to scientists at the National Institutes of Health, who followed 200 people through a Thanksgiving-to-New Year's stretch.

Granted, many of the people in their study never lost the extra holiday pound they gained, meaning that 20 Christmases can add up to 20 extra pounds. But what happens with your weight over the holidays is absolutely in your control—indulgence or not. The researchers reported that those in the study who were most active from late November through December later reported the greatest weight loss and were in fact unlikely to gain any weight to begin with.

People who are most successful at preventing holiday food blowouts use a variety of strategies to keep from going overboard. One of those approaches, according to Kirschenbaum, is not to eat everything willy-nilly but to go for foods that are specific to the holidays and worth the indulgence—for example, "a dish that you can only get one time a year," he says, "or one that nobody but your grandmother makes, and it's totally unique, something really special." Scope out the situation at a party or buffet and remind yourself, "I can have the Rice Krispies bars anytime, but I don't usually see linzertorte."

For Fay Reiter, a certified social worker based near Princeton, New Jersey, one of the best strategies during the holidays is to eat small portions. "A big amount isn't going to taste better than a small amount," she says. In fact, eating too much and not feeling good afterward defeats the purpose. "Why ruin something that could be enjoyable? Eat a small amount that tastes good and walk away feeling good, too."

Keeping up physical activity is important as well—and not just because it burns calories. "When you exercise," Reiter says, "you're making time for yourself."

Healthful holiday eating isn't just about avoiding pitfalls. It's also about enjoying some high-nutrient foods that you don't typically have at other times of the year. For example, a modest slice of pumpkin pie has enough vitamin A to meet the Daily Value for that nutrient (in the form of beta-carotene) twice over. Turkey

Holiday Strategies

- Indulge in special occasion seasonal foods rather than foods you can have at other times of the year.
- Eat small portions.
- Maintain physical activity.
- Enjoy high-nutrient holiday foods.
- Don't fear the food.

has plenty of high-quality protein, along with iron, zinc, and other essential minerals. Oysters, another traditional Christmastime favorite, are excellent sources of zinc and vitamin B12. And pecans and chestnuts mixed into pies and stuffings make their own nutrient and fiber contribution. Furthermore, their fat isn't the saturated kind that leads to clogged arteries.

The holidays are also vegetable season. A report from Britain's Cancer Research Campaign goes so far as to state that Christmas dinner is the only meal of the year where children are served an adequate amount of vegetables.

In other words, 'tis the season to enjoy the food, not to fear it. Even if you do go overboard here and there, the world won't come to an end. And neither will your commitment to staying fit and healthy. 　　　　　　　　*—Larry Lindner*

10 HOLIDAY DISHES YOU'LL BE HAPPY TO HAVE

It's true. Pumpkin pie, stuffing, fruitcake, spiced pecans, and other holiday dishes pack a fair amount of fat and calories. But what's not often highlighted is that many of these foods are also good sources of some essential nutrients, providing significant percentages of the Daily Values for iron, fiber, and several vitamins and minerals. Check out the numbers below.

Holiday Treat	Daily Value Percentage
1 slice pumpkin pie	237% of vitamin A, 15% of calcium
½ cup Brussels sprouts	80% of vitamin C, 14% of fiber
1 slice fruitcake	9% of iron
½ cup cranberry sauce	6% of fiber
6 oysters	212% of vitamin B12, 178% of zinc, 25% of iron
3 ounces roasted turkey breast (skin removed)	34% of niacin, 27% of vitamin B6
1 ounce roasted chestnuts	18% of vitamin C
1 ounce pecans	10% of zinc
1 sweet potato (baked with skin)	498% of vitamin A, 47% of vitamin C, 14% of fiber
½ cup creamed spinach	17% of vitamin C, 13% of calcium

Respectfully Revising Mom's Holiday Recipes

Even though our favorite Mom foods replenish our spirits and remind us how nice it is to be cared for, they sometimes need a little reinvention along the way to reflect today's healthier cooking styles. We think you'll like these new lightened versions of some holiday favorites. And we're sure that Mom will be pleased.

FRUITED PORT-CRANBERRY SALAD

    1   envelope unflavored gelatin
    ½   cup port or other sweet red wine
    2   (3-ounce) packages cranberry-flavored gelatin
    ¼   teaspoon ground ginger
    ¼   teaspoon ground allspice
    2   cups boiling water
    1   (16-ounce) can whole-berry cranberry sauce
    ½   cup ice water
    1½ cups finely chopped Granny Smith apple (about 1 large apple)
    1   (14-ounce) package frozen unsweetened raspberries, thawed
    1   (8¼-ounce) can crushed pineapple in juice, drained

1. Sprinkle unflavored gelatin over port; set aside. Combine cranberry gelatin, ginger, and allspice in a large bowl; stir well. Stir in boiling water and port mixture. Add cranberry sauce and ice water; stir well. Chill 30 minutes.

2. Combine apple, raspberries, and pineapple; stir into gelatin mixture. Pour into an 8-cup gelatin mold; chill 4 hours or until set. To unmold, dip mold into hot water for 5 seconds; invert onto serving platter. Yield: 12 servings (serving size: 1 slice).

CALORIES 178 (1% from fat); FAT 0.2g (sat 0g, mono 0g, poly 0.1g); PROTEIN 2.3g; CARB 41.3g; FIBER 2g; CHOL 0mg; IRON 0.4mg; SODIUM 63mg; CALC 10mg EXCHANGES: ½ Starch, 2 Fruit

SAUTÉED GREEN BEANS AND ONIONS WITH BACON

    1   pound green beans, trimmed and halved crosswise
    4   bacon slices
    1   (16-ounce) bottle cocktail onions, drained
    2   teaspoons sugar
    ½   teaspoon dried thyme
    1½ tablespoons cider vinegar
    ¾   teaspoon salt
    ¼   teaspoon black pepper

1. Cook beans in boiling water 4 minutes or until crisp-tender. Rinse with cold water; drain and pat dry.

2. Cook bacon in a skillet over medium-high heat until crisp. Remove bacon from pan, reserving 2 tablespoons drippings in pan; crumble bacon, and set aside. Add onions to drippings in pan; cook 3 minutes, stirring occasionally. Add sugar and thyme; cook 3 minutes or until onions are golden, stirring occasionally. Add beans; cook 2 minutes. Add vinegar, salt, and pepper; toss to coat. Stir in crumbled bacon just before serving. Yield: 8 servings (serving size: ½ cup).

CALORIES 59 (46% from fat); FAT 3g (sat 1.1g, mono 1.4g, poly 0.4g); PROTEIN 2.2g; CARB 6.5g; FIBER 1.2g; CHOL 4mg; IRON 0.8mg; SODIUM 621mg; CALC 24mg EXCHANGES: 1 Vegetable, ½ Fat

SQUASH-RICE CASSEROLE

8	cups sliced zucchini
1	cup chopped onion
½	cup fat-free, less-sodium chicken broth
2	cups cooked rice
1	cup fat-free sour cream
1	cup (4 ounces) shredded reduced-fat sharp Cheddar cheese
¼	cup (1 ounce) grated fresh Parmesan cheese, divided
¼	cup Italian-seasoned breadcrumbs
1	teaspoon salt
¼	teaspoon black pepper
2	large eggs, lightly beaten

Cooking spray

1. Preheat oven to 350°.

2. Combine first 3 ingredients in a Dutch oven; bring to a boil. Cover, reduce heat, and simmer 20 minutes or until tender. Drain; partially mash with a potato masher. Combine zucchini mixture, rice, sour cream, Cheddar cheese, 2 tablespoons Parmesan cheese, breadcrumbs, salt, pepper, and eggs in a bowl; stir gently. Spoon zucchini mixture into a 13 x 9-inch baking dish coated with cooking spray; sprinkle with 2 tablespoons Parmesan cheese. Bake at 350° for 30 minutes or until bubbly.

3. Preheat broiler.

4. Broil 1 minute or until lightly browned. Yield: 8 servings (serving size: 1 cup).

CALORIES 197 (25% from fat); FAT 5.5g (sat 2.7g, mono 1.5g, poly 0.4g); PROTEIN 12.7g; CARB 24g; FIBER 1.4g; CHOL 65mg; IRON 1.5mg; SODIUM 623mg; CALC 209mg EXCHANGES: 1 Starch, 1 Vegetable, 1 Medium-Fat Meat

APPLE-GLAZED PORK LOIN ROAST WITH APPLE-HAM STUFFING

As dramatic as a crown roast of pork may be, a boneless pork loin roast is just more practical today. It's leaner, easier to find, and simpler to prepare. We used lean ham instead of pork sausage for the stuffing and added a piquant glaze and more spices.

STUFFING:

6   cups (½-inch) cubed white bread (about 8 slices)
1   tablespoon butter or margarine
1¼ cups diced ham (about 6 ounces)
½   cup chopped onion
⅓   cup chopped carrot
⅓   cup chopped celery
½   teaspoon dried thyme
½   teaspoon dried rosemary
1   garlic clove, minced
1½ cups chopped Granny Smith apple
¼   teaspoon salt
¼   teaspoon black pepper
1   cup apple juice

ROAST:

3   pounds boned pork loin roast
1   tablespoon garlic powder
1   teaspoon ground cinnamon
1   teaspoon ground cumin
¾   teaspoon salt
½   teaspoon ground allspice
¼   teaspoon ground ginger
¼   teaspoon black pepper
Cooking spray
⅔   cup apple jelly
2   teaspoons minced peeled fresh ginger
1   teaspoon grated lemon rind

1. Preheat oven to 400°.

2. To prepare stuffing, arrange bread cubes in a single layer on a jelly roll pan. Bake at 400° for 6 minutes or until toasted; set aside. Melt butter in a large nonstick skillet over medium-high heat. Add ham; sauté 4 minutes or until lightly browned. Add onion and next 5 ingredients; cook over medium-high heat 5 minutes or until tender. Add apple, salt, and ¼ teaspoon pepper; cook 2 minutes. Add bread cubes and apple juice to stuffing mixture, stir gently. Set aside.

3. To prepare roast, trim fat from pork. Combine garlic powder and next 6 ingredients in a small bowl; rub evenly over pork. Place pork on a broiler pan coated with cooking spray; insert meat thermometer into thickest portion of pork. Bake at 400° for 30 minutes. Combine jelly, ginger, and lemon rind in a small bowl. Brush jelly mixture over roast. Spoon stuffing onto broiler pan around pork. Cover with foil, and bake at 400° for 15 minutes; uncover and bake an additional 15 minutes or until thermometer reaches 155°, basting pork occasionally with jelly mixture.

Cover and let stand 10 minutes before slicing. Yield: 10 servings (serving size: 3 ounces pork and ½ cup stuffing).

CALORIES 396 (38% from fat); FAT 16.8g (sat 6g, mono 7.3g, poly 2.1g); PROTEIN 32g; CARB 27.9g; FIBER 1.7g; CHOL 100mg; IRON 2.5mg; SODIUM 676mg; CALC 50mg
EXCHANGES: 2 Starch, 3 Medium-Fat Meat

JALAPEÑO CORN BREAD

- 1 teaspoon vegetable oil
- Cooking spray
- 1¼ cups all-purpose flour
- 1¼ cups yellow cornmeal
- 2 tablespoons sugar
- 1 tablespoon baking powder
- 1 teaspoon salt
- 1 teaspoon ground cumin
- 1 cup fat-free milk
- ½ cup chopped red bell pepper
- ½ cup minced seeded jalapeño pepper
- 3 tablespoons butter or margarine, melted
- 2 tablespoons minced fresh cilantro
- 2 large eggs, lightly beaten
- 1 (7-ounce) can whole-kernel corn, drained

1. Preheat oven to 425°.

2. Coat a 10-inch cast iron or heavy ovenproof skillet with oil and cooking spray. Place pan in a 425° oven for 7 minutes.

3. Lightly spoon flour into dry measuring cups; level with a knife. Combine flour and next 5 ingredients in a bowl. Combine milk and remaining ingredients in a bowl; add to cornmeal mixture, stirring just until moist. Pour batter into prepared pan. Bake at 425° for 25 minutes or until a wooden pick inserted in center comes out clean. Cool in pan 5 minutes on a wire rack. Remove from pan. Yield: 12 servings (serving size: 1 wedge).

CALORIES 174 (25% from fat); FAT 4.9g (sat 2.3g, mono 1.5g, poly 0.7g); PROTEIN 4.9g; CARB 28.1g; FIBER 1.4g; CHOL 45mg; IRON 1.8mg; SODIUM 416mg; CALC 105mg
EXCHANGES: 2 Starch, ½ Fat

Party On

Treats offered at holiday parties and special family celebrations may be tempting, but they can wreak havoc with your weight-loss plan. Here are some tricks for maintaining control during social occasions.

- Eat a regular meal before you go to a party. Then you won't be hungry and tempted to overindulge in snacks and sweets.
- Don't skip meals during the day to "save up" for overeating at the party.
- Keep a glass of water or sugar-free soft drink in your hand at all times. It's harder to eat when one hand is busy holding a glass.
- If you drink alcohol, choose low-sugar mixers such as sugar-free soft drinks, diet tonic water, club soda, seltzer, or water.
- Don't stand next to the serving table all night. Move to another place in the room.
- Enjoy conversation. When your mouth is busy talking, it's not busy eating.
- Drink lots of water before a party. You'll feel full and be less tempted to snack.
- Offer to bring a low-fat dish to the party.
- Fill up on low-calorie, high-fiber foods, such as fresh vegetables and fruits. But go easy on the vegetable dips and cheese.
- If you must have something sweet, go ahead and have a little taste. Sometimes just a small bite is enough to satisfy your sweet tooth.
- Keep the fat content of your regular meals especially low during the holidays to balance the extra fat that you may get in party foods.

PARTY PICKS

Choose these low-fat, low-sugar party foods when you're looking over the party spread.

Fruits
- Apple wedges
- Grapes
- Pear slices
- Pineapple
- Strawberries

Vegetables
- Broccoli florets
- Carrot sticks
- Cauliflower
- Celery sticks
- Cherry tomatoes
- Squash slices
- Zucchini slices

Breads and Starches
- Breadsticks
- French bread
- Low-fat potato chips
- Low-fat tortilla chips
- Melba rounds
- Pita bread wedges
- Plain crackers
- Plain rolls
- Pretzels

Dips
- Black bean dip
- Salsa

Meats, Poultry, and Seafood
- Lean roast beef
- Pork tenderloin
- Roasted turkey
- Boiled shrimp

Chapter 72

Vacation Blues

"Any time I go on a vacation, I gain back
the pounds I worked so hard to lose!"

Secret: Recreational Respites

Ah-h-h Spa

A spa visit used to mean Spartan schedules, measly rations, torturous exercise sessions, and eat-this-way-or-else lectures. One primary goal united all these activities: weight loss. That's why they were called "fat farms," a nickname that stuck until well into the 1980's.

But spas have become much more user-friendly. Today, many fall into the "resort spa" category—hotels at which, between rounds of golf, poolside sunbathing, and late-night stints in the nightclub, you may get a quick massage or facial, have a "spa cuisine" lunch from the mostly non-light menu, or play around in a souped-up fitness center. Even most "destination spas"—where the more traditional regimen of health-boosting treatments, exercise, and light eating is the only attraction—have relaxed both dietary restrictions and fitness requirements.

Spas today are more like year-round summer camps for grownups. Especially for women, they've become destinations of choice, where mothers and daughters, sisters and sisters-in-law, or groups of old friends can retreat from the day-to-day and do a bit of bonding. But men, too, are catching on: The percentage of male spa visitors has been increasing steadily since 1999.

ALTERNATIVE HEALTH CARE

One of the biggest reasons behind the increased interest in spas, besides the push from a core market of baby boomers, is the growing interest in alternative health care. Many spas nowadays are staffed with a host of alternative as well as mainstream health professionals, including nutritionists, herbalists, M.D.s, acupuncturists, psychologists, and chiropractors. At Canyon Ranch in Tucson, Arizona, and the Berkshire Mountains of western Massachusetts, the price of a package not only includes facials and other pampering services, but a consultation with "health and healing" practitioners who might, for instance, help you with your chronic backaches. Services such as these are becoming so popular that mind/body medical expert Pamela Peeke, M.D., who is affiliated with the National Institutes of Health's Office of Alternative Medicine, has begun working with the International Spa Association (ISPA) to offer guidance on merging alternative and traditional medicine.

> One of the biggest reasons behind increased interest in spas is the growing interest in alternative health care.

THE TAKE-HOME MESSAGE

Many spas also host evening seminars on healthy-living topics such as stress management. This teaching element is what separates the newer breed of American spas from those in Europe. "When you go to a European spa, they do things to you," says Gary Milner, director of development for Canyon Ranch. "The American spa wants to show you how to do things for yourself."

Emerging especially strongly in the new spa curriculum is the role of the spa dietitian. In the old days, when most spa-goers struggled under a daily limit of 800 calories or so, staff dietitians essentially played food police. Now they are taking on a bigger challenge: teaching their guests lessons that stick, beginning in the spa restaurant. While mandatory calorie counts are passé, portions help guests get a realistic view of serving sizes. One spa serves up a highly effective visual—a 2-ounce hamburger (that is described on the menu as having 9 grams of saturated fat) the circumference of a Coke can. The point: If you eat a typical restaurant burger, you could be getting 30 to 40 grams of saturated fat.

Another take-home lesson is that eating healthfully can be pleasurable. "Spa-goers want to know what food can do for their health," says Michel Stroot, executive chef at the Golden Door in Escondido, California. "When tofu is on the menu, about one-third of the guests choose it." But it has to taste—and look—good, so spa chefs boost flavor with herbs, salsas, and coulis that have little or no added fat, and use colorful veggies and sauces to enhance presentation. Many spas also offer cooking instruction, where guests learn it doesn't take a culinary degree to re-create spa cuisine at home.

Even when a spa staffer is doing things to you—giving you a facial, for instance, or a massage—it's with an eye toward teaching you how to do it for yourself. Estheticians in spas nowadays are going beyond the cosmetic application of moisturizers, emphasizing preventive maintenance and repair. Products and on-site treatments are primarily aimed at one thing: reducing the effects of aging. But keep your perspective. Facials involving oxygen, collagen, fruit acids, and vitamins may be in vogue, but lasting effects are unlikely, especially with only one or two applications over the course of a spa stay.

THE POWER OF TOUCH

Massage and other total-body treatments such as salt scrubs are also enlisted to battle aging. Still the number-one spa service, basic massage is getting new twists with aromatherapy and indigenous herbs and music. At the Grand Wailea Hotel, Resort & Spa in Maui, for example, the Lomi Lomi massage, accompanied by native Hawaiian music, offers legendary healing and relaxing effects. Thai massage, which incorporates rhythmic breathing and assisted stretching, and watsu, a type of massage performed in a warm, shallow pool, offer the spa-goer even more creative ways to destress.

While some studies have suggested that massage can have therapeutic value and some facials may minimize (but not eliminate) wrinkles, most benefits depend on your perception of the experience. "There's data that shows there are immunological changes that result from just being touched, but we don't have enough studies yet to know if many of the treatments are truly effective. There could be a placebo effect," says Samuel D. Benjamin, M.D., director of the University Center for Complementary and Alternative Medicine at the State University of New York-Stony Brook. Costs permitting, though, Benjamin encourages patients to experiment with pampering. "No one," he says, "has ever been admitted to a hospital for an overdose of pleasant experiences."

Ah, but pampering can be addictive. After a few days at a spa, you may not look any younger or be any healthier. But you'll feel as if you are.   —*Victoria Clayton*

10 Active Vacations

Whether they're spent right in your own backyard or halfway around the world, vacations offer a well-deserved respite from the stresses of everyday life. But instead of passively taking in the scenery from the seat of an automobile, ship, or tour bus, why not put yourself right into the action? Hike a part of the Appalachian Trail, paddle the shores of Alaska's Prince William Sound, or bicycle through French wine country. Not only will you experience breathtaking scenery, you'll also give your body a challenging physical workout.

Adventure travel companies like American Wilderness Experience, BackRoads, Earthwatch, Journeys International, and Overseas Adventure Travel, to name a few, offer active vacation packages to suit every fitness level. Better yet, they plan all the details for you. Still, if you have the time and inclination, don't rule out setting up your own personalized trip. Look to special interest magazines—tennis, golf, mountain biking, skiing, kayaking, travel—for ideas. Or use our mini-top 10 guide to help you get started.

1 **Two Wheel Adventures** Cycling vacations run the gamut from easy to challenging depending on the terrain you choose. Package trips typically provide equipment, room, and board, all for one price; you can spend as little as a couple of hundred dollars biking the wine country of North Carolina's Blue Ridge Mountains or spend thousands of dollars for a European cycling adventure. Keen on creating your own trip? *Bike* magazine calls these the best mountain biking towns stateside: Eugene, Oregon; Asheville, North Carolina; Austin, Texas; Colorado Springs, Colorado; Ithaca, New York.

2 **The Walking World** In big cities like New York, Paris, and Rome, it's almost easier to navigate by foot than by car. And so seeing the sights becomes a walking vacation of sorts. But travel companies are seeing a surge in another kind of walking vacation, one that lets travelers explore the island of Crete, Ireland's stunning Connemara region, or the glaciers of Switzerland, all on foot. It's not just the appeal of unspoiled countryside that beckons walkers, but the chance to stay in one spot and really get to know it intimately. Popular walking tour companies: Cross Country International, Country Walkers, BackRoads.

3 **Trail Mix** If walking on the flatlands or gently rolling hills seems too tame, consider taking a hike. National parks are a good place to find trails; the setting and level of difficulty are yours to decide. Or maybe you'd like a unique locale. One company leads a trek in Bhutan, a tiny country nestled between India and Tibet. As you meander through rhododendron forests and climb a wooded path that leads to a sacred monastery perched on top of a mountain, your feet and mind learn firsthand of a little known and isolated culture.

4 **Scaling Rocks and Mountains** Some folks may need the challenge of climbing Mount Everest, but for most of us a smaller mountain will do. Less specialized equipment is needed and climbs aren't so grueling. New Hampshire boasts the White Mountains. Colorado has seven "fourteeners," mountains that reach over 14,000 feet high, for traversing. But if it's an introduction into rock climbing you're looking for, check out www.rockclimbing.com, a grass roots effort run by climbers telling other climbers about where and when to climb.

5 **Back in the Saddle** If horseback riding is your ideal way of getting up close and personal with a wide expanse of the great outdoors, go for it. Surprisingly, this sport lets you burn roughly 360 calories per hour. Check out companies that package horseback adventures: American Wilderness Experience, Equitor (a Wyoming company with over 600 trips), or Boojum Expeditions with trips to Mongolia, Argentina and China. Or contact the Dude Rancher's Association (www.duderanch.org) for a directory of over 100 member dude ranches with accommodations ranging from working cattle ranches to luxurious resorts.

6 **Winter Pursuits** Snowboarding and downhill skiing can burn close to 600 calories per hour; energy demands are about the same for cross-country skiing and snowshoeing. But the latter two pursuits give you a chance to slow down and really see the scenery and wildlife around you. The Trapp Family Lodge (www.trappfamily.com) in Vermont has one of the most extensive cross-country and snowshoe trail systems in the country. For more adventure, log on to www.yellowstone.net for information on trails in the land of Old Faithful.

7 **Pick Your Paddle** Avid canoers and kayakers often fantasize about far away places—the Norwegian fjords or Russia's Lake Baikal. But closer to home destinations like Nevada's Lake Mead, Alaska's Prince William Sound, or Canada's Bonnet Plume River can be easier on the travel budget. So too are trips planned in your own neck of the woods. Check out http://canoekayak.about.com, the website of *Canoe & Kayak* magazine, for more ideas.

8 **Spa Work Out** While some spas are all about pampering, many offer intense fitness programs both indoors and out. Red Mountain Spa in Utah, for example, is a prime destination for mountain bikers and avid hikers. Kripalu Center for Yoga & Health offers spa-style yoga retreats in the bucolic countryside of Massachusetts. For a yearly wrap-up of spa offerings, check out *Spa Finder* magazine (www.spafinder.com). Another great resource: *Fodor's Healthy Escapes*. (See "Ah-h-h Spa" on page 465.)

9 **Sporting Schools** It's not hard to find tennis courts or golf courses in just about any vacation destination. But if you really want to bring your game to the next level, dozens of schools will put you through the paces. One tennis school in Kentucky jokes that it's "no vacation" since participants go through daily bone-grinding drills meant to improve their game. Golf schools are much the same. You can go into an intense program or one that lets you take activity at your own pace. Check tennis and golf magazines for their annual ratings of the top institutions.

10 **Assorted Activities** Can't decide which of these active vacation styles suit you? Well, maybe you don't have to pick just one. The latest trend in active travel is the "multisport" vacation, a trip with several different activities—kayaking, cycling, rafting, hiking—all packaged into one glorious outdoor location. The scenery's the same as from the motor coach, but instead of seeing the water from a distance, you're paddling right in it. And instead of sitting on your rear, you're shaping it up by hiking. The enjoyment factor might be similar to the sit-down tour, but the feelings of accomplishment and your connection to the place you visit will be a whole lot stronger.
—Maureen Callahan

RECIPE INDEX

SUBJECT INDEX

Portion sizes, 406-407
Potatoes, 229
Poultry, 134
Pregnancy, 19, 100, 213
Protein, 89-92

Resveratrol, 240

Self-esteem, 20
Shrimp, 217, 218, 268
Snacking, 31, 171, 414-419
Soy, 113, 174. *See also* Tofu.
Spices, herbs and, 144, 146
Strength training, 27, 32, 114, 334, 338-346
    See also Muscle.
Stress, 31, 101, 121
Success stories, weight-loss, 34-56
Sugar, 76-78
Sunscreen, 113
Supplements, vitamin and mineral, 71, 72, 95,
    98-102
Sweets, 394-405. *See also* Desserts.

Tempeh, 90, 232
Tofu, 90, 138, 223, 225
Tortillas, 138, 231, 270, 301
Turkey, 134, 259, 303

Vacation, 465-470

Vegetarian diets, 221
Vitamins
    A, 68-69, 180, 182, 264
    C, 68-69, 111, 172, 209, 236, 261, 264
    E, 68-69, 276
    D, 110
    Multivitamins, 98-102

Walking, 24, 49, 50, 56, 105, 110, 337, 366-368,
    468, 469. *See also* Pedometers.
    and daily activity, 356-359
Weight, healthy, 21-24
Weight gain, 19, 24, 29, 30, 457-459
    carbohydrates, 73-74, 229
    holiday, 457-459
    stress-related, 31
    women, 19, 29-30
Weight loss
    benefits, 18-20
    body shape, 21-24
    calcium, 94
    fiber, 80
    journal, 36, 124, 309-310
    successful, 12-14, 34-56
Weight training. *See* Strength training.
Winter squash, storage, 280
Wild rice, 287

Yoga, 376-388

EDITORIAL CONTRIBUTORS

Karen Baar is coauthor of *The Circadian Prescription* (Putnam).

Madonna Behen is the health director at *Woman's Day* magazine.

Laura Billings is a freelance writer and has also been published in *Health, Mademoiselle, Outside,* and *Self* magazines.

Ed Blonz, M.S., Ph.D., writes "On Nutrition," a column syndicated in more than 600 newspapers.

Marc Bloom is a senior writer for *Runner's World* and a frequent contributor to *The New York Times.*

Bill Buettler is a visiting professor of journalism at Ohio University's E.W. Scripps School of Journalism in Athens. His work has appeared in *Men's Journal, Sports Illustrated,* and *The New York Times Book Review.*

Maureen Callahan, M.S., R.D., is a registered dietitian and trained professional chef who writes frequently about food and nutrition. She is the director of Callahan Culinary Communications.

Karen Cicero is a freelance writer whose work has also appeared in *Child, Prevention,* and *Self.*

Rod Davis is the former executive editor of *Cooking Light.*

Lisa Delaney is the executive editor of *Health* and the former editor of CookingLight.com.

Jim Fobel is an award-winning author and recipe developer. His most recent books include *Jim Fobel's Old-Fashioned Baking Book: Recipes from an American Childhood* and *Jim Fobel's Big Flavors.*

Kim Goad is a freelance writer whose work has also appeared in *Allure* and *Town & Country.*

Megan Othersen Gorman is a freelance writer whose work has also appeared in *Men's Health* and *Runner's World.*

Bill Gottlieb is the author of *Alternative Cures: From 300 of America's Top Doctors and Natural Healers, The Most Effective Home Remedies for 160 Health Problems* (Rodale). He writes frequently for *Men's Health, Readers' Digest, Health,* and *Self.*

Jennifer Pitzi Hellwig, M.S., R.D., is a freelance writer based in Rhode Island.

Melissa Ewey Johnson is a former *Cooking Light* assistant editor.

Wayne Kalyn is the editorial director of health books at *Readers' Digest.*

Carol Kutik, M.A., is the director of Exercise and Education at SportsFirst, Inc., Baptist Health System. She is an ACM and ACE certified fitness trainer.

Larry Lindner is the executive editor of the *Tufts University Health & Nutrition Letter* and teaches writing at Tufts University School of Nutrition Science and Policy.

Michele Mann is a freelance writer and former assistant health and fitness editor at *Cooking Light.*

Michele Meyer is the winner of the American Society of Journalists and Authors Outstanding Service Article Award and has also written for *Better Homes and Gardens, Men's Health, Metropolitan Home,* and *Self.*

Beth Witrogen McLeod is the author of *Caregiving: The Spiritual Journey of Love, Loss and Renewal* (John Wiley & Sons).

Gin Miller is the creator of step aerobics and a Reebok Master Trainer.

Tracey Minkin is a freelance writer who has written for *Outside* and *Men's Journal.*

Liz Neporent is a pesonal trainer and coauthor of *Fitness for Dummies* (IDG Books).

Linda Rao is a freelance writer based in Allentown, Pennsylvania. Her work has also appeared in several national magazines including *Prevention.*

Su Reid is a former *Cooking Light* editorial assistant.

Tamara Schryver, M.S., R.D., is a registered dietitian and the former editor of *Dietitian's Edge,* a trade publication for registered dietitians.

Carole Sugarman writes about nutrition for *The Washington Post* and other publications.

Tracy Teare is a freelance writer who also writes for *Shape, Fit Pregnancy, Walking,* and *Self.*

Jim Thornton is a contributor to *Cooking Light.*

Kerri Westenberg is a former *Cooking Light* assistant editor.

Selene Yeager is the author of *The Doctor's Book of Food Remedies* (Rodale) and a contributing editor for *Prevention.*

Winifred Yu is a freelance writer in Albany, New York, and a contributor to *Cooking Light.*